GREENWOOD
and
MOUNT OLIVET

CEMETERIES

GREENWOOD and
MOUNT OLIVET

CEMETERIES

Fowlerville, Michigan

✱✱✱✱✱✱✱✱✱✱✱✱✱✱

Transcribed Records

Compiled by

MILTON CHARBONEAU

Livingston County Genealogical Society

Howell, Michigan, 1985

Library of Congress Cataloging-in-Publication Data

Charboneau, Milton, 1926-
 *Greenwood and Mount Olivet cemeteries,
Fowlerville, Michigan.*

   Includes index.
   1. Fowlerville (Mich.)--Genealogy. 2. Registers
of births, etc.--Michigan--Fowlerville. 3. Greenwood
Cemetery (Fowlerville, Mich.) 4. Mount Olivet
Cemetery (Fowlerville, Mich.) 5. Inscriptions--
Michigan--Fowlerville. I. Title.
F574.F78C47 1985   929.5'09774'36   85-19832

Manufactured in the United States of America

Published by LIVINGSTON COUNTY GENEALOGICAL SOCIETY
              P.O. Box 922, Brighton, Michigan 48116

Contents

Illustrations

INTRODUCTION

Greenwood cemetery at Fowlerville

This cemetery lies about a mile west and north of
the village of Fowlerville, Michigan in Handy township
and contains most of the pioneer families of the area.

The cemetery is divided into two areas: The Original
sections and the New sections.

The original plot contains sections "A" and "B" and
and the Civil War monument. All the re-burials from the
"Old" cemetery are here. A Potters Field is located at
the rear of section A.

The new part contains sections "1", "2", "3", "5",
"8", and "9" of which the first three sections are full.
Sections 1 and 2 contain burials after 1920, with the
other numbered sections containing more recent burials.

There is a modern Veteran's plot at the head of section
number 3. There is a special Babyland plot in section 9.

Section 4, 6 and 7 are at present empty with but a
few grave sites sold. Many lots in these sections are
not platted as yet.

The Mausoleum is in the left hand corner of section 1,
with the entrance directly from Cemetery road.

- - - - - -

The author has attempted to faithfully transcribe the tombstones
just as they are written. The office records are also copied as
written. It is left up to the reader to make any corrections.

Special acknowledgement is made to the staff at the village of
Fowlerville office. We thank them for their valuable assistance
and cooperation.

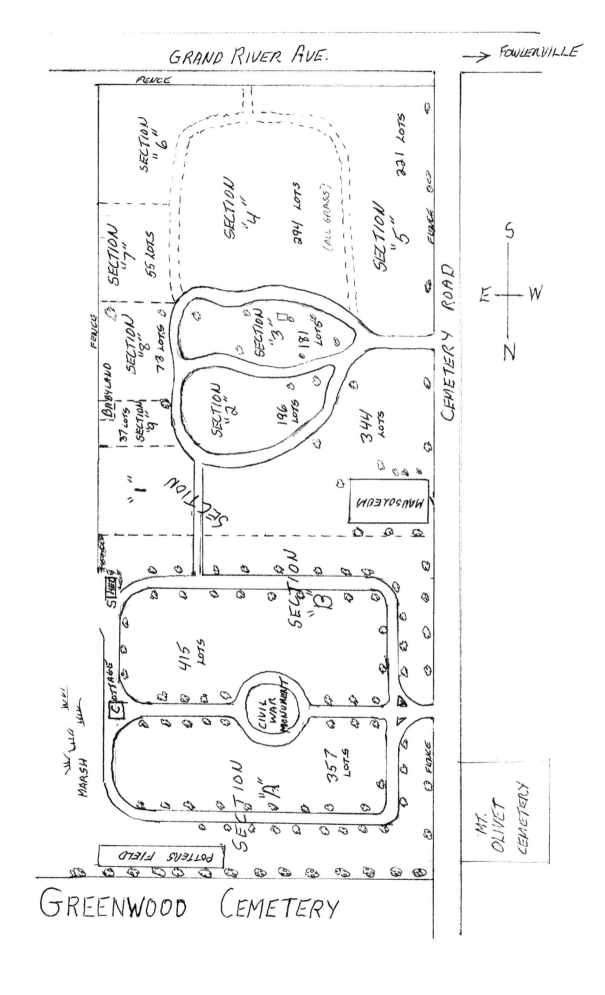

GRAND RIVER AVE.

→ FOWLERVILLE

FENCE

SECTION "6"

SECTION "4"
394 LOTS
(ALL GRASS)

SECTION "7"
55 LOTS

SECTION "5"
231 LOTS

SECTION "8"
73 LOTS

SECTION "3"
181 LOTS

SECTION "2"
196 LOTS

344 LOTS

SECTION "9"
37 LOTS

BABYLAND

FENCES

SECTION "1"

MAUSOLEUM

CEMETERY ROAD

S
E — W
N

SHED

COTTAGE

SECTION "B"
415 LOTS

CIVIL WAR MONUMENT

MARSH

SECTION "A"
357 LOTS

FENCE

MT. OLIVET CEMETERY

POTTERS FIELD

GREENWOOD CEMETERY

History of the OLD cemetery at Fowlerville

The "old" cemetery as it was called was deeded to the township of Handy by the Fowler family. On June 9, 1859 Mary Fowler, widow of John B Fowler gave an acre of land in the southeast corner of the southwest quarter of section 11, Handy township for the sum of One dollar and a cemetery lot for members of the Fowler family.

This grave yard was located just east of the village limits of that day and just north of Grand River road.

In the deed, Mary, Ralph, Rufus H and Lisle Fowler all signed over the land to the trustees of school district number Six which was to have control over the burial ground. On the school board at that time were Sam G Palmerton, Marchal A Porter, James M Long, William H Evans, George Fowler, William Falful and Harvey Metcalf.

Many years later District #6 turned over the cemetery ground to the village of Fowlerville who took over its care. In 1881 possibly because of future growth of the village, the village council decided to purchase land for a new cemetery. Several offers were made to sell land adjoining this old cemetery but they were turned down in favor of a new location outside the village limits.

After the new land was purchased and surveyed the council decided in May of 1883 to "allow parties owning lots in the old cemetery and wishing to remove the remains of departed friends be allowed to exchange such lots for lots in the new cemetery with the lots in the old grave yard to be deeded to the village of Fowlerville." This motion by the council suggest that it left it up to the relatives and friends to have the bodies removed and re-interred in sections A and B of the new cemetery. It would also account for the fact that several graves were missed and the bodies of these missing persons still lie beneath the original site. The records show that Mr. S S Abbott who purchased the old cemetery land was paid for removing several of the bodies after he had purchased the land in 1901.

One article on the removal of bodies is found in the pages of the Fowlerville Review newspaper of June 19, 1896. "In removing the bodies from the old cemetery to the new one the remains of Mrs. Sarah B Mitchell who died July 20, 1857 at age 56 were found to be in remarkable state of preservation. The remains had been buried in a metallic casket and her features, hair, eyebrows and the cloths in which she was buried were as perfect as could be so that anyone who knew her would have no difficulty recognizing her. Mrs. Mitchell had came to Fowlerville from Cincinnati, Ohio with her daughter Margaret and bought the farm owned in 1896 by Mr. O D Weller, west of Fowlerville. She had some wealth and built a house that still stood. She spent the summer here and then returned to Cincinnati. A few years later the daughter returned to Fowlerville with the remains of her mother. She did not stay and 16 years later sold the house and never returned."

It appears that for almost twenty years bodies were being removed from the old cemetery and re-interred in Greenwood.

On Oct. 21, 1901 the village of Fowlerville sold the old cemetery land to Spridon S Abbott for $100 and it became part of the village of Fowlerville. Even the "old timers" of today have no memory of it.

One unwritten tale of folklore relates that Ralph Fowler, founder of the village of Fowlerville who then lived across the road from the old cemetery decided that he did not want to be buried in the new cemetery which he called a "swamp." So when he and his wife died they were buried on their own land. Much later the bodies were removed to section "1" of Greenwood cemetery but the stones were not placed there but left on his homesite. So no stone marks the final resting place of the village's founder.

- - - - - - -

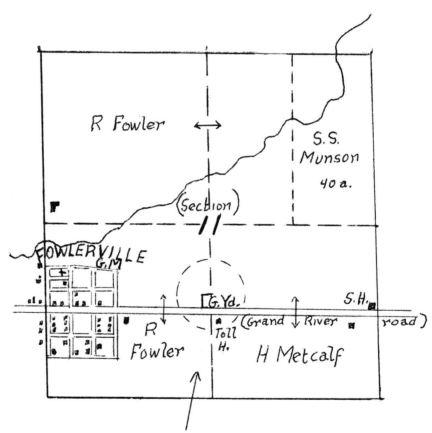

Location of Old cemetery on 1859 wall map.

History of GREENWOOD Cemetery

The Old cemetery had served the village of Fowlerville for many years. As time passed and the village grew the need for a larger burial ground became apparent. In 1881 a petition was presented to the voters to purchase a new site for a larger cemetery. The president of the village at the time was Frank Rounsville. The council moved to levy a tax of $1000 on village property to purchase a site for a grave yard which the citizens passed on March 14, 1881. A Committee made up of Peck, Walton and Hughes were to find a site.

From an "Early History of Fowlerville" article found in the Review newspaper of June, 1936 it states , "Various sites were offered for a cemetery. Mr. S Gilliam offered four acres adjoining the old cemetery." Mr. S L Bignall also offered five acres adjoining the old cemetery while George Fisher offered to set out 40 lots complete with walks for $10 a lot. Mr. Benjamin offered a site and S M Faunce had eight acres east of eight acres Mr. Starkey offered to sell to the committee. The council almost bought this land of Starkey but his neighbors objected and the offer was withdrawn.

William H Shorman offered ten acres on the northwest corner of his farm in section 12 for $100 an acre. In December of 1881 the council accepted the land. The article went on to say, "it is not expected that the purchase and location will suit all our citizens but the council has done what is best in their judgement. They certainly selected a fine piece of land and one that can be filled up and beautified at a small expense." Meanwhile Alonzo Fields was appointed sexton of the new site while Mr. Dopkins would serve as sexton of the old cemetery.

Nothing was done to the site till the spring of 1882 when the land was surveyed into lots by E P Hodge and his helper Ruel Curtis. The stakes were put in and then the land was seeded to hay. A fence contract was let out and by fall the north, south and east fences were built. J Ashley Dodge and F H Starkey supplied the boards and L J Hall supplied some 300 fence post. A H Philo helped build the fence.

During this time a cemetery committee was set up to procure deeds and receipts for lots in the new cemetery. This burial ground was first called "Oakwood" with C Y Peck as trustee. By June of 1883 the west side fence was in place, made up of pickets. The first crop of hay was sold to O N Benjamin for $20. Others who worked on the fence were Dillen Pettinger, James H Place, W H Wert and O H Jones. In the spring of 1884 James Place set out 520 trees around the cemetery land at a cost of $62. The name of the place was changed to Greenwood cemetery by the village council.

The village Ordinance book which contains laws passed by the council gives some insight on how the cemetery was maintained and controlled. In April 1886 control of the land is handed over to a cemetery board whose members are appointed for three years, on a stagger basis. They are to sell lots and take care of interments. They report to the village council once a year.

Another ordinance states that all lots have to be paid in cash. (cost $5 a lot) except persons exchanging lots in the old cemetery for ones in the new land. Only full lots are to be sold. Lot owners are allowed to enclose their lots in a wall, hedge or fence not over three feet high and decorate the lot with planted shrubbery as long as the roots of plants did not extend to other lots. The cemetery board had the power to remove these plants. No grave site could be raised over a foot high.

Still another law set aside lots 19 to 30 in section "A" for a potters field. A $100 fine was set for mutilating or destroying graves or tombstones.

The council appointed William Shorman as sexton in 1884. He was to dig and fill graves at $2.50 each as his salary. They also told the cemetery board to build a bier.

Nothing else is known of the early days of this cemetery. It seems that a small cottage building was constructed in the back which still stands there today. This was first used as a mausoleum in the winter where bodies could be stored until the ground was thawed for burial.

Map of Handy
township, 1875

note:
Old cemetery
section 11

Greenwood
cemetery
section 12

GREENWOOD CEMETERY

"The Cottage"

Sections A & B

Later Greenwood Cemetery History

In 1922 the village of Fowlerville bought the rest of the northwest quarter of the southwest quarter of section 12 from Merritt N Cook for $3700 which was platted as the New Sections of the cemetery. The burial ground now extends along Cemetery road as far as Grand River Avenue. A large expanse of this land near the highway is in grass space. Just last year some of this was surveyed for more lots.

A township record book for 1921 to 1942 gives several bills paid by the township for funeral expenses and work of tiling, surveying and labor on the road along side the New addition of Greenwood cemetery. Archer C Grover and John S Vogt received burial care money. In 1928 Memorial Day activities were taken over from the GAR whose men had all died and given over to the American Legion group. For the first few years the township paid for the flags placed on the veteran's graves.

During these years J J Hendron acted as township health officer. Frank Ulter and Grant DeForest were listed on the cemetery board.

The Sextons

Over the years there have been several sextons. Besides Field and Shorman already mentioned there was Ott "Mickey" McDaniel who served till 1959. The office of the cemetery had been in the cottage building earlier but during his time the office was moved into the mausoleum. Wayne Eaton served as sexton till 1962, then Grant DeForest till 1968.

The present sexton is Ron Fickens and his crew who are part of the department of Public Works for Fowlerville village. In more recent years the cemetery office has been located in the village offices.

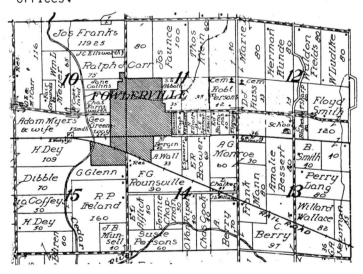

Map of Handy township, 1915

note;
Mt. Olivet &
Greenwood
section 11, 12

Old cemetery
is gone

INDEX

INDEX   Greenwood cemetery

unknown male	A-344	ALEXANDER-Alzina	1-175
ABBEY-Carolyn T	A-19	Eva E	1-186
ABBOTT-Arlie A	A-217	Infant son	A-222
Bert L	B-5	Minnie	1-186
Bess L	B-5	Robert T	1-186
Clara	B-394	William	1-175
ERnest C	B-5		1-186
Erwin J	A-97	ALGER- Anna E	3-58
Franklin B	B-395	ALLBRIGHT-Gertrude M	2-117
Fred K	B-394	Ida R	2-117
Gertrude	A-217	James H	2-117
Irving	A-91	Wayne E	2-117
Iva B	A-91	ALLEN-Albert E	B-81
Janette	A-91	Amy L	3-94
Louie	A-217	Anna L	1-54
Maria C	B-5	Bertha V	B-390½
Mary E	A-217	Burr	1-46
Matilda M	B-395	Charles G	A-53
Milo M	A-217	Clesson S	1-55
Ruth E	B-394	Coye T	1-55
Spridon	B-5	Cressa Newman	1-149
ACKER-Eugene M	2-14	Etta E	A-53
Margaret A	2-14	Frank H	1-270
ADAMS-Carrie	B-64	George H	A-53
George L	b-64	J, Mrs.	A-305
Irene M	A-69	Joel B	1-149
	1-69	Leona M	1-55
Jaunita S	A-69	Mabel	1-46
	1-69	Mary	A-53
Ruth Elizabeth	A-235	Maude	1-149
ADDISON-Edward C	3-46	Minnie E	1-55
Grace M	3-46	mother	B-81
ALBAUGH-Agnes I	3-159	Nellie B	B-81
Lawrence G	3-159	Raymond A	B-408
ALBERT-Carolyn J	2-154	Ray W	1-54
Karen A	2-154	Rose A	b-81
ALDRICH-Adelaide	A-148	Ruth E	B-408
Bessie C	A-261	Stanley K	1-270
Earl W	A-260	William E	B-390½
Elias	A-106	ALLHOUSE-Ardale L	3-170
Frank R	B-13	George C	3-170
Fred W	A-261	ALLISON-James R	3-124
Hugh G	B-309½	Mamie L	3-124
J H	A-147	Marcus B	1-223
Leslie L	A-260	Viola A	1-223
Lottie L	A-260	ALSBRO-Charles	B-35
Mabel C	B-309		B-48
Mert W	A-260	Eliza	b-48
Robert N	A-260	infant	A-340
		Mather	A-340
		Polly	B-48
		William	b-48

INDEX   Greenwood cemetery

BARBER-Nellie B	B-22
Orren	b-22
Sylvester	B-22
BARCUS-Ethel	A-131
George T	A-131
Sarah M	A-131
BARCHUS-Georgiann	B-401
BARDEN- Charles	A-312
BARNARD-Edward C	B-262
Ella M	B-78
Eunice	B-78
Harry L	B-379
Ida M	B-379
infant	B-379
Irene M	B-379
Lucy A	B-262
Neil G	A-215
William	B-78
BARNETT-Ila E	A-67
Russell	A-67
BARRY-Doris A	B-156
Elsie B	B-156
George W	B-156
Matilda	A-28
BARTEG-Evelyn	B-173
BARTIG-Charles A	1-93
Luella J	1-93
Marymae	3-136
Robert E	3-136
Rutherford B	3-136
BARTLETT-Julia	1-23
Robert	1-23
BARTON-Emmett J	1-218
BARTOW-Charles K	3-104
Merle D	3-104
BATES-Donald Lee	3-38
Helen	b-203
BATRAM-Emily A	B-413
Mark W	B-413
BAYES-Leta Blasick	1-242
Phyllis M	1-242
BAYS-Samuel	A-350
BEACH-Addie L	B-68
Frank	1-205
Helen Kinsman	1-205
BEAN- Chloe	B-298
James	B-298
BECKER-Lessie M	1-74
Roy I	1-74
BEEBE-Adelbert J	A-198
Ella	A-198
L H	A-197

BEEBE-Sarah	A-198
S S	A-197
BEHR-Herbert C	8-16
Lois B	8-16
BEHRINGER-Robert D	3-1
BELEC-Garnet M	1-226
Joseph H	1-226
BELKNAP-Olive Coles	B-64
BELL-Amelia	1-139
Amy, Mrs.	B-12
Bert J	1-124
Clyde	1-139
Eliza A	1-139
Eugene	2-100
Grace	2-100
Helen	2-100
John	1-139
Lola	2-161
Louise M	1-124
Malinda	2-100
Philip A	1-139
Russell E	b-12
William	B-72
BELLINGER-Allen B	A-159
Clara	A-159
Ira	A-159
BENEDICT-Chester Omar	B-404
Gertrude Coll	B-404
BENJAMIN-Agnes E	B-101
Albert D	B-101
Andrew J	1-272
Arthur E	A-19
Bertha A	A-19
Burnette	A-139
Carolyn T	A-19
Cecil L	B-243
Charity	1-272
Charles N	3-59
Charley L	Maus.
Clarence W	2-77
daughter	B-102
David	A-139
Edna L	A-288½
Edwin	A-139
Ernest D	Maus.
Ella	A-55
Ellen I	B-243
Ellen M	A-139
Erdine	B-244
Eugene	B-101
Fame	2-132
Florence	2-77

INDEX   Greenwood cemetery

INDEX   Greenwood cemetery

INDEX   Greenwood cemetery

CADMUS-Susan M	A-312	CARR-Albert B	B-201
CADWELL-Alice M	A-15	Amarilla	Maus.
Charles H	A-15	Cordelia J	B-201
Cornelius	B-134	D A A-232	
Eula F	A-15	Eldorus	B-201
CALKINS-Alice	1-43	Erwin P	2-130
Freely	B-233	Fame	2-130
Harry G	2-36	Ida P, Mrs.	A-232
Ima H	2-36	Julius	Maus.
infant	B-233	Maria J Kirkland	B-97
Ira W	B-283	Mary	B-204½
Lula Mae	B-233	Orr E	B-97
Orville	1-43	Robin K	B-97
Sarah	B-233	Thomas N	B-201
CAMERON-Claude	B-254	CARSON-Jessie A	1-190
George E	A-167½	Percy E	1-94
Herbert	B-254	CARTER-Albertie	A-128
John H	B-254	CARUSI-baby girl	3-109
Leo V	B-266½	John Jr.	B-303½
Lyle	A-171½	CARVER-Todd Allen	A-11
Otie B	A-167½	CASADY-Amos B	2-126
Ruth M	B-254	Clarence B	3-118
	B-266½	Frank J	2-127
Tressa L	B-254	Lillian H	2-126
CAMPBELL-A V P	A-227	Maggie	2-127
Egbert	A-227	Ross M	2-127
Hawthorn	A-22	Ruth E	3-118
Lois W	3-52	Wanda Jo	2-127
L W	B-96	CASTERTON-Blanche E	A-11
Marion	A-227	Mildred	A-11
Susan	A-227	Roy W	A-11
W Bruce	3-52	CASWELL-James H	A-158½
CANFIELD-Abigail	B-211	CAVANAUGH-Basil	1-276
female	B-211	Fern S	1-276
Hazel M	1-90	Rose Mary	1-276
Howard A	1-90	CEPHELUS-Ernestine	B-362
J A	B-211	Gustave	B-362
Louis J	B-211	CHALKER-Horace	A-346
Judson A	B-211	Julia E	unk.
CARDOTT-Curtis Edgar	A-179		A-346
Effie	A-179	Llewellyn	1-215
Martha	B-363	Matilda	A-346
CAREY-Frank L	1-118	Mary	1-215
Lyda A	1-118	Thomas	A-346
CARLSON-Bonnie Lee	2-2	CHAMBERS-Milo S	3-114
John W	2-129	Ruby A	3-114
CARMER-William	unk.	CHAPLIN-Betsey	B-197
CARPENTER-Beverly E	3-129	Betsey L	A-197
Martin L	B-121	G W	B-197
Mary	A-165	Willie	B-197
Susan I	B-121		

{31}

		INDEX		Greenwood cemetery

DEAN-Glen W	1-261	DERATANY-Leo G	B-39
Gussie W	A-77	DETERDING-Edward G	A-75½
Helen A	B-372	DeTROYER-Laurence R Sr.	1-99
James O	B-372	DEVINE-Dorothy	B-255½
Laura E	1-261	Edna R	1-114
Lavina	A-60	Fred J	1-114
Morris D	A-60	Gladys	B-255
Vance	1-261	James	B-255
DeANGELO-Agnes Howard	1-93	Mary J	B-255
DEFENDORF-Byron	A-94	Patrick	B-255
Edgar D	Maus.	William	B-255½
Eugene A	Maus.	DEWAR-Mary	1-48
Hulda A	A-94	William	1-48
Jessie M	Maus.	DeWATERS-David R	1-80
DeFOREST-Allen	1-267	Richard K	1-80
Arthur	5-46	DEY-A Eugene	B-165
Elmer	1-209	Anna	B-183
Ernest J	3-74	B Elda	Maus.
Eva L	5-46	Cecil A	Maus.
Grant H	3-151	Charles O	B-183
Jane	1-209	Clementina	1-142
Mabel I	3-74	Deo	B-183
Martie F	1-224	George A	B-165
Natashia T	3-166	Henry N	1-142
Susan M	3-151	Lida May	B-165
William N	1-224	Nettie	B-165
William	1-209	Olive	B-183
DEHART?-D Martha	B-217	Pierson W	B-183
DeLANDY-Edwin R	B-2	DEZESS-Claude	B-247
DeLINE-Wanetta	1-132	John	B-247
DeMARAIS-Caleb R	3-84	Mabel	B-167
M Agnes	3-84	Velma C	B-247
DEMEREST-Alta M	B-86½	DIAMOND-Agnes	A-233
LaVerne	B-86½	Ellen I	A-233
Lintsford	B-6	Francis I	A-230½
Matilda	B-6	Henry	A-233
Mary J	B-6	Henry G	A-233
DENDEL-Donald	1-6	DIBBLE-baby	1-38
DENIKE-Doris L	3-101	Benjamin	A-270
Henry W	3-101	Earl	A-270
DENNIS-Clara	A-332	Edith	A-270
Darwin	A-332	Elizabeth	i-38
DENSON-Algenons	B-59	Francis A	A-270
Alonzo	B-59	George E	B-231
Edward	B-59	Harriett	1-38
Lydia	B-59	Lavern	1-38
William	B-59	twins	1-38
DENSMORE-Mary L	2-8	William Harold	1-38
William C	2-8	William J	1-38
DENTON-Charles	1-41	DICKERSON-Kate	B-304
Colleen	1-41		

{32}

INDEX   Greenwood cemetery

FERGUSON-William	A-238
Zoe	B-229
FERNLESS-Martha	A-59
FERRIN-Bernard L	A-136
Dorothy E	2-68
Edmond M	2-68
father	A-136
Grace L	2-66
Harry S	2-66
mother	A-136
Ronald D	2-67
FERRINGTON-Ella M	3-54
FEWLASS-Ella	A-55
George B	A-55
	A-59
Jane	1-209
Martha	A-59
Martha L	A-55
FICHTENBERG-Neva B	B-266
FIELD-William Allen	2-55
FIELDS-Alonzo	A-225
Anna	B-177
baby	A-191
Bertha E	A-191
Catherine	A-225
Della E	A-191
Earl H	A-191
Edward L	A-191
Henry	A-225
Henry W	A-191
infant son	A-192
Mary A	B-235
Seth W	B-235
Waldon S	B-177
FINCH-James Edward	A-46
Joseph	B-262
Susan	B-262
FINKBEINER-Mary	A-188
FINKHEENER-Mary	A-189
FINLEY-Annie	unk.
FISCHER-Fred W	B-376
Julia M	B-376
FISH-Ida May	A-283
FISHER-Ada	B-14
Alma L	B-194
Andrew	B-219
Andrew H	Maus.
Bill	B-219
Blanche E	3-46
Daniel W	B-14
Eliza	B-14

FISHER-Ella B	Maus.
George L	Maus.
Hattie	B-194
Hannah A	B-14
Harvey C	3-46
infant dau.	B-194
John D	B-194
Mabell	B-194
William G	B-14
FLADOM-Emil	3-87
FLANIGAN-Emma	1-253
William	1-253
FLEURY-Joseph D	1-229
FLURIA-C H	1-229
Emily	1-229
FLYNN-Thomas J	unk.
FORCE-Claude	A-253
David	A-253
father	A-253
Fred	B-257
Hollis N	B-221
James	A-231
Jane	A-231
Mary	A-253
mother	A-253
William	B-258
FORD-Bernice D	1-123
Buell D	A-123
	1-122
Richard B	1-123
FORSTER-Jane	A-138
FOSTER-Alice E	3-111
baby	B-294
Claude	B-394
Dortha V	B-171
Eva Richmond	B-294
Ira E	1-72
Leona	B-171
Lean G H	1-72
Martin R	1-200
Mary M	1-72
Myra M	1-72
Richard A	1-98
Steven E	8-59
Susan	unk.
Viola	1-200
W	A-138
Wesley B	3-111
FOWLE-Florence L	1-163
FOWLER-Alonzo	B-121
Alta A	B-87½

{36}

INDEX   Greenwood cemetery

FOWLER-Charles	B-85	FRAZIER-James W	3-93
Dollie	2-57	FREDENBURG-Richard E	3-2
Effie	1-105	Thelma	A-9
Eielin	B-85	FRENCH-Ketha Odomia	B-155
Elvie Wooden	1-3	Signa B	B-155
Floss	B-385	FRETZ-Elsie E	A-203½
Frank	1-105	Floss M	A-107
Hellen	B-85	Thomas M Jr.	A-203½
Ina	1-106	Thomas M Sr.	A-203½
Joanna	B-4	FREY-William	B-353
John B	B-88	FRY-infant son	B-353
Laura	A-168	FRYANY-Catherine	A-190
Lewis	A-192	Charles	A-190
Lewis Wilber	1-4	Daniel	A-190
Martha Smith	B-87	Sarah	A-190
Mary, Mrs.	B-85	FRYE-Lucille M	A-234½
Mary Smith	B-88	Plyn E	A-234½
Milburn	B-85	FUESLEIN-John V	3-157
Nettie	A-152	Virgiline	3-157
Nettie Huck	A-126	FUHR-Bertha E	B-242
Polly	B-121	FULKERSON-Ezra A	3-77
Polley	B-385	Lois M	3-77
Ralph	B-87	FULLER-Clara M	2-26
Rufus H	B-86	Clarence J	2-25
Silas	A-152	Duane	2-27
Silas H	B-87½	Elizabeth R	2-25
Vera M	1-4	Ethel B Burley	3-68
Walter	B-85	Judith Ann	3-68
W H H	B-385	Julian B	Maus.
Wilbur	1-3	Matilda H	Maus.
William	1-106	Milburn Wells	3068
FOX-Francis A	5-41	Wells	2-26
FRANKLIN-Mary E	2-9	FURBUSH-Cardlyn	1-97
	9-3		
FRANKS-Addie M	2-92		
Anna J	B-232		
Dusty Donald	2-106	GABLER-Esther E	5-5
Ella J	A-243	Homer L	5-5
George D	2-92	GAFFIELD-Agnes	A-233
Gean D	B-360	GAGE-Carrie	B-375
Gean E	B-361	Clay W	B-375
Joseph	A-243	Ellen M	B-375
	B-243	Virginia	B-375
Joyce M	A-243	William	B-375
Louisa	2-106	GALARNEAW-Roger Dale	1-267
Myrtie A	B-360	GALBRAITH-Clinton R	3-85
Nelson	2-106	Florence G	3-85
FRANSON-Carl E	2-51	James W	3-85
Charles E	2-51	Pearl E	2-150
Helga	2-51	William Wayne	2-64
Thomas C	2-51	William W	2-150

INDEX   Greenwood cemetery

INDEX   Greenwood cemetery

HALE-Orman Bennett	2-31		HANDY-Jobes	A-293
Rachel A	B-193		Mary	A-293
son	B-193		William	B-48
HALEY-Andrew	1-17		HANIGAN-Ephraim	1-232
HALL-Belle	A-156		Maude I	A-146
Blanche M	B-142½		HANNA-Claude H	1-332
Dell Clara	B-251		Esther M	1-332
George S	B-135½		William A	1-331
Helen F	3-79		HANNAGAN-Joseph H	1-232
James B	3-69		HANSON-Charles A	1-174
James M	A-156		Charles F	3-110
John H	B-142½		Crystal	8-20
Joseph P	A-4		Donald G	8-20
Julia	A-156		Elva A	3-110
Kenneth T	1-297		Flora May	1-174
Luetta M	A-158		Grace	1-102
Lula Straws	B-126		Henry V	1-173
MargARET L	3-79		Margaret A	1-173
Merrell D	A-158½		Norma E	3-111
Minnie A	A-158		William F	1-174
Orla B	A-158		HARDING-Alice J	A-184
Sophia A	1-80		HARDY-Monah	2-120
HALLER-Martha H	A-265½		Maude M	3-7
Ralph J	A-265½		Purl C	3-7
HALLOWAY-Peter	1-244		HARFORD-Alice	3-91
HAMBURGER-Fred J	2-32		George	3-91
Mary L	2-32		Wilson	3-98
HAMELL-Anthony S	A-196		HARMON-Ann	8-35
Emma	A-196		Charles	A-248
HAMILL-infant son	A-186		Colleen	1-14
HAMILTON-Claude D	B-67		Dorothy V	B-146
David	A-216		Edgar	1-14
Emily	A-216		Elmer	8-35
Ethel Gardner	B-67		Henry	B-146
Eva Disbrow	A-216		Henry S	B-146
George D	B-70		Julia	B-146
infant	A-216		Ruth	1-14
Jacob D	A-216		HARREN-baby	1-198
Josephine	B-70		HARRIS-Bernie G	2-142
Romine G	3-92		Clara V	2-142
HAMLIN-Rose V	2-165		Daniel	B-24
Willard J	2-165		David K	unk.
HANDY-Calvin	B-48		Edward	B-161
Calvin, Mrs.	A-340		Mary A	B-27
Charles	B-48		Meade	B-24
Charles G	A-176		Sarah M	B-161
Harriet Jane	A-176		HARRISON-Anna, Mrs.	A-57
Eliza	B-48		baby	B-199
Ida	A-68		Clarence	B-199
Ira	A-68		Ethel D	B-214½
James E	A-176		infant son	B-199

INDEX   Greenwood cemetery

HICKS-Celestia	A-274	HOLMES-Mae E	1-112
Geraldine	B-219½	Marian L	1-190
John	B-219½	Nina C	1-190
HIGDON-Ruth L	B-95½	Norman	1-179
Tyler M	B-95½	Orra H	1-112
HILDEBRANT-Minnie	B-81	Orville T	1-190
HILDERBRANT-Catherine	A-16	Otilla	1-179
HILDRETH-Esther	A-221	Ralph A	1-112
HILL-Anna M	3-57	Samuel R	2-83
Clara S	1-277	Warren S	1-117
Gary Lee	3-25	HOLT-Gertrude L	1-226
James B	3-25	Laverne G	1-226
Julia M	3-25	Myrtie B	1-226
Mabel	2-72	Roy J	1-226
Mary	B-26	HOPKINS-Etta	1-215
Ralph C	3-57	Pennilla	B-59
Ralph Charles	3-157	wife	B-58
Sameul	2-72	William	B-58
HILLMAN-Frederick	1-42	William J	2-32
Inez	1-42	HORTON-Bessie M	2-113
Ray M	2-54	Blanche E	A-84
Sarah C	2-54	Caleb	A-240
HINER-Edward Marvin	3-4		A-285
HISSONG-Joe S	3-136	Carol D	A-84
Sylvester	3-136	Carrie Peckens	B-200
HOAG-Arvin Nelson	1-69	Elizabeth	A-83
B F	Maus.	Gerald E	2-125
Charles	1-69	H	A-285
Martha E	Maus.	infant	A-393
HOAGLAND-Ella M	B-358	June	A-285
Fred C	B-358	Libbie	A-235
HODGE-Amelia	B-45	Lettie C	A-240
Arissa	B-45	Rollin S	A-84
Celia	B-45	Roy D	2-113
Dora B	B-45	Stephen R	A-83
Erastus	B-45	Verlyn L	A-84
HODGES-James M	B-46	Wilfred D	A-202
Lafayette	B-46	William	A-285
Prima	B-46	HOSKING-Freda C	A-270½
HOFFMAN-Mildred	2-75	John N	A-270½
HOISINGTON-Gale	2-108	HOSKINS-Wm. Bradford	3-104
Kendall D	2-108	HOUSE-Amasa G	A-232
Merideth G	2-108		A-236
Nancy Lee	2-108	Archie G	1-153
Pearl H	2-108	baby boy	A-236
Shirley E	2-108	Cynthia	A-232
HOLLOWAY-Carrie	1-244		A-236
Peter	1-244	E A	A-236
HOLMES-Fred	moved	Eddie	A-232
Genevieve B	1-117	Eddie Jr.	A-232
Ida B	1-179	Edward E	A-185
Jennie	2-83	Florence J	3-142
Lorenzo D	1-179	Ilah G	B-282

HOUSE-infant	A-185	HUCK-William H	B-381
Loretta	B-46	William L	B-381
Lyle K	A-185	Winnie O	2-157
Marjorie I	A-185	HUDSON-Jan	1-333
Nellie K	A-185	HUFF-Arvilla S	B-252
Rex	3-142	Charlotte	B-333½
Ruth L	1-153	Joseph S	B-252
Sanford E	A-236	Raymond D	B-333½
Tho	A-232	HUGHES-Allen D	A-104
HOUSTON-Kimberly Jo	3-50	Annie D	B-100
HOWARD-Agnes B	1-93	Arvid H	A-104
Ernest B	1-93	Blanche A	3-86
Inez B	A-61	Donna J	5-3
HOWE-Ida Mae	B-235½	Delia M	B-110
Lorin D	B-235½	Eliza	A-201
HOWELL-Carrie	B-311	Floyd T	5-3
F Emmet	B-311	Goldie B	3-18
Maxine	B-311	Harriet	B-47
HOYLAND-Garth	B-46½	J D	B-110
Mark Eric	B-46½	Minnie D	B-110
HOYT-Charles H	B-397	Norman	A-201
Curtis C	B-249	HUMPHREY-Earl	A-281
Estella	B-249	HUMRICH-Carl Raymond	2-104
Euphemia	B-205	HUNT-Eliza	1-183
Hannah L	B-342	Jessie	1-183
Leila H	B-397	Lester	1-183
Rex F	B-397	Nellie	1-183
Theodore	B-249	Stanley	1-183
Thomas J	B-342	Wesley	1-183
Ella R	B-249	HUSCHKE-Anna E	B-313
HUBBARD-Finley Allen	1-99	Carl A	B-313½
Martha J	1-99	Edith	1-21
HUBER-Joseph H	B-99	Henry	A-276
Relta Hyne	B-99	Fred	B-384½
HUCK-Alta Ruth	2-28	Fredrick	3-157
Barbara E	B-381	Grace	B-384½
Catherine	B-380	Henry	1-21
Charles D	B-380	John F	B-158
Countess Marie	A-126	Katherine A	B-313½
	2-28	Louis H	B-313
Eddie Lee	2-28	Margaret	B-313
Frank Sr.	B-380	Mary	A-276
Harry J	2-28		B-158
Leonard	A-126	Millie M	B-158
	B-380	Roy H	B-312½
Leonard A	2-28	Rudolph	B-313
Mabel V	B-381	HUSS-David J	B-373
Mary A	B-380	Elizabeth	B-373
Nettie	A-126	Melinda Mastic	B-373
Terri Lee	3-167	HUTCHINS-Helen Irene	A-212
Wilbur E	2-157	HUTCHKISS-Anila	1-35

INDEX   Greenwood cemetery

INDEX   Greenwood cemetery

INDEX   Greenwood cemetery

{53}

INDEX   Greenwood cemetery

NASS-Arnold A	2-170	NICHOLS-Jeramiah	B-278½
Margaret M	2-170	Louise F	B-185
NEELY-Elizabeth, Mrs.	A-122	Lucy C	A-178
Emilyn	A-196	Marian D	1-187
Ezra	1-17	Mary	B-278
Merion E	A-122	mother	B-278
NELSON-Alice	2-22	Oscar	B-277
Carrie M	2-62	Rhoda J	B-278
Clinton James	A-58	Rollin C	B-185
Harriet	A-58	Seth A	B-185
Helen M	1-53	NICKERSON-Frances	A-82
Henry Eugene	2-62	Joanna A	A-82
John J	1-53	NICKLOY-Irene T	B-199
Loyce M	1-232	Martin D	B-199
NEWKIRK-Anna M Jeffrey	3-36	NIELSON-Helmar	1-121
John "Lin"	A-197	Minnie H	1-121
NEWMAN-Alvis	A-338	NIXON-Clark P	3-61
Amelia	A-140	Hathe M	3-61
Ann	A-119	NORDMAN-Frank Z	2-45
Annie E	B-131½	Laura C	2-45
Bertha	A-140	NORTHRUP-Mrs.	B-140
Cressa Mae	1-49	NORTON-Jimmie	A-191
Daniel	B-171	NOVAK-Ronald	1-251
D R	B-131	NUNN-Jaunita L	8-20
Elwin E	B-131½	Ray L	8-20
Ethel	Maus.	NYGREN-Bernard L	3-153
George A	Maus.	Hazel E	3-54
Hattie	A-119	Louis L	3-54
Henry	A-112	Pearley E	3-153
Irving P	A-140	W William	3-54
Leah W	1-150		
Lilla	B-131		
Lodema	A-112		
Martha R	A-179		
Mary E	Maus.	ODELL-Florence	B-226
Sarah	B-131	O'DELL-Claude L	B-355
Thomas	A-119	Cora Bell	B-255
	A-343	Miles S	B-355
William	A-119	Susie D	1-315
NEWSOME-George H	B-286	O'DONNELL-Frank E	2-110
Ida May	B-286	Ola M	2-110
NEWTON- James	A-192	OESTERLE-Asenath B	2-151
Newell	B-123	Bertha Westmoreland	
Thurza M Dailey	B-123		B-153
William F	B-123	Charles C	2-151
NICHOLAS-Catherine	B-106	O'GRADY-Bernard	B-403
NICHOLS-Ada J	Maus.	Leroy	B-403
Adreannie	B-277	OLIVER-Ivan E	1-67
Albert M	A-178	Mary I	1-67
Charles E	B-278½	Robert J	1-67
Chester E	A-178	Roy H	1-67
Frank D	Maus.	OLSEN-Carl C	2-85
Hillyard	B-278	Fred F	2-82
		Sarah C	2-82
		Wilburt E	B-62

{57}

READ-Elizabeth	A-132	RIACE-Dema	1-269
Loothda	B-128	RICH-Bernard C	1-51
REASON-Alice M	A-15	Elden B	1-51
RECTOR-Bert W	A-204	Jessie S	1-51
Caroline A	A-203	Leona L	1051
Charles H	A-204	Robert E	1-51
Ward A	A-203	RICHARDSON-Lewis Andrew	B-239½
William H	A-203	RICHMOND-Addie Irene	2-54
REDFIELD-Bessie M	L-176	Addie Meader	2-78
Betsy	1-185	Bertha A	2-9
Carrie	1-185	Celia A	B-294
Gladys I	1-176	Deak Daniel	2-78
Ivan W	1-185	Dora Blanch	A-160
Jay	1-185	Eva	B-294
J B	1-176	Geo Russell	A-160
L	1-176	infant son	A-160
William	1-185	Jay T	B-294
REDIGER-Selma	B-364	Melvin	1-5
REDINGER-Florence A	3-86	Millie	2-78
Lyle C	3-86	Ola May	A-160
Wayne K	1-315	Ray W	2-9
REED-E B	B-78	Russell L	2-78
Jessie Lint	B-400½	RICHTER-Fred	A-196
Richard	B-82	Lena	A-196
REESE-Bessie L	A-210	Wayland	A-222½
Bessie Louise	A-217	RICKETT-Jennie G	2-113
Isaac M	A-210	S Reynolds	2-113
REILLY-Eva M	B-283	RIDER-C Cecil	2-99
REIMANN-Charles	2-105	Charley A	2-99
Grace	2-105	Fred P	1-279
RENDER-Kathrine B	Maus.	Goldie May	1-279
Walter E	Maus.	Hattie	2-99
RENN-Bertha	2-104	Viola B	1-279
Carl	2-104	RIES-Ozonna Lou	B-404½
RENT-M	B-216	Vetha M	B-404½
REX-John A	B-389	Wayland C	B-404½
REXIN-Caroline	1-160	RIFE-Friedarica	A-74½
Floyd	1-160	George W	A-74½
REYHL-Arden D	B-365	Jennie	3-169
Christian F	B-364	Herman	3-169
Donald E	B-365	RILEY-Frank S	Maus.
Ernest C	B-365	Grace	Maus.
Frank A	B-364	RIPPLE-Burton V	A-247½
Fred	1-16	Nellie E	A-247½
Ida	1-16	RISCH-Ann	A-202
Irene	1-16	Herman L	B-392½
Richard	B-364	Ida G	B-392½
Ruth M	B-365	RISDON-Donna E	A-47
Selma	B-364	Iva	A-47
William	1-16	Orla D	A-47
REYNOLDS-Ileta	1-124	Orman D	A-47
Raymond R	1-124	Russell	1-3
		Treva	1-3

Greenwood cemetery

RUDNICKI-Andrew	1-44		SAVAGE-Katie E	B-56
Jane Lena	1-44		Maurice	B-56
Kate	1-44		SAWYER-Eliza	B-163
Lena	1-44		SAYLOR-Joyce A	B-122½
RUDOLPH-C F	Maus.		Robert J	B-122½
Cora L	Maus.		SCHAADT-Larry L	2-84
RUGGLES-Archie E	1-133		SCHAFER-Florence M	3-40
Artie R	A-235		Joseph H	3-40
Elizabeth J	B-388		SCHAFFER-Abagal	A-239
Fanny M	A-235		SCHLAACK-Hal M	B-202
George A	B-388		SCHLAAK-Vera	B-202
Hannah S	1-133		SCHMIDT-Frank F	A-85
John M	A-235		Olga M	A-85
K Donald	1-133		Stanley F	A-85
RUSSELL-Daisy	3-138		SCHNEEBERGER-Carrie R	B-231½
Don G	3-138		Fred C	B-231½
Halsey	2-123		SCHNEIDER-Albert	B-269
Henry D	2-74		Conrad	B-270
Mayme C	2-74		Elizabeth	B-269
Timothy Wayne	2-124		Fred H	B-252½
RUSSOLL-Henry	B-309½		George H	B-269
RUTTMAN-August	2-97		Gladys Cook	1-246
Byron August	3-133		John	B-269
John	1-12		Mae	B-384
Laurens	1-12		Martha	B-270
Mary G	2-97		Ruth L	B-252½
RYAN-infant boy	8-37		SCHOOLEY-Sarah Jane	unk.
			SCHULTZ-Wanda Jo	2-127
			SCOON-Edith M	3-169
			SCOTT-Alfred Emmons	1-192
SABIN-Abigail H	A-165		Alice Long	1-192
Alice	A-318		Nina M	B-54½
Devilla	1-198		Reginald	1-192
Dollie Dee	A-164		SCRIPTURE-Abbie E	A-321
Elizabeth	B-199		Amanda	A-321
Ellen	1-198		Samuel	A-321
Ernest D	1-198		SELFRIDGE-Florence I	A-70
father	A-164		George A	A-70
Fred	A-151		SESSIONS-Alva P	A-257
grandmother	A-164		Hannah P	A-257
Harold D	1-198		Lydia	A-257
Louanna	A-165		William H	A-257
mother	A-164		SEXTON-James A	2-34
Smith E	A-165		SEYFREID-Sopha V	2-53
Virginia D	1-198		William F	2-53
William J	A-164		SEYMOUR-Ed	1-273
SAGE-B E, Mrs.	B-11		Eda L	B-298½
Caroline S	B-73		Fran Louise	B-396
William	B-73		Fred J	B-298½
SANCHO-David D	3-46		George	A-214
SATTERLA-Glen H	2-13		Mary	A-214
Ina	2-13		Newton	A-214
SAUNDERS-Aaron	B-45		SEYMOURE-Lillie	1-273

INDEX   Greenwood cemetery

INDEX   Greenwood Cemetery

INDEX   Greenwood cemetery

INDEX   Greenwood cemetery

INDEX   Greenwood cemetery

INDEX   Greenwood cemetery

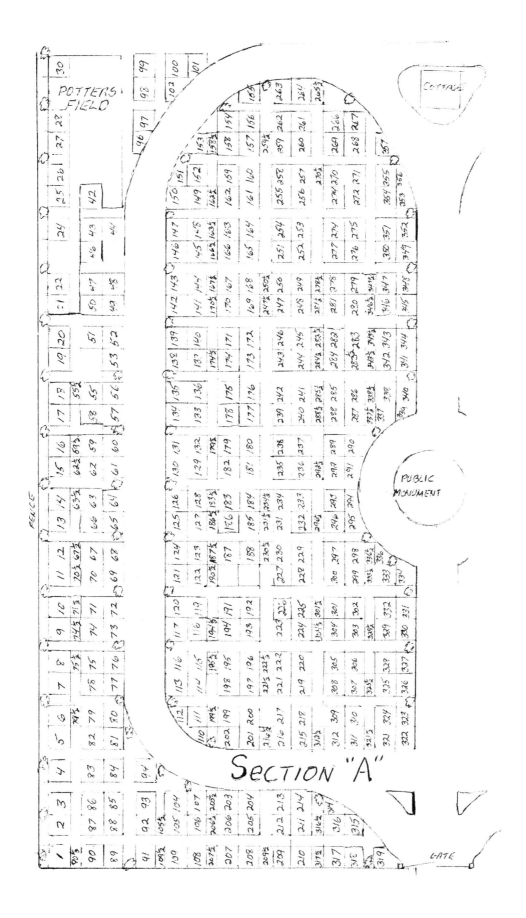

POTTERS FIELD

SECTION "A"

PUBLIC MONUMENT

FENCE

COTTAGE

GATE

GREENWOOD CEMETERY

General View

Section A

SECTION "A"

lot #
1 LOGAN
   Alice E Logan "mother"   b-Ohio   res. Webberville
   1894-1920   d-Feb. 4, 1920 age 26, appendicitis

   double stone;
   Samuel C Logan   "Samuel Cyrus" b-Mi.   res.-Wayne
   1868-1959   d- 4-5-59 age 91
   Ella C Logan   res.-Lansing
   1873-1930   d-Aug. 23, 1930 age 53
2 PIERSON
   Robert, 1857-1919   b-N.Y.   res.-Fowl.
                                   d-June 20, 1919 age 62
   Ella, 1866-1955   "Ella R" b-N.Y.   res.-Fowl.
                                   d- 1-12-55 age 88

   on monument-Pierson
3 SMITH
   Hillyard,   (FLT emblem)   res.-Fowl.
   1890-1947   d-Feb. 1, 1947 age 56
   Elizabeth, 1898-1919   (Mrs. Hilliard Smith)b-Mi. res.-Detroit
                                   d- 1-5-1919 age 19, spinal mengitis

   on monument-Smith
                                   female, Smith   res.-Fowl.
                                   d-Feb. 13, 1943, stillborn
4 HALL
   Joseph P Hall   b-Mi.   res.-Iosco
   1883-1919   d-March 3, 1919 age 36
5 WATERS
   Byrde, 1876-1956   "Bertha E" b-Mi.   res.-Oakland Co.
                                   d- 2-23-56 age 80
   David, 1855-1941   "David D"   Res.-Pontiac
                                   d-Jan. 25, 1941 age 85
   Libbie, wife of D Waters   not listed
   1855-1904
   on monument-Waters

                                   (Libbie Waters)b-Mi.   res.-Salem
                                   d-Apr. 30, 1920 age 45, cancer
6 CRIPPEN
   Isaac, 1837-1928(GAR emblem)   b-Mi.   res.-Conway
                                   d-Mar. 21, 1923 age 84
   Elizabeth, 1846-1919   b-N.Y.   res.-Conway
                                   d-April 11, 1919 age 72
   Myrtle, 1868-1926   res.-Fowl.
                                   d-April 20, 1926 age 58
   on monument-Crippen
                                   (Emma Ada Crippen)b-Mi.   res.-Ingham Co.
                                   d- 7-13-61 age 75
7 WITT
   no stones   (Herman Peters)b-Germany
                                   d-Oct. 13, 1919 age 89
                                   (John C Peters)b-Mi.   res.-Fowl.
                                   d-Sept. 5, 1925 age 65
                                   (John W Peters)   res.-Grand Rapids
                                   d-Jan. 1, 1932 age 42

Section "A"
lot #
8   LASHER
     double stone;
     Ollie D Lasher   res.-Fowl.
     1889-1968   d- 1-20-68 age 78
     Edwin H Lasher   res.-Handy
     1877-1964   d- 12-28-64 age 87
                                     (Ruth M Lasher) res.-Fowl.
                                     d-Nov. 17, 1919, stillborn
                                     (Clare Lasher)b-Mi.   res.-Conway
                                     d-Oct. 30, 1920 age 2 hours

9   EWING
     John E Ewing   "John Ezra"   res.-Alma
     Cfr. Cas. Det. 160 Dep.Brig.   d-age 85
     World War 1
     Oct. 20, 1882-Dec. 21, 1967
                                     (Rosella Ewing) res.-Fowl.
                                     d- 5-24-66 age 79
     Lyle Rogers   "Lyle D"   res.-Cadillac
     1905-1964   d- 1-25-1964 age 58
                                     (Thelma Fredenburgh) res.-Eaton Co.
                                     d- 3-17-70 age 55

10   ROGERS--SULKOWSKI
     Elmer J Rogers   b-Mi.   res.-Fowl.
     1889-1921   d-May 15, 1921 age 31
     double stone;
     Fred A Sulkowski   "Fred August"   res.-Liv. Co.
     1901-1972   d- 1-13-72 age 70
     Ivah B Sulkowski   "Ivah Belle"   res.-Howell
     1889-1970   d- 5-6-70 age 80
                                     (Carl E Steele)   res.-Fowl.
                                     d-Apr. 26, 1929 age 11mo. 19days, pnue.

11   CASTERTON
     double stone;
     Roy W Casterton   res. Howell twp.
     1895-1928   d-Dec. 22, 1928 age 33, pnue.
     Blanche E Casterton   (Blanche E Grant) res.-Liv. Co.
     1896-1973   d- 7-14-73 age 76
     Mildred Casterton   "Mildred E" b-Mi.   res.-Fowl.
     1917-1920   d-March 31, 1920 age 3
     Charles D Warren   res.-Lansing
     Michigan Phmi. USNR   d-age 48
     World War 2
     Oct. 30, 1923-Nov. 25, 1971
                                     (Todd Allen Carver) res.-Lansing
                                     d- 6-29-68 age 1 day

12   MUNSELL--HENRY
     double stone;Munsell
     Lawson W, 1861-1939   res. Ann Arbor
                                     d-Oct. 19, 1939 age 78
     Mary L, 1863-1944   res.-Fowl.
                                     d-Aug. 7, 1944 age 79
     on monument-Henry
     Rose, 1866-1943   (Rose Amelia Henry) res.-Fowl
                                     d-May 17, 1943 age 76
     Eugene, 1866-1929   (Eugene Henry) res.-Howell twp.
                                     d-Jan. 15, 1929 age 63, flu

Section "A"   Greenwood cemetery
lot #
13   WILLOVER
      no stones   (Maudeline Willover)b-Mi. res. Lansing
                                         d-Dec. 1, 1920 age 26, peretinitis
                                         (infant girl, Dogue)
                                         d-stillborn, burial May 24, 1938
                                         (Alice Plummer) res. Ann Arbor
                                         d-Oct. 6, 1939 age 65
                                         (Richard Plummer) res. Fowlerville
                                         d-March 20, 1941 age 3½

14   BETTERLY
      Ray L Betterly   "Raymond L" b-Mi. res. Lansing
      1875-1957   d- 12-15-1957 age 82
      Lillie M Betterly   "Lillie May" b-Mi. res. Conway
      1878-1921   d-March 21, 1921 age 42
      Bertha M Betterly   res. Lansing
      1886-1945   d-Feb. 27, 1945 age 58
      on monument-Betterly
15   CADWELL
      Charles H Cadwell "father"   not listed
      1881-
      Eula F Cadwell "mother"   res. Lansing
      1885-   d-Nov. 29, 1940 age 55
      on monument-Cadwell
      Alice M Reason   b-Mi. res. Lansing
      1908-1921   d-June 3, 1921 age 13
                                         (male Faunce?) removed from old cem.
                                         d-age 8 months, scarlet fever
                                         (Charles Faunce)
                                         d-April 23, 1889 age 31, consumption

16   KEENMON
      double stone;-Keenmon
      Charles H, "father"   b-Germany   res. Cohoctah
      1857-1921   d-June 29, 1921 age 65
      Catherine E, "mother"   (Catherine E Hilderbrant) res.Pontiac
      1862-1946   d-July 20, 1946 age 83
17   KUEHNLE
      Robert H Kuehnle   b-Mi.   res. Howell twp.
      1914-1921   d-July 19, 1921 age 7, accident
      Henry M Kuehnle   b-Mi.   res. Howell twp.
      1877-1921   d-July 19, 1921 age 43, accident
      Jeannette Kuehnle   res. Toledo, Ohio
      1878-1949   d-Dec. 31, 1949 age 71
18   BAMFORD
      Ephriam Bamford "father"   res. Fenton
      1872-1947   d-April 24, 1947 age 74
      Dora Bamford "mother"   b-England res. Tyrone
      1874-1921   d-March 25, 1921 age 47
19   BENJAMIN
      Bertha A, "mother"   b-Mi. res. Macomb Co.
      1869-1957   d- 3-11-57 age 87
      Arthur E, "father"   b-Mi.   res. Fowlerville
      1872-1922   d-Jan. 8, 1922 age 49
      on monument-Benjamin

{76}

lot #
19 continued
    Carolyn T Kennedy "daughter"   (Carolyn T Abbey) res. Highland Park,Mi.
    1906-1949   d-Nov. 10, 1949 age 43
    Emeline and Franklin Crawford -see lot A-54
                                    (Matilda Berry)
                                    d- 4-15-1871 age 19 (listed on A-21)
                                              removed from lot 85 of old cemetery
                                    (Otto Madison) b-Handy
                                              no date-removed fron old cemetery

20 KILPATRICK
                                    (infant son of Jesse Killpatrick)
                                              no date-removed fron old cem.

21 "potters field"
    no stones   (Amanda Sweet)
                                    d-age 19, no date, removed from old
                                                        cemetery
                                    (Frank L Baker) b-Mi. res. Handy
                                    d-Feb. 4, 1908 age 2, pnue.
                                    (David Clare Jones) res. Fowlerville
                                    d-July 19, 1911 age 2

22 "potters field"
                                    (Hawthorn Campbell)
                                    burial-?
                                    (Thomas Weller)   (no information)
                                    (Alice Epley)b-Mi. res. Handy
                                    d-Feb. 1, 1921 age 40 days
                                    also two remains marked to
                                    Tom Weller from lot 29 of old cem.

23 empty
24 LONSBURY   "potters field"
    Ira Lonsbury   b-N. Y   res. Fowlerville
    1814-1902   d-March 4, 1902 age 87y,4m,9d
                                          listed in old record as A-53(?)
                                    (infant, Dunham)b-Fowlerville
                                    d-March 31, 1902 age 22 days

25 "potters field"
                                    (Eligah Chapman)
                                    d- 10-23-74 age 78--from old cemetery
                                    (Charles William McEwan jr.)b-Mi.
                                    d- 11-21-61 age 1 hour

26 "potters field"
                                    (Alvin C Blakslee) res. Fowlerville
                                    burial Dec. 23, 1923 age 1 hour

27 "potters field"
                                    (John Blatten)b-Germany res. Iosco
                                    d-Dec. 6, 1899 age 65
                                    (Daniel D Waite) res. Handy
                                    d-Feb. 1, 1900 age 89

28 "potters field"
                                    (Earl Daniels)
                                    d-April 6, 1885 age 7 months,diptheria
                                    (Frank C Martin)   res. Ann Arbor
                                    d-Sept. 16, 1887 age 24,killed by cars
                                    (Lewis Levins) b-New York
                                    d-Oct. 30, 1887 age 75

Section "A"   Greenwood cemetery
lot #
28 continued   (William Bowen)
                                    d-April 13, 1885 age 7
                                    (Frederick Bowen)
                                    d-April 19, 1885 age 4
                                    (Etta Bowen)b-Fowlerville
                                    d-Jan. 8, 1887 age 3 of burns
                                    (Ervin Daniels)
                                    d-April 11, 1885 age 9,diptheria
                                    (Matilda Barry)
                                       removed from lot 85 old cemetery
                                    (Julia A Faunce) from old cemetery
                                    d-1863 age 34, typhoid fever
                                    (unknown male)b-Handy
                                    d-May 4, 1893, stillborn
29   empty
30   (Calvin Lockwood)b-N. Y. res. Fowl.
                                    d-Feb. 20, 1904 age 70 (listed lot 38½)
31 to 41, part of "potters field" are empty
42   SHERMAN
                                    (Job Sherman)   no data
                                    also two unknown bodies marked to
                                    Job Sherman, from lot 69 of old cem.

43   STICKLES--SWIFT
                                    (George Stickles)
                                    d- 1-13-64 age 4, from old cemetery
                                    (Deliah Stickles)
                                    burial 7-18-66 from old cemetery
                                    (Orsan Swift)
                                    d-12-20-74 age 67, from old cem.

44   SMITH
     double stone; Smith   res. Iosco
     Thomas E, 1867-   d-May 8, 1941 age 78
     Cora E, 1871-1939   res. Iosco   "Cora Ida"
                                   d-April 4, 1939 age 68
                                   (William Smith) res. Iosco
                                   d-Feb. 18, 1937 age 69
                                   (Margaret Lamoreaux)b-Ireland,res. Iosco
                                   d-March 11, 1921 age 90

45   empty
46   PHILLIPS
                                    (Carrie A Phillips) res. Jackson
                                    d-May 15, 1945 age 65
                                    (Shirley May Phillips) rest Clayton
                                    d-Oct. 17, 1936 age 6 months
                                    (male Phillips) res. Jackson
                                    d-March 28, 1953
                                    (Isaac F Herrington)
                                    d- 4-26-57 age 3 from lot 53 old cem.
                                    (James Edward Finch)b-Fowlerville
                                    d- 9-2-1918 age 2 months
                                    (Dorothy Lord) res. Fowlerville
                                    d- 10-27-1918 age 7 months, pnue.

Section "A"   Greenwood cemetery
lot #
47   BODINE--RISDON

                              (Hiram Bodine) parent may be Orla Risdon
                              d- 3-10-76   from old cemetery
                              (Iva Risdon) res. Livingston Co.
                              d- 7-2-74 age 79
                              (Orla D Risdon) b-Mi. res. Fowl.
                              d- 12-19-75 age 81
                              (Orman D Risdon) b-Mi. res. Fowl.
                              d-Oct. 29, 1921 age 3
                              (Donna E Risdon) res. Fowlerville
                              d-June 30, 1926 age 6 months, pnue.

48   GLOVER
     Kenneth H Glover   b-Mi. res. Handy
     1891-1920   d-Feb. 19, 1920 age 29
     Barbara B Glover   b-Germany res. E. Lansing
     1867-1951   d-Dec. 15, 1951 age 84
     Archie M Glover   "Archie Milan" b-Mi. res. Handy
     1863-1924   d-May 22, 1924 age 61
     on monument-Glover
49   GLOVER
     double stone; Glover
     Carl E, 1894-1982 (masonic)   res. Livingston Co.
                              d- 12-10-82 age 88
     Dora F, 1899-19-   (O.E.S)   not listed
50   DOUGLAS
                              (Mary E Douglas)
                              d- 3-29-69 age 33 from old cemetery
                              (Abigail Chapman) no data-from old cem.

51   CRANE--FEAR
     Marcia A, "mother"   (Marcia A Crane) res. Webberville
     1851-1928   d-Aug. 22, 1928, cancer
     Frank J, "father"   (Frank J Crane)b-N. Y.   res.Handy
     1850-1923   d-Sept. 21, 1923 age 73
                              (Sarah B Mitchell)
                              d- 7-20-57 age 56 from old cemetery

52   FEAR--CRANE
     William E, 1871-1957   (William E Fear)b-Mi. res. Fowl.
                              d- 3-25-59 age 88
     Mary M, 1875-1918 "mother"   (Mrs. Wm. Fear)
                              d- 2-2-1918 age 41, pnue.
     Lois M, 1875-1960   no record
53   ALLEN
     George H, "father"
     Etta E, "mother"
     on monument--Allen
     George H, 1870-1943   res. Iosco
                              d-April 24, 1943 age 72
     Etta E, 1875-1968   res. Livingston Co.
                              d- 12-31-68 age 93
     double stone; Allen
     Charles G, 1900-1972   res. Livingston Co.
                              d- 7-27-1972 age 72 killed-airplane crash
     Mary, 1903-1972   d- 7-27-1972 age 69   "   "   "
     Michael R Smith "our baby"   res. Iosco
       1948   d-Feb. 21, 1944 age 0, burial 1944

Section "A"   Greenwood cemetery
lot #
54   BENJAMIN

                        (Franklin H Crawford) (stone on lot A-19)
                        d-age 9 months   from old cemetery
                        (infant female, Sweet) res. Owasso
                        d-May 13, 1930 stillborn
                        also a women & child from lot 93 of
                        the old cemetery, removed by S S Abbott

55   BAILEY--FEWLASS
      Martha L Fewlass "wife"   not listed
      1872-1947
      George B Fewlass "husband"   not listed
      1866-1919
      Claire Blossom Bailey   "Claire A"   res. Detroit
      June 11, 1887-Feb. 19, 1966   burial 2-21-66 age 78
      James I Bailey   not listed
      Dec. 17, 1887-Aug. 2, 1955
      Ella Bailey Benjamin   res. Fowlerville
      Sept. 18, 1855-Sept. 12, 1936   d-age 81
on monument--Bailey-Benjamin
            James I, 1887-1955
            Claire Blossom, 1887-1966
            Ella Fewlass Bailey, 1855-1936
                        (Mary A Bowan)
                        d-age 48 of consumption, burial 1898
                               removed from Briggs cemetery

56   McDANIELS
      double stone--McDaniels
      John, 1865-1933   res. Fowlerville
                                        d-Feb. 1, 1933 age 63
      Nellie , 1881-1932   "nellie J" res. Fowlerville
                                        d-July 16, 1932 age 51
                                        (Bernard J Daniels)b-Mi. res. Fowl.
                                        d- 9-25-1917 age 9 months
                                        (Lois M Lear)b-Mi. res. Shiawasee Co.
                                        d- 7-21-1960 age 84

56½   GRIFFIN--NELSON
      on monument-Griffin-Nelson
                Frank S, 1864-1937 not listed
                Louise Bailey, 1879-1968 not listed
                Clinton J, 1883-1949 not listed
                Harriet Bailey, 1886-1959 not listed
57   HARRISON
      P Franklin Harrison   res. Shiawasee Co.
      1873-1949   d-Sept. 26, 1949 age 77
      Mrs. Anna Harrison   res. Shiawasee Co.
      1895-1973   d- 4-18-73 age 75, burial from Bancroft
                                        (L D Harrison) male, res. Ann Arbor
                                        d-June 5, 1949 age 22
                                        (John Ray) b-Mi. res. Barryton
                                        d- 7-19-1917 age 62

Section "A"   Greenwood cemetery
lot #
58

                                   (Harriet L Nelson)b-Mi. res. Ann Arbor
                                   d- 2-17-59 age 72 (cremated-Oct. 5-59)
                                   (Clinton Jones Nelson)b-Mi. res. Ann Arbor
                                   d- 12-9-49 age 66 (cremated-Oct. 5, 1959)

59   BAILEY-FEWLASS

                                   (Martha Fernless)? res. Meridan twp.
                                   d-Jan. 1, 1947 age 74
                                   (Geo. B Fewlass) b-Mi. res. Lansing
                                   d-June 29, 1919 age 52

59½

                                   (Perry D Lang) res. Handy
                                   d-June 4, 1945 age 72
                                   (Clare Leroy Lang) res. Howell
                                   d-July 1, 1951 stillborn
                                   (Martha Estella Lang) b-Mi. res. Liv. Co.
                                   d- 9-8-62 age 78, burial 10-2-62

60   DEAN
     double stone;-Dean
     Aaron L, 1898-1962   b-Mi. res. Liv. Co.
                                   d- 6-12-1962 age 64
     Arloa R, 1902-1977   res. Mesa, Arizona
                                   d- 7-1-1977 age 75
     Lavina Dean   res. Conway
     1862-1936   d-Feb. 13, 1936 age 72
     Morris D Dean   res. Conway
                                     d- 3-2-1917 age 61

61   WEST--GRANT
     Ila May Austin   not listed
     1901-1913
     Eva West   (Mrs. Eva West)b-Mi. res. Lansing
     1885-1919   d-Oct. 16, 1919 age 34 of burns
     Ada E Grant   "Ada G" res. Lansing
     1854-1927   d-Dec. 4, 1927 age 73
     Bryan Grant   b-Mass. res. Lansing
     1854-1917   d- 1-6-1917 age 79
     on monument--West-Grant

                                   (Inez B Howard) res. Lansing
                                   d-Feb. 21, 1934 age 54

62   DORMER
     William H, 1854-1917   not listed
     Sarah E, 1859-1933   res. Handy
                                     d-Oct. 6, 1933 age 75 in accident
     R D Dormer   res. Clinton Co.
     1882-1971   d- 4-20-71 age 88
     on monument-Dormer
62½   LANG
     Julia C Lang   b-Mi. res. Handy
     1919-1963   d- 5-22-63 age 44 of burns-train accident
     Ford T Lang   not listed
     1914-19-
     Perry D Lang   not listed
     1872-1945
     M Estella Lang   not listed
     1884-1962

Section "A"   Greenwood cemetery
lot #
63   KLEIN
      William Klein   "Wm. F," b-Mi. res. Conway
      1878-1956   d- 1-26-56 age 65
      Clara Klein   "Clara E," b-Mi. res. Howell
      1880-1957   d- 4-16-57 age 77
      Mildred V Klein   (Mildred Viola Kline)b-Mi. res. Cohoctah
      1908-1917   d- 9-15-1917 age 8, diptheria
      Gladys M Klein   b-Mi. res. Ann Arbor
      1910-1917   d= 8-29-1917 age 6
63½   PLUMMER
      double stone;-Plummer
      Frank, 1900-1970   res. Howell
                                         d- 5-12-70 age 69
      Naomi, 1901-1963   res. Fowlerville
                                         d- 11-6-1963 age 61

64
                                         (infant daughter) of W A Brooks
                                         d-April 21, 1907   res. Fowlerville

65   ROGERS
      double stone;-Rogers
      Henry A, 1843-1915   b-Mi. res. Fowlerville
                                         d- 12-8-1916 age 71
      Adelia, 1865-19-   (Adelia Rogers Bickford) res. Fowl.
                                         d-May 18, 1948 age 82
                                         (Vern Rogers)b-Mi. res. Fowl.
                                         d- 4-29-1917 age 28
                                         (George Rogers)b-Mi. res. Fowl.
                                         d- 9-19-1958 age 73

66   WYCKOFF
      Frederick Clayton, 1918-1919   b-Mi. res. Fowlerville
                                         d-April 8, 1919 age 7, pnue.
      Esther Leone, 1917-1917   b-Mi. res. Handy
                                         d- 5-25-1917 age 2 months
      Ila May, 1923-1923   b-Mi. res. Lansing
                                         d-Aug. 16, 1923 age 4 months
      Charles R, 1920-1935   not listed
      "mother"
      "father"
      on monument-Wyckoff
              Richard T, 1895-1974   res. Lansing
                                     d- 3-10-74 age 78
              Harriet A, 1898-19-   not listed
67   PULLEN--VAN VERST
      Clyde L Pullen   b-Mi. res. Lansing
      1869-1913   d- 4-30-13 age 43, suicide
      Jennie Pullen   res. Lansing
      1865-1939   d-age 74   burial Feb. 1, 1939
      Russell Barnett   "Russell E"b-Mi. res. Lansing
      Oct. 31, 1916-Nov. 21, 1916   d-age 3 weeks
      Ila E Van Verst "wife"   res. Bradenton, Florida
      1895-1973   d- 8-3-73
      on monument--Van Verst-Barnett-Pullen

Section "A"   Greenwood cemetery
lot #
67½ LAUTERBACH
     double stone;-Lauterbach
     Emil M, 1888-1962 (vet)   b-Mi.   res. Ingham Co.
                                      d- 2-25-62 age 73
     Luella G, 1894-1983   res. Ingham Co.
                                      d- 4-27-1983 age 88, burial from Lansing

68   PALMERTON
     William Palmerton "father"   b-Mi. res. Lansing
     1836-1907   d-May 24, 1907 age 70
     May Palmerton "mother"   (Mrs. Wm. Palmerton) b-on the high seas
     1836-1915   d- 5-3-1915 age 77   res. Conway
                                      (Ida Handy)b-Mi. res. Howell twp.
                                      d-Feb. 20, 1907 age 46
                                      (Ira Handy)b-Mi.   res. Fowlerville
                                      d- 9-18, 1911 age 23, suicide

69   SHORMAN
     double stone;-Shorman
     Isaac, 1868-1948 "father"   res. Webberville
                                      d-Feb. 29, 1948 age 79
     Hattie C, 1876-1964 "mother"   res. Ingham Co.
                                      d- 7-23-1964 age 87
     Effie I, 1895-1903   (Effie I Shorman)b-Mi. res. Conway
                                      d-Dec. 25, 1903
     J C, 1905-1910 (male)   (J C Shorman)b-Mi. res. Fowl.
                                      d-June 22, 1910 age 4, pnuemonia
     Irene M Shorman Adams "mom"   listed on lot 1-69
     1900-1972
     Jaunita S Adams "baby"   not listed
                                      (infant son of I M Shureman)res. Fowl.
                                      d- 8-17-1913 stillborn

70   HAYNER
     Harriet, 1841-1916   b-N. Y res. Conway
                                      d- 9-5-1916 age 74
     Andrew J, 1842-1919   listed on lot 70½
     on monument-Hayner
     George A Selfridge   b-Mi. res. Conway
     1870-1921   d-Feb. 4, 1921 age 50
     Florence I Selfridge Bullen   res. Jackson
     1879-1966   d- 2-21-66 age 86, burial from Lansing
70½ HAYNER
     double stone;-Hayner
     W Elmer, 1868-1954   b-Mi. res. Lansing
                                      d- 6-8-54
     Helen E, 1872-1941   "Helen Edith" b-Handy res. White Oak
                                      d-Aug. 6, 1941 age 65
                                      (Andrew J Hayner)b-N. Y. res. Conway
                                      d-March 19, 1919 age 77

71   ECKHART--STOW
     Frances
     George
     Dora
     Cleve

Section "A"   Greenwood cemetery
lot #
71 continued
    on monument-
        G Cleve Eckhart   b-Mi.   res. Handy
        1884-1920   d-Aug. 30, 1920 age 35
        Dora B Eckhart   res. Livingston Co.
        1886-1976   d- 8-17-1975 age 88, burial 8-20-75
        George F Stow   res. Livingston Co.
        1884-1974   d- 1-2-1974 age 89
        Frances L Stow   res. Conway
        1885-1935   d-age 49, burial Oct. 7, 1944
                                     removed from Miller cemetery

71½

                         (Clifford Rogers)b-Mi. res. Fowl.
                         d-April 28, 1953
72 KNICKERBOCKER--ABBOTT
    George A,   (George A Knickerbocker)res. Fowl.
    died Mar. 3, 1936 age 79y, 5m, 19d   burial same day, age 69(?)
    Florence E,   (Florence E Knickerbocker)res. Fowl.
    died Apr. 27, 1928 aged 54y, 6d   burial April 30
    Charles E,   (Charles E Abbott) b-N. Y. res. Fowl.
    died Sept. 10, 1916 aged 77y, 7m, 8d   burial 9-13
    Martha A, wife of Charles E Abbott   b-Mi. res. Handy
    died April 25, 1905 aged 57yrs, 10mos & 21 days   Burial Apr. 28
    on monument-Knickerbocher-Abbott
73 KLECKNER
    J K   see below
    Caroline Kleckner   res. Fowlerville
    1848-1931   d-Jan. 29, 1931 age 82
    Minnie B Kleckner   "Minnie Bell" b-Mi. res. Fowl.
    1872-1917   d- 6-22-1917 age 44, pnuemonia
    Rosa May Kleckner   res. Fowlerville
    1880-1926   d-Dec. 30, 1926 age 46
    James Kleckner   see monument
    Co. A, 48th Pa. Inf.
    on monument-Kleckner
              Edward J, son of J & C Kleckner   not listed
              born Oct. 12, 1875, died Oct. 11, 1881
              James Kleckner   not listed in records
              born Apr. 26, 1817, died Feb. 16, 1881
74 KLECKNER
    E J K   see lot 73
                         (Wm. Kleckner) burial (?)
                         old records list a male-lot A-73 & A-174
74½ RIFE
    George W Rife   b-Mi.   res. Livingston Co.
    Ohio, Pvt. Co. F, 17 Rect. Infantry, Spanish American war
    Dec. 5, 1875-March 8, 1956   burial 3-11-56 age 80
    Friedarica Rife   b-Mi. res. Iosco
    April 2, 1879-May 8, 1953
75 STEINACKER
    double stone;-Steinacker
    Adam, 1851-1927   res. Cohoctah
                         d-July 7, 1927 age 75

    Amelia, 1854-1929   res. Cohoctah
                         d-May 13, 1929 age 74

Section "A"   Greenwood cemetery
lot #
75 continued
      Leland, 1913-1923   (Leland Steinacker)b-Mi. res. Cohoctah
                                     d-Dec. 11, 1923 age 10, diptheria
                                     (Charles Steinacker) res. Oceola
                                     d-Oct. 2, 1948 age 85

75½ DETERDING
      Edward G Deterding   b-Mi. res. Livingston Co.
      March 10, 1891-September 13, 1956   d-age 65
76   BRAVENER
      Robert, 1847-1905   b-Mi. res. Cohoctah
                                     d-Aug. 5, 1905age 48

      Emma, 1860-1935   (Emma Jordon) res. Howell
                                     d-March 22, 1935 age 74

      Homer R,   b-Mi. res. Fowlerville
      Aug. 18, 1901-Sep. 4, 1909   d- of typhoid, age 8
      on monument-Bravener

                                     (Leonard Daniels)b-Mi. res. Howell twp.
                                     d- 3-7-1915 age 3 weeks
                                     (Ina M Soule) res. Ingham Co.
                                     d- 2-23-78, ashes buried at head of Emma
      Charley Steinacker   no record
      1863-1914   (may be buried on lot 78)
                                     (George Bunting Jr.) res. Howell
                                     d-Nov. 1909 age 1, heart failure
                                               burial Nov. 4, 1909

77   DEAN
      Bert J, 1864-19-   (flt emblem)not listed
      Gussie W, 1860-1914   res. Howell twp.
                                     d- 11-3-1914 age 54

      on monument-Dean
78   STEINACKER
      Elizabeth, "wife"   res. Cohoctan (listed as lot B-78)
      1853-1929   d-April 2, 1929 age 75, pnue.
      Frederick, "husband"   b-Germany res. Howell
      1847-1915   d- 11-6-1915 age 68
      on monument-Steinacker

                                     (Wilber Sticknacker) res. Jackson
                                     d-Jan. 20, 1937 stillborn
                                     (Florence Steinacker)b-Mi. res. Cohoctah
                                     d-July 28, 1919 age 3 months

79   CONIWAY
      Mr. John D Coniway   b-Mi. res. Locke twp.
      1846-1916   d- 8-23-1916 age 70
      Florence E Coniway   res. Lansing
      1866-1941   d-Oct. 28, 1941 age 74
79½ CRIPPEN
      W Irving, 1876-1960   (Washington Irving Crippen)b-Mi.
                                     d- 1-20-1960 age 83 res. Ingham Co.

      Emma A, 1883-1961   no record
80   WILLETT
      Mary Willett   b-England res. White Oak, Ingham Co.
      1857-1915   d- 6-19-1915 age 58, cancer
                                     (Harriet Willett) burial ?

Section "A"   Greenwood cemetery
lot #
81   BRAVENER
     double stone;-Bravener
     William, 1855-1915   b-Canada   res. Fowlerville
                                 d- 8-7-1915 age 60
     Mary E, 1869-1963   res. Florida
                                 d- 12-12-1963 age 94
     double stone;-Bravener
     Lavern D, 1895-   not listed
     Eva A, 1908-   not listed
82   NICKERSON
     Johanna A Nickerson "mother"   not listed
     1886-19-
     Frances McLosey "daughter" (Frances McLosey Nickerson)b-Mi.
     1908-1916   d- 2-26-1916 age 8, typhoid res. Fowl.
83   HORTON
     Stephen R, 1850-1912   no record
     Elizabeth, 1863-1951   res. Fowlerville
                                 d-Aug. 21, 1951 age 88
     Alta H Minkley   res. Charlotte
     1886-1971   d- 8-10-71 age 85
     on monument-Horton
84   HORTON
     double stone;-Horton
     Rollin S, 1879-1975   res. Livingston Co.
                                 d- 6-3-75 age 95
     Blanche E, 1888-1975   res. Livingston Co.
                                 d- 1-26-75 age 86
     Verlyn L Horton   res. Fowlerville
     1926-1967   d- 11-17-67 age 38
     Carol D Horton   res. Wayne Co.
     1952-1974   d- 7-28-74 age 21
     William C Durfee (masonic) res. Handy
     1864-1949   d-April 11, 1949 age 79
85   SCHMIDT
     Frank F, 1869-1951   res. Howell
                                 d-July 15, 1951 age 82
     Olga M, 1879-1961   "Olga Martha"b-Mi. res. Liv. Co.
                                 d- 11-28-61 age 82
     Stanley F, 1901-1915   b-Mi.   res. Howell
                                 d- 10-9-1915
     on monument-Schmidt
86   CUMMISKEY
     Rhea M Cummiskey   res. Handy
     1899-1963   d- 12-4-1963 age 64
     Ernest Cummiskey   res. Howell
     1893-1966   d- 9-9-66 age 73
     Mary, "mother"   "Mary C"   res. Iosco
     1872-1947   d-Dec. 12, 1947 age 75
     Barney, "father"   b-Mi.   res. Iosco
     1858-1917   d- 10-27-1917 age 59
     on monument-Cummiskey (masonic emblem)

Section "A"   Greenwood cemetery
lot #

87   STAGE
     triple stone;-Ash
     Larkos, 1891-19-   (Larkos W Ash) res. Petoskey
                                   d- 7-19-1983 age 92
     baby, 1933   (baby boy, Ash) res. Conway
                                   d-stillborn burial March 29, 1933
     Gay, 1890-1973   res. Howell
                                   d- 3-3-73 age 82
     Nellie S, 1866-1945   (Nellie Snell Stage) res. Conway
                                   d-Jan. 23, 1945 age 79
     William R, 1861-1917   no record
     on monument-Stage- WRS

                                   (Latella Mapes)b-Mi. res. Lapeer
                                   d- 7-5-59 age 87

88   SNELL
     John W, 1838-1915   "John Sr." b-England res. Conway
                                   d- 12-6-1915 age 77
     Charlotte, 1843-1920   b-England res. Fowlerville
                                   d-May 4, 1920 age 77

     on monument-Snell

                                   (Paul Snell) res. Fowlerville
                                   d-June 1, 1928 age 6, drowned by mother

89   SNELL
     Fred S, "father"   res. Fowlerville
     1868-1926   d-Sept. 28, 1926 age 58, accident
     Latella "mother"   no record
     1872-1959
     on monument-Snell

90   DINGMAN
     Edwar Dingman   "Edward" b-Conway res. Fowl.
     1868-1941   d-Sept. 5, 1941 age 73
     Gracie M Dingman   b-Mi. res. Fowlerville
     1873-1918   d- 10-18-1918 age 45
                                   (Jessie McLucus) male, res. Fowl.
                                   d-age 32, burial Oct. 9, 1938

91   ABBOTT
     double stone;-Abbott
     Irving, 1855-1926   no record
     Janette, 1851-1923   b-Mi. res. Fowlerville
                                   d-Dec. 10, 1923 age 74, typhoid
     Iva B, wife of G B Abbott   (Mrs. Guy Abott)b-Mi. res. Lansing
     1894-1919   d- 12-30, 1919 age 26
92   BENNETT
     W Sterling Bennett "our son" "Wilbur S" b-Mi. res. Detroit
     1907-1916   d- 9-3-1916 age 8
93   CROFOOT
     double stone;-Crofoot
     George V, 1883-1963   b-Mi. res. Ingham Co.
                                   d- 9-12-63 age 79
     Emma S, 1885-1976   "Emma Selma" res. Ingham Co.
                                   d- 9-17-1976 age 91
     Edmund S, "son"   b-Mi. res. Iosco
     1907-1915   d- 9-4-1916 age 9

Section "A"   Greenwood cemetery
lot #
93 continued
    George D Ward   "George Dwight" res. Howell
    1945-1966   d- 9-30-66 age 21, fracture of spine
                                                   burial 10-3-66 from Stockbridge

94 DEFENDORF
    double stone;-Defendorf
    Dr. Byron, 1839-1929   res. Chelsea
                                       d-June 12, 1929 age 89
    Hulda A, 1847-1913   b-N. Y   res. Chelsea
                                                   removed from Chelsea cemetery
97
                                       (Erwin(?) J Abbott)b-Mi. res. Fowl.
                                       d-Jan 20, 1926 age 71
98 to 103 are empty-not used
104 HUGHES
    Ellen D Hughes "mother"   (Mrs. A H Hughes)b-Mi. res. Fowl.
    1847-1915   d- 4-16-1915 age 68
    Arvid H Hughes "father"   b-Mi.   res. Fowlerville
    1841-1918   d- 10-12-1918
105 MUNSELL
    Arthur G Munsell   b-Mi.   res. Handy
    1881-1954   d- 1-8-1954 age 72
    Bessie L Munsell   b-Mi.   Res. Livingston Co.
    1882-1962   d- 8-16, 1962 age 80
    Gertrude Mary Munsell   b-Mi. res. Howell twp.
    1905-1920   d-Feb. 5, 1920 age 15, pnuemonia
    Beatrice Munsell   res. Handy
    1911-1911   d-Jan. 21, 1911 age 9 days of deformity
105½ LEARY
    double stone;-Leary
    Donald C, 1904-1956   b-Mi. res. Ann Arbor
                                       d- 9-11-56 age 52
    Olis M, 1917-   not listed
106 DURFEE
    Harry G Durfee   no record
    Sep. 30, 1872-Nov. 28, 1909
    Etta M Durfee   no record
    Dec. 16, 1879-
    Elias Durfee "father"   no record
    Co. E, 26 Mich. Inf.
    Jennie Durfee "mother"   "Laura J" res. Fowlerville
    Jan. 12, 1852-Mar. 6, 1932   d-age 80
    on monument-Durfee
107 PALMER
    Minnie Palmer   b-Mi.   res. Fowlerville
    1893-1921   d-July 25, 1921 age 28 of T.B.
    double stone;-Palmer
    George E, 1857-1929   res. Fowlerville
                                       D-Dec. 8, 1929 age 72
    Catherine G, 1859-1939   (Catherine Perkins Palmer)res. Fowl.
                                       d-March 12, 1939 age 79
    Floss M Fretz "daughter"   not listed
    1896-19-
                                       (Ora J Palmer) res. Handy
                                       d-May 29, 1907 age 3 weeks

108 SIDELL
    Will M, 1868-1945 "father"   res. Fowlerville
                                    d-Feb. 18, 1945 age 76

    L Audrey, mother"   "Lillian Ardy" res. Fowlerville
    1871-1941   d-June 2, 1941 age 70
    Pierson W, 1889-1963   b-Mi.   res. Fowlerville
                                    d- 9-30-1963 age 74

    Julia M, 1887-1957   res. Ann Arbor
                                    d- 9-4-1957 age 70

    on monument-Sidell

                                    (Clarence M Hale) res. Handy
                                    d-May 27, 1905 age 1 month 22 days
                                    (Fred W Pettet)
                                    burial 6-19-1943 age 74

109 SIDELL
    Nellie M, 1895-1940   res. Flint
                                    burial 6-4-1940 age 45

    Lillian, 1916-1918   "Lillian E" b-Mi.   res. Handy
                                    d- 11-12-1918 age 2, flu
    Floyd D, 1893-1973   res. Bradenton, Florida
                                    d- 5-21-1973 age 79

    on monument-Sidell
109½ SIDELL
    Dorathy A, 1907-1982   res. Livingston Co.
                                    d- 2-25-1982 age 74

    Leslie W, 1906-19-   not listed
    on monument-Sidell
110 GRIFFIN-PLASS
    Rose M Griffin   b-Mi.   res. Fowlerville
    Mar. 23, 1883-Jan. 22, 1914   d-age 30 of pnuemonia
    double stone;-PLASS
    Dorothy E, 1911-1966   "Dorothy Elizabeth" res. Pontiac
                                    d- 12-16-1966 age 55
                                    (infant male,Plass) res.Fowl.
                                    d-Jan. 21,1933 stillborn

111 LAMOREUX
    baby Plass, 1933   see above lot (stone on lot 111)
    John Lamoreux   b-N. Y.   res. Handy
    May 7, 1841-May 10, 1922   d-age 81
    "mother"
    on monument-Lamoreux
        Elizabeth M,   b-N. Y.   res. Handy
        born Sept. 15, 1815, died Apr. 23, 1898   age 80
                                    burial 5-17-1896(?)
        Thomas Lamoreux   b-N. Y.   res. Iosco
        died June 10, 1884 aged 63 years   burial Nov. 11, 1920
                                    removed from Mapes cemetery

    "father"
112 NEWMAN
    Lodema Newman   b-Mi.   res. Fowlerville
    1857-1906   d-Feb. 19, 1906 age 47
    Henry Newman   b-Mi.   res. Fowlerville
    1854-1923   d-April 21, 1923

Section "A"   Greenwood cemetery
lot #
112 continued
    Leona Jackson "mother"   res. Fowlerville
    1901-1938 (Amer. Leg. Aux.)   d-age 37, burial Sept. 21, 1938
    Charles H Jackson   "Charles Hiram" b-Mi. res. Montcalm Co.
    Michigan Cpl. Co. M, 338 Infantry, World War 1
    July 23, 1893-Jan. 12, 1957   d-age 63
                                    (Kenneth Charles Jackson)b-Mi. res. Fowl.
                                    d-Apr. 19, 1919 age 2_(?) of pnue.

113 PULLEN
    Levi Pullen   b-Maine   res. Fowlerville
    1810-1910   d-Jan. 4, 1910 age 99
    Emily Pullen   b-N. Y.   res. Fowlerville
    1828-1913   d- 2-21-1913 age 85
    Mary Emily Pullen   res. Racine, Wisconcin
    1850-1939   d-June 16, 1939 age 88
    Selden Burgess Pullen   "Burgess" b-Mi. res. Fowl.
    1848-1916   d-5-21-1916 age 67 (listed lot 114)
    Jennie B Pullen   res. Racine, Wisconcin
    1875-1935   d-Dec. 29, 1935 age 61, burial May 8, 1936
                                    (Amy Rose Pullen) (might be Amy & Rose)?
                                    burial 10-31, 1963(ashes)

114 PULLEN
    Milton H Pullen   b-Mi. res. Howell
    1842-1916   d- 8-7-1916 age 73
    Margaret E Pullen   b-N. Y.   res. Handy
    1849-1883   d-July 8, 1883 age 32 of typhoid
                                         burial 7-10-1893 from Howell

115 HENRY
    Ella M, his wife   (Ella Mariah Van Riper Henry)
    1855-1900   b-Webster twp, Wash. Co. res. Fowl.
                                    d-May 5, 1900 age 44

    Gilbert Henry   no record
    1849-1915

                                    (Nellie M Henry) res. Howell
                                    d-Jan. 5, 1929 age 67, concer

116 BOWERS
    Martha E Bowers   "Martha Elizabeth" b-Mi. res. Detroit
    1876-1920   d-Dec. 24, 1920 age 44
    Bradley R Bowers   b-N. Y.   res. Fowlerville
    1845-1922   d-May 7, 1922 age 77
    Deborah M, wife of B R Bowers   b-N. Y.
    born Mar. 12, 1850, died July 12, 1896   age 46
    Elizabeth A Dickinson "mother" b-N. Y.
    born Aug. 19, 1824, died Mar. 19, 1896   burial Nov. 21, 1896
    on monument-Bowers
                                    (infant of Fred Bowers) b-Handy
                                    d-May 10, 1899 age 7 hours
117 PLIMPTON
    Hiram A Plimpton (KOMT emblem) b-N. Y.   res. Handy
    born May 12, 1854, died Nov. 18, 1897   age 43
    Hiram,   a headstone
    Ruth M Wieand   "Ruth Marie" res. Livingston Co.
    1914-1968   d- 12-22-68 age 53
    Richard C Wiend   "Richard Charles" b-Howell, res. Howell
    1938-1939   burial April 15 or 18, 1939 age 1

Section "A"   Greenwood cemetery
lot #
117 continued
                                      (Dexter N Wieand) res. Liv. Co/
                                      d- 1-6-78 age 61
                                      (Sarah J Maleitzke)res. Hartland
                                      d- 12-9-1915 age 54
118 TEACHWORTH
                                      (Ward Teachworth) b-N. Y. res. Fowl.
                                      d-Feb. 8, 1899 age 66 of pnuemonia
                                      (Eliza Ann Teachworth)b-Mi. res. Conway
                                      d-Nov. 1, 1920 age 76
119 NEWMAN
    William Newman "father"   no record
    born Dec. 15, 1812, died Mar. 15, 1870
    Ann Taylor Newman "mother"   b-England res. Fowlerville
    born May 28, 1817, died Dec. 26, 1899   age 81
    Hattie, dau. of W & A Newman   (Mrs. Wm. Leedle)b-Salem,Mi. res. Byron
    born Oct. 17, 1851, died July 10, 1900   age 49
    on monument-Newman

                                      (Thomas Newman) b-England res. Fowl.
                                      d- 3-28-1915 age 68
120 PLASS
    "mother"
    "father"
    on monument;-Plass
        Edgar Plass   b-N. Y. res. Newark, N. Y.
    b-Feb. 15, 1825, d-Aug. 22, 1902   burial Dec. 25, 1902
        Charlotte Ann Plass   b-N. Y. res. Conway
    b-July 8, 1824, d-May 13, 1899   age 75
121 GRANT
    double stone;
    Herbert Stanley, 1867-1947   (Herbert Stanley Grant)res. St. Petersburg
                                      d-Aug. 25, 1947 age 79 (in Florida)_
    Ellen Abbott, 1869-1902   (Ellen May Grant)b-Mi. res. Handy
                                      d-Nov. 4, 1902 age 33, heart failure
    on monument-Grant
122 NEELY
    Merion E Neely   "Myrton E" b-Mi. res. Fowlerville
    born Sept. 18, 1872, died Aug. 7, 1903   age 30
                                      (Mrs. Elizabeth Neely)b-N. Y. res. Fowl.
                                      d-April 1, 1901 age 68y, 9m, 13d
123 BALL-WICKMAN
    Dewitt C Ball "father"
    1823-1872   removed from Benjamin cem. 4-28-1904
    Mary J, wife of Dewitt C Ball   b-Mi. res. Fowlerville
    1832-1903   d-May 3, 1903 age 70
    Anna Ball Wickman   "Anna M" res. Fowlerville
    1866-1947   d-March 27, 1947 age 81
    James F Wickman   b-Mi. res. Fowlerville
    1848-1918   d- 12-23-1918 age 70
    on monument-Ball

                                      (Buell D Ford)b-Mi. res. Howell
                                      d-age 57, ashes buried 4-20-1960

Section "A"   Greenwood cemetery
lot #
124 BOYD
     John L Briggs   res. Fowlerville
     1850-1926   d-Aug. 30, 1926 age 76
     Millie Lasher   res. Fowlerville
     1852-1928   d-Jan. 11, 1929 of flu, bur. Jan. 14, 1929
     a blank stone   (Elizabeth Boyd) res. Conway
                                d-Aug. 9, 1932 age 89
     Henry, 1832-1902   (Henry P Boyd)b-Mi. res. Conway
                                d-Dec. 3, 1902 age 70

     on monument-Boyd
125 LUDTKE
     Amalie Ludtke "mother"   "Amalie A" b-Germany,res. Handy
     1850-1903   d-May 26, 1903 age 53
     Wm. F Ludtke "father"   b-Germany   res. Germany(?)
     1848-1921   d-Jan. 24, 1921 age 72, pnue. bur. Jan. 26
                                (Emily Elizabeth Ludtke)b-Mi. res. Handy
                                d- 2-18, 1913 age 1 of pnuemonia
                                (Lois Lud(t)ke) b-Mi. res. Handy
                                d-June 27, 1910 age 6 months, of T.B.
                                (Matie A Ludtke)b-Mi. res. Handy
                                d- 7-15, 1915 age 14 months
                                (Olga Lang Ludtke)b-Germany, res. Handy
                                d-June 26, 1911 age 26
                                (Wm. F Ludtke)b-Germany, res. Handy
                                d- 2-16-1913 age 35, suicide by shotgun
                                (Levi S Ludtke)b-Mi. res. Handy
                                d- 1-10-1916 age 17 days of pnue.

126 HUCK
     double stone;-Huck
     Leonard Huck   b-Livingston Co. res. Fowlerville
     1868-1901   d-May 4, 1901 age 33y, 8m, 27d
                                         removed from Fleming
     Nettie Huck Fowler   "Nettie B" b-Mi. res. St. Johns
     1870-1960   d- 3-27-1960 age 90
                                (Countess Marie Huck) b-Mi. res. Handy
                                d-Feb. 20, 1924 age 2 days

127 WHITE
     Ernest W,   b-Howell   res. Howell
     Jan. 27, 1899-June 3, 1901 d-age 21 of menengitis
     Jennie M, wife of Chester W White   b-Inham Co. res. Fowl.
     Nov. 24, 1875-Dec. 15, 1901 d-age 26 of T. B.
     Chester W White "father"   b-N. Y. res. Fowlerville
     1866-1920   d-June 19, 1920 age 54, killed
     Minnie B White "mother"   (Minnie B Tucker) res. Lansing
     1878-1943   d-June 9, 1943 age 65
     on monument-White
128 DAVIS
     Hiram B, 1832-1902   (Hiram B Davis)b-N. Y. res. Handy
                                d-Aug. 7, 1902 age 69y, 9m, 17d
     Sarah A, "mother"   (Mrs. H B Davis)b-N. Y. res. Handy
     1837-1918   d- 9-21-1918 age 80
     Henry Rd. Davis   res. Handy
     1857-1932   d-May 21, 1932 age 75
     Otis L Davis   b-Mi. res. Lansing twp.
     1876-1956   d- 1-2-1956 age 79
     on monument-Davis

Section "A"   Greenwood cemetery

lot #
128 continued

                                    (Albertie Carter) female, b-Mi.res. Fowl.
                                    d-Sept. 19, 1910 age 47

129 WESTPHAL--ECKHART
     Lucile, 1908-1917   (Lucile Westphal) b-Mi. res. Ingham Co.
                                d- 4-19-1917 age 9

     Pauline, 1900, 3mos, 7ds   (Pauline E Westphal)b-Leroy, Ingham Co.
                                d-Dec. 31, 1900 age 3m, 4d.

     on monument-Eckhart-Westphal

                                (Albert H Westphal)b-Mi. res. Ingham Co.
                                d-Feb. 22, 1919

130 WESTPHAL--ECKHART
     Albert A, 1866-1955   (Albert A Westphal)b-Mi. res. Ingham Co.
                                d- 6-6-55 age 88

     Ann E, 1880-1959   (Ann Elizebeth Westphal)b-Mi. res. Fla.
                                d- 1-17-1959 age 78

     Frank, 1861-1932 "motner" (Frank A Eckhart) res. Fowlerville
                                d-Aug. 26, 1932 age 70

     William, 1853-1915 "father" (Wm. Eckhart) res. Handy
                                d- 1-23-1915 age 62, heart attack

     on monument-Eckhart-Westphal
131 BARCUS
     George T Barcus   res. Fowlerville
     1860-1946   d-Feb. 22, 1949 age 85
     Sarah M Barcus   res. Livingston Co.
     1874-1968   d- 2-15-1968 age 93
                                (Ethel Barcus)b-Mi. res. Fleming
                                d-Sept. 14, 1903 age 17

132 FAUNCE
     Sumner M, 1822-1914   b-Mass. res. Fowlerville
                                d- 10-24-1914 age 92

     Elizabeth, 1821-1902   (Elizabeth Read Faunce)b-Mass
                                d-May 23, 1902 age 81y, 2m, 15d

     John M, 1857-1936   res. Handy
                                d-Nov. 6, 1936 age 79

     Emma J, 1861-1939   "Emma Jane" res. Handy
                                d-July 26, 1939 age 78

     on monument-Faunce
133 MUSSON
     Joe,
     Sarah,
     F J Hawkes   (Fred Hawks) res. Fowlerville
     1869-1926   d-June 26, 1926 age 50, auto accident
     on monument-Musson
        Josepn Musson   b-Lincolnsnire, England, res. Fowl.
     May 5, 1844-Oct. 27, 1901 d-age 47y, 5m, 22d, blood poison
        Sarah, his wife   (Sarah Hawkes Musson)b-Mi. res. Fowl.
     May 9, 1852-June 23, 1924 d-June 23, 1923 age 71
134 CURTIS
     infant son of F H & J L Curtis b-Mi. res. Conway
     1882   burial Nov. 25, 1902,
                                        removed from home in Conway twp.

Section "A"   Greenwood cemetery
lot #
134 continued
     Julia L, wife of F H Curtis   b-Mi. res. Cohoctah
     1858-1912   d-July 13, 1912 age 53, in operation
     Frank H Curtis   res. Fowlerville
     1852-1936   d-Sept. 20, 1936
     on monument-Curtis
135 WERT
     Wm. C Wert   b-New Jersey, res. Webberville
     Co. D, 9 Mich. Inf.   d-July 9, 1903 age 78
                                      (Mary E Wert)b-N. Y. res. Webberville
                                      d-Aug. 10, 1903 age 67
                                      (Loren Tutman) male, b-Mi. res. Conway
                                      d-Oct. 12, 1909 afe 50, fall in a barn
136 FERRIN
     Bernard L,   b-Mi. res. Fowlerville
     born Mar. 26, 1915, died Jan. 2, 1916   age 9 months
     mother, 1844-1920   "Louisa" b-N. Y. res. Fowlerville
                                      d-Sept. 10, 1920 age 75
     father, 1837-1917   "Olonzo" b-N. Y. res. Fowlerville
                                      d- 1-2-1917 age 79
     on monument-Ferrin
                                      (Hattie Keller) res. Toledo
                                      d-Sept. 24, 1937 age 76
137 SOULE
     Geo. W Soule "father"   b-Mi. res. Cohoctah
     1853-1901   d-Dec. 29, 1901 age 48, pnuemonia
     Gaddie A Soule "mother"   (Caddie Soule Bird) res. Fowl.
                                      d-Jan. 11, 1930 age 62
                                      (Sarah Roff) b-London, Eng. res. Fowl.
                                      d-June 25, 1897 age 74
     on monument-Soule
138 KEARNEY
     Jane Kearney, wife of Wm. Forster   no record
     1854-1909
     Annie E Kerney "mother"   b-Ireland, res. Handy
     1832-1909   d-Jan. 19, 1909 age 77
     John Kerney   b-Ontario, res. Handy
     1823-1903   d-July 3, 1903 age 80
     Annie E Kerney   no record
     1832-
                                      (Wm. F Kearney)b-Mi. res. Handy
                                      d- 3-6-1917 age 46 of T B
                                      (W Foster)male, b-Canada, res. Ont.
                                      d-April 20, 1921 age 70
139 BENJAMIN
     Burnette, 1860-1945   res. Fowlerville
     1860-1945   d-Dec. 21, 1945 age 85
     David, 1836-1907   "George David" b-N. Y. res. Fowl.
                                      d-June 21, 1907 age 70
     Ellen M Benjamin   b-Mi. res. Handy
     1836-1903   d-July 18, 1903 age 67
     Edwin, 1866-1916   "Edwin H" b-Mi. res. Pontiac
                                      d- 1-30-1916 age 49
     on monument-Benjamin

Section "A"   Greenwood cemetery
lot #
140 NEWMAN
     Amelia, 1851-1934   res, Fowlerville
                                d-Sept. 4, 1934 age 81

     Bertha, 1881-1902   no record
     Irving P, 1849-1936   res. Fowlerville
                                d-Dec. 19, 1936 age 87

     on monument-Newman
141 WALLACE
     John, "father"   b-Mi. res. Fowlerville
     1837-1918   d- 4-22-1918 age 81
     Amelia, "mother"   b-N. Y. res. Fowlerville
     1837-1920   d-Jan. 22, 1920 age 82
     James H Wallace   res. Fowlerville
     1862-1932   d-Mar. 24, 1932 age 69
     on monument-Wallace
142 MINKLEY
     Edwin C Minkley   b-Mi. res. Green Oak twp.
     Nov. 11, 1885-Jan. 1, 1960   d-age 74
     Rex W Minkley "husband & father"   res. Detroit
     1884-1935   d-June 21, 1935 age 51
143 GIBSON
     George W, 1851-1929   no record
     Ada L, 1853-1935   res. Jackson
                                d-May 5, 1935 age 81
     on monument-Gibson (reverse side-Randall)
144 RANDALL--FENN
     double stone;-Fenn
     Clarence O, 1872-1959   no record
     Grace A, 1877-1952   b-Mi. res. Handy
                                d-May 19, 1952 age 74
     M E Randall   "Elizabeth" b-Mi. res. Fowl.
     1845-1925   d-April 1, 1925 age 80
     W R Randall   "William" b-Handy, res. Fowl.
     1850-1918   d- 5-30-1918 age 68
     on monument-Randall (resverse side-Gibson)
145 LEAICH
     George H Leaich   b-Mi. res. Williamston
     July 4, 1866-Mar. 14, 1923   d-age 57
     Daisy M Leaich   b-Mi. res. Handy
     Feb. 17, 1871-Mar. 11, 1904   d-age 33
     on monument-Leaich

                                (Glen J Leach) b-Mi. res. Lansing
                                d-Mar. 6, 1920 age 30 days

146 LING
     Mary,
     on monument-Ling
        George W Ling   res. Williamston
        1867-1946   d-Sept. 20, 1946 age 78
        Mary C Ling   b-Canada, res. Handy
        1875-1902   d-Feb. 12, 1907 age 32
        Julia A Ling   b-Mi. res. Ingham Co.
        1865-1956   d- 2-14, 1956 age 90
        Maude I Hanigan   b-Mi. res. Lansing
        1888-1918   burial 5-10-1918

Section "A"   Greenwood cemetery
lot #
147 MANNING
     William H Manning(FLT emblem)   res. Fowlerville
     1867-1927   d-May 3, 1927 age 60
     Charles W Manning   no record
     1872-1928
     Dimmarius Manning   res. Handy
     1844-1934   d-July 1, 1934 age 89
     L L Manning   "Levi L" b-N. Y. res. Handy
     born July 8, 1838, died Sept. 21, 1904   age 66
     (on stone behind above)
              Levi Manning, Co. F, 11 Mich. Inf.
     on monument-Manning
148 ALDRICH
     mother,
     father,
     Eva D Duncan   "Eva Delia" b-Mi. res. Conway
     1866-1952   d-June 10, 1952 age 85
     George Duncan   res. Handy
     1860-1937   d-July 23, 1937 age 77
     on monument-Aldrich
        J H Aldrich   "Joseph" b-N. Y. res. Handy
        1833-1914   d- 10-28-1914 age 81
        Adelaide, his wife   "Frances Adelaide" b-Mi. res. Handy
        1840-1904   d-Mar. 5, 1904 age 62
149 COLLINS
     Miles H Collins   b-Mi. res. Charlotte
     1847-1920   d-May 4, 1920 age 73
149½ DUNCAN

                                     (George J Duncan) res. Howell
                                     d- 8-11-1971 age 67
150 COWIE
     Ethan L Cowie (on a metal tag) res. Fowlerville
     born Oct. 7, 1878, died Dec. 25, 1934   age 56, heart failure
     mother, 1860-1920   (Mrs. J D Cowie)b-South Bend, Ind.
                                     d-May 30, 1920 age 60   res. Fowl.
     father, 1857-1921   (Joseph D Cowie)b-England,
                                     d-Nov. 4, 1921 age 63 res. South Bend
     on monument-Cowie
151
                                     (Fred Sabin) b-England, res. Fowl.
                                     d-April 21, 1921 age 86
152 FOWLER
     Silas Fowler   b-Mi. res. Ann Arbor
     1863-1920   d-Aug. 17, 1920 age 57
     Nettie Fowler   res. Ypsilanti state hospital
     1864-1947   d-Jan. 12, 1949 age 84
153 ROTH
     George Roth   b-N. Y. res. Hamburg twp.
     1853-1924   d-July 24, 1924 age 71
     Kate Roth   "Catherine" b-Canada, res. Fowl.
     1844-1924   d-Sept. 6, 1924 age 80

Section "A"   Greenwood cemetery
lot #
154 GARDNER
     Eva Gardner   res. Fowlerville
     1869-1938   d-age 69   burial April 26, 1938
                                        (Edward Gardner) res. Fowl.
                                        d-May 22, 1948 age 57
                                        (Judson Bullis) b-Mi. res. Detroit
                                        d-Feb. 12, 1922, cancer

155 MAAS
     Katherine Maas "mother"   b-Mi.   res. Livingston Co.
     1868-1957   d- 2-10-57 age 88
     Joseph Maas "father"   res. Howell twp.
     1869-1928   d-Oct. 20, 1928 age 59
     Henry C Maas   res. Whitmore Lake
     Pvt US army, World War 1   d-age 75
     Oct. 22, 1896-Apr. 26, 1975
156 HALL
     Julia Merrell "mother"   "Julia Ann" res. Fowlerville
     1835-1925   d-July 27, 1925 age 90
     Belle Hall   b-Mi.   res. Livingston Co.
     1864-1955   d- 12-11-1955 age 91
     James M Hall   res. Fowlerville
     1859-1932   d-July 4, 1932 age 72
                                        (George H Buckley) res. Fowl.
                                        d-Feb. 24, 1937 age 79

157 WILSON
     Brazilla H Wilson   res. Fowlerville
     1887-1927
     (behind stone above) Brazilla H Wilson
                         Michigan Pvt 338 Inf. 88 Div.
                         June 24, 1927
     Emma J Wilson "mother"   res. Franklin twp. Lenewee Co.
     1854-1931   d- 5-6-1931 age 78
     Daniel S Wilson "father"   b-Mi.   res. Fowlerville
     1859-1920   d-Dec. 17, 1920 age 61
     Nora E, 1884-1969   res. Kalamazoo, Mi.
                                        d- 9-14-1969 age 84

     on monument-Wilson
158 HALL
     triple stone;-Hall
     Orla B, 1894-1966   res. Fowlerville
                                        d- 1-5-1966 age 71
     Minnie A, 1895-1976   res. Howell (listed on lot 158½)
                                        d- 4-25-1976 age 80
     Luella M, 1920   "Luella Marie"b-Mi. res. Fowl.
                                        d-Oct. 20, 1920 age 9 days
                                        (James A Caswell) (listed on lot 158 also)
                                        d- 12-17-1963 age 98

158½ HALL
                                        (Merrell D Hall) res. Mason, Mi.
                                        d- 5-16-1975 age 84

Section "A"   Greenwood cemetery
lot #
159 BELLINGER
     Ira Bellinger
     1864-1913   burial Nov. 17, 1936, removed
                                                from Perry,Mi.

     Clara Bellinger   "Clara A" res. Lansing
     1862-1940   d-Dec. 10, 1940 age 78
     Allen B Stewart "father"   b-Mi.   res. Handy
     1859-1903   d-April 26, 1903 age 44
     on monument-Bellinger
160 RICHMOND   (Melvin L Richmond)b-Mi. res. Liv. Co.
     no stones   d- 9-2-1962 age 65
                                       (Geo. Russell Richmond)b-Mi. res. Fowl.
                                       d-Sept. 28, 1920 age 4 hours
                                       (Dora Blanch Richmond)b-Mi. res. Fowl.
                                       d-June 18, 1921 stillborn
                                       (infant son of Melvin Richmond)
                                       d-Jan. 1, 1923 stillborn res. Fowl.
                                       (Ola May Richmond) res. Fowlerville
                                       d- 4-17-1967 age 67
                                       (infant male, Krumm)res. Fowl.
                                       d- 9-2-1954, of shock
                                       (Linda Marie Stringer)res. Williamston
                                       d- 2-16-1966 age 8 months

161 KUEHNLE
     double stone;-
     George L Kuehnle   res. Flint, Mi.
     1873-1943   d-May 9, 1943 age 70
     son Leslie   res. Flint
     1924-1930   d-Feb. 2, 1930 age 6
     Martha A, wife of G L Kuehnle no record
     1873-1912
     on monument-Kuehnle (right side)
        Gertrude Mildred, 1894-1902 (Gertrude Lockwood)b-Handy, res. Toledo
                                       d-Feb. 22, 1902 age 7y, 7m, 13d
        Martha A, 1873-1912

                                       (infant of Geo. Kuehnle)res. Handy
                                       d-Nov. 25, 1902 at childbirth
                                       (infant dau. of Geo. Kuehnle)res. Howell
                                       d-May 20, 1904 stillborn

162 STEWART
     on monument-Stewart (left side)
        Lyman, 1835-1913
        Martha A, 1837-1909
        Allen B, 1859-1903   no record
     Martha, wife of Lymam Stewart b-Handy res. Handy
     1837-1909 "mother"   d-Jan. 25, 1909 age 72
     Lyman Stewart "father"   no record
     1835-1913
162½ DUNCAN
     double stone;-Duncan
     George J, 1904-1971   no record
     Clella A, 1896-19-   not listed

Section "A"   Greenwood cemetery
lot #
163 BENNETT
     Helen M Bennett   b-Mi. res. Handy
     1903-1904   d-Aug. 3, 1904 age 1, burial Sept. 2.
     Allie J Meabon   b-Mi. res. Livingston Co.
     1872-1958   d- 1-24-1957 age 85
     George F Bennett   b-Mi. res. Oceola twp.
     1867-1916   d- 6-22-1916 age 47
163½ WINEGAR
     double stone,-Winegar
     Jay F, 1877-1948   "Jay Franklin" res. Handy
                                    d-Sept. 4, 1948 age 71

     Marion A, 1884-1953   b-Mi. res. Handy
                                    d- 9-8-1953 age 69
164 SABIN
     Dollie Dee Warner   "Dollie S" b-Mi. res. Brighton
     dau. of W & A Sabin   d-age 58
     born Oct. 9, 1849, died Dec. 9, 1907
     father   (William Sabin) b-N. Y. res. Brighton
                                    d-May 21, 1902 age 89y, 11m, 4d
     mother   no record
     grandmother   no record
                                    (William J Sabin) res. Highland Park
                                    d-March 9, 1928 age 80

165 WERT--MINKLEY
     double stone;-
         William H Wert   "Wm. Henry" res. Brighton
         Civil War veteran, Sgt.   d-Jan. 3, 1931 age 90
         1840-1931
         Louanna Sabin, wife of W H Wert   b-Youngstown, N. Y. res. Fowl.
         1843-1896   d-Dec. 15, 1896 age 53
                                        (held in vault) burial 4-12-1897
     Rorilla Minkley   "Roxilla V" b-Mi. res. Oakland Co.
     Sept. 25, 1866, Nov. 27, 1960 d-age 95
     on monument-Wert-Minkley
     Mary Carpenter   no record
     born in 1790, died Apr. 11, 1875
     on monument
         Abigail H Sabin   (Abigail H Sabine)
         born June 13, 1822, died Apr. 30, 1892
                                    removed from Benjamin cemetery with
                                    two children(?) and another person(?)
     Smith E Sabin(stone flat on ground)   no record
     born Sept. 13, 1851, died May 28, 1856
     aged 4yrs, 8mos & 15days
166 CROOPE
     Viva, 1904 "our baby"   b-Mi. res. Lansing
                                    d-Feb. 9, 1904 age 5, burial Apr. 17.
     Adelaide, 1880-1954 "wife"   (Adlaide Meese)b-Mi. res. Williamston
                                    d- 3-8-1954 age 76
     Clarence C, 1872-1928 "husband"   res. Lansing
             (FLT emblem)   d-June 18, 1928 age 56, heart failure
     Delia L Croope   res. Dewitt
     1846-1934   d-April 5, 1934 age 88

Section "A"   Greenwood cemetery
lot #
166 continued
    Henry Croope   b-Pa.   res. Conway twp.
    1826-1915   d- 10-4-1915 age 89
    on monument-Croope-(with masonic emblem)
166½ CROOPE
    Charles D Croope   b-Mi.
    1883-1963   d- 7-20-1963 age 79
    Ellen Croope   "Ellen A" res. Delhi twp, (Lansing)
    1885-1973   d- 1-14-1973 age 88
167 PITTS
    Phebe, "mother"   res. Leroy twp.
    1835-1900   d-May 13, 1900 age 65
                                                removed from Benjamin cemetery

    father   no record
    Wayne Cameron "baby"   "Wayne J" b-Mi. res. Iosco twp.
    1921-1924   d-Feb. 15, 1924 age 2, pnuemonia
    on monument-Pitts
        Irving Pitts   no record
        1868-1908
        Mary E, 1869-1957   no record
167½ CAMERON
    double stone;-
    George E Cameron   "George Ernest"b-Mi. res. Handy
    1884-1952   d-June 13, 1952 age 68
    Otie B Cameron   res. Livingston Co.
    1889-1980   d- 2-23-1980 age 90
168 DUNN
    double stone;-Dunn
    Joshua Jr. 1862-1900   b-Handy, res. Marion twp.
                                        d-April 28, 1900 age 38
    Laura F, 1867-1946   (Laura Fowler Wooden) res. Owasso
                                        d-Aug. 23, 1946 age 78
    double stone;-Dunn
    Gerald E, 1895-1967   res. Perry twp.
                                        d- 1-16-1967 age 71
    Anna B, 1895-1966   res. Shiawassee Co.
                                        d- 2-4-1966 age 70
169 DUNN
    double stone;-Dunn
    Mellen J, "father"   b-Marion twp. res. Iosco twp.
    1836-1909   d-June 16, 1909 age 73
    Margaret E, "mother"   b-Sussex Co. N. Y. res. Iosco twp.
    1836-1922   d-Sept. 2, 1922 age 86
    double stone;-Dunn
    Mell C, 1879-1950   res. Fowlerville
                                        d-Feb. 15, 1950 age 70
    Anna, 1873-1938   b-Iosco twp. res. Iosco
                                        d-age 65   burial 12-9-1938
170 JUDD
    Ozias, 1859-1945   "Ozias C" res. Handy
                                        d-April 27, 1945 age 85
    Eva E, 1875-1940   res. Handy
                                        d-March 20, 1940 age 64, cancer

{100}

Section "A"   Greenwood cemetery
lot #
170 continued
    Martha M, 1865-1933   res. Handy
                                    d-March 3, 1933 age 67, insane

    mother
    father
    on monument-Judd
        Seth H Judd   res. Handy
        1824-1900   d-June 10, 1900 age 45, pnue.
        Frances M, 1833-1914   b-Mi.   res. Handy
                                    d- 11-5, 1914 age 81
                                    (infant dau. of D Judd) res. Handy
                                    d-April 25, 1905 at birth

170½ JUDD
    Arthur F Judd   "Arthur Fear"b-Mi. res. Liv. Co.
    1909-1961   d- 5-5-1961 age 51
171 BURRIER
    double stone;-Burrier
    M Delmer, 1867-1956   "Milo Delmer" b-Mi. res. Howell twp.
                                    d- 5-22-1956 age 88

    Emily A, 1871-   res. Howell
                                    d- 6-27-1965 age 95

171½ CAMERON

                                    (Lyle Cameron) res. Liv. Co.
                                    d- 4-23, 1983 age 67

172 BURRIER
    E D, infant son of A M & R C Grant   b-Conway
    died Dec. 28, 1884 aged 1mo, 28ds   removed from Conway cem. 1899
    Eva Hazel Wright   res. Ann Arbor
    Aug. 29, 1899-Dec. 6, 1936   d-age 37
    F B, infant son of G W & A A Wright "Floyd B" b-St. Clair Co.
    died Apr. 7, 1894 aged 4ms, 18ds   removed from Conway cem. 1899
                                    (may have died April 11, burial Apr. 14)
    Allie A Wright   res. Ann Arbor
    Aug. 26, 1871-Apr. 22, 1940   d-age 68
    Rev. Geo. W Wright   res. Ann Arbor
    Sept. 21, 1866-May 27, 1942 age 75
173 BURRIER
    George W, MD.   (George W Burrier)b-Conway, Res. Clair,Mi.
    1863-1899   d-June 5, 1899 age 35, heart failure
    mother
    father
    Mary E Gordon (star emblem)   res. Detroit
    1858-1939   d-age 80   burial Jan. 4, 1939
    on monument-Burrier
        David,   b-Ohio   res. Fowlerville
    born Sept. 2, 1826, died Nov. 20, 1905   d-age 79
        Evey,(female)   b-Pa. res. Fowlerville
    born Dec. 4, 1830, died Mar. 5, 1902   d-age 71

Section "A"   Greenwood cemetery
lot #3
174 BURRIER
     Laban P Gordon (FLT emblem)   b-Mi.   res. Fowlerville
     1858-1915   d- 7-18-1915 age 57
     Pearl A Burrier   b-Mi.   res. Handy
     1884-1953   d- 12-26-1953 age 69
     Eva S Burrier   res. Handy
     1857-1933   d-May 4, 1933 of flu
     Simon P Burrier (FLT emblem)   b-Ohio   res. Handy twp.
     1854-1912   d- 12-29-1912 age 58
174½ RADDATZ
     double stone;-Raddatz
     Louis C, 1886-1948   res. Cohoctah twp.
                                   d- 11-4-1948 age 62 of T B

     Winnie B, 1888-1979   Res. Livingston Co.
                                   d- 11-12-1979 age 91

175 WILLIAMS
     Chas. F, "father"   b-N. Y.   res. Fowlerville
     1848-1919   d-Aug. 15, 1919 age 72
     Eunice E, "mother"   b-Mi.   res. Fowlerville
     1850-1916   d- 8-12-1916 age 66
     Milton P, 1880-1901   "Milton Palmer"b-Liv. Co. res. Fowl.
                                   d-July 9, 1901 age 21y, 1m, 15d of T B.
     Clark F, 1872-1872   b-Fowlerville (removed from old cemetery
                                   to lot B-53, then burial in this lot later
                                   d-Aug. 1872 age 4 mo. burial 8-11-1872
     R C Palmer   "Richard C" res. Fowlerville
     1829-1850   d-July 26, 1850 age 22
                                   removed from Briggs cem. burial 1902

     on monument-Williams
176 HANDY
     Charles G,   b-Handy, res. Owasso, Mi.
     Jan. 31, 1853-Oct. 14, 1899   d-age 46
     Harriet Jane,   res. Ypsilanti, Mi.
     May 17, 1856-Mar. 28, 1933   d-age 77
     James E Handy   res. Pontiac
     April 2, 1851-Dec. 9, 1926   d-age 69
     on monument-Handy
177 CONVERSE
     triple stone;-Converse
     Fred L, 1875-1957   "Fredrick Lynden"b-Mi. res. Liv. Co.
                                   d- 3-16-1957 age 82
     Hattie S, 1875-1941   res. Handy
                                   d-Dec. 28, 1941 age 66
     Cecil, 1899, infant of Fred Converse   b-Handy
                                   d-May 7, 1899 age 2 weeks
178 NICHOLS
     triple stone;-Nichols
     Chester E, 1876-1949   res. Detroit
                                   d-Aug. 16, 1949 age 73
     Lucy C, 1849-1899   b-Brighton, res. Fowlerville
                                   d-Nov. 26, 1899 age 50 of T B.
     Albert M, 1842-1901   no record
     (behind above stone) Alb't Nichols
                         Co. C, 2 N. Y Mto. rifles

{102}

Section "A"   Greenwood cemetery
lot #
179 BRISTOL
     Lorenzo, son of Henry & Martha Bristol   "Lorenzo Norman"
     died June 4, 1901 aged 23yrs, 7mos, & 8 days   b-Handy, Res. Fowl.
     Martha R, "mother"   (Martha R Newman)b-Mi. res. Fowl.
     1853-1920   d-March 24, 1920 age 66
     on monument-Bristol

                                  (Effie Cardotte) b-Mi. res. Lansing
                                  d-age 57   burial Nov. 19, 1938
                                  (Curtis Edgar Cardott)b-Mi. res.Lansing

179½ FAUNCE--THATCHER
     double stone;
     Clarence S Faunce   res. Livingston Co.
     1898-1974   d- 8-2-1974 age 75
     Gerald E Thatcher   not listed
     1915-
180 ROBERTS
     George B   (George Burr Olmsted Roberts)res. Handy
     12-31-1844--4-8-1899   d-April, 1899 age 54
                                     removed from vault, burial 6-10-1899

     Cordelia Roberts   no record
     1846-1921
     Lena Stewart   "Lena B" b-Handy, res. Pontiac
     1867-1941   d-Sept. 23, 1941 age 73
     Byron Stewart   "Byron B" res. Lansing
     1871-1965   d- 12-28-1965 age 94
     on monument-Roberts
181 METCALF
     Etta Metcalf   "Etta D" b-Fowlerville, res. Fowl.
     1881-1898   d-Dec. 25, 1898 age 16
                                 (Harvey Frank Metcalf)b-Fowlerville
                                 d-Sept. 17, 1899 age 8 months 23 days

182 WALTER
     Hattie E Walter "mother"   b-Mi. res. Fowlerville
     1840-1923   d-March 13, 1923 age 82
     Israel Walter "father"   b-Wa__(?) Co. Ohio
     1840-1900, Co. K, 18th Mich. Inf.   d-April 9, 1900 age 60
     (stone behind above) Isr'l Walters, Co. K, 18 Mich. Inf.
                                 (Arthur G Walters)res. Traverse City,Mi.
                                 d-Feb. 6, 1934 age 53
                                 (John G Wolter) res. Fowlerville
                                 d-Aug. 2, 1932 age 67

183 MASTIC
     Frank B Mastic   b-Mi. res. Fowlerville
     1863-1900   d-May 23, 1900 age 36 of T B.
     on monument-Mastic

                                 (Cora Dunn)b-N. Y. res. Howell twp.
                                 d-April 12, 1906 age 31 in childbirth
                                 (Alice Stackweather) res. White Oak
                                 d-Dec. 20, 1936 age 71
                                 (Mrs. Angeline Coleman)b-Mi. res. White Oak
                                 d- 12-20-1917 age 75

Section "A"   Greenwood cemetery
lot #
183½
                              (Frederick Wickman) res. Battle Creek
                              d-Jan. 16, 1949 age 60
                              (Glen P Haskins) retired vet
                              d-overseas, burial March 8, 1949
                              (Leon Mastic)b-Mi. res. Fowl.
                              d- 10-20-1958 age 69, pnuemonia

184 WHITAKER
     Elvira, 1834-1899   b-N. Y.   res. Handy
                              d-June 26, 1899 age 66, neart trouble

     on monument-WhitAKER
                              (Ila Mae Grant)b-Mi. res. Lansing
                              d- 10-21-1913 age 12, appendicitis
                              (Alice J Harding)res. Lansing
                              d-Oct. 22, 1927 age 64
                              (G. A. Whittacre)male, b-Mi.res. Lansing
                              d- 2-22-1915 age 84

185 HOUSE
     Edward E, 1865-1919   b-Mi.   res. Handy
                              d-May 26, 1919 age 51 of flu
     Nellie K, 1871-1949   "Nellie M" res. Mt. Morris
                              d-Nov. 27, 1949 age 79
     infant son of E & N House "our baby"   "Edwar" b-Handy twp.
     July 27, 1896-July 29, 1896
     Marjorie I, 1903-1965   "Marjorie Isabell" res. Fowl.
                              d- 12-25-1965 age 61
     Lyle K, 1899-1982   res. Livingston Co.
                              d- 6-14-1982 age 82

     on monument-House
186 SMITH
     no stones   (Harrison H Smith)b-N. Y. res. Handy
                              d-May 20, 1899 age 70
                              (Maria Jennett Hattie Smith)
                              d-Dec. 27, 1902
                                   removed from cemetery in Plymouth,Mi.
                              (Frank B Smith)b-Mi. res. Howell
                              d-age 50   (possibly in 1915)?
                              (infant son of Thomas & Ruth Hamill)
                              d-Nov. 18, 1923 stillborn res. Handy

186½ SMITH
     double stone;-Smith
     Harry H, 1867-1943 (FLT emblem)res. Fowlerville
                              d-June 18, 1943 age 75
     Nellie, 1867-1953   b-Mi.   res. Ann Arbor
                              d-Feb. 3, 1953 age 85

187 ORTH
     John H Ortn   "John Henry" b-Mi. res. Leroy, Ingham Co.
     Aug. 26, 1856-Dec. 17, 1912   d-age 56
     Anna C Orth   "Mrs." b-Mi.
     Oct. 12, 1861-Nov. 21, 1917
     on monument-Orth (masonic emblem)

Section "A"   Greenwood cemetery
lot #
187½ WICKMAN--HASKINS
    Glen P Haskins   (see lot 183¼)
    Micnigan Pfc. 135 Inf. World War 11
    Dec. 13, 1924-July 10, 1944
    Frederick Wickman (Amer. Leg. emblem)   no record
    1881-1949
188 ORTH
    Rev. John Orth   b-N. Y. res. Sparta, Mi.
    1831-1912   d-Jan. 4, 1912 age 82
    Anna K Ortn   (Mrs. A Katherine Orth)D-Germany
    1832-1899   d-April 11, 1899 age 68 res. Howell
    Mary Finkbeiner   no record
    1861-1930
    on monument-Orth
189
    no stones   (Leonard A Mosner)b-N. Y. res. Fowl.
                                     d-June 16, 1898 age 72
                                     (Alice L Mosner)b-Mi. res. Detroit
                                     d-Sept. 28, 1910 age 72
                                     (Mary Finkheener) res. Detroit
                                     d-April 23, 1930 age 68, cancer

190 FRYANT
    no stones   (Sarah Fryant) res. Fowlerville
                                     d-March 11, 1898
                                     (Charles Fryant)b-N. Y. res. Fowl.
                                     d-Nov. 9, 1904 age 88
                                     (Catherine R Fryant) res. Fowlerville
                                     d-Feb. 14, 1928 age 71
                                     (Daniel Fryant) res. Oceola
                                     d-Nov. 2, 1942 age 85

190½ DUNCAN
    double stone;-Duncan
    Frank R, 1899-1964   d- 7-29, 1964 age 65, burial from Florida
    Bernice G, 1898-1964   "Bernice Grant" res. Florida
                                     d- 5-5-1964 age 66, burial from Florida

191 FIELDS--DODGE
    Earl H Fields   "Earl Henry" res. Howell
    1887-1940   a-age 53   burial June 17, 1940
    Bertha E Fields   res. Vermontville
    1887-1970   d- 5-19, 1970 age 82
    Edward L Fields   b-Iosco, res. Lansing
    1868-1940   d-Nov. 8, 1940 age 72
    Della E Fields   b-Mi. res. Fowlerville
    1867-1925   d-Sept. 30, 1925 age 57
    Henry W Fields   no record
    1862-1895
    baby Fields, 1911-1911   no record
    on monument-Fields
                                     (Wm. Robinson)res. Fort Payne(?)
                                     d- 10-1-1896
                                     (Clara Robinson) res. Fowlerville
                                     d-Oct. 16, 1878 age 9
                                         removed from the old cemetery
                                     (Jimmie Robinson) res. Fowlerville
                                     d-April 14, 1863 age 2, from old cem.

Section "A"   Greenwood cemetery
lot #
191 continued

                        (William Robinson) res. Fowl.
                        d-March 14, 1877 age 55, from old cem.
                        (Jimmie Norton) res. Fowlerville
                        d-April 5, 1883 age 72, from old cem.
                        (Almeda J Minto)female, res. Union City
                        d-Sept. 11, 1924 age 76

192 ROBISON (or Robinson)
     William Sr. 1822-1877   burial March 1877 age 55
     Eliza, 1839-1933   (Eliza Robinson)res. Fowlerville
                               d-Dec. 25, 1933
     William Jr. 1875-1898   burial 10-1896
     Clara, 1869-1878   d-lo-16-1878 age 9
     James Newton   "Jimmie"
     1811-1883   burial 4-1883 age 72
     Hannah, wife of Lewis Fowler b-Mi.   res. Fowlerville
     1863-1908   d-Nov. 22, 1908 age 45
     James, 1861-1863   "Jimmie" burial 4-1863 age 2
     on monument-Robison

                        (infant son of Earl Fields)
                        res. Grand Ledge,Mi.
                        d-Nov. 10, 1911 stillborn

193 GOULD
     Lieut. J G Gould   "John G" b-Erie, Pa. res. Grayling
     Co. K, 9th Mich. Inf.   d-Jan. 1885 age 57,overdose of morpnine
                                    removed from old cemetery
     Soph
     Surviah N, wife of J G Gould "Sophia"b-Bell Isle, N. Y. res. Fowl.
     died March 28, 1881 aged 38yrs, 1mo & 28dys   from old cemetery
                        (Licander Phillips)listed on lot 194
                               burial ? removed from old cem.
                        (Lulu E Taylor) res. Lansing
                        d-age 73   burial Jan. 15, 1938
                        (Rose Gould)b-Fowlerville
                        d-1873 age 6, from old cemetery
                        (Martial Gould)burial ?
                            listed on lot 194, from old cem.
                        (Joyce Gould)burial ? from old cemetery
                            listed on lot 194
                        (Helen Gould) burial ? from old cemetery
                            listed on lot 194

194 WILLIAMS
     John D Williams   b-N. Y   res. Handy
     1840-1924   d-April 11, 1924 age 83
     Catherine Williams   res. Handy
     1850-1940   d-age 89   burial July 11, 1940
     John T Williams (FLT emblem) no record
     1878-1920
     on monument-Williams
194½
     no stones   (Jessie J Williams)b-Mi. res. Ingham Co.
                               d- 6-27-1955 age 77

{106}

Section "A"   Greenwood cemetery
lot #
195 BOYD
     John N.
     Lucinda
     on monument-Boyd
         John N Boyd   b-Conneceires, N. Y. res. Cohoctah
         1822-1895   d-Nov. 6, 1895 age 73
         Lucinda, wife of John N Boyd   b-N. Y.   res. Fowlerville
         1827-1906   d-Aug. 29, 1906 age 79
195½
     no stones   (Fred C Bowers) res. Caledonia
                                        d-Aug. 27, 1949 age 82
196 RICHTER--HAMMELL
     Anthony S Hamell   b-Boston, Mass. res. Fowlerville
     born Oct. 11, 1855, died Dec. 1, 1898   d-age 43, consumption
     Emma Hammell   (Emilyn Neeley)b-Mi. res. Fowl.
     1852-1921   d-May 21, 1920 age 69
     Lena, 1874-1921 "mother"   b-Mi. res. Fowlerville
                                         d-July 30, 1921 age 47
     Fred, 1871-   "father"   res. Ingham Co.
                                         d-Nov. 11, 1948 age 79
     on monument-Richter
197 BEEBE
     father
     mother
     John L Newkirk "Lin"   b-Mi. res. Samaria, Mi.
     Nov. 26, 1861-Sept. 22, 1900   d-age 39, typhoid
     on monument-Beebe
         L H Beebe   (Levi H Beebe)b-N. Y. res. Munith
         born July 17, 1823, died Feb. 3, 1895   d-age 73
         S S Beebe   no record
         born Jan. 24, 1831, died Aug. 15, 1910
                                         (Betsey L Chaplin)b-Mi. res. Fowl.
                                         d-July 18, 1902 age 64y, 2m, 16d
198 BEEBE--SPENCER
     Adelbert J Beebe   res. Fowlerville
     1856-1935   d- 9-18-1935 age 79
     Ella Beebe   res. Fowlerville
     1858-1934   d-June 23, 1934 age 75
                                         (Sarah Beebe)b-N. Y. res. Harbor Springs
                                         d-Aug. 15, 1910 age 78
     double stone;-Spencer
     A Clifford, 1876-1964   "Ashley Clifford"b-Fowlerville
                                         d- 2-13-1964 age 88
     Edith L, 1879-1975   burial 1-25-1975
                                         (infant male,Spencer)res. Fowlerville
                                         d- 9-6-1915 stillborn
                                         (Bessie L Snedicor) res. Fowlerville
                                         d- 3-6-1965 age 86
199 COOPER
     Robert L Cooper   b-Mi.   res. Wyandotte
     1904-1957   d- 5-17-1957 age 52

Section "A"   Greenwood cemetery
lot #
199½ LAMOREAUX
    double stone;-Lamoreaux
    Dr. Charles H, 1855-1942   res. Fowlerville
                                 d-May 15, 1942 age 87

    Eudora M, 1860-1926   no record
200 COOPER
    Aaron W Cooper, MD   b-Canada, res. Fowlerville
    Co. G, 11 Mich. Vol. Inf.
    1840-1922   d-Dec. 17, 1922 age 82
    Amity Cooper   res. Fowlerville
    1847-1928   d-Dec. 18, 1928 age 81
    Lydia Wines Cooper   "Lydia H" res. Detroit
    1872-1940   d-March 19, 1940 age 67
    Ashley Cooper (masonic emblem) "James Ashley" res. Wayne
    1872-1961   d- 2-1-1961 age 84
201 HUGHES--CHENEY
    Eliza Hughes   "Eliza J" b-Mi.   res. Fowlerville
    1848-1914   d- 11-17-1914 age 66
    Helen C Cheney   "Helen V" res. Fowlerville
    1860-1929   d-Feb. 28, 1929 age 71
                                   (Norman Hughes)b-Mi. res. Fowl.
                                   d-Nov. 25, 1921 age 78

202 DURFEE
    Edith Durfee Grindling   "Edith Ethaline"b-Mi. res. Ontario,Cal.
                                   d-May 20, 1924 age 57

    Anna Durfee Risch   "Anna B"b-Mi. res. Howell
                                   d-Aug. 26, 1904 age 34

    mother
    father
    on monument-Durfee
        Emery Durfee   b-N. Y. res. Handy (listed onlot 203)
        1820-1904   d-Dec. 31, 1904, burial Jan. 3, 1905
        Cordelia Durfee   b-N. Y.   res. Handy
        1827-1911   d-April 19, 1911 age 83
    Wilfred D Horton   b-Mi.   res. Conway twp.
    1905, aged 6mos.   d-Feb. 18, 1906
203 RECTOR
    on monument-Rector (front) Voegt (reverse)
    William H Rector   b-Mi.   res. Lansing
    1855-1917   d- 5-16-1917 age 62
    Caroline A Rector   b-Mi.   res. Charlotte
    1860-1952   d-June 22, 1952 age 91
    Ward A Rector   res. Charlotte
    1890-1939   d-age 48   burial Jan. 9, 1939
203½ FRETZ
    double stone;-Fretz
    Thomas M Jr. 1917-1973   d- 9-4-1973 age 55 in Clare, Mi.
          married August 23, 1948
    Elsie E, 1924-   not listed
    Thomas M Fretz Sr.   no record
    Nov. 22, 1888-May 18, 1964

Section "A"   Greenwood cemetery
lot #
204 RECTOR
     Charles H Rector   b-Mi.   res. Fowlerville
     1879-1902   d-Sept. 28, 1902 age 23y, 6m, 18d
     Bert W Rector   b-Mi.   res. Charlotte
     1881-1952   d-May 13, 1952 age 71
205 VOGTS
     Elwin, 1915-1937 "darling"   (Elwin L Wallace) res. Howell
                                   d-Feb. 13, 1937 age 21, killed in accident
     Fred N Vogts   "Fred C" b-Mi. res. Jackson Co.
     1900-1952   d-Nov. 15, 1952 age 52
     Lewis C Vogts   b-Mi.   res. Norfolk, Virginia
     1876-1907   d-July 30, 1907 age 30, spinal mengitis
     on monument-Vogts
206 VOEGT
     Clara Voegt   (Clara Vogt)b-Mi. res. Iosco twp.
     1825-1905   d-Aug. 19, 1905 age 80 (was in lot 203)
     Augustus Voegt   (August Vogts)b-Germany, res. Fowl.
     1824-1910   d-Sept. 30, 1910 age 86
     on monument-Aug. Vogt

                                   (John Knoop)b-Mi. res. Cohoctah
                                   d-Jan. 5, 1921 age 26
206½ SMOCK
     Ashley G Smock   b-Mi. res. Livingston Co.
     Michigan Pvt. Co. M, 77 Infantry, World War 1
     Dec. 16, 1895-April 29, 1962 d-age 67
     Arloa A Smock   not listed
     Jan. 11, 1901-
207 McGAULEY
     Mark McGauley "father"   b-Mi. res. Livingston Co.
     1875-1961   d- 12-25-1961 age 86
     Ina May McGauley "mother"   res. Fowlerville
     1877-1946   d-Jan. 26, 1946 age 68
                                   (Johnny McGauley)b-Mi. res. Handy
                                   d- 10-30, 1918 age 14 of flu
                                   (Martin McGauley)b-Ireland,res. Handy
                                   d- 10-30, 1918 age 74

207½ SIDELL
     Sam M, 1892-1977   res. Genesee Co.
                                   d- 2-18-1977 age 84
     Mary E, 1895-1972   "Mary G" res. Livingston Co.
                                   d- 3-6-1972 age 76

     on monument-Sidell
208 PETTIT
     Adelia, 1825-1918 "mother"   b-Mi.   res. Handy
                                   d- 4-17-1918 age 92
     William H, 1853-1933   res. Handy
                                   d-Sept. 2, 1933 age 79
     Fred, 1868-1943   "Fred W" res. Fowlerville
                                   d-June 16, 1943 age 74

     on monument-Pettit
209 TANNER
     Cleve   b-Mi.   res. Fowlerville
     (on stone benid above)Cleve Marshall Tanner
                         Michigan Fireman, 3 cl, USNRF
                         September 25, 1918   d-age 32 of flu

Section "A"   Greenwood cemetery
lot #
209 continued
    on monument-Tanner
        Cleve M, 1886-1918
        Marshall S, 1855-1928   res. Fowlerville
                                     d-March 24, 1926 age 78

        Rhoda D, 1855-1925   b-Mi.   res. Fowlerville
                                     d-Nov. 24, 1925 age 70

209½ PHILLIPS
    double stone,-Phillips
    Albert J, 1899-1977   res. Livingston Co.
                                     d- 4-3-1977 age 78
    Esther M, 1901-1966   res. Fowlerville
                                     d- 8-9-1966 age 64

210 REESE--GEHRINGER
    double stone;-Reese
    Isaac M, 1863-1945   res. Howell
                                     d- 7-10-1945 age 82
    Bessie L, 1864-1951   burial 10-14-1951
    double stone;-Gehringer
    Theodore J, 1903-1979   "Theodore Joseph"res. Howell
                                     d- 5-31-1979 age 75
    Dollie L, 1906-1978   res. Washtenaw Co.
                                     d- 11-25-1978 age 72
                                     (Melvin T Gehringer)res; Howell
                                     d-May 21, 1931 age 22 days
                                         (burial at head of stone above)
                                     (Charlie F Meyers) res. Howell
                                     d-Jan. 27, 1937 age 71

211 DURFEE
    H Orel Durfee   "Henry O" res. Howell
    1883-1934   d-March 20, 1934 age 50,heart trouble
    Myrtle B Durfee   (Myrtle B Durfee Gresehover)res.Denver
    1890-1981   d-1-19-1981 age 90
    Henry H Durfee   res. Cohoctah
    1850-1931   d-Aug. 8, 1931 age 80
    Saville M Durfee   b-Mi.   res. Oceola twp.
    1850-1921   d-Feb. 24, 1921 age 70
    Dorothy E Durfee   res. Howell
    1917-1921   d-Aug. 10, 1921 age 3
                                     (infant son of Oral Durfee)res. Handy
                                     d-June 3, 1910 age 1 day, pnuemonia

212 GRIFFIN
    Daisy D, 1877-1908   (Daisy D Durfee)b-Illinois,res. Howell
                                     d-May 6, 1908 age 30
    William I, 1880-1957   "Wm. Ira" b-Mi.
                                     d- 4-1--1957 age 75
    Agnes H, 1889-1946   res. Howell
                                     d-Oct. 25, 1946 age 57
    Helen I, 1920-1947   (Helen Irene Hutchins)res. Howell
                                     d-Aug. 17, 1947 age 26
    on monument-Griffin
        William I Griffin, 1880
        Daisy D, his wife, 1877-1908

Section "A"   Greenwood cemetery
lot #
213 TUCKER
        triple stone;-Tucker
        John M,   res. Detroit
        Feb. 18, 1840-June 29, 1924
        Caroline J,   "Caroline Jane"b-Pa. res. Detroit
        July 17, 1843-Feb. 7, 1902   d-age 59
        Elmer,   no record
        Aug. 18, 1864-Dec. 30, 1864
214 SEYMOUR
        Newton Seymour   b-Mi.   res. Handy
        1848-1926   d-Feb. 20, 1926 age 77
        Mary Seymour   "Mary Grace" res. Fowlerville
        1851-1939   d-Dec. 26, 1936 age 88
        George Seymour   "Newton George" res. Fowlerville
        1883-1967   d- 3-18-1967 age 85
                                           (W H Bakewell)male, b-N. Y. res. Handy
                                           d-March 4, 1899 age 82

215 BARNARD--BARRY
        Neil G, son of M L & E A Barnard "Neal"b-Fowlerville,res. Detroit
        born Dec. 21, 1885,died Mar. 24, 1887 (record says d-March 22 age 1)
216 HAMILTON
        Jacob D Hamilton   b-Churorgh Co. N. Y.res. Fowl.
        1834-1899   d-Aug. 31, 1899 age 65
        Eva Disbrow Hamilton   "Eva May"   removed from old cemetery
        1854-1883   d-May 2, 1883 age 27 in childbirth
        and infant daughter   no record
        Emily Hamilton   b-Pa.   removed from old cemetery
        1807-1873   d-May 17, 1873 age 66
        David Hamilton   b-Pa.   removed from old cem.
        1807-1869   d-July 18, 1869 age 62
        on monument-Hamilton
216½ GOTTERMAN--RICHMOND

                                           (Harold F Burgert) res. Livingston Co.
                                           d- 1-25, 1976 age 77

217 ABBOTT
        Arlie A, 1872-1873   removed from Marion cemetery
        Gertrude, 1884-1884   removed from Marion cemetery
        Louie, 1875-1875   removed from Marion cemetery
        Mary E Abbott   b-Huron Co.(Ohio or Mi.)? res. Detroit
        1850-1918   (Mrs. Milo Abbott)burial 5-29, 1918 age 65
        Milo M Abbott   b-Huron Co. Ohio, res. Fowlerville
        1843-1898   d-Jan. 11, 1898 age 54
        (behind stone above)M M Abbott, Co. H, 22 Mich. Inf.
        on monument-Abbott

                                           (Bessie Louise Reese) res. Howell
                                           d-Oct. 14, 1951 age 86

218 GUY
        B W Lawrence   no record
        died Mar. 8, 1868 (rest buried)
                                           (Sarah Elizabeth Lawrence)b-N. Y
                                           d- 9-6-1914 age 80   res. Fowl.
                                           (Nellie Bristol)b-Greenfield ?
                                           d- 11-20-1896 age 46
                                           (Kattie Whitbeck) res. Meridian
                                           d-April 1870 age 1 from old cem.

Section "A"   Greenwood cemetery
lot #
218 continued
                                        (Spencer Guy) b-Highland
                                        d-Oct. 7, 1873 age 2 from old cem.
                                        (George Guy)b-Handy
                                        d-Aug. 11, 1875 age 2 from old cem.
                                        (Lottie Guy)b-Handy
                                        d-Sept. 12, 1876 age 9 months
                                                removed from old cemetery
                                        (Brad Guy)b-N. Y. res. Howell,Mi.
                                        d-Jan. 10, 1912 age 65
218½
        no stones   (Margaret L Line)b-Mi. res. Conway twp.
                                        d-March 19, 1953 age 79
219 SPENCER
        N S (broken stone)
        I M S
        on monument-Spencer
            Norman Spencer   b-N. Y. res. Fowlerville
              died Oct. 5, 1872 aged 72yrs   d-age 75, removed from old cemetery
            Amanda M, wife of Norman Spencer   b-N. Y. res. Fowlerville
              died March 10, 1876 ae 72ys, 1mo & 28ds   d-age 75, from old cem.
                                        (Lottie F Spencer)
                                        burial 7-10-1862   from old cemetery
        Edith E, dau. of W C & L E Spencer   b-Fowlerville
        died Apr. 7, 1874 aged 5yrs, 5ms & 5ds   removed from old cemetery
        Frankie M, daughter of W C & L E Spencer   b-Fowlerville
        died Mar. 5, 1872 aged(rest missing)   d-age 83, from old cem.
        Fanie M, daughter of W C & L E Spencer   "Fannie"
        died July 10, 1862 aged 2yrs, 3mos, 11ds   from old cemetery
220 SPENCER
        James P Spencer   b-N. Y.   res. Fowlerville
        1844-1921   d-Feb. 25, 1921 age 76
        Lillian S Spencer   res. Fowlerville
        1852-1934   d-March 7, 1934 age 81
        Bessie L Stark   no record
        1878-1965
        William J Stark   res. New York
        1874-1928   d-July 14, 1928 age 53
        on monument-Spencer
                                    (Edith L Spencer)res. Livingston Co.
                                    d- 1-23-1975 age 95
221 PULLEN
        Emily A Pullen   b-Mi.   res. Fowlerville
        1849-1924   d-Feb. 27, 1924 age 74
        Cleve S Pullen   res. Detroit
        1880-1928   d-June 8, 1928 age 47
        William H Pullen   b-Mi.   res. Fowlerville
        1840-1905   d-Sept. 9, 1905 age 65
        Sergt. of Co. I, 5th Mich Vol. Inf.GAR
        (behind stone above) Serg't. W H Pullen, Co. I, 5 Mich. Inf.

Section "A"   Greenwood cemetery
lot #
221 continued
    (on Wm. H Pullen stone)
    in memory of Merritt F Pullen, born Aug. 25, 1842
    Co. I, 5th Mich. Vol. Inf. GAR, killed in action
    at Williamsburg, Va. May 5, 1862
    Esther, daughter of W & S A Hildreth   (Ester Hildveth)b-Fowl.
    died July 31, 1863 aged 11yr, 4ms & 21ds   (record says age 8 months)?
                                        removed from old cemetery
                                        (Cliff Moore)b-Fowlerville
                                        d-July 22, 1880 age 1, from old cem.
                                        (Elizabeth Barabee)b-Lima, N. Y.
                                        d-Sept. 20, 1895 age 76   res. Fowl.

221½ WOODLEY
    double stone;
    Bob, 1885-1960   "Clarence A"b-Mi. res. Livingston Co.
                                        d- 1-25, 1960 age 74
    Clara, 1884-1975   res. Genesee Co.
                                        d- 12-22-1975 age 91

222 THAYER
    Laura S Thayer "mother"   no record
    1832-1896
                                        (Laura Thayer) res. Handy
                                        d-July 4, 1866, removed from old cemetery
    Joseph Thayer "father"   res. Handy
    1830-1896   d-Jan. 29, 1896 age 66
    on monument-Thayer
                                        (William Thayer) res. Oregon
                                        d-Sept. 28, 1928 age 65, insane
                                        (infant son of Wm. Alexander Sr.)
                                        d- 3-27, 1914 stillborn   res. Handy

222½ GREEN
    Charles L Green   "Charles Lawrence" res. Fowlerville
    1876-1948   d-Jan. 22, 1949 age 72
    Lillian Green   b-Mi. res. Livingston Co.
    1882-1962   d- 9-7-1962 age 80
                                        (Wayland Richter) res. Kalamazoo,Mi.
                                        d-Oct. 29, 1947 age 40(?)

223 ELLSWORTH--POLL
    on monument-Ellsworth
                                        (John Ellsworth)no information(see below)
    on monument
       A B MacGregor MD   b-Canada, res. Cheboygan,Mi.
    Alexander B MacGregor   (same person as above)
    Apr. 27, 1875, July 14, 1914   d-age 39 in railroad accident
224 ELLSWORTH
    John Charles Ellsworth   res. Fowlerville
    Aug. 24, 1847-Sept. 22, 1939   d-age 92
    Emily French Ellsworth   ("emma" Mrs. John C Ellsworth)b-Mi.
    Feb. 28, 1854-Apr. 12, 1912   d-age 58
    on monument-Ellsworth

Section "A"   Greenwood cemetery
lot #
225 FIELDS--STANLEY
     Alonzo Fields   b-N. Y.
     1821-1891   d-Jan. 10, 1892 age 69
     Catherine Fields   "Mrs." res. Stockbridge
     1834-1913   d- 10-29-1913
     Sophia Stanley   no record
     1855-1923
     James K Stanley   b-Mi. res. Ocean Side, California
     1850-1922   d-Dec. 12, 1921 age 71
                               (Henry Fields)b-Unadilla, res. Fowl.
                               d-June 20, 1895 age 33, consumption
                                         removed from old cemetery

226
     no stones   (Oliver Griggs)b-N. Y. res. Fowl.
                               d-Feb. 3, 1893 age 57
                               (Mrs. Lucy E Griggs)b-Livingston Co/
                               d-March 2, 1901 age 57y, 4m, 9d
                               (Herbert A Griggs)b-Mi. res. Fowl.
                               d- 11-24-1916 age 50
                               (Lena Griggs)b-Handy, res. Hart
                               d-Nov. 22, 1950 age 73

227 CAMPBELL
     Egbert Campbell   b-Mi. res. Bambridge, Berion Co.
     1852-1901   d-Nov. 15, 1901 age 49
     Violetta Giddings   d-1901? age 49?
     1864-1926
     A V P Campbell
     1822-1905   burial ? d-age 83
     Susan Campbell   res. Fowlerville
     1830-1897   d-May 10, 1897 age 67
     Marion Campbell   b-Unadilla, res. Holland
     1853-1896   d-Jan. 13, 1896 age 42(or 43)
                               (Frances M Giddins)res. Fowlerville
                               d-Aril 30, 1926 age 63

228 GLENN
     infant son of C J & N S Glenn no record
     died Dec. 1, 1873 aged 21 days
                               (Charles J Glenn)b-N. Y. res. Belding
                               d-Oct. 20, 1893 age 68

229 WATKINS
     Mathew,   "Mathew G"b-England, res. Locke
                               d-July 23, 1895 age 75
                                         removed from old cemetery
     Mary E,   (see next entry)
     G Watkins   (Mary G Watkins) res. Pontiac
     1818-1908   d-July 23, 1908 age 90
     on monument-G Watkin
230 ROSE
     J S Rose   "Justin S" b-N. Y. res. Fowlerville
     Co. H, 5 Mich. H A   d-Nov. 8, 1904 age 70
     mother
     on monument-Rose
     M E Rose   "Maud E" b-Hamden, N. Y. res. Handy
     1838-1896   d- 3-24-1896 age 58, cancer

Section "A"   Greenwood cemetery
lot #
230 continued

                                    (James W Rose) b-Mi. res. Grand Rapids
                                    d-Jan. 3, 1901 age 33y, 7m, 1d, of injury
                                    (Charles Rose) b-N. Y. res. Fowl.
                                    d-Jan. 2, 1911 of typhoid age 52

230½ DIAMOND
    Francis I Diamond(on metal tag)"Francis Ione" res. Livingston Co.
    born 1910, died 1977 age 67   d- 10-8-1977, burial from Howell,Mi.
231 McMANUS
    M R McManus   no record
    Co. L, 3rd Mich. Cav.

                                    (Abbey McManus) res. Handy
                                    d-Jan. 17, 1896 age 82
                                    (Jane Force)b-Mi. res. Fowlerville
                                    d- 8-20-1915 age 72
                                    (James Force) b-Mi. res. Fowlerville
                                    d- 6-27-1917 age 77
                                    (Mary Gardner)b-Genoa twp. res. Fowl.
                                    d-March 16, 1900 age 49, apoplexy

231½ McDANIELS
    triple stone;-McDaniels
    Arthur, 1875-1909   res. Howell
                                    d-Nov. 12, 1909 age 34
                                    removed from Howell cem. burial 1944
    Jewell, 1903-1906   res. Howell
                                    d-April 29, 1906 age 2
                                    removed from Howell cem. burial 1944
    Maude, 1877-1971   res. Chelsea
                                    d- 1-16-1971 age 93

232 PEEK
    G Y Peek   "Christopher Y"b-Mi. res. Fowl.
    1844-1921   d-March 20, 1921 age 76
    Mary Peek   (Mary Lewis Peek) res. Fowlerville
    1844-1927   d-Oct. 30, 1927 age 81
    Emma Peek   res. Fowlerville
    1870-1930   d-Aug. 30, 1930 age 60 of T B.
    D A Carr   no record
    born 1859, died 1885

                                    (Mrs. Ida P Carr)b-Unadilla, res. Detroit
                                    d-Oct. 5, 1894 age 36
                                    (infant son, Peek)res. Detroit
                                    d-Aug. 8, 1932, premature
                                    (Lizzie Drew)b-White Oak
                                    d-Dec. 5, 1893 age 39, cancer
                                    (Amasa G House)b-N. Y.
                                    d-Dec. 6, 1893   removed from old cem.
                                    (Cynthia House) from old cemetery
                                    burial 12-6-1893
                                    (Eddie House)
                                    burial 12-6-1893 from old cemetery
                                    (Eddie House Jr.) d-age 1
                                    burial 12-6-1893 from old cemetery
                                    (Tho? House) d-Dec. 6, 1893 age 1 hour
                                    burial 12-6-1893, removed from old cem.

Section "A"   Greenwood cemetery
lot #
233 DIAMOND--GAFFIELD
     Agnes,   (Agnes Gaffield)b-Fowlerville
                                     d-July 27, 1895 age 4 montns
                                             removed from old cem.(?)

     Henry,   "Henry C" b-Fowlerville
                                     d-Jan. 2, 1900 age 25 days
     Ellen I, 1850-1924   b-Mi.   res. St. Louis, Mo.
                                     d-Sept. 14, 1924 age 74
     Henry G, 1850-1918   b-Fowlerville, res. Vestenburg
                                     d- 6-6-1918 age 68
     on monument-Diamond
234 BENNETT
     Caroline Bennett "mother"   b-Mi.   res. Fowlerville
     1843-1911   d-March 22, 1911 age 68
     David D Bennett "father"   res. Lansing
     1838-1924   d-Dec. 6, 1924 age 86
                                     (Norman Bennett)b-N. Y, res. Fowl.
                                     d-March 30, 1904 age 82
                                     (John Layton)b-N. Y. res. Handy
                                     d- 1-6-1896 age 76, from old cemetery

234½ FRYE
     double stone;-Frye
     Plyn E, 1891-1979   "Plyn Elias" res. Genesee Co.
                                     d- 6-8-1979 age 87, burial from Linden
     Lucile M, 1904-   not listed
235 RUGGLES--ADAMS
     mother   no record
     mother   no record
     "Artie R" J M Ruggles
     on monument-Ruggles
         John M Ruggles   b-N. Y.   res. Handy
         died June 3, 1899 aged 75yrs, & 26dys
         Fanny M, his wife   res. Montrose, Mi.
         died Aug. 7, 1909 aged 76y, 3m, 21d
                                     d-Aug. 6, 1908, burial 8-8-1908
                                     (Libbie Horton) res. Lansing
                                     d-July 12, 1933 age 77
                                     (Ruth Elizabeth Adams)b-N. Y. res. Fowl.
                                     d-Oct. 18, 1897 age 85
                                     (Michael McManus)b-Ireland
                                     d-age 73, burial from old cemetery
                                     (Eliza McManus)b-Green Oak twp.
                                     d-age 17, removed from old cemetery
                                     (Martha McManus)b-Handy (listed lot 231)
                                     re-burial from old cemetery-no date

236 HOUSE
     A G House   "Amasa G"
     Co. B, 1st Mich. S S
     double stone;
     Amasa G House   b-N. Y. res. Handy
     died Nov. 18, 1871 aged 71yrs, 1mo, 21ds
                                     removed from old cemetery Dec. 6, 1893
     Cynthia House   b-N. Y.
     died March 9, 1857 aged 36yrs? 8mos, 21ds
                                     removed from old cemetery Dec. 6, 1893

Section "A"
lot #
236 continued
   E A House   "Eddie" b-Handy
   Co. B, 26th Mich. Inf.   d-of army wound
                      removed from old cemetery Dec. 6, 1893
   Sanford E House   "Sanford Emery" b-Mi. res. Fowl.
   1848-1921   d-July 1, 1921 age 73
   Co. I, 9 Mich.

                     (Eddie House)
                     d- age 1, burial Dec. 6, 1893 from old cem.
                     (male) ? no name, d-age 1 month
                     removed from old cemetery Dec. 6, 1893
                     (infant daughter of Ed Dunn)res. Handy
                     d-Jan. 8, 1904 age 8 days,
                     (burial on W S House lot)

237 COLLINS
   Carrie, daughter of Noel & Maria Collen
   died Sept. 30, 1854 aged 2yrs, 6mos,& 10 days
   (this stone leaning against stone below)
                     (old cemetery record list Carrie Coffey
                     d-1861   b-Handy removed from old cem.)
   Almira, wife of John W Collins   b-Handy   d-of cancer
   died Sept. 4, 1865 aged 19y, 1m, & 11dys   removed from old cem.
   Libbie S Collins   "Elizabeth"b-Handy, res. South Bend, Ind.
   dies Aug. 12, 1879 aged 32yrs, 8mos, 22dys   d-age 36
   libbie
   mother
238 FERGUSON
   Joseph Ferguson   b-Utica, N. Y. res. Fowlerville
   1804-1896   d-July 8, 1898 age 94
   Emeline Ferguson   b-N. Y. res. Fowlerville
   1826-   d-April 17, 1905 age 79
239 BRISTOL
   Richard G, 1830-1912   b-N. Y. res. Fowlerville
                     d- 7-21-1912 age 82
   Henry N, 1855-1913   b-Mi. res. Fowlerville
                     d- 3-5-1913 age 57

   on monument-Bristol
   Salina, daughter of Richard & Alma Bristol(this stone leaning on mon.)
   died Aug. 21, 1851 aged 4 years b-Handy,d- of a deformity
                     removed from the old cemetery
                     (Mrs. Emma Head) res. Fowlerville
                     d-Oct. 25, 1919 age 66
                     (Hiram Bristol)b-Onandaga, N. Y.
                     d-age 88, burial ? from old cemetery
                     res. Cohoctah
                     (Sallie Bristol)b-Genesee Co. N. Y.
                     d-age 86, removed from old cemetery
                     (Alma Bristol)
                     d-age 36, burial 1874, removed from
                     the old cemetery
                     (Emerson Bristol)b-Handy
                     d-age 6, removed from old cemetery
                     (infants (2)Bristol) from old cemetery

Section "A"   Greenwood cemetery
lot #
239 continued

                        (Delia Bristol)b-Livingston Co. res. Fowl.
                        d-Jan. 17, 1906 age 55
                        (Abagal Schaffer)
                        d-July 23, 1897
                        (Justus Fales) d-age 70

240 WHITNEY--CORY
     Orison G Whitney (FLT emblem)   "Orson C" res. Locke
     1852-1931   d-April 19, 1931 age 78
     Sophia R, wife of O C Whitney   "Rose Sophia"b-Mi. res. Locke twp.
     1852-1923   d-May 8, 1923 age 71
     Caleb Horton   removed from old cemetery to lot A-285
     died May 11, 1859 aged 64 years & 5mos   moved here May 18, 1900
     on monument-Whitney-Cory

                        (Lettie C Horton) removed from lot A-285
                        d-Jan. 7, 1862 age 7 weeks
                        (Mrs. Caleb Horton)b-Newark, N. J.
                        d-Sept. 3, 1865 buried in old cem.
                        then to lot A-285, then here 1900
                        (all the Hortons first buried-old cem.)

241 WELLER
     Oscar D, 1832-1904   b-Mi. res. Handy
                                      d-Jan. 3, 1904 age 71
     Harriet E, 1839-1922   "Harriet Elizabeth" b-Mi. res. Fowl.
                                      d-Dec. 25, 1922 age 83
     Benjamin Weller   no record
     died Feb'y 16, AD 1860 in the 65 year of his age
     Emma. daughter of O D & C P Weller   "Emma N"b-Handy, res. Handy
     died Oct. 21, 1865 aged 10yr, 5mo, & 8?dys   buried 1874 from old cem.
     (this stone is leaning on Warren H, stone)
     Warren H, son of OD & C P Weller   "Warren Henry"b-Handy
     died July 25, 1854   d-age 2 months, removed from old cem.
     Cordelia P, wife of Oscar D Weller   b-Handy
     died Sept. 2, 1859 aged 25 years   removed from old cemetery
     on monument-Weller
242 LING
     Ida A Ling   "Ida Worden Ling"b-Handy
     1-22-1858--2-15-1900   d-age 42 in Saginaw
     John Ling   res. Webberville
     1850-1933   d-April 9, 1933 age 81
     on monument-Ling

                        (Bert H Ling)res. Wyandotte
                        d- 11-9-1963 age 87
                        (Minnie Ling) res. Webberville
                        d-Dec. 19, 1930 age 73
                        (Minnie N Ling) res. Wyandotte
                        d- 4-4-1956 age 79
                        (Gottlieb Keuhnle)b-Germany,res. Toledo
                        d-Feb. 24, 1921 age 80, burial Mar. 3.

Section "A"   Greenwood cemetery
lot #
243 FRANKS
     Joyce M, wife of Joseph Franks b-Handy
     1850-1898   d-June 29, 1898 age 48, burial Aug. 2.
     Joseph   no record
     1845-1914
     Ella J, 1861-1927   res. Webberville
                                     d-Nov. 27, 1927 age 66

     on monument-Franks
244 MATTHIESEN
     John, "father"   b-Germany, res. Fowlerville
     1854-1938   d-age 84, burial Oct. 30, 1938
     Anna M, "mother"   res. Fowl.
     1853-1927   d-Oct. 11, 1927 age 74
     double stone,-Matthiesen
     Herman H, 1880-1955   b-Mi. res. Oceola
                                     d- 4-17-1955 age 74
     Mattie E, 1886-1967   b-Howell
                                     d- 9-22-1967 age 81

     on monument-Matthiesen

                                     (Abram Swanson)b-Mi. res. Howell
                                     d-May 15, 1911 age 76
                                     (Abraham Swanson)b-Sweden,res. Howell
                                     d-April 29, 1895 age 76

245 VAN BUREN
     Martin G Van Buren   (see lot 246)
     Michigan 2d Lt. Co. K, 63 Pioneer Inf. World War 1
     March 7, 1896-July 5, 1964
     Lida M,
     George M, 1866-1957   b-Mi. res. Ingham Co.
                                     d- 1--16-1957 age 91
     Effie C, 1867-1954   b-Mi. res. Fowlerville
                                     d- 4-21-1954 age 85
     on monument-Van Buren
         Lida M, wife of G M Van Buren   b-(or) res. Conway?
         1872-1896   d- 4-16-1896 in childbirth
246 VAN BUREN
     Sarah O, 1831-1915   res. Handy (no other information)
     Martin, 1826-1885
     on monument-Van Buren
         in memory of Martin Van Buren   res. Fowlerville
         who died Sept. 27, 1885 aged 59ys, 5m, 4d
                                     removed from Benjamin cemetery-
     on monument-Dunn
         Daniel Dunn   (David Dunn)b-Maine
         1806-1876   d-Nov. 4, 1876, removed from Howell 1898
         Cnristina, his wife   b-Boston, Mass.
                                     d-1895, removed from Howell 8-19-1898
247 DUNN
     Joshua Dunn   b-Maine res. Handy
     1829-1898   d-Aug. 14, 1898 age 69
     Frances M, wife of Joshua Dunn b-Maine res. Handy
     1836-1902   d-March 30, 1902 age 66
     on monument-Dunn

Section "A"   Greenwood cemetery
lot #
247 continued

                              (infant Dunn)b-Mi. res. Fowlerville
                              d-Jan. 20, 1907 age 1 day, pnue.
                              (John Dunn)res. Detroit
                              d-April 14, 1942 age 76
                              (Wayne Dunn)b-Mi. res. Detroit
                              d- 7-1-1913 age 21 by drowning

247½ RIPPLE
     double stone;-Ripple
     Burton V, 1902-1966   res. Ovid, Mi.
                                 d- 12-16-1966 age 64
     Nellie E, 1915-   not listed
                                 (Carl Gifford Dunn)res. Grand Rapids
                                 d- 4-4-1978 age 37

248 LAUDE--KUNDE
     Edith M, 1899-1923   (Edith M Laude)b-Mi. res. Fowlerville
                                 d-March 11, 1923 age 24
     Carl, 1843-1904   (Carl F Kuhnde) b-Germany, res. Handy
                                 d-June 10, 1904 age 61
     Henry, 1897-1907   (Henry HLaude)b-Mi. res. Handy
                                 d-June 19, 1907 age 10
     Amelia, 1840=1919   (Amelia F Kunde)b-Germany,res. Bennington
                                 d-Oct. 8, 1919 age 79
     Herman A, 1859-1926   (Herman G Laude)b-Germany, res. Handy
                                 d-Feb. 12, 1926, age 66
     Alvina, 1864-1895   (Alvina Laude)b-Germany, res. Lansing
                                 d-Sept. 21, 1895, consumption
     Charles, 1895   (Charles H Laude or Chas. Harmon Laude)
                                 d-Aug. 31, 1895   res. Lansing
                                        removed from old cemetery
     Carl, 1903   (Carl Laude)b-Mi. res. Handy
                                 d-Dec. 24, 1903 age 7 months
     Paulina, 1870-1904   (Paulina Laude)b-Germany, res. Handy
                                 d-March 8, 1904 age 27

     on monument-Laude-Kunde
249 BRISTOL
     daughter of F Bristol   (June Bristol)
     May 5, 1852 aged 13yrs, (?) 25ds   removed from old cemetery
     Mabel, dau. of L & E M Bristol
     died Feb. 1, 1884 aged 7m, 6d   d-2-15-1884, removed from old cemetery
     Avery U Bristol   "Avery Urile"b-Mi. res. Fowlerville
     1869-1907   d-Aug. 17, 1907 age 38, apoplexy
     Ellen M Bristol   (Mrs. Levi Bristol)b-Mi. res. Fowl.
     1847-1915   d- 4-19-1915 age 67
     Levi Bristol   b-Canada, res. Fowlerville
     1836-1911   d-Dec. 4, 1911 age 75
                                 (unknown Bristol) no information
                                        removed from old cemetery

250 DUNN
     Edward M Dunn   res. Livingston Co. infirmary
     1866-1942   d-Nov. 19, 1942 age 76
     Elijah T Dunn   b-Maine, res. Fowlerville
     Co. K, 9 Mich. Inf.   d-Feb. 10, 1910 age 70

Section "A"   Greenwood cemetery
lot #
250 continued
    Louisa A Dunn   b-N. Y.   res. Handy
    1842-1908   d-Feb. 17, 1908 age 65
    on monument-E T Dunn
250½ DUNN
    M Ethel Dunn   res. Ingham Co.
    1891-1974   d- 11-14-1974 age 83, bur. from Lansing
    Clayton R Dunn   b-Mi. res. Ingham Co.
    1888-1958   d- 6-21-1958 age 69
251 MINICK
    M F Minick   no record
    1829-1909
    S B Minick   "Samuel Sr." b-Pa. res. Handy
    1829-1902   d-Sept. 7, 1901 age 72
    on monument-Minick
252 MINICK--Elliot
    Isaac Minick "husband"   (record says he died Nov. 20, 1898)
    born Feb. 25, 1859, died May 19, 1898   d-age 39, bur. 11-21-1898
                                 (Ellen Minnick Sharp)b-Canada
                                   d-June 29, 1903 age 39 res. Locke twp.
                                   (Glades Elliot) b-Conway
                                   d-Feb. 18, 1899 age 8 months
                                   (Eva May Elliot)D-Ingham Co.
                                   d-June 24, 1901 age 1m, 14d
                                   res. Watertown, Ingham Co.
                                   (William J Bommer)b-Mi. res. Fowl.
                                   d-June 19, 1904 age 37
253 FORCE
    Claude Force   b-Fowlerville, res. Fowlerville
    died Nov. 29, 1900 aged 21ys, 13d   d- of gunshot in head
    father
    mother
    (a old footstone)
                                   (David Force)b-Vermont, res. Handy
                                   d-Oct. 11, 1901 age 84
                                   (Mary Force)D-Canada, res. Fowl.
                                   d-Sept. 15, 1854 age 25
                                   (Frances Force)b-Germany, res. Fowl.
                                   d-March 7, 1907 age 42
                                   (Charles Bowen)b-Handy
                                   d-June 17, 1854 age 18
                                   (Lucy Bowen)
                                   d-Nov. 18, 1865 age 16
                                   (Edwin Bowen)b-Handy(?)
                                   d-Oct. 23, 1882 age 77
                                   (Eliza Bowen)b-Quebec, Canada
                                   d-March? 17, 1891 age 76
                                   (Emeline Lewis)b-Mi. res. Fowl.
                                   d-Sept. 3, 1907 age 61
                                   (Ealga Ione Griswold)b-Mi. res. Fowl.
                                   d-May 30, 1923 age 3m, 4d

Section "A"   Greenwood cemetery
lot #
254
        no stones   (Nettie Minnick)res. Hennepin, Minn.
                                     d-May 5, 1935 age 64 of T B.
                                     (Samuel W Minnick)b-N. Y. res. Handy
                                     d-Feb. 5, 1903 age 42
                                     (children of S W Minnick)res.Handy
                                     burial April 18, 1903
                                     removed from the residence
                                     (Neil Minnick)b-Mi. res. Fowlerville
                                     d-Aug. 9, 1920 age 23

255 RADDATZ
     mother   no record
     Otto M, 1907-1908   b-Mi. res. White Oak
                                     d-July 7, 1908 age 8 months

     double stone;-Raddatz
     Louis, 1862-1946   res. Fowlerville
                                     d-April 19, 1946 age 84
     Pauline, 1869-1949   res. Farmington
                                     d-March 24, 1949 age 79
                                     (Frederick Raddatz)res. Cohoctah
                                     d-March 4, 1909 age 76

256 SMITH
     Nick Smith "our father"   "Nicholas"
     1847-1894   d-Dec. 23, 1894
     Mort Palmatier   b-Mi. res. Handy
     1846-1911   d-Aug. 9, 1911 age 64
     double stone;
     Laura E Jacklin "mother"   no record
     1857-1947
     Charles Wm. Smith "son"   res. Handy
     1883-1947   d-April 26, 1947 age 63
                                     (William Livermore)b-Mi. res. Lansing
                                     d-Feb. 19, 1921 age 67

257 SESSIONS
     Wm. H Sessions   b-N. Y. res. Fowlerville
     1835-1920   d-June 27, 1920 age 84
     Lydia Sessions   "Lydia S"b-Mi. res. Handy
     1836-1913   d-5-23-1913 age 76
     double stone;-Sessions
     Alva P, 1866-1936   "Alva Peck"res. Fowlerville
                                     d-July 8, 1939 age 72, cancer
     Hannah P, 1867-1943   res. Fowlerville
                                     d-April 19, 1943 age 75
                                     (Willie Sessions)b-Mi. res. Handy
                                     d- 12-18-1915 afe 1
                                     (Ella Wendell) res. Lansing
                                     d-Jan. 18, 1947 age 80

258 BESSERT
     double stone;-Bessert
     Max C, 1876-1916 "father"   b-Mi. res. Conway
                                     d- 6-11-1916 age 39
     Catherine, 1875-1948 "mother"   "Kate" b-Germany, res. Lansing
                                     d-July 4, 1948 age 73

Section "A"   Greenwood cemetery
lot #
259 PETERSON
     Ida May Ferguson   res. Detroit
     1869-1939   d-Dec. 13, 1939 age 70
     Dora Coffey   res. Livingston Co.
     1854-1941   d-Jan. 10, 1941 age 87
     (a grave)?   no record
     Carl Peterson   res. Ann Arbor
     1886-1939   d-Sept. 14, 1939 age 53
259½ POLOM
     double stone;-Polom
     Robert M, 1901-1966   res. Royal Oak
                               d- 2-23-1966 age 64

     Gertrude W, 1905-   not listed
260 LING--ALDRICH
     double stone;-Ling
     Hiram, 1856-1938   d-age 82 burial June 29, 1938
     Fannie, 1857-1936   "Fannie E" res. Fowlerville
                               d-Sept. 18, 1935 age 78
     H Ling (a footstone)   (Hiram also listed as "Kuam")
     Lottie L Aldrich   b-Mi.   res. Fowlerville
     1882-1952   d-Aug. 13, 1952 age 70
     Mert W Aldrich   b-Mi. res. Livingston Co.
     1872-1956   d- 11-24-1956 age 84
     Leslie L Aldrich   "Leslie Lisle"b-Mi.
                               d-Nov. 26, 1909 age 2
     Earl W Aldrich   b-Mi.   res. Detroit
                               d- 2-24-1918 age 3 months
                               removed- to lot 260, Oct. 24, 1921
                               (Robert N Aldrich)b-Mi. res. Detroit
                               d-July 1, 1923 age 5 months, pnue.

261 ALDRICH
     double stone,-Aldrich
     Fred W, 1897-1952   "Fred Watson"b-Mi. res. Linden
                               d-May 30, 1952 age 54
     Bessie C, 1900-1976   (Bessie Haviland) res. Livingston Co.
                               d- 7-2-1976 age 76, burial from Linden
262 BIRKENSTOCK
     father
     mother
     Charles
     Fred, 1881-1947   res. Oceola
                               d-Jan. 8, 1947 age 65

     on monument-Birkenstock
        Conrad Birkenstock   b-Germany, res. Fowlerville
     Sept. 14, 1845-Sept. 9, 1914 d-age 72, removed from Genoa cem.
        Elizabeth Birkenstock b-Mi.   res. Fowlerville
     May 16, 1846-Dec. 17, 1926 d-age 80
        Charles Birkenstock   b-Mi.   res. Fowlerville
     Oct. 26, 1874-Jan. 26, 1909 d-1910 age 28
                               (removed from Genoa cem. by John Vogts)

Section "A"   Greenwood cemetery
lot #
263 SMITH
     Mary M Smith "wife"   b-Mi.   res. Inkster
     1910-1956   d- 6-29-1955 age 44
     Fay Smith   no record
     1923-1924
264 EVANS--ALRICH
     double stone;-Evans
     Benjamin H, 1893-1927   res. Cohoctah
                                      d-Dec. 19, 1927 age 34, cancer of foot
     Florence K, 1896-1983   (Florence K Phillips)res. Livingston Co.
                                      d- 1-30-1983 age 86
     Benjamin Evans Jr.   (Benjamin Wilmer Evans)res. Fowl.
     1924-1925   d-Aug. 10, 1925 age 9 months
     Otto Jr, son of Otto & Florence McDaniels (Otto James McDaniels)
     May 1931   d-May 8, 1931 age 1 day, premature
                                      res. Conway

265½ HALLER
     double stone;-Haller
     Ralph J, 1911-   not listed
     Martha H, 1915-   not listed
266 McCULLOUGH
     no stones   (Roy Emerson Palmteer)b-Mi. res. Fowl.
                                      d-Nov. 17, 1921 age 13, typhoid

267 BOWEN
     Mary M Bowen "wife"   no record
     1856-1923
     Levant Bowen "husband"   b-Mi.   res. Fowlerville
     1848-1925   d-June 25, 1925 age 77
                                      (Oren Bowen)b-Mi. res. Handy
                                      d- 6-30-1914 age 76
                                      (Henry Bowen) res. Ionia
                                      d-Oct. 6, 1932 age 82
                                      (Mary Ellen Pitts)b-Mi. res. Shiawasee Co.
                                      d- 1-26-1957 age 87

268 SMITH
     Linnie B Smith "mother"   (Lenna Smith)b-Mi.   res. Handy
     1891-1928   d-Sept. 7, 1923 age 32, appendacitis
     George E Smith "father"   res. Durand
     1890-1965   d- 3-9-1965 age 74
269 HEINEMAN--AVIS
     (a grave?)
     (a grave?)
                                      (Alta A Heineman)b-Mi. res. Fowl.
                                      d-Aug. 4, 1921 age 30
                                      (Kingsley Avis)res. Fowlerville
                                      d-Dec. 17, 1936 age 76
                                      (Ellen Avis)res. Fowlerville
                                      d-April 7, 1941 age 79

Section "A"   Greenwood cemetery
lot #
270 DIBBLE
     no stones   (Edith Dibble) d-age 6, diptheria
                                         burial?, removed from old cemetery
                                         (Benjamin Dibble)b-Pa. res. Fowl.
                                         d- 8-24-1915 age 70
                                         (Francis A Dibble) res. Fowlerville
                                         d-Nov. 16, 1926 age 82
                                         (Earl Pittinger) d- age 3, diptheria
                                         burial ?, removed from old cemetery

270½ HOSKING
     double stone;-Hosking
     John N, "father"   b-Mi. res. Wayne
     1885-1953   d-June 4, 1953 age 67
     Freda C, "mother"   b-Mi. res. Livingston Co.
     1889-1957   d- 11-3-1957 age 67
271 BOWEN
     David, 1806-1864   d-Jan. 20, 1864 age 53
                                         removed from old cemetery
     Betsey, his wife   d-April 3, 1880 age 67
     1813-1880   removed from old cemetery
     Huldah A, his wife   no record
     1840-1923
     David Jr. 1839-1913   no record
     7 little Bowen children   (George Bowen)
     moved from old cem.   d-Aug. 1873 age 4
                                         (Ein(?) Bowen)b-Handy
                                         d-Dec. 1874 age 11 months
                                         (Rosetta Bowen)b-Handy
                                         d-Aug. 15, 1870 age 1
                                         (Herman Bowen)b-Handy
                                         d-May, 1874 age 3 montns

     on monument-Bowen
                                         (David Bowen)b-Mi. res. Fowlerville
                                         d- 5-12-1918 age 79
272 DORMER
     Mina F, dau. of W H & S E Dormer   no record
     died Oct. 9, 1877 aged 4m & 12ds
     Elizabeth J, wife of Philip Dormer   res. Leroy, Ingham Co.
     died Apr. 18, 1858 aged 20yrs, 6ds   removed from old cemetery
                                         (May have been 5 remains removed
                                         from the old cemetery with Elizabeth)
     Willis L, son of P & E J Dormer   no record
     died Aug. 15, 1858 aged 6ms, 18ds
                                         (no name-Dormer)b-Handy
                                         d-Aug. 27, age 2 months(?)wnooping cough

273 BESSERT
     Chris L, 1866-1953 "father"   b-Germany, res. Handy
                                         d-June 24, 1953 age 86
     Anna A, 1864-1936 "mother"   res. Fowlerville
                                         d-April 12, 1936 age 71
     Otto, 1874-1921 "brother"   b-Germany, res. Fowlerville
                                         d-Jan. 28, 1921

Section "A"   Greenwood cemetery
lot #
273 continued
    Caroline, 1832-1893 "mother"   b-Germany, res. Howell
                                      d-April 7, 1893 age 60
    August, 1836-1923 "father"   b-Germany, res. Conway
                                      d-Jan. 26, 1923 age 86

    on monument-Bessert
274 SHEPHERD
    Olive S Shepherd   res. Owasso   (listed on lot 277)
    1880-1950   d-April 29, 1950 age 70
    Fred C Shepherd   no record
    1884-19-
    Hatty Curtis   no record
    1857-1936
                                      (Olive Corbett)b-Ohio, res. Fowl.
                                      d-June 16, 1902 age 77y, 6m, 6d
                                      (Celestia Hicks)b-Palmyra, Onio
                                      d-Oct. 25, 1873 age 25 res. Ovid
                                      removed from old cemetery
                                      (Sarah J Moore)b-Ovid, res. Kalamazoo
                                      d-May 29, 1873 age 27-from old cem.

275 BESSERT
    Louis, 1841-1916 "father"   "Ludwig" b-Germany, res. Fowl.
                                      d- 3-28-1916 age 74
    Amelia, 1855-1926 "mother"   res. Fowlerville
                                      d-July 10, 1926 age 71
    Anna, 1889-1911   b-Mi. res. Fowlerville
                                      d-June 6, 1911 age 22
    Eva, 1887-1917   b-Mi. res. Fowlerville
                                      d- 8-20-1917 age 30
    Wilhelm Janke "father"   no record
    1821-1910
    Frank,   no record
    Oct. 22, 1879-July 22, 1880
    Henry, 1891-1892   no record
    on monument-Bessert
276 MALEITZKE
    Fred G Maleitzke "father"   res. Handy
    1851-1928   d-Oct. 2, 1928 age 76, pnuemonia
    Rebecca Maleitzke "mother"   b-Mi. res. Handy
    1855-1921   d-May 20, 1921 age 65
    mother, 1805-1883   (Mary Maleitzke)b-Germany
                                      d-Dec. 29, 1883 age 78
    Eva L, dau. of E & H Huschke   b-Mi. res. Handy
    1906-1907   d-March 13, 1907 age 3 months
    Shirley F, son of E & H Huscnke   no record
    1912-1915
    on monument-Maleitzke

                                      (Henry Huschke) res. Iosco
                                      d- 6-28-1915 age 3
    Dorothea Janke "mother"   no record
    1817-1881

Section "A"   Greenwood cemetery
lot #
276 continued

    (Edward Smith or Luitze)b-Detroit
    d-Jan. 11 or Feb. 11, 1896 age 13 months
    res. Handy, by covenant with F Maleitzke
    (Ines Smith)b-Handy
    d-Feb. 12, 1896 in childbirth

277 CORBETT

    (Olive S Shepherd) see lot 274

on monument-Corbett
  Ora H Corbett   b-Worchester, Mass.
  June 13, 1822-Oct. 17, 1891 d-age 69
  Olive, wife of Ora H Corbett
  Dec. 11, 1821-   burial Oct. 20, 1891
  Mary C, wife of L B Hicks   "Cebestia"
  Apr. 11, 1848-Oct. 25, 1873 burial Oct. 29, 1873, from old cem.
  Sarah J, wife of S S Moore   b-Ovid, res. Kalamazoo
  June 25, 1846-May 29, 1873 d-age 27 (listed lot 274)
                   removed from old cemetery

Sarah J,
Mary C,
Ora H, (all footstones)
    (Hattie Curtis) res. Owasso
    d-Feb. 28, 1933 of old age

278 SHARPE
  Thos. G Sharpe (vet)   "Jr." res. Fowlerville
  1880-1934   d-Jan. 15, 1934 age 53
  Laura H Sharp Russell   (Laura James)
  1880-1973   d- 3-28-1973 Howell,Mi.
  William H James DDS   res. Howell twp.
  1885-1976   d- 2-21-1976 age 90
  Clarence H Sharp   not listed
  1904-
  on monument-Sharpe
278½ SHARPE
  Esther D Sharpe   not listed
  1917-
  Thomas G Sharpe III   not listed
  1917-
279 PLUMB
  E C Plumb   (E C or E L Plumb)b-N. Y.
  Co. C, 1st Mich. L A   d-Oct. 18, 1893 age 67   res. Williamston
  Phoebe M, wife of Enos C Plum b-N. Y.   res. Conway
  1839-1889
    (Eunice C Plumb)b-N. Y, res. Conway
    d-March 13, 1889 age 49
    (E C & Eunice records mixed up ???)
    (W C or A C Taylor)res. Williamston
    d-Oct. 12, 1895

280 RAY
  Walter B, 1829-1887   res. Fowlerville
                     d-Nov. 25, 1887 age 58
  Mary, 1829-1917   (Mrs. Walter B Ray)b-Mi. res. Barryton
                     burial 11-15-1917
  D E Ray   "Daniel E" res. Stanton
  1862-1935   d-Aug. 9, 1935 age 73

Section "A"   Greenwood cemetery
lot #
280 continued
    double stone;
    Anna M Robertson   res. Detroit
    1868-1926   d-Jan. 8, 1926 age 59
    Grace R McMurchy   res. Detoit
    1872-1940   d-age 68   burial Sept. 16, 1940
281 Scott J Humphrey (masonic)   b-Mi.   res. Howell
    1869-1953   d- 10-26-1953 age 84
    Mary J Humphrey "mother"   b-Mi.   res. Howell twp.
    1836-1924   d-Jan. 11, 1924 age 89
    Jacob Humphrey "father"   b-N. Y. res. Howell twp.
    1819-1892   d-Aug. 28, 1893 age 70
                                  (Earl Humphrey)b-Howell
                                  d-July 3, 1882 age, removed from door-yard

281½ LINE
    double stone;-Line
    William, 1870-1944   res. Cohoctah
                                  d-March 28, 1944 age 73
    Margaret, 1874-1953   no record
282 COLBURN
    T Matilda Eggleston "daughter" b-Mi.   res. Fowlerville
    1882-1912   d-June 26, 1912 age 29, paralysis
    Orpha E Copeland "mother"   no record
    1850-
    Arvilla Colburn, his wife   b-Mi.   res. Fowlerville
    1841-1913   d- 5-29-1913 age 72
    Justus Colburn   no record
    1839-1895
    (behind stone above)Justus Colburn, Co. F, 9th Mich. Inf.
    on monument-Colburn
        Justus Colburn
        born July 21, 1839, died Apr. 21, 1895, Co. F, 9th Mich. Inf.
        James Gordon
        born Mar. 16, 1837, diedin Andersonville,Ga. June 28, 1864
        Co. D, 6th Mich. Cav.
282½
    no stones   (Martin George Van Buren) res. Livonia
                                  d-7-5-1964 age 68
283 FISH
    no stones   (Ida May Fish)b-Conway
                                  d-Sept. 7, 1891 age 7 months
283½ BENJAMIN (full lot)?
    Eone L, 1875-1875   (see Edna, below)
    Electa,
    Julia E,   no record
    Marvin,
    Matilda, 1809-1895   no record
    on monument-Benjamin
        Marvin Benjamin   b-N. Y.   res. Fowlerville
        born May 4, 1836, died July 6, 1916   d-age 80
        Co. K, 9th Mich. Inf. GAR

Section "A"   Greenwood cemetery
lot #
283½ continued
      on Monument-(continue)
          Electa Swarthout, wife of Marvin Benjamin   b-Putnam
          died Jan. 30, 1890 aged 46yrs, 5mos, 10 days
          Edna L, daughter of Marvin & Electa Benjamin   b-Handy
          died Jan. 8, 1875 aged 3mos, 15 days   (removed from Coffrin cem.)
          Libbie Snyder, wife of Marvin Benjamin   no record
          died Oct. 12, 1870 aged 24yrs, 6mos, 14 days
284 BENJAMIN
     Harvey, 1809-1893   b-N. Y.
                                    d-June 19, 1893 age 84
     Orisa L, 1848-1861   "Orsel L" b-Handy
                                    d-June 5, 1861 age 12
     O Edwin, 1853-1902   "Oren E" b-Mi. res. Detroit
                                    d-Aug. 1, 1902 age 48y, 11m, 14d
     Mary, 1878-1897   "Mary E" b-Flint, res. Handy
     on monument-Benjamin
                                    (Matilda Benjamin)b-N. Y. res. Handy
                                    d-April 6, 1895 age 86
                                    (Justus Colburn)b-N. Y.
                                    d-April 21, 1895
285 HORTON
     J H H   (all removed from old cemetery)
     A A H
     father
     (behind above stone) J C Horton, Co. A, 6th Mich. Cav.
     on monument-Horton
         Ira C Horton   res. Sioux City
         born Fed. 12, 1833, died Sept. 8, 1895   (from old cemetery)
         Jane H Horton   b-England
         1835-1858   d-Sept. 15, 1852 age 23 in childbirth
                                    burial Sept. 18, 1854
         Amelia A Horton   b-Putnam, res. Stanton
         1840-1872   d-Dec. 25, 1872 age 32
         Manning S Horton   no record
         1861-1907
                                    (H? Horton)male, res. Minneapolis, Minn.
                                    d-May 29, 1907 (may be Manning S)
                                    (Wm. Horton)burial ? from old cemetery
285½ RICHMOND
     Leeanna Crawford Richmond   res. Livingston Co.
     1929-1972   d- 7-13-1972 age 43
286 CRAWFORD
     triple stone;-Crawford
     George M, 1843-1893   b-Damon(?)   res. Ball Mt. Oakland Co.
                                    d-Aug. 16, 1893 age 59
     Mary E, 1851-1928   (Mary E Whithead)res. Handy
                                    d-April 30, 1928 age 77
     May E, 1887-1903   "Eva May" b-Mi. res. Handy
                                    d-March 21, 1903 age 15
     (behind above stone) G M Crawford, Co. K, 22nd Mich. Inf.
                                    (Hugh L Crawford)res. Webberville
                                    d-Sept. 14, 1927 age 2 hours,premature
                                    (Emma D Miner)
                                    d-March 25, 1898 (in vault, bur.May 26.)

Section "A"   Greenwood cemetery
lot #
287 WHITNEY
     blank stone
     blank stone
     on monument-Whitney (masonic emblem)
          Geo. W Whitney   res. Oakland Co.
          died Sept. 13, 1885 aged 44 years, 22nd Mich. Vol. Inf.
          Eliza J, wife of Geo. W Whitney
          died June 16, 1885 aged 43yrs
          Will M Shorman
          1866-1896   d- 4-23-1896
          Myrtle L Whitney
          Myrtle L Shorman
          Myrtle L Simpson   b-Mi.   res. Handy
          1869-1904   d-Feb. 18, 1904 age 34 in childbirth
     double stone;
          Myrtle L   (Myrtle L Simpson) see above
          Herbert W   (may be her baby, record unclear
                                       probably died in few days)

          Will M,
288 WHITNEY
     father
     mother
     on monument
          Chas. Whitney   res. Handy
          born Mar. 24, 1813, died Mar. 17, 1880
          Lydia A Whitney   "Mrs." b-Palmyra, N. Y.
          born Sep. 8, 1820, died Nov. 9, 1894   d-age 74, from old cemetery
          Seymour C Whitney   res. Fowlerville
          1861-1947   d-Sept. 14, 1947 age 86
          M Adella, wife of S C Whitney res. Fowlerville
          1859-1925   d-June 7, 1925 age 66
288½ WHITNEY
          Susie Pearson Whitney   "Susie M" b-Mi. res. Livingston Co.
          1865-1961   d- 7-4-1961 age 96
                                      (Edna L Benjamin) removed from Coffen cem.
                                      d-Jan. 8, 1875 age 3m, 10 d
                                      burial 1-10-1872 (?)
                                      (Jerry V Cory)b-Mi. res. Locke twp.
                                      d- 3-22-1956 age 77
                                      (Mary Lydia Cory)b-Mi. res. Ingham Co.
                                      d- 12-15-1954 age 70 (listed lot B-288½)

289 MINER
     Ezra A Miner "father"   b-N. Y.   res. Owasso
     1820-1903   d-June 18, 1903 age 83
     Anna M Miner "mother"   "Anna Mira" res. Handy
     1826-1894   d-Aug. 31, 1894 age 68
     William J Miner "husband"   res. Fowlerville
     1846-1931   d-July 15, 1931 age 84
     Emma Miner "wife"   "Emma D" res. Fowlerville
     1849-1898   d-March 25, 1898, pnuemonia
                                      (baby, Farr) res. Fowlerville
                                      d- 3-1-1918 stillborn
                                      burial in lot b-335, then here 1921

Section "A"   Greenwood cemetery
lot #
290 HAYNER
     C G Hayner   "Conrad C" b-Cohoctah
     Co. D, 8th Mich. Cav.   d-Sept. 2, 1888 age 44
                                   removed from Howell vault 1--18-1888
     Carrie A, 1850-1928   res. Fowlerville
                                   d-May 24, 1928 age 77 of T B.

     on monument-Hayner
291 DODGE
     (a grave)   no record
292 DENNIS
     on monument-Dennis
         Darwin L, 1850-1892   b-Salem, res. Detroit
                                   d-Oct. 29, 1893 age 41, bur. 11-1-93
         Clara A, 1853-1893   b-Highland, res. Detroit
                                   d-March 1, 1893 age 39

292½ MIKS
     double stone;-Miks
     Joe, 1922-   "dad"   not listed
         married Aug. 19, 1944
     Clara E, 1926-1980 "mom"   "Clara A" res. Livingston Co.
                                   d- 9-4-1980 age 53

293 WHITE
     Mercy, wife of G W Joles   (Mary Jobes)b-N. Y.
     died Feb. 13, 1872 aged 59yrs, 5ms, & 22ds   removed from old cemetery
     double stone;
     Mary White
     born Sept. 14, 1815, died Apr. 11, 1891   d-March 11, age 73
     F White   no record
     born Nov. 16, 1818
                                   (Jonn D White)b-N. Y. res. Pinckney
                                   d-Feb. 4, 1899 age 81

294 GREEN
     Myron G Green   res. Marquette, Mi.
     born Oct. 3, 1849, died Dec. 12, 1932   d-age 83
     Patience E Green   no record
     born Feb. 26, 1849, died Dec. 9, 1903
     on monument-Green
                                   (Luther Childs)b-Otsego, N. Y.
                                   d-Aug. 5, 1900 age 85 res. Freeport, Mi.
                                   (Angeline Child)b-N. Y.
                                   d-April 10, 1862 age 45
                                   burial 10-22, 1888 from Braten cem.
                                   (Amanda Child)b-Stueben Co. N. Y.
                                   d- June 25, 1888 age 26 of fits
                                   burial 10-22-1888, moved from Braten cem.

295 HYNE--HASTINGS
     on monument-G Hyne
     Geo. E Hyne "father"   b-Mi.   res. Fowlerville
     May 22, 1855-Nov. 28, 1918   d-age 63
     Anna Hyne "mother"   no record
     Nov. 27, 1860-Aug. 15, 1913
     Charles W, son of G E & A S Hyne   b-Fowlerville
     age 11ms   d-April 20, 1901 age 5m, 5d
                                   removed from lot 298, Nov. 1, 1901

Section "A"   Greenwood cemetery
lot #
295 continued
                                    (A J Hastings)
                                    d-1887   later removed to Howell cem.
                                    (Allen Hastings)
                                    d-Feb. 15, 1886 age 55, removed--
                                    (Rose Hastings)
                                    d-Dec. 5, 1878 age 10, diptheria
                                    (the Hastings bodies removed to Howell)

296 GREEN
     Lyman E   res. Greenville
     June 10, 1853-May 24, 1898   d- of consumption
     Esther A Green   b-N. Y. res. California
     born Apr. 29, 1827, died Feb. 19, 1910   burial May 23, 1910
     Nelson H Green   "Nelson B" b-Williamston
     May 1, 1824-Sep. 8, 1891   d-Sept. 4, 1891 age 67, burial Sept. 6.
     on monument-Green

                                    (Elizabeth F Green)b-Genoa, res. Genoa
                                    d-age 2 of diptheria
                                    (Phobe J Dodge) res. Flint
                                    d-Oct. 27, 1934 age 77

296½ DUNSMORE
     double stone;-Dunsmore
     Ralph M, 1923-1980 (masonic)   d- 9-24-1980 age 56
     Connie M, 1932-   not listed
297 HEAD
     Jennie Head   res. Fowlerville
     born Nov. 21, 1858, died Dec. 23, 1943   d-age 85
     William Head   b-N. Y.
     born Feb. 5, 1821, died Feb. 22, 1892   d-age 71
298 HYNE
     C G Hyne "fatner"   "Claude G" b-Mi. res. Detroit
     1883-1921   d-May 17, 1921, shot wounds
     S E Hyne "mother"   "Susie" res. Detroit
     1883-1942   d-June 19, 1942 age 58
     G H Hyne "son"   "George H" res. Ferndale, Mi.
     1907-1947   d-July 13, 1947 age 39
     Wm. Williams   b-Norway
     U S Navy   d-1877 age 38, consumption
                                    removed from old cemetery

     on monument-Hyne (BPOE emblem)
                                    (Louis Williams)b-Norway, res. Fowl.
                                    d-Dec. 22, 1900 age 84
                                    (Charles Williams)b-Buffalo, N. Y.
                                    d-Dec. 22, 1886 age 33, consumptiom
                                    res. Ionia
                                    (Emma Williams)b-Norway
                                    d-Jan. 28, 1892 age 73

299 COOPER--BURNETT
     E F C
     Josephine Miller "wife"   res. Chicago, ill.
     1856-1942   d-April 5, 1942 age 87

Section "A"   Greenwood cemetery
lot #
299 continued
    double stone;-Burnett
    George N, 1878-1936   res. Harvey, Cook Co. Ill.
                                 d-March 24, 1936 age 58
    Avon B, 1879-1949   res. Lake Forest, Ill.
                                 d-Dec. 12, 1944 age 65
    on monument-Cooper
        Elisha F Cooper   b-Grass Lake, Mi.
        died Nov. 28, 1887 aged 41yrs, 2m   burial 12-30-1887
                                 (Christen Cooper) burial Dec. 8, 1887
300 SMITH
    Georgie, "son"   "George C" b-Handy
                                 d-Oct. 10, 1876 age 10 months
                                 removed from old cemetery

    double stone;-Smith
    Byron G, 1869-1953   b-Mi. res. Fowlerville
                                 d- 12-2-1953 age 84
    Abbie M, 1873-1961   "Abbie May" b-Mi. res. Jackson Co.
                                 d- 2-9-1961 age 87 (listed on lot 301)
                                 (Inez Smith)b-Handy
                                 d-Feb. 12, 1896 age 26 in childbirth

301 BENNETT
    Maria Louesa Bennett   "Maria Louisa" b-N. Y. res. Duluth, Iowa
    1832-1913   d- 5-8-1913 age 80
    Lafayette L Bennett   b-Genesee Co. N. Y. res. Pontiac
    1833-1892   d-Feb. 21, 1892 age 59
    Mary E Bennett   res. East Lansing, Mi.
    1860-1930   d-Aug. 25, 1930 age 70
    on monument-Bennett
                                 (Ida Davis)b-Unadilla
                                 d-Dec. 29, 1891 age 36

301½ REBHOLZ
    double stone;-Rebholz
    Charles V, 1908-1973   "Charles Vernon" res. White Oak twp.
        married Nov. 6, 1937   d- 8-15-1973 age 65
    Bernice I, 1903-   not listed
302 WALKER
    Carrie A, daughter of Benjamin G & Mary A Walker   no record
    "our darling sister"
    died March 21, 1863 aged 17 years, 6mo & 19ds
303 MUNSON
    on monument-
        Samuel S Munson   b-Saratoga, N. Y. res. Fowlerville
        died Feb. 2, 1887 aged 87y, 5m, 2d
        Phebe Ann Walker, wife of S S Munson   "Phoebe A"
        died May 7, 1887 aged 84y, 8m, 1d   burial March 9, 1887
        Susan Adelaide   see other stone
        Aug. 4, 1829-Dec. 13, 1913
        *Melvin C, Feb. 22, 1862
        *Charles H, Oct. 16, 1862
        *Benjamin G, Feb. 25, 1864
        *died in the Army

Section "A"   Greenwood cemetery
lot #
303 continued
    Edwin W,
    S Adelaide Munson, wife of James B Lowe   b-Mi. res. Marquette
    Aug. 4, 1929-Dec. 13, 1913   (Mrs. Addie Lowe) d-age 84
                                    (Eri Spencer)b-N. Y. res. Au Train
                                    d-Aug. 7, 1906 age 85
    on monument-(reverse side)
        Isabella M Loveland   no record
        died Oct. 20, 1867
        Clara G Fowler   no record
        Feb. 4, 1870
        Edwin W, Nov. 8, 1873   no record
        Amanda M,   no record
        died Jan. 15, 1847
        Ida D, Apr. 18, 1849   no record
        Albert S, Apr. 20, 1849   no record
        Lydia W Munson   no record
        Mar. 24, 1824-Mar. 26, 1909
304 SPENCER
    Lydia W Spencer   no record
    1824-1909   (may be Lydia Munson listed lot 303)?
    Ery M Spencer   see lot 303
    1823-1906
    Lucy E, wife of E M Spencer "our mother"   b-N. Y. res. Fowl.
    died Sept. 23, 1860 aged 39yrs and 1 da   removed from old cem.
    on monument-Spencer
        Ery M, 1823-1906
        Lydia W, 1824-1909
        Lucy E, 1821-1860
        Emma Doucette, 1850-1935   (Emma Spencer Donetta)res. Marquette
                                    d-March 4, 1935 age 85
        Jennie A, 1862-1944   res. Marquette
                                    d-Aug. 23, 1944 age 82
304½ WHITE
    no stones   (Edward White) res. Livingston Co.
                                    d- 7-8-1973 age 38
305 LOCKWOOD
    Vance I, 1874-1895   b-Fowlerville, res. Fowlerville
                                    d-Oct. 5, 1895 age 21
    James G, 1876-1928   no record
    James A, 1846-1914   no record
    Arloa H, 1849-1921   b-Mi. res. Fowlerville
                                    d-June 11,1921 age 72

    on monument-Lockwood
                                    (Mrs. J Allen)b-N. Y.
                                    d-April 14, 1864 age 94-from old cem.
                                    (Mrs. Eliza Tanner)b-N. Y.
                                    d-of cancer, burial 4-19-1864
                                    removed from old cemetery
                                    (A A Lockwood)b-N. Y.
                                    d-April 12, 1862 age 54-from old cem.

Section "A"   Greenwood cemetery
lot #
306 LOCKWOOD
     Alanson B, 1823-1869   no record
     Elizabeth, 1824-1876   no record
     Francis E, 1850-1900   (Mrs. Francis Mann)b-N. Y. res. Saginaw
                                      d-Oct. 8, 1900 age 50
     Calvin, 1833-1904   no record
     Co. K, 9 Mich. Inf.
     on monument-Lockwood (on lot 305-306)
307 KEENMON
     John Keenmon   b-Germany
     1825-1887   d-Jan. 26, 1887 age 62
     Caroline Keenmon   b-Germany, res. Howell
     1834-1906   d-Nov. 31, 1906 age 72
     Louis Keenmon   b-Mi. res. Howell
     1863-1921   d-April 11, 1921 age 57
308 REESE
     Julia E Reese   b-N. Y. res. Fowlerville
     died June 4, 1912   d-age 63
     James H Reese   b-N. Y. res. Fowlerville
     1834-1906   d-Dec. 6, 1906 age 71
     (behind stone above)Jas. H Reece, Co. B, 8 Mich. Inf.
309 GRANT
     on monument-
        Lucy M Grant   b-Conn.
        born at Hartford Ct. April 31, 1813
        died-   d- May 24(?)1859, burial July, 1859
                                      removed from old cemetery
        Wm. W Grant
        born at Howell, Mich. May 13, 1848
        died May 2, 1870   burial 7-187-, removed from old cem.
        Walker L Grant   (listed as "W W")
        born at Howell, Mich. Mar. 10, 1846
        died July 7, 1870   d-age 23 of consumption
        Joseph Grant   b-Newark
        born at Newirk, N. J Sept. 27, 1808
        died Dec. 25, 1859   d-age 52
                                      (L. W Grant)b-Howell, res. Handy
                                      d-July 7, 1887 age 25, consumption
                                      (Elmer Tucker)b-Handy
                                      d-Dec. 30, 1864 age 4 months
                                      burial 1-2-1864, removed from old cem.
                                      (Ruby A Tucker)b-Mi. res. Fowlerville
                                      d-Feb. 8, 1909 age 73
                                      (Giles G Tucker)b-Mass. res. Fowlerville
                                      d-May 4, 1909 age 79
310 ELLIOTT--PLACE
     John Elliott   b-Canada, res. Gaylord, Mi.
     1832-1908   d-Nov. 17, 1908 age 76
     (behind stone above) John Elliot, Miss. Marine Brigade
     Bridget Elliott   b-Canada, res. Gaylord
     1830-1902   d-Nov. 22, 1902 age 72

Section "A"   Greenwood cemetery
lot #
310 continued
      Kate J Elliott   res. Pontiac
      1860-1930   d-June 21, 1930 age 70
                                      (Clarrilla Place)res. Howell
                                      d-Feb. 27, 1871, consumption
                                      removed from old cemetery

311 COFFEN
      U C
      Uriah Coffen   b-N. Y.
      died May 16, 1883 aged 64yrs

                                      (Catherine Coffin)b-Pa. res. Handy
                                      d-Aug. 14, 1901 age 84
                                      (Debery Eldrich)female, b-N. Y/
                                      d-March 5, 1891 age 75

312 ELDRIDGE--BARDEN
      Deborah Eldridge   no record
      born Oct. 16, 1815-Mar. 5, 1891
      Mildred E Hagadorn   "Ethel Mildred"b-Mi. res. Fowlerville
      1887-1904   d-Aug. 30, 1904 age 17,
                                      burial on Barden lot
                                      (Charles Barden)b-N. Y. res. Fowl.
                                      d-Sept. 20, 1907 age 58 of injury
                                      (Susan M Cadmus)b-N. Y. res. Fowl.
                                      d-Nov. 1, 1903 age 81

312½ EDDY
double stone;-Eddy
      Charles, 1883-1976   res. Pontiac
                                      d- 8-20-1976 age 93

      Dencie P, 1885-1973   res. Howell
                                      d- 12-13-1973 age 88
313
      empty
314
      no stones   (Emeline Burkhart)b-Lockport,N. Y.
                                      d-Jan. 1, 1887 age 56
                                      a charity grant lot

315 TRYON
      on monument-Tryon
      Hannah M Tryon "wife"   res. Handy
      1849-1939   d-Feb. 11, 1937 age 87
      Spencer Tryon "husband"   b-Mi.   res. Williamston
      1851-1906   d-June 19, 1906 age 55
316 AFFLECK
      George Affleck "son"   b-Mi.   res. Fowlerville
      1856-1961   burial 12-29, 1906 from another cem.
      Ella Affleck "dau."   b-Mi.   res. Fowlerville
      1863-1865   burial 12-29, 1906 from another cem.
      John P Affleck "father"   b-N. Y. res. Fowlerville
      1823-1889   burial 12-29, 1906
                                      transfered from another cemetery
      Lydia L Affleck "mother"   b-England, res. Fowlerville
      1832-1908   d-Oct. 12, 1908 age 76
      Elisha L Affleck "son"   res. Fowlerville
      1860-1928   d-Aug. 6, 1928 age 58

{136}

Section "A"   Greenwood cemetery
lot #
316½ AFFLECK--CHAPMAN
     Jennie A Chapman "wife"   b-Mi. res. Oakland Co.
     1867-1959   d- 5-4-1959 age 92
     Frank E Chapman "husband"   res. Arizona
     1864-1950   d-Jan. 10, 1950 age 86
     on monument-Affleck-Chapman
317 ATKINS
     George, 1860-1941   b-Canada, res. Ypsilanti
                                    d-Aug. 5, 1941 age 81

     Belle, 1869-1941   (May Belle Mapes Atkins)res. Hartland
                                    d-May 27, 1941 age 72

     Iila, 1894-1917   "Lila" b-Mi. res. Fowlerville
                                    d- 3-19-1917 age 22 of T B.

     on monument-Atkins
317½ EATON
     double stone-Eaton
     Lehman J, 1911-   not listed
     Myrtle Dale, 1906-   not listed
318
     no stones   (Alice Sabin)b-Mi. res. Handy
                                    d- 7-14-1913 age 30
                                    (Henry Curtis)b-Ohio, res. Fowlerville
                                    d-March 8, 1920 age 72
                                    (Hattie Curtis) res. Ypsilanti
                                    d-Jan. 10, 1945 age 96

319 CURTIS
     Henry Curtis   no record
     1847-1920
     Hattie Curtis   no record
     1848-1945
     Alice Curtis   no record
     1882-1906
321 SCRIPTURE
     blank stone   (Amanda Scripture)b-N. Y.
                                    d-March 20, 1894 age 60-from old cem.

     Bert E Scripture (masonic)   "Bert Edwin" res. Fowlerville
     1866-1939   d-April 8, 1939 age 72
     Ellen H Scripture   res. Fowlerville
     1876-1967   d- 7-30-1967 age 91
321½ DAVIDS
     double stone;-Davids
     William L, 1911   not listed
     Elsie E, 1912-   not listed
322 METCALF--SCRIPTURE
     on monument
        Cornelia W, dau. of H & E A Metcalf   b-Fowlerville
        died June 19, 1872 ae 24ys & 3ms   d-June 21, epilepsy
        Abby E, dau. of S & A F Scripture   b-Fowlerville
        died Apr. 15, 1870 ae 1yr, 8mo & 8ds   d- of congestion
        Harvey Metcalf   b-Mass.
        died Mar. 28, 1878 aged 83ys, 3ms, 8d
        Samuel Scripture   b-N. Y or N. H.
        died Sept. 25, 1872 aged 45yrs, & 5mos d- of dropsy
                                    (all above removed from old cemetery)

Section "A"   Greenwood cemetery
lot #
322 continued
    On monument-(continued)
        infant son of S & A F Scripture   b-Fowlerville
        died Jan. 10, 1872 aged age 16 days
                                (record shows d-Dec. 25, 1871)
    blank stone
    blank stone
    (behind stone above) Sam'l Scripture, Co. D, 6th Mich. Cav.
                                (Evelin Metcalf) burial 12-7-1890
                                (Emeline Metcalf) b-N. Y.
                                d-Dec.5, 1890 age 80
323 PLACE--ELLIOTT
    on monument-Place-Elliott
    James H Place   b-N. Y. res. Fowlerville
    1836-1909   d-Jan. 5, 1910 age 73, bur. Jan. 7, 1910
    Angeline, wife of James H Place   b-Genesee Co. N. Y.
    1836-1894   d-Jan. 13, 1894 age 57(listed lot 324)
    Charles, infant son of Mr. & Mrs. James H Place   (infant-no data)
    1874-1874
324 ELLIOTT--PLACE
    Charles F Elliot   b-Sterling (?)
    1866-1896   d-April 16, 1896 age 30(listed lot 323)
    Annabelle, wife of Charles Elliot   res. Howell
    1871-1943   d-Oct. 23, 1943 age 72(listed lot 323)
    Frank S, son of Mr. & Mrs. James H Place   b-Fowlerville, res. Fowl.
    1857-1898   d-Dec. 4, 1898 age 41
    Mary E, wife of   no record
    died June 1, 1852 aged 76yrs
    Harry, inft. son of Mr. & Mrs. C F Elliott   no record
    1895-1895
325 DINTURFF--LANE
    Frank Dinturff Lane   res.Fowlerville
    1858-1950   d-Aug. 25, 1950 age 91
    Nevada Read Lane   res. Fowlerville
    1864-1943   d-July 22, 1943 age 78
    Harry Read Lane   res. Ann Arbor
    1891-1939   d-July 29, 1939 age 49, fractured neck
    Irma Marle Lane   b-Mi. res. Fowlerville
    1901-1904   d-Oct. 8, 1904 age 3, diptheria
325½ LANE
    Vera Lane Henry   not listed
    1889-19-
326 DINTURFF
    Daniel W Dinturff (masonic)   b-N. Y. res. Fowlerville
    1830-1909   d-Feb. 22, 1909 age 78
    Mary M Dinturff   b-N. Y. res. Fowlerville
    1830-1911   d-Dec. 3, 1911 age 81
    on monument-Dinturff-(right side) Lane-(left side)

Section "A"   Greenwood cemetery
lot #
327 DREW
     H D
     on monument-Drew
          in memory of Isaac C Drew by his adored wife   b-N. H.
          Oct. 27, 1816, died Apr. 3, 1885   d-age 65, consumption
          to the memory of our beloved mother
          Hannah Dunnville   b-England
          born Mar. 16, 1824, died Sept. 7, 1884   d-age 57
     I C D
                                   (Lizzie Drew)b-White Oak
                                   d-Dec. 5, 1893 age 39
                                   (Jane Drew)b-N. Y. res. Conway
                                   d-June 3, 1893 age 73
                                   (Frank Drew)b-Mi. res. Wyandotte
                                   d- 12-6-1917 age 65

328 MARTIN
     Mamie E, dau. of A A & M J Martin   "Mary B"
     1873-1879   d-Dec. 28, 1879 age 6. from old cem.
     Andrew A Martin   b-Ireland
     1838-1875   d-Nov. 2, 1875 age 37, typhoid
                                   removed from old cemetery
     Mary Jane Martin
     1842-1907   d-Jan. 18, 1907
     double stone,-Butterfield
     A I, 1869-1955   b-Mi.   res. Fowlerville
                                   d- 2-17-1955 age 85
     Lillian N, 1870-1956   res. Howell
                                   d- 2-6-1956 age 86
     Ford, son of A I & L M Butterfiled   no record
     age 8mos, 18 days
     on monument-Martin
329 BROWN--GREENAWAY
     James A Brown   b-Chatauqua, N. Y.
     died May 1, 1887 aged 50ys, 9ms, 28ds   (listed lot 330)
     Sarah F Brown Greenaway   "Sarah Frances" b-Mi. res. Fowl.
     died Dec. 27, 1917 aged 71ys, 10ms, 15ds (listed lot 330)
     Mabel   b-Fowlerville
     died Mar. 11, 1876 aged 6m, 22d   (listed lot 330)
     infant babes,   no record
     died Dec. 24, 1876
     children of J A & S F Brown
     Temple K Brown "doctor"   res. Lansing
     1879-1935   d-Feb. 26, 1935 age 58
329½ BISHOP
     Vance Wells Bishop   res. Livingston Co.
     Pvt. U S Army, World War 1
     1897-1976   d- 9-11-1976 age 79, bur. from Howell
330 BROWN--GREENWAY
     on monument-Brown

Section "A"   Greenwood cemetery
lot #
331 PULVER--NICHOLS
     Edwin S, 1858-1929   (Edwin S Nichols) res. Handy
                               d-Dec. 19, 1930 age 73
     Myrtie V, 1863-1917   (Myrtie V Nichols)b-Mi. res. Iosco
                               d- 2-20-1917 age 52, cancer
     Jesse Pulver   no record
     1819-1884
     Phylinda, his wife   b-N. Y.
     1826-1886   d-March 30, 1885 age 60, consumption
332 SHORMAN
     Rachel G, "dau."   (Rachel G Kast)b-N. Y. res. Lansing
     1849-1907   d-Aug. 4, 1907 age 58
     William H, 1826-1889   b-N. Y.
                               d-April 10, 1889 age 63
     Susan, 1829-1908   res. Conway
                               d-March 29, 1908 age 79

     on monument-Shorman
                               (Clara Dennis)b-Highland, res. Detroit
                               d-March 1, 1898 age 39
                               (Darwin Dennis)b-Salem, Oakland Co.
                               d-Oct. 29, 1893 age 41, typhoid
                               res. Detroit
                               (Ervin Pitts)b-Mi. res. Handy
                               d-Sept. 5, 1908 age 40

333 BLACKMER
     S Thurlow Blackmer   "Sears Thurlow" res. Fowlerville
     1869-1948   d-Nov. 21, 1948 age 74(listed lot 334)
     Deo M Blackmer   res. Fowlerville
     1892-1967   d- 1-19-1967 age 74
     Ethel M Blackmer   res. Indiana
     1890-1976   d- 4-23-1976 age 86
     Betty Beatrice Blackmer   b-Mi. res. Milan, Mi.
     Sept. 21, 1916-Dec. 1, 1916 d-age 2 months
333½ DUNHAM
     double stone;-Dunham
     Scott D Sr. 1920-1975   res. Livingston Co.
          married Oct. 16, 1937 d- 10-15-1975 age 55
     Ruth V, 1920-   not listed
334 MINTO--BLACKMER
     William Bruce Minto "father" res. Fowlerville
     1846-1936   d-April 19, 1936 age 90
     Almeda Jane Minto "mother" no record
     1848-1924
     Blanche Minto Olmstead   res. Fowlerville
     1885-1938   d-age 53   burial May 25, 1938
     Matie E Blackmer   b-Mi.   res. Fowlerville
     1870-1956   d- 7-30-1956 age 86
                               (Helen K Simpson)res. Jackson
                               d-Jan. 17, 1942 age 48

Section "A"   Greenwood cemetery
lot #
336 CARR
     Dr. O C Carr   "Ora" res. Pontiac
     1870-1946   d-Jan. 7, 1946 age 76
     Cora M, 1867-1876   d-Nov. 21, 1876 age 29
                                     removed from Antrim Co. cem. 1904
     Tama E, 1851-1928   res. Genoa twp.
                                     d-Sept. 22, 1928 age 77
     Dewitt C, 1843-1907   b-Rhode Is. res. Fowlerville
                                     d-June 7, 1907 age 63, typhoid
     Anna L, 1870-1943   res. Genoa twp.
                                     d-July 18, 1943 age 62(listed on 336½)

     on monument-Carr
336½ ADAMS
     Chas. L Adams   "Charles Lyman" res. Detroit
     1902-1943   d-Aug. 24, 1943 age 40
     Arlene M, wife of Chas.   (Arlene M McClung) res. Lansing
     1905-1966   d- 8-5-1966 age 61, kidney failure
337 GALE
     on monument-Gale
        Susan F Gale   b-Mi.   res. Detroit
        Aug. 25, 1849-July 5, 1900   d-age 49
     Mary T Gale   "Mary C" res. Fowlerville
     born July 17, 1850, died Nov. 15, 1928   d-age 78
     Wm. B Gale   res. Columbus
     born Jan. 25, 1848, died Nov. 22, 1933   d-age 85
337½ CRAWFORD
     double stone;-Crawford
     George L, 1908-   not listed
     Martha D, 1915-1972   res. Wayne Co.
                                     d- 1-7-1972 age 56, pnuemonia
338 RATHBUN
     on monument-
        Bessie, dau't. of S J & Alice B Sheran (Bessie Snerman)b-Handy
        died Oct. 22, 1884 aged 9mos & 11dys   removed from old Briggs cem.
        Alice Bell Newman   b-Handy
        died Feb. 18, 1890 aged 27ys, 6ms & 2ds   d-of consumption
     Belle
     Fred   (Fred Rathbun) res. Wayne
     1850-1930   d-March 4, 1930 age 70, pnuemonia
     Bessie
                                     (Alvis? Newman)burial 2-20-1889
                                     (this may be record of Alice Newman)
                                     (Sarah Ferguson) res. Flint
                                     d-Jan. 4, 1946 age 77

     father
     (behind this stone) O J Rathbun, Co. O, 9th Mich. Inf.
     mother
     Charley

Section "A"   Greenwood cemetery
lot #
338 continued
    on monument-Rathbun (other side)
        Oscar J Rathbun   b-Oakland Co.
        died Oct. 10, 1865 aged 39yrs, 11mo   removed from old Briggs cem.
        Marinda Rathbun   b-N. Y. res. Fowlerville
        Apr. 2, 1820-Feb. 12, 1911 d-age 84
        Charley J Rathbun   "C J" res. Milwaukee
        died Feb. 26, 1889 aged 24yrs, 20dys   d-in railroad accident
338½ CRAWFORD
    double stone;-Crawford
    Spencer G, 1880-1956   b-Mi. res. Livingston Co.
                                    d- 5-20-1956 age 75(listed lot 337½)

    Mattie E, 1888-1968   res. Livingston Co.
                                    d- 9-22-1968 age 80

339 BALDWIN
    on monument-Baldwin
    (cement log stone)   (Emiline R Baldwin)res. Williamston
                                    d-Aug. 24, 1906 age 69
    J G B   (J G Baldwin) res. Fowlerville
    1827-1895   d-Sept. 8, 1895 age 68-from old cem.
340 WIXSON--ALSBRO
    Edward Wixson   no record
    1864-1918
    Helen Alsbro   no record
    1837-1915
    on monument-Wixson

                                   (Ada Wixon)b-Mi. res. Fowlerville
                                   d- 2-7-1954 age 89
                                   (infant of Mathew Alsbro)
                                   d-age 3, scarlet fever
                                   removed from old cemetery
                                   (Mathew Alsbro) res. Detroit
                                   d-Dec. 25, 1922
                                   (Mrs. Calvin Handy) b-N. Y.
                                   d-Nov. 29, 1886 age 79

341 HARRIS
    David,   "infant" b-Lansing, res. Lansing
                                   d-Sept. 1, 1894
    D K Harris
    born Dec. 11, 1836, died Nov. 9, 1862
                                   (Mary Prime) res. Fowlerville
                                   d-Nov. 22, 1930 age 83
342 KUEHNLE
    Charlie, father of Stella Kuehnle   b-Ann Arbor
    1866-1892   d-April 12, 1892 age 25 by falling tree
    on monument-Kuehnle
    Anna Maria "our mother"   b-Germany
    wife of G Kuehnle
    died Apr. 19, 1889 aged 47 years
    Amelia,   res. Toledo, Ohio
    1867-1924   d-Feb. 13, 1924 age 4

Section "A"   Greenwood cemetery
lot #
342 continued
        Gottlieb Kuehnle "our father"   no record
        died Feb. 28, 1921 aged 80 years, 1mo & 12ds
                                    (R B Kuehule)b-Howell, res. Handy
                                    d-Aug. 27, 1899 age 1m, 27 days
                                    (Norman Kuehnle)b-Handy
                                    d-Dec. 16, 1886 stillborn
342½ McNeil
        Stella McNeil Macomber   not listed
        1892-19-
        W Webb McNeil (masonic)   res. Ann Arbor
        1886-1946   d-July 16, 1946 age 59
343 Horton
        E Tracy Horton   no record
        died Aug. 28, 1886 aged 28yrs, 5mos, 5ds
        William M Horton   no record
        Captain, 26 Mich. Inf. (GAR)
        1843-1915
        Loana Horton   "Clarsia" res. Fowlerville
        1846-1935   d-Mar. 19, 1935 age 88
        Jay G Horton (masonic)   res. Fowlerville
        1876-1949   d-Oct. 14, 1949 age 73
                                    (infant son of Jay Horton)b-Mi. res. Fowl.
                                    d-Feb. 8, 1909, premature

343½ HORTON
        Lena M Horton   res. Fowlerville
        1877-1943   d-Apr. 8, 1943 age 66

344 BURKHART
        F Hillery Burknart   b-N. Y. res. Fowlerville
        1827-1912   d-April 23, 1912 age 84
        Emeline, wife of F H Burkhart b-Lockport, N. Y.
        1830-1887   d-Jan. 1, 1887 age 56, consumption
        on monument-Burknart
                                    (male, no name) res. Fowlerville
                                    d- 10-23-1914 stillborn

345 LEAVENS
        mother
        father
        on monument-Leavens
            Lewis Leavens   b-N. Y. res. Fowlerville
                                    d-Oct. 30, 1887 age 75
            Anna,   b-N. Y.
                                    d-June 28, 1886 age 48
                                    (Sarah Leavens) res. Fowlerville
                                    d-Sept. 15, 1932 age 78

346 CHALKER
        no stones   (Thomas Chalker) res. Fowlerville
                                    d-July 14, 1931 age 74
                                    (Horace Chalker)b-Vermont
                                    d-Jan. 1, 1898 age 71(listed lot 347)

Section "A"   Greenwood cemetery
lot #
 346 continued

                              (Julia Chalker)b-Locke, res. Locke
                              d- age 10   removed from old cem.
                              (Matilda Chalker)b-N. Y. res. Fowl.
                              d-May 19, 1920 age 88
                              (Phoebe A Day)b-Locke, res. Plainfield
                              d-Oct. 9, 1887 age 26, consumption
                              removed from Howell cem.
346½ OWENS
    Martin Francis Owens   res. Detroit
    Michigan Pvt. U S Marine Corps
    Aug. 14, 1890-March 31, 1964   d-age 73
    Helen Marjorie Owens   res. Detroit
    beloved wife and mother
    Jan. 2, 1892-Mar. 6, 1970   d-age 78
347 HERNING--MANNING
    Eve B & Hesmond   "Eve" b-Mi. res. Minnesota?
    wife & inf. son of Ray C Hoisington
    1885-1912   d-in childbirth
    mother   (Mary L Herning)b-Germany, res. Handy
    1825-1899   d-Feb. 27, 1899 age 71
    (blank)   (Albert Herning)b-Cohoctah
    born Apr. 26, 1856, died Dec. 8, 1891   d- of a gun accident,age 31
    little Gerald, son of W & A Manning   "Jerald W" res. Fowl.
    1902-1906   d-Feb. 20, 1906 age 3 of burns
    Augusta T Manning   res. Fowlerville
    1858-1929   d-Aug. 22, 1929 age 71
    on monument-Herning
347½ OWENS
    J Edward Owens "beloved son"   "James Edward" res. Detroit
    nov. 16, 1919-Feb. 12, 1942   d-age 22
348 RUEL
    George Ruel   b-Scotland, res. Fowlerville
    1826-1885   d-Aug. 25, 1885 age 58, insanity
    (behind stone above)Geo. Ruel, Co. H, 14th Mich. Inf.
    Helen Ruel   "Mrs." b-Canada, res. Fowlerville
    1836-1915   d- 12-6-1915 age 79
    on monument-Ruel
        George Ruel, Co. H, 14 Mich. Vol. Inf.
        died Aug. 25, 1885 aged 59yrs
    double stone;-Williams
    Stephen D, 1861-1933   res. Detroit
                                    d-March 11, 1933
    Nellie R, 1866-1928   res. Dearborn
                                    d-Feb. 17, 1928 age 61
349 GILLAM
    Samuel Gillam
    died Dec. 24, 1885 aged 56yrs   burial May 8, 1886, removed from Howell
    Adella M Gillam   "Della"
    died June 21, 1882 aged 16 years (d-June 21, 1881, bur.June 23, 1881
    Margurette Everett Southerton   no record
    died Oct. 25, 1879 aged 34yrs
    on monument-Gillam

{144}

Section "A"   Greenwood cemetery
lot #
350 BAYO
     Samuel Bayo   (Samuel Bays)
     died Aug. 1, 1872 aged 27ys, 9ms & 9ds
351 PULCIPHER--GILLAN
     John H Pulcipher   res. Owasso
     1849-1927   d-Jan. 9, 1927 age 77
     Della Pulcipher   "Alma D" res. Owasso
     1852-1930   d-June 1, 1930 age 78
     Morgan Campbell   b-Unadilla, res. Detroit
     1855-1890   d-April 26, 1890 age 34
352 WELLER--SIMMONS
     Julia A Weller   b-N. Y.
     born May 31, 1823, died Aug. 27, 1885 (d-Aug. 29, 1885 age 60
                                         removed from yard
     George P Weller   b-Lodi, Mi.
     born July 1, 1827, died Mar. 13, 1894   d-age 66
     no name   (infant son of Geo. P Weller)
     born Jan. 5, 1877, died Dec. 26, 1893   burial ?
     Charles D Simmons   b-Auburn, Mi. res. Conway
     1850-1885   d-April 25, 1885 age 35
     Ada E Simmons   no record
     1869-1876

                                         (Freddie Simmons) res. Owasso
                                         d-Dec. 26, 1893 age 17
                                         (infant, Weller)b-Albion
                                         d-Jan. 31, 1900 age 12 hours

353 HOUSE
     Walter B House   "Walter Bigelow" b-Mi. res. Fowl.
     1853-1921   d-July 11, 1921 age 67
     Anna J House   b-Mi. res. Fowlerville
     1866-1924   d-Nov. 18, 1924 age 68
354 BOWEN
     Rex Edward Taylor   no record
     May 24, 1948
     Mary Jane Taylor   b-Mi.   res. Livingston Co.
     1951-1960   d- 11-7-1960 age 9 of Leukemia
     double stone;-Bowen
     Emerson, 1855-1923   no record
     Francis, his wife   b-Mi.   res. Pinckney
     1862-T904   d-Oct. 24, 1904 in childbirth
                                         (Roland H Bowen)b-Mi. res. Pontiac
                                         d- 10-10-1915 age 9 days
                                         (Eva Monroe)b-Mi. res. Pontiac, Mi.
                                         d- 5-13, 1913 age 1, pnuenonia
                                         (Allis Bowen)b-Handy
                                         d-Oct. 17, 1887 age 9
                                         (Delia Bowen)b-Mi. res. Oceola twp.
                                         d- 8-22-1916 age 25, appendacitis

355 STEVENS
     Libbie and Melissa Stevens   "Melissa" b-Handy
                                         d-May 13, 1890 age 20 of measles
                                         "Libbie" res. St. Johns, Mi.
                                         d-Jan. 8, 1930 age 54, cancer

Section "A"   Greenwood cemetery
lot#
356 HOUSE
     no stones   (Ruth Anna Westmoreland)b-Mi.
                                  d-July 19, 1922 age 7 res. Fowl.
357 BABBETT
     double stone;-
     Lamott,   "Lamont" Res. Peoria, Ill.
     died Nov. 7, 1871 aged 20y & 11m &11d   d-of railroad accident
                                  burial ?, removed from old cemetery
     Romer,   "Homer" b-Branch Co.
     died Mar. 17, 1872 aged 10yrs & 1ms & 28d   from old cemetery

                    - - - - - - - - - - -
                            End

MARSH

COTTAGE

SHED

PUBLIC MONUMENT

SECTION "B"

GATE

GREENWOOD CEMETERY

General View

Section B

Section "B"   Greenwood cemetery
lot #
2   COBLEY
     father   (B____ Cobley)b-Mi. Res. Fowl.
     1840-1918   d- 9-2-1918 age 77
     mother   (Mary F Cobley)b-N. Y. res. Fowl.
     1842-1903   d-Nov. 18, 1903 age 59
     Edwin R DeLanoy   b-Mi. res. Fowlerville
     1854-1925   d-Sept. 5, 1925 age 71
     Hubert L Cobley   res. Livingston Co.
     Apr. 5, 1905-Sept. 30, 1980 d-age 75
     on monument-Cobley
2½   COBLEY
     double stone;-Cobley
     Wilbur Henry, 1879-1944   res. Fowlerville(listed lot 2)
                                 d-Dec. 26, 1944 age 65
     Emma Catherine, 1881-1967   res. Fowlerville
                                 d- 3-2-67 age 86
3   PALMERTON
     on large monument-Palmerton (lot 3 & 4)
                                 (Luretta Sweet)b-Vermont, res. Fowl.
4   PALMERTON
     Blanch E Palmerton Rounsville b-Fowlerville
     1871-1895   d-Aug. 25, 1895 age 24, consumption
                                 removed from old cemetery
     Joanna Fowler Palmerton   b-Mi. res. Fowlerville
     Oct. 18, 1839-Sept. 22, 1917 d-age 77
     George W Palmerton   no record
     died Jan. 2, 1870 aged 12yrs, 10ms & 4ds
     Lozia J, daughter of Geo. W & Joanna Palmerton   no record
     died Feb. 3, 1872 aged 7 years & 11ms
5   ABBOTT
     Bess L Abbott   b-Mi. res. Tucson, Az
     1883-1960   d-Jan. 31, 1960 age 75, bur. 2-5-60
     Ernest C Abbott   "Ernest J" (listed lot 6)
     1876-1877   d-Feb. 16, 1877 age 4 months
                                 removed from old cemetery
     Bert L Abbott   removed from old cem.
     1874-1895   d-June 18, 1895 age 21, appendacitis
     Maria C Abbott   "Myria" res. Fowlerville
     1846-1928   d-Sept. 19, 1928 age 82
     Spiridon S Abbott   res. Fowlerville
     1847-1926   d-July 12, 1926 age 76
6   DEMEREST--ABBOTT
     Mary J Demerest   "Mary Jane" b-Mi. res. Handy
     1858-1921   d-Nov. 26, 1921 age 69
     Lintsford B Demerest   "L B" b-Mi. res. Handy
     1848-1928   d-Nov. 3, 1923 age 80
     Matilda A Demerest   res. Iosco twp.
     1850-1885   d-Nov. 6, 1885 age 34, typhoid
                                 removed from Munsell cemetery

Section "B"
lot #

7   ROUNSVILLE
     Wm. E Rounsville   b-N. Y.
     died Dec. 14, 1867 aged 13ys, 10m, 9ds   d-age 43, typhoid
     Silvia M, wife of W E Rounsville   "Sylvia M" b-N. Y.
     died May 4, 1869 aged 39yrs, 11mo, 16ds   from old cemetery
     little Clyde, infant son of F G & H M Rounsville   b-Fowl.
     died Mar. 17, 1884 aged 6 days (removed from old cemetery)
     Rose S, dau. of F G & H M Rounsville   "Rose E"
     died Mar. 8, 1884 aged 8yrs, 2m, 23ds   d-Mar. 10, bur. May 12-84
     Frank G, 1848-1929   see lot 8
     Helen, wife of F G Rounsville   res. Fowlerville
     1849-1888   d-May 20, 1893
                                 burial ?, removed from house

8   ROUNSVILLE
     Anna, 1877-1896   b-Fowlerville, res. Fowl.
                                     d-June 10, 1896 age 18

     Leah N, 1878-1951 (OES)   "Leah Nora" res. Fremont, Ohio
                                     d-Apr. 20, 1951 age 78

     Claud G, 1874-1937 (masonic)   res. Fowlerville
                                     d-Sept. 10, 1937 age 63

     on monument-Rounsville

                                     (F G Rounsville) res. Fowlerville
                                     d-Jan. 6, 1929 age 80

9   WALTON
     Edwin E Walton
     1828-1887   d-Dec. 5, 1887 age 59
     Hannah M Walton   res. New Jersey
     1833-1909   d-May 20, 1909 age 75

10   WALTON
     America B Walton   no record
     1860-1913
     Jay G Walton   "Jay C" b-Mi. res. Pomona, Cal.
     1856-1915   d- 9-2-1915 age 60, bur. 9-14-15
     on large monument-Walton

11   SAGE
     Mrs. B E Sage   "Betsey E" b-Lockport, N. Y.
     born Apr. 24, 1815, died Feb. 4, 1887   d-age 72 res. Detroit

12   BELL
     Russell E Bell   b-New Hampshire
     born Oct. 13, 1835, died Oct. 14, 1880   d-age 45
     (part of a inscription-"dear husband")
                                     (Mrs. Amy Bell)b-Mi. res. Detroit
                                     burial 1914?
     on monument-Bell

13   POWERS--ALDRICH
     Caleb T Powers   "C T" b-N. Y.
     1816-1887   d-Jan. 24, 1887 age 74
     Eliza, wife of C T Powers   b-N. Y.   res. Handy
     1818-1893   d-Jan. 3, 1893 age 75
     Frank R Aldrich   res. Detroit
     born Jan. 4, 1840, died July 30, 1893   d-age 53,bur. 8-2-93

13 continued
    Phidelia, wife of James Sweet   b-Wallingford, Vt.
    1810-1897   (Phildelia "Eddy" Sweet)
                                d-April 8, 1897 age 88

    James Sweet   b-Vermont
    1820-1899   d-Apr. 23, 1899 age 79, water accident
    on monument-Aldrich

                                (Frank Plummer)res. Fowlerville
                                d-Jan. 16, 1947 age 79

14   FISHER
    William G Fisher   b-Mi.   res. Fowlerville
    1874-1914   d- 7-28-1913 age 40, bur. 7-3--13
    Ada Fisher   res. Fowlerville
    1873-1927   d-April 2, 1927 age 52
    Eliza Fisher   (Eliza Fisher Stacy)b-N. Y.
    1830-1887   d-Aug. 8, 1887 age 69
    Hannah A Fisher   res. Fowlerville
    1852-1928   d-May 4, 1928 age 75
    Daniel W Fisher   no record
    1850-1918
15   FAUNCE
    on monument-Faunce
        Julia Ann, 1831-1864   "Julia A" b-Handy
                              d-1863 age 34, typhoid, from old cem.
        Julia A, 1864-1871   (listed-no lot or section)
                              d-age 8, scarlet fever, from old cem.
        Rosena, 1860-1888   (Mrs. Rosena Perry)b-Handy, res. Venes?
                              d-June 8, 1888 age 28, consumption
                              burial Nov. 26, 1901 from lot 114
        Charley H, 1854-1889   b-Handy
                              d-Apr. 23, 1889 age 34, consumption
        Sophia J, 1828-1892   no record
        William H, 1819-1897   b-Mass.
                              d-March 14, 1897 age 77
        Maretta E, 1866-1941   res. Handy
                              d-April 25, 1941 age 74
16   McLEOD
    no stones   (Sarah McLeod)b-Scotland
                                d-Jan. 7, 1887 age 76
17   WYATT
    Catherine Wyatt "mother"   b-N. Y.   res. Fowlerville
    born Jan. 24, 1824, died Apr. 13, 1907   d-age 83
    Deborah J, wife of J L Williams   res. Fowlerville
    1864-1932   d-Sept. 22, 1932 age 68, pnue.
19 BOWMAN
    F R B   (F R Bowman)b-Staton, Prussia
                                d-Aug. 28, 1887 age 63, malaria

    on monument-Bowman

                                (Ida Bowman)b-N. Y.
                                d-March 4, 1888 age 30
                              (Julia A Bowman)b-Newark, N. J.
                              d-April 16, 1898 age 73 res. Handy

{151}

Section "B"   Greenwood cemetery
lot #
19 continued
                              (Charles Bowman) res. Fowlerville
                              d-Feb. 21, 1930 age 74
                              (Mrs. O J Ewers)b-Mi. res. River Rouge
                              d- 6-8 -1914 age 28, cancer
20   BRANDT
     on monument-Brandt
         Annie A Brandt   see below
         died Sep. 9, 1875 aged 34y, 9m
                              (Mrs. H G Brandt) res. Fowl.
                              burial Oct. 10, 1887-from old cem.
21   KING
     Jenette, wife of William H King   b-N. Y. res. Leroy, mi.
     died Mar. 15, 1864 aged 36yrs, 2ms, 15ds   removed from old cem.
     (stone broke off) wife of E R Powell   no record
     & daughter of Ezekial & Lucy King
     died Nov. 14, 1862 aged 33yrs, 5ms, & 4ds
     Lucy, wife of Ezekiel King   b-Elizabethtown, Ontario, res.Howell
     died Aug. 24, 1869 aged 70yrs & 19ds   from old cemetery
     Ezekiel King   b-Seneca, N. Y. res. Brighton
     died Sept. 24, 1885 aged 85yrs, 7ms & 28ds
22   BARBER
     Syvester U Barber   no record
     Corp. 22 Mich. Inf.(WW II emblem)
     July 4, 1916
                              (Bertram Barber)   from old cemetery
                              d-Jan. 14, 1882 age 1
                              (Nellie B Barber)b-Handy
                              d-Sept. 23, 1877 age 7, from old cem.
                              (Ernest B Barber)b-Handy
                              d-Sept. 18, 1877 age 2, heart trouble
                              removed from old cemetery
                              (Lina J Barber)b-Handy
                              d-Sept. 30, 1890 age 3, from old cem.
                              (Morva Barber)female, b-Mi. res. Putnam
                              d-Dec. 16, 1904 age 63, consumption
                              (Orrin Barber)b-N. Y. res. Webberville
                              d- 7-4-1916 age 80
                              (Orval Goss)   removed from old cem.
                              d-May, 1870 age 72
23   PEARSON
     Hiram
     Martha J.
     on monument-Pearson
         Hiram Pearson   res. Handy
         Aug. 26, 1818, Dec. 18, 1899   d-age 81
         Martha J Pearson   b-N. Y.
         Aug. 1825-Feb. 10, 1889   d-age 64
                              (Richard Pearson)b-Mi. res. Detroit
                              d- 12-29-1918 age 4½

Section "B"   Greenwood cemetery
lot #
24   HARRIS
      "our boy"
      husband)   (Daniel W Harris)d-Sept. 6, 1888 age 34
      on monument-Harris
          our only boy Meade, son of D W & M E Harris   b-Burns, Mi.
          died Aug. 8, 1885 aged 9yrs, 11mo, 12ds   d-by smothering
25   PALMERTON
      Harvey O, son of _____ & Lucy Palmerton   no record
      died Jan. 13(?) 1865 aged 15(?)yrs, 5ms & 14(?)ds
      U S (this stone broken and crumbled)
      (behind stone above) H O Palmerton, Co. K, 9th Mich. Inf.
      Nettie Palmerton   "Nettie Del"b-Handy, res. Oceola
      1864-1941   d-Oct. 31, 1941 age 76
      Zidania Marsh Palmerton   res. Pontiac
      1846-1940   d-age 92, burial May 17, 1940
      L S Palmerton   "Lorenzo" b-Ohio, res. Fowl.
      1844-1921   d-Jan. 4, 1921 age 76
26   WARNER
      George Warner   b-Mi.   res. Conway
      1842-1920   d-Feb. 8, 1920 age 78
      Mary E Warner   b-Cohoctan
      1847-1890   d-Aug. 8, 1890 age 43
                                     (Mary Hill) res. Lansing
                                     d-Dec. 30, 1929 age 25, bur. Jan.2-29
27   MELVIN
      Susan, 1821-1887   b-N. Y.   res. Handy
                                     d-March 1, 1887 age 65
      Fidelia "mother"   "Fidelia Emeline"b-N. Y. res. Fowl.
      1854-1919   d-Dec. 1, 1919 age 65
      Dewitt "father"   "Dewitt C" res. Handy
      1859-   d-June 21, 1936 age 82
      on monument-Melvin
                                     (Roy C Melvin)b-Mi. res. Handy
                                     d- 10-11-1914
                                     (Mary A Harris) res. Pontiac
                                     d-Feb. 7, 1930 age 68

28   DUNSTON--MOWER
      infant son of W J Dunston   b-Howell
      died Nov. 1889   d-stillborn
      on monument-Mower
          Calista Mower   (Celesta Vines?)
          died Oct. 7, 1891 aged 71ys, 2ms,& 12ds   d-age 72
      Calista
      (behind stone above) C M
29   MILLER--SMITH
      Ida B Smith   b-Mi. res. Grand Rapids
      1869-1920   d-March 21, 1920 age 50
      Frank Miller   b-Ohio, res. Ionia, Mi.
      1856(?)-1886(?)   d-July 27, 1885 age 25

Section "B"   Greenwood cemetery
lot #
30   HERNING
     Augusta, 1859-1887   res. Fowlerville
                                     d-Jan. 19, 1888 age 30, bur. 1-22-88
     Louis, 1857-1897   "Lewis F" b-Detroit, res. Fowl.
                                     d-Dec. 22, 1897 age 40
     on monument-Herning
31   GLENN
     (badly busted stone-with a large base) (Nelson A Glenn) b-N. Y.
     (broken footstone-N G)   d-Dec. 1, 1870-removed from old cem.
     Charlie E, son of G H & F A Glenn   no record
     died Jan. 24, 1889 aged 2y, 5m, 27d
                                     (Flora Glenn)b-Mi. res. Fowlerville
                                     d-Jan. 21, 1905 age 9, diptheria
                                     (Anna Eliza Glenn)b-N. Y. res. Fowl.
                                     d-March 11, 1920 age 88
32   GLENN
     Elmina, wife of Geo. M Glenn   no record
     died Nov. 16, 1882 aged 24yrs, 15dys
                                     (Cecil Glenn)b-Mi. res. Fowlerville
                                     d- 12-23-1912 age 6 months
                                     burial 5-10-1913 from the vault
                                     (George Glenn)b-Mi. res. Fowlerville
                                     d- 2-8-1916 age 60
33   TORREY
     Margaret S, dau. of S B & E Torrey   b-N. Y. res. Unadilla
     born Nov. 11, 1835, died July 15, 1845   d-July 15, 1846
                                     burial July 17, 1846
     Seth B Torrey   b-N. Y.   removed from Unadilla cem.
     born May 18, 1799, died Nov. 17, 1869   d-age 70
     Eliza S, wife of S B Torrey   no record
     born Sept. 24, 1804, died April 11, 1895
     (laying next to stone above- a footstone-J R J (?)
     on monument-Torrey
34   MAYCOCK
     father
     mother
     on monument-Maycock
         Frederick, 1831-1911   d-Jan. 5, 1911
         Eliza E, 1836-1916   b-N. Y.   res. Handy
                                     d- 2-7-1915 age 79, bur. 2-9-1915
35   SMITH--ALSBRO
     Irene A, "wife"   b-Mi.   res. Handy
     1897-1921   d-March 22, 1921 age 23, blood poison
     Charles H, 1893-1976   res. Handy
                                     d- 5-24-1976 age 82
     a slab   (Henry Fay Smith)b-Mi. res. Fowl.
                                     d-Jan. 28, 1924 age 16 months
     Morna C, "daughter"   "Momes"
     1916-1918   d- 11-2-1918 age 2, flu
     on monument-C H Smith
                                     (Charles Alsbro)b-Handy
                                     d-Oct. 14, 1867 age 4, typhoid
                                     removed from old cemetery

Section "B"   Greenwood cemetery
lot #
36   JONES
     little Johney   (John R Jones) listed twice
                                   d-Oct. 1, 1867 age 8 months
                                   burial 1867 from Unadilla cem
     Richard Jones   "Richard H" b-Fowlerville
     died Apr.(?) 17, 1867 aged 26yrs, 3mos & 1dys
                                   d-Apr. 17, burial Apr. 19, 1867
                                   of consumption, from Unadilla
     (behind stone above) R H Jones, Co. K, 9th Mich. Inf.
37   DAVENPORT
     Stillman Davenport "father"   b-N. Y.   res. Fowlerville
     Co. K, Mich. Cav.
     1848-1925   d-Jan. 4, 1924 age 74, bur. 1-6-24
                                   (Nellie J Davenport)b-N. Y. res. Fowl.
                                   d-Jan. 25, 1906 age 44

38   JONES
     Miles T Jones   b-Handy
     1848-1867   d-April 29, 1867 age 19, consumption
     Philo, 1846-1864   no record
     Mercy, wife of John M Jones   "Mary A (orB)" b-Wayne Co. N. Y
     1811-1890   d-Aug. 8, 1890 age 76 res. Bancroft
     John M Jones   b-N. Y.
     1811-1866   d-Feb. 11, 1866 age 55
39   SHOOTER
     no stones   (Clinton B Shooter)res. Ingham Co.
                                   d- 11-11=1883 age 74
                                   (Leo G Deratany)res. Handy
                                   d-July 5, 1927 age 1y, 9m, 20d
                                   in auto accident

40   TITMUS
     no stones   (George Glyndon Titmus)b-Mi. res. Iosco
                                   d-June 2, 1921 age 19 months
                                   (Blanch Eline Titmus)b-Mi. res. Detroit
                                   d-age 3 in 1923

41   WALLENDER
     Rose M Wallender "mother"   "Rose Marie" res. Ingham Co.
     February 22, 1949-January 8, 1979   d-age 29
43   GEE
     Alonzo R Dakins   "Alonzo Roland" res. Marshall, Mi.
     Montana Pvt. 38 Co., 166 Depot Brigade, World War 1
     Oct. 19, 1888-Feb. 6, 1955   d-age 66
     Nettie E Gee "mother"   "Nettie Edith"
     1885-1924   no information
     Ira G Gee "father"   "Ira Gilbert" b-Mi, res. Liv. Co.
     1883-1961   d- 9-5-1961 age 78
44   COPELAND
     Junior, son of F E & B A Copeland   b-Mi. res. Conway
     died Dec. 31, 1920 aged 2ms, & 25ds   burial Jan. 3, 1921
     double stone;-Copeland
     Frank E, 1883-1940   "Frank Ernest" res. Conway
                                   d-age 57 burial June 24, 1940

     Bertha A, 1891-19-   not listed

{155}

45   HODGE
      Dora B Hodge Ross   b-Fowlerville, res. Bay City, Mi.
      1880-1900   d-Oct. 16, 1900 age 20 in childbirth
      on monument-Hodge
         Erastus, 1821-1904 age 82   b-N. Y.   res. Fowlerville
                                       d-April 2, 1904
                                       (Amelia Hodge)b-Handy
                                       d-age 2, whooping couch-from old cem.
                                       (Celia Hodge)b-Handy
                                       d- age 3 months, bur. ?-from old cem.
                                       (Arissa Hodge)b-N. Y. res. Fowlerville
                                       d-Sept. 27, 1922 age 70
                                       (Aaron Saunders)res. Handy
                                       d-Dec. 3, 1875-removed from old cem.
                                       (Mrs. Hiram Elliott) res. Handy
                                       d- 12-23-96 age 66

46   HODGES
      father   (James M Hodges) removed from old cem.
      1816-1866   d-April 15, 1866 age 50, consumption
      mother   (Prima Hodges) res. Lansing
      1818-1906   d-Aug. 1, 1906 age 88
      Jane A Parish   no record
      1844-1926
      Loretta House   res. Fowlerville
      1857-1936   d-Sept. 30, 1936 age 79
      Lafayette, son of J M & B O Hodges
      died Mar. 20, 1862 ag'd 4ys, 4ms   d-of measles
                                       removed from old cemetery
      James F, son of Samuel & Jane A Stevens   no record
      died Aug. 26, 1865 aged 1yrs, 3ms & 26 days
      (on reverse side of stone above) "Frankie
                                       (Frank Stevens)res. Handy
                                       d-1865, age 2 removed from old cem.
      on monument-Hodges
46½   MOSES
      double stone;-Moses
      Lewis A, 1882-1941   "Lewis Albert" b-Hillsdale
                                       d-July 31, 1941 age 59 in accident
                                       res. Lansing
      Bessie M, 1890-1941   "Bessie May" b-Fowl. res. Lansing
                                       d-June 14, 1941 age 51, cancer
                                       (Garth Hoyland) res. Lansing
                                       d-April 16, 1945 age 0
                                       (Mark Eric Hoyland)b-$\overline{M}$i. res. Ingham Co.
                                       d- 4-28-1961 stillborn

47   McDANIELS
      James McDaniels "father"   b-Cambridge, England, res. Fowl.
      1864-1943   d-July 17, 1943 age 79
      Delilah McDaniels "mother"   b-Mi.   res. Fowlerville
      1867-1925   d-Dec. 25, 1925 age 58
      Otto McDaniels "son"   res. Fowlerville
      1897-1966   (vet emblem)   d- 3-15-1966 age 68

Section "B"   Greenwood cemetery
lot #
47 continued
    Hiram Bowen   b-Canada
    Co. E, 5th Mich. Inf.   d-Sept. 3, 1889 age 51
                                        (infant McDaniels)
                                        d-Jan. 29, 1899 age 7 days
                                        (Harriet Hughes)b-N. Y.
                                        d-age 38, consumption-from old cem.

47½ TOBIN
    double stone-Tobin
    James, 1876-1952   "James A" b-Mi. res. Fowlerville
                                        d-May 11, 1952 age 75
    Hazel, 1887-1961   "Hazel B" b-Mi. res. Livingston Co.
                                        d- 4-29-1961 age 73

48   ALSBRO--HANDY
    Calvin C, 1796-1875   (Calvin C Handy)
                                        d-May 31, 1875 age 79-from old cem.
    Patience E, 1806-1886   (Patience Handy) no record
    (on same stone with Calvin)
    Eugene H Gibson   b-Livingston Co. res. Greenville
    1851-1918   d- 6-18-1918 age 66
    Ella P Gibson   res. Howell
    1854-1940   d-Feb. 17, 1940 age 85
    Polly, 1825-1918   (Polly Alsbro)b-Mi. res. Fowl.
                                        d- 3-9-1918 age 92
    WilliAM, 1821-1913   (Wm. Alsbro)b-N. Y. res. Fowl.
                                        d- 3-5-1913 age 91
    Charles, 1848-1853   no record
    Eliza, 1829-1853   no record
    on monument-Handy-Alsbro
49   CRAIG
    J M Craig   "John M" b-Scotland, res. Hamburg
    died June 11, 1878 aged 62y, 2m, 27d (d-June 13, bur. June 15, 1887)
    (behind stone above) J M Craig, Co. B, 9th Mich. Inf. (d-age 63)
                                        (Ella Craig)b-Handy
                                        d-Sept. 16, 1861 age 9 months
                                        (Mrs. Sarah Craig)b-Scotland
                                        d-age 61, burial ?   res. Handy

50   KENYON
    Carrie, 1874-1912   no record
    father
    mother
    on monument-Kenyon
      A C Kenyon   res. Detroit
      1833-1915   d- 2-8-1915 age 81
      Ann E, his wife   "Ann Elizabeth" res. Leroy,Mi.
      1834-1906   d-Jan. 29, 1906
50½ BULLIS
    double stone;-Bullis
    Fred, 1884-1947   res. Flint
                                        d-Jan. 4, 1947 age 62
    Ellen, 1891-1951   "Ellen R" res. Fowlerville
                                        d-May 16, 1951 age 59

Section "B"   Greenwood cemetery
lot #
51   PAGE--PEEK
     I Page
     (behind stone above) Isaac Page, Co. E, 25th Mich. Inf.
     Julia E
     on monument-Page
         Isaac Page   res. Webberville
         12-25-1829--2-5-1896   d-of wound in shoulder
         Julie I, wife of Isaac Page   res. Bancroft
         8-6-1847--12-26-1915
     double stone;-Peek
     Frank J, 1874-1927   res. Bancroft
                                          d-April 29, 1927 age 51, cancer
     Maude A, 1878-1953   (Maud Peek Page Mills)b-Mi.
                                          d-Arp. 27, 1953, operation
                                          res. Bancroft
     on monument-Gladden
     Rosa, dau. of Wm. & H D Gladden   b-Ionia, res. Detroit
     died Mar. 6, 1886 aged 3ms, 28ds (d-Mar. 7, 1887, bur. 3-9-87
     Ernest, son of Wm. & H D Gladden   no record
     died Mar. 3, 1881 aged 3y, 6m, 24d
     (footstone-E G)   (Emrey Gladden) b-Fowlerville
                                          d-age 3y, 3m, bur. ? (may be above)
51½ McDANIELS
     double stone;-McDaniels
     William H, 1885-1950   res. Howell
                                          d-July 13, 1950 age 64
     Ann May, 1882-1962   (Ann May Martel)b-Mi. res. Ingham Co.
                                          d- 1-8-1962 age 79
52   RANDALL
     Jannett, wife of E P Randall   res. Fowlerville
     1853-1931   d-March 15, 1931 age 79
     Edwin P Randall   b-Mi.   res. Fowlerville
     1848-1920   d-March 11, 1920 age 71
     Hariett E, wife of E P Randall b-England, res. Fowlerville
     1849-1911   d-Feb. 19, 1911 age 62
     baby, 1874   b-Conway
                                     d-Dec. 2, 1874
                                     burial 1-10-1894, removed from Conway
     on monument-Randall
53   WILLIAMS
     Lucretia A, wife of J L Williams   b-Howell
     born Sept. 26, 1859, died June 7, 1894   d-age 36, consumption
     on monument-
         John L Williams   res. Fowlerville
         1850-1936   d-July 1, 1936 age 86
         Esther A, his wife   b-Mi.   res. Fowlerville
         1859-1916   d- 5-25-1916 age 57
         Paul L, 1897-1913   res. Fowlerville
                                     d- 12-21-1913 age 17
         Iva May, 1876-1880   b-Handy
                                     d-Jan. 9, 1881 age 4, disentary
53½
     no stones   (John T Williams)b-Mi. res. Fowl.
     (stone on lot A-194)   d-May 23, 1920 age 42 of a fall

Section "B"   Greenwood cemetery
lot #
54   VEALEY
     Frank Vealey   b-Wayne Co. res. Detroit
     born Apr. 2, 1854, died Mar. 11, 1889   d-age 34, railroad accident
     Emma Vealey   b-Handy
     born Jan. 28, 1859, died June 22, 1890   d-age 31
     on monument-Vealey
                                     (Lloyd B Vealey)res. Clinton Co.
                                     d- 1-10-1982 age 95
                                     (infant son of Ernest D Benjamin)
                                     d-Jan. 10, 1924 stillborn, b-Fowl.
54½ VEALEY--SCOTT
     Paul P Vealey "son"   "Paul PATRICK" b-Mi. res. Webberville
     1919-1956   d- 1-3-1956 age 36, gunshot in head
     Nina M Scott "mother"   b-Mi. res. Eaton Rapids
     1898-1956   d- 3-14-1956 age 57
55   BOWEN
     no stones (just a ladies Aux. V F W emblem)
                                     (Saran Bowen) res. Handy
                                     d-July 25, 1937 age 80
                                     (Amasa Bowen)b-N. Y. res. Handy
                                     d- 12-5-1914 age 83
                                     (Mary A Bowen)res. Handy
                                     burial 1898, removed from Briggs cem.
                                     (listed as Bowan on lot A-55)
                                     (Catherine D Vealey)res. Livingston Co.
                                     d- 9-2-1977 age 6
56   WYATT
     George Wyatt   b-N. Y.   res. Fowlerville
     1823-1906   d-March 28, 1906 age 82
     Edwin Wyatt   b-N. Y.
     1853-1856   d-1854 age 20 months, burial Sept.1854
                                     removed from old cemetery
     Maurice Savage   "Morris" b-Irelamd, res. Fowl.
     1844-1871   d-1864 age 25, consumption, bur. 1865
                                     removed from old cemetery
     Katie E Savage   b-Fowlerville
     1869-1884   d-April 1882, age 16-from old cemetery
                                     (Johnie Van Verst)b-Fowlerville
                                     d-May, 1873 age 8 months
                                     burial May 1876, removed from old cem.
57   BOWEN
     no stones   (Almond Woodard) res. Iosco
                                     d-March 1870, typhoid-from old cem.
                                     (Lenard F Woodard)
                                     d-1862 age 21 months-from old cem.
                                     (Annetta Woodard)d-Aug. 15, ? age 3½ mo.
                                     burial ?, removed from old cemetery
                                     (Elmer Woodard)b-Handy,
                                     d-Jan. 26, 1900 age 32 res. Cleveland,O
                                     (Anna Atkins) d-1894
                                     removed from old cemetery

Section "B"   Greenwood cemetery
lot #
57 continued

                                    (Sarah Bowen)b-Cohoctah
                                    d-Jan. 10, 1880 age 35-from old cem.
                                    (Louisa Bowen) res. Webberville
                                    d-March 12, 1899 age 55-from old cem.
                                    (Mary M Bowen)b-Mi. res. Fowl.
                                    d-Jan. 27, 1923 age 67

58   HOPKINS
     William Hopkins and wife   "Wm. P" b-N. Y. res. Marion twp.
                                    d-March 10, 1899 of old age
                                    "Permille" b-N. Y.
                                    d-July 30, 1893 age 81
                                    (James I Bailey)b-Mi. res. Highland Park
                                    d- 8-2-1955 age 67 (stone on lot A-55)
                                    (Augustis Weller)
                                    d-Dec. 1867 age 4-removed from old cem.
                                    (Vada Weller)b-Handy
                                    d-1864 age 4, whooping cough
                                    removed from old cemetery

59   DENSON
     on monument-Denson
        Edward Denson   no record
        born Feb. 8, 1833, died in U S service, Oct. 17, 1864
        enlisted in Co. B, 3rd Cavelrey, Sep. 1861
        Algenons Denson   b-England
        born Aug. 20, 1797, died Feb. 12, 1883 removed from old cemetery
        Lydia Denson   "Mrs." b-England, res. Fowlerville
        born Sep. 19, 1797, died Aug. 22, 1888 d-age 90
        William Denson   b-England, res. Fowlerville
        born July 20, 1839   d- 7-24-1914 age 75
                                    (Alonzo Denson)b-England
                                    d-age 89, burial ?, removed from old cem.

60   WILLIAMS
     no stones   (Jamie L Williams) res. Fowlerville
                                    d-Nov. 11, 1893 age 45 of poisoning

61   LOREE
     Sara Skutt   (Sarah Loree)b-Handy
     b-Jan. 27, 1875, d-June 10, 1898   d-age 23
     Ray L Skutt   b-Mi. res. Fowlerville
     1897-1918   d- 9-26-1918 age 20 of flu
     Cavalry-Marine, USA
     (behind stone above) Ray Scutt, Michigan, Seaman 2 cl, USNRF
                          September 26, 1918
     Mary, 1841-1924   (Mary Orphelia Loree)b-N. Y. res. Fowl.
                                    d-Feb. 16, 1924 age 83
     Isaac, 1834-1897   b-Stueben Co. N. Y. res. Iosco twp.
                                    d-Feb. 9, 1897 age 53, consumption
     (behind stone above) Isaac Loree, Co. F, 1 Mich. S.S
                                    (John E Loree)burial 1873
                                    removed from old cemetery

Section "B"   Greenwood cemetery
lot #
61 continued
    double stone;-
    John E,   (John E Loree)b-Handy
    born May 13, 1877, died Sep. 8, 1881   d-age 4, from old cemetery
    Nellie E,   b-Handy
    born Apr. 3, 1872, died Sep. 1, 1873   d-age 17 months, typhoid
    on monument-Loree

                                     (Iva Bird)b-Iosco, res. Iosco
                                     D-Aug. 16, 1898 age 6 montns, menangitis
                                     (stone is on lot B-181)

62 HAWKEY
    Susan F, wife of J Hawkey "mother"   b-Handy
    June 1, 1857-Jan. 16, 1890   burial-same day, d-age 32
    Joseph Hawkey "father"   no record
    Dec. 18, 1853-Apr. 4, 1892
    Wilbert Elmer, loyal son of Elmer & Rose D Olson   b-Mi.
    died(?) 1903   d-Sept. 14, 1903 age 5 months
                                   res. Lansing

63 MILEM
    Mary A Milem "mother"   (Mary A Milan)b-N. Y.
    died May 3, 1891 aged 58yrs   d-age 57
                                   (William Milan)b-England, res. Fowl.
                                   d-Feb. 18, 1908 age 85

64 ADAMS
    William A Coll   "Wm. Alfred" res. Livingston Co.
    1881-1969   d- 2-22-1969 age 87
    double stone;
    George L Adams   res. Fowlerville
    1855-1930   d-Nov. 3, 1930 age 75
    Carrie Adams   (Carrie Tanner Adams)
    1860-1945   d-Aug. 10, 1945 age 85
    Mildred J Coll   "Mildred Jane" res. Fowlerville
    1894-1965   d- 2-9-1965 age 70
    Olive Coles Belknap   no record
    Oct. 3, 1826-June 1863

                                   (two remains never removed from the
                                   old cemetery-supposed folks of
                                   G L Adams wife-children age 2 & 10
                                   children of Cnester Bell-Knop

65 ROBERTS
    Eliza J, daughter of Wm. & E Roberts   no record
    died June 4, 1869 aged 18yrs, 5ms & 1d
                                   (William Roberts)b-Salem, Ohio
                                   d-March 21, 1887 age 66y, 6m,consumption
                                   res. Jefferson Co. __?

66 ROBERTS
    blank stone (lays flat on ground)
    mother
    monument;-

Section "B"   Greenwood cemetery
lot #
66 continued

                                        (Eliza Jane Roberts)b-OhiO
                                        d-May 30, 1884 age 35
                                        (John A Roberts)b-Ohio, res. Fowl.
                                        d-April 2, 1912 age 57
                                        (Eva Roberts)b-Ohio, res. Fowlerville
                                        d-April 26, 1912 age 94
                                        (Jessie J Bristol)b-Ohio, res. Handy
                                        d-Sept. 21, 1899 age 26, brights
                                        (Hattie Dunn)b-Ohio, res. Handy
                                        d-Sept. 3, 1896 age 26, consumption

67   HAMILTON
      Claude D Hamilton   res. Fowlerville
      1872-1939   d-Sept. 2, 1939 age 67
      Ethel Gardner Hamilton   "Ethel D"
      1873-1935   d-Sept. 30, 1935 age 62
68   BEACH
      Addie L Beach   b-Iosco, res. Milford
      1869-1894   d-Sept. 2, 1894 age 26 in childbirth
69   SMITH
      Genevieve H Smith   b-Mi.   res. Livingston Co.
      1875-1960   d- 2-1-1960 age 84
      Ford E Smith DDS   res. Fowlerville
      1879-194u   d-age 67   burial July 27, 1940
70   HAMILTON
      George D Hamilton   GAR   res. Fowlerville
      1847-1929   d-July 20, 1929 age 82
      Josephine Hamilton   "Marie Josephine" res. Fowlerville
      1852-1932   d-March 10, 1932 age 79
      on monument-Hamilton
71   MALTBY
      Vera O Maltby   "Vera Lena" b-Fowlerville
      1899 aged 26ds   d-March 1, 1900 age 23 days
      Lena Maltby "mother"   b-Mi. res. Lansing
      1874-1906   d-June 23, 1906 age 32
      on monument-Maltby
                                     (Marcella M Maltby) res. Ionia
                                     d-July 1, 1929, pnuemonia
                                     (Martha Maltby) res. Cheboygan
                                     d-July 11, 1935 age 30
                                     (Richard Maltby) res. Lansing
                                     d-June 17, 1942 age 45
                                     (Harold D Turbine)b-Mi. res. Lansing
                                     d-Aug. 28, 1922 age 1 month

72   BELL
                                     (William Bell)b-British Isles
                                     d-Nov. 18, 1886 age 76

Section "B"   Greenwood cemetery
lot #
73   SAGE--BOWER
     William Sage   removed from old cemetery
     died (rest of stone broken off)d-Sept. 19, 1871 age 54, consumption
     Caroline S Sage   res. Handy
     1831-1915   d- 12-23-1915 age 84
     Carrie J Bowers   res. Royal Oak
     1862-1964   d- 3-21-1964 age 103
     Benjamin M Bowers   res. Fowlerville
     1855-1938   d-age 82   burial June 21, 1938
     Lyle Avery, son of B M & C J Bowers   b-Handy
     died Aug. 31, 1881 aged 5mos & 18ds   removed from old cem.
74   COLLINS
     Mary Jane Collins   res. Fowlerville
     1850-1937   d-April 21, 1937 age 87
     James L Collins   GAR   b-Canada, res. Fowlerville
     1845-1905   d-June 24, 1905 age 59 of T B
     (behind stone above) J L Collins, Co. B, 30 Micn. Inf.
     Charles H Collins   "Charles Henry"
     died April 9, 1863 aged 21ys, 5ms & 18ds   burial July 13, 1871
     (part of inscription "dear son"   removed from old cem.
     Novada Collins Woods   res. Fowlerville
     1869-1941   d-Jan. 6, 1941 age 72,bur. Dec. 9,1941
     Michael J Woods   res. Fowlerville
     1869-1942   d-Feb. 7, 1942 age 72
     Waneata M Rogers   b-Mi.   res. Livingston Co.
     1904-1963   d- 2-14-1963 age 59
                                     (Charles L Collins)b-N. Y.
                                     d-July 11, 1871 age 82-from old cem.
                                     (Elizabeth Collins)b-Maryland
                                     burial July 13, removed from old cem.

74½ COLLINS
     double stone;-Collins
     J Clair, 1879-1958   b-Mi.   res. Fowlerville
                                    d- 9-18-1958 age 78

     Carrie M, 1881-1956   b-Mi.   res. Livingston Co.
                                    d- 4-20-1956 age 75

75   HAWLEY
     Robert,
     father
     on monument-Hawley (on lot 75 & 76)
         Rev. James Hawley   b-England
         died Nov. 1, 1855 aged 43yrs   removed from old cemetery
         Margaret, wife of Rev. James Hawley   (Margaret M Silsby)b-Eng.
         died Mar. 1, 1888 aged 72yrs   res. Stockbridge
                                     (Lena L Stevens)b-Conway, res. Fowl.
                                     d-April 7, 1878 age 9-from old cem.
                                     (Dorcia A Stevens)b-Fowlerville
                                     d-Oct. 7, 1885 age 6 months
                                     removed from old cemetery

Section "B"   Greenwood cemetery
lot #
75½ OSAN
     double stone;-Osan
     George, "father"   res. Livingston Co.
     1884-1976   d- 12-21-1976 age 92
     Helen "mother"   res. Ypsilanti twp.
     1893-1966   d- 8-28-1966 age 73
76   HAWLEY
     James L Hawley, Co. G, 3 Mich. Cav.   no record
     wife
     on monument-Hawley
        Mary K, wife of J L Hawley b-Mi.
        died May 6, 1888 aged 30yrs d- of measles
        Robert, 1851-1914
     (near monument a WRG, No. 22, 1883 emblem)
77   WORTHINGTON
     James A Worthington   b-N. Y.   res. Marion twp.
     1837-1910   d-Nov. 6, 1910 age 73
     Nancy J Worthington   b-Mi.   res. Fowlerville
     1841-1907   d-Jan. 15, 1907 age 65
     Chester C Worthington   b-Handy, res. Howell
     1870-1905   d-Aug. 5, 1905 age 34
     Sarah R, wife of M ? Jeffery b-Hartland
     died May 15, 1883 aged 18ys, 5ms, 13ds   burial 4-12-1893
                                   removed from Coffey cemetery

     on monument-Worthington
78   BARNARD
     Corp'l E B Reed   "Edward B" b-Howell, res. Conway
     Co. B, 1st Cal. Inf.   d-Sept. 8, 1886 age 52, consumption
     double stone;-Barnard
     William "father"   "Wm. Milo" b-N. Y. res. Fowlerville
     1829-1898   d-Oct. 3, 1898 age 70
     Eunice "motner"   b-Mi.
     1836-1917   d- 4-26-1917 age 80
                                   (Ella A Barnard)b-Mi. res. Detroit
                                   d-May 30, 1909 of pnuemonia
                                   (Wm. Harold Krause)b-Fowl. res. Fowl.
                                   burial Oct. 1898
78½ SORENSON
                                   (Thorvald Sorenson) res. Livingston Co.
                                   d- 10-19-1978 age 92
79   GRAHAM
     little Gertrude-Jacob & Mary Graham   (Gertrude Graham)b-Mi.
     born Oct. 27, 1900, died July 5, 1903   d-age 3, scalded
                                   res. Williamston twp.
     Mary Graham   "Mary Viola" res. Lansing
     1868-1948   d-Dec. 2, 1948 age 80
     Jacob Graham   res. Williamston
     1850-1933   d-March 16, 1933
     Hattie A, wife of Jacob Graham b-Redford, Mi.
     born Dec. 28, 1858, died May 5, 1882   (d-May 5, 1881 age 79
     Marth H Graham   b-Mi.   res. Howell
     1882-1954   d- 5-13-1954 age 72

Section "B"   Greenwood cemetery
lot #
79½ OSAN
     double stone;-Osan
     Rudolph, 1910=1981   res. Ingham Co.
                                     d- 1-8-1981 age 70

     Julia, 1920-   not listed
80   GRAHAM
     John W Graham   b-N. Y.
     died July 6, 1889 aged 22yrs & 11d   d-age 32
     Arthur Graham Sr.   b-Ireland
     born 1799, died Apr. 1st, 1891   d-age 97
     Jane Graham   b-Ireland
     born 1815, died Nov. 5, 1888   d-age 70
     Thomas H, son of A & J Graham b-Ireland
     died June 3, 1872 aged 30yrs, 2ms, & 21ds d- of war wound
     Co. G, 1st Mich. Infantry   removed from old cemetery
     (behind stone above) T H Graham, Co. G, 1st Mich. Inf.
     Normie, son of J W & H L Graham   b-Handy
     died Jan. 7, 1891 aged 5ys & 7ms
     on monument-Graham
          Thomas H, son of A & J Graham
          died June 3, 1872 aged 30yrs, 2ms & 21ds
81   ALLEN
     (a wood sign)"mother" 6-9-82   no record
     Minnie E, wife of W Hildebrant b-Mi.   res. Fowlerville
     1876-1913   d- 11-26-1913 age 36
     Albert E Allen (LFATA emblem)   res. Howell twp.
     Aug. 19, 1849-July 21, 1912   d-age 63
     Rose A Allen (LFATA emblem)   res. Fowlerville
     May 29, 1856-Mar. 17, 1927   d-age 69
     Nellie B Allen   b-Stockbridge
     May 29, 1886-Dec. 4, 1887   d-age 1
     on monument-Allen
82   REED
     no stones   (Richard Reed)b-Ireland, res. Fowl.
                                     d-Oct. 21, 1887 age 73

82½ ROBINSON
     double stone;-Robinson
     Mark Adam, 1963-1981   res. Howell
                                     d- 8-24-1981 age 17, head injury
83   CLARK
     father
     mother
     on monument-Clark
          Samuel Clark
          died Oct. 9, 1856 aged 43ys, 4ms & 5dys (from old cemetery)
          Charlotte A, wife of Samuel Clark   removed from old cem.
          died June 14, 1874 aged 67ys, 3ms & 28dys
                                     (d-June 4, burial June 6, 1874)
                                     (Jane Clark)b-N. Y. res. Kalamazoo
                                     d-Dec. 5, 1923 age 85

Section "B"   Greenwood cemetery
lot #
83½ MONKRESS
     no stones   (Crystal Leona Monkress) res. Howell
                                   d- 10-20-1971 age 48
84   STEPHENS
     Lamah W Stephens   "Luman W" b-N. Y. res. Gaylord, Mi.
     died Aug. 21, 1881 aged 45yrs, 8ms, 18ds   d-of burns
                                   removed from old cemetery
     Bessie May, dau. of J___ & H___ Stephens   b-Fowlerville
     died Apr. 16, 1881 aged ___, 28ds   d-age 1
     (stone quite illegible)
                                   (Harriett Stephens)b-N. Y.
                                   d-Nov. 28, 1903 age 51
85   FOWLER
     no stones   (Ralph Fowler) burial ?
                                   (Mrs. Mary Fowler) burial ?
                                   (Milburn Fowler) burial 4-1-1891
                                   (Emielin Fowler)b-N. Y.
                                   d-Oct. 14, 1893 age 47
                                   res. Grand Rapids, Mi.
                                   (Walter Fowler) res. Detroit
                                   d-March 30, 1891 age 47
                                   (Charles Fowler)b-Mi. res. Fowl.
                                   d-Jan. 29, 1906 age 67
                                   (Hellen Fowler)b-Ohio, res. Fowl.
                                   d-Sept. 9, 1905 age 60
86   FOWLER
     Rufus H Fowler   res. Fowlerville
     1839-1926   d-March 15, 1926 age 87
86½ DEMEREST
     LaVerne J Demerest   res. Detroit
     1882-1965   d- 8-24-1965 age 83
     Alta M Demerest   res. Fowlerville
     1875-1966   d- 11-6-1966 age 90
87   FOWLER
     Ralph
     Martha S,
     on monument-Fowler (east side)
        Ralph Fowler   no record
        1809-1887
        Martha Smith Fowler   no record
        1808-1846
87½ FOWLER
     Alton A Thomas   "Alton Alfred, Jr." res. Brighton
     1921-1965   d- 10-15-1965 age 44
     Silas H Fowler   res. Detroit
     1906-1965   d- 4-11-1965
88   FOWLER
     John B,
     Mary S,

Section "B"   Greenwood cemetery
lot #
88 continued
      on monument-Fowler (on lot 87 & 88)
            John B Fowler   no record
            1811-1842
            Mary Smith Fowler   no record
            1810-1887
91   BIGNALL
      S L B
      Margaret
      on monument-Bignall
            S L Bignall Sr.   b-Vermont, res. Fowlerville
            1802-1877   d-April 18, 1877 age 75
            Betsey E, his wife   b-N. Y. res. Unadilla twp.
            1803-1846   d-Jan. 28, 1846 age 42 in childbirth
            Polly Jane, their dau.   b-Unadilla, res. Unadilla
            1843-1846   d-June 11, 1846 age 3
            S L Bignall   "Solomon L" b-Mi. res. Fowlerville
            1834-1918   d- 4-1-1918 age 83
            Edith S, 1855-1860   d-Oct. 12, 1860 age 4, diptheria
            Katie E, 1857-1863   b-Dexter, res. Unadilla
            their children(of S L & Phebe)
            Margaret, wife of S L Bignall   res. Fowlerville
            1846-1936   d-July 8, 1936 age 91
92   BIGNALL
      S L B Sr.
      Betsey
      Polly J,
      Katie
      Edith
      Phebe   (all these removed from Unadilla cem.
                                        burial Oct. 12, 1899
93   AUSTIN
      Abel S Austin MD "father"   b-N. Y. res. Flint, Mi.
      1835-1908   d- Oct. 20, 1908 age 70
      Emma C Austin "mother"   "Mrs. Abel"
      1836-1920   burial 9-12-1920
94   FEE
      baby son of Robert L & Eva M Fee   b-Detroit
      1920   burial Oct. 16, 1902 from Detroit
95   SHARP--LAROWE
      double stone;-LaRowe
      Floyd, 1875-1953   b-Mi. res. Lansing
                                        d- 12-26-1953 age 78
      Catherine, 1877-1964   res. Lansing
                                        d- 12-5-1964 age 87
      double stone;-Sharp
      William F, 1863-1932   res. Fowlerville
                                        d-May 4, 1932 age 73, pnuemonia
      Hattie L, 1869-1957   "Hattie Louise" b-Mi. res. Liv. Co.
                                        d- 6-1-1957 age 88
                                        (Ella Grover) res. Handy
                                        d-Feb. 17, 1941 age 67

Section "B"   Greenwood cemetery
lot #
95½ HIGDON
     double stone;-Higdon
     Tyler M, 1888-1960 (Masonic)   b-Mi.   res. Livingston Co.
                                     d- 5-17-1960 age 72
     Ruth L, 1892-1980 (Star emblem)   res. Mt. Clemens,Mi.
                                     d- 11-18-1980 age 88
96
     no stones   (Derrick Slater) b-N. Y. res. Fowl.
                                     double entry-d-Aug. 25, 1907 age 69
                                               d-May 25, 1909 age 70
                                     (L W Campbell) male, res. Lansing
                                     d-May 21, 1912, diabetes
97   CARR
     double stone;-Carr
     Orr E, son of Luther & Mary Parker Carr   res. Handy
     1859-1937 "father"   d-Sept. 11, 1937 age 78
     Maria J, dau. of George & Jane Cobb Kirkland   res. Fowlerville
     1852-1931 "mother"   d-Feb. 23, 1931 age 78
     double stone;-Carr
     Robin K, son of Orr E & Maria J Carr   "Robin Kirkland"b-Mi.
     1887-1961   d- 6-25-1961 age 74 res. Liv. Co.
     Goldie Ann, dau. of Harriet & Oscar Baker res. Genesee Co.
     1884-1973   d- 11-28-1973 age 89
98   BROWN
     no stones   (Minnie Brown)b-Canada, res. Fowl.
                                     d-May 31, 1893 age 49
98½ LUCAS
     double stone-Lucas
     George R, 1895-1963   "Geo. R Sr." b-Mi. res.Livingston Co.
                                     d- 4-15-1963 age 67
     Eva H, 1894-1967   "Eva Harriet" res. Fowlerville
                                     d- 7-16-1967 age 73
99   HYNE--HUBER
     Joseph Henry Huber   res. Fenton
     1865-1926   d-April 23, 1926 age 61
     Retta Hyne Huber   "Retta I" res. Detroit
     1865-1947   d-June 19, 1947 age 81
     Hannah Hyne Curtis "Ma"   b-Brighton, res. Toledo, Ohio
     Dec. 25, 1851-Sept. 14, 1900 age 48
     on monument-Huber
     mother
     father
     on monument-Hyne
         Frederick Hyne   b-Germany, res. Detroit
         1827-1905   d-Nov. 1, 1905 age 78
         Harriet, his wife   b-N. Y.   res. Fowlerville
         1828-1896   d-Oct. 25, 1898 age 70
99½ ROBERTSON
     no stones   (Nora Smyth)
                                     d- 3-5-1973 age 35 at Bowling Green, O.

Section "B"   Greenwood cemetery
lot #
100 LAMB
     Simen D Lamb   "Simeon D" b-N. Y. res. Fowlerville
     born Sept. 3, 1845, died Dec. 25, 1893   d-age 52, bur.-12-27-98
     Harriet Austin   "Harriet Amanda" b-N. Y. res. Fowl.
     1853-1924   d-May 5, 1876 age 16, consumption
     Charles E Lamb   res. Fowlerville
     1877-1950   d-Feb. 13, 1950 age 72
     on monument-Lamb
101 BENJAMIN--DuBOIS
     Eugenie,   (Eugenie DuBois)b-Mi. res. Canidria(?)
                                     d-July 8, 1890, consumption   res. N. Y.
     on monument-Benjamin (on lot 101-2)
        Albert D Benjamin   no record
        1842-1876
        Agnes E Benjamin   no record
        1871-1875
     on reverse side of monument
        Eugenie Benjamin DuBois
        died July 8, 1890 aged 46 years
102 BENJAMIN-DuBOIS
     daughter of A D & E Benjamin   no record
     died Apr. 8, 1879 ae 2y, 4m, 20d
     Albert D,
     (behind stone above) Lieut. A D Benjamin, 30tn Mich. Inf.
102½ HADLEY
     double stone;-Hadley
     Dorr L, 1902   no record
     Frances S, 1902-1979   res. Livingston Co.
                                     d- 10-4-1979 age 77
103 GARDNER
     Annette Irene, 1863-1923   b-Mi.   res. Fowlerville
                                     d-Feb. 20, 1923 age 60
     Austin R, 1844-1922   b-N. Y.   res. Fowlerville
                                     d-Aug. 20, 1922 age 77
     Mary, 1846-1891
     on monument-Gardner
        Mary, wife of A R Gardner   b-Putnam
        Aug. 29, 1846-July 29, 1891 d-age 45, burial Aug. 13, 1891
103½ PERROUD
     double stone;-Perroud
     Joseph G   res. Bradenton, Florida
     Jul. 28, 1906-Apr. 26, 1976   d-age 69
     Carla E,   res. Livingston Co.
     Dec. 11, 1907-Jun. 9, 1976   d-age 68
104 GARDNER
     Helen Irene, 1880-1955   b-Mi.   res. Fowlerville
                                     d- 8-17-1956 age 75
105 KEENER
     no stones   (Charles C Keener)b-Fowlerville
                                     d-Oct. 12, 1891 age 7 months

Section "B"   Greenwood cemetery
lot #
106 Taylor
     Ruby, dau. of Mr & Mrs S Z Taylor   (Ruby Myrtle Taylor)b-Fowl.
                                        d-Oct. 29, 1886 age 2
                                        (Henrietta Taylor) res. Lansing
                                        d-Sept. 29, 1930 age 76
                                        (Catherine Nicholas)b-Ohio
                                        d-Sept. 20, 1888 age 60, consumption
                                        res. Bell Oak
106½ PERROUD
     double stone;-Perroud
     Daniel A, "husband"   res. Livingston Co.
     1949-1981   d- 4-20-1981 age 31, heart trouble
     Sue A, "wife"   not listed
     1950-
107 GRAHAM--FEAR
     Thomas B, 1842-1919   no record
     Christine G, 1847-1933   (Christine G Fear) res. Iosco
                                    d-Sept. 21, 1933 age 86
     Chas. W Graham   b-Ireland
     1843-1890   d-April 23, 1890 age 47
     Co. A, 9th Mich. Inf.
     on monument-Graham-Fear
107½ BUTLER
     no stones   (Lois E Butler) res. Livingston Co.
                                    d- 4-28-1960, bur. from Williamston
108 HALE
     no stones   (Nellie Maud Hale)b-Farmington
                                    d-Oct. 21, 1891 age 18 in childbirth
                                    (Bernie Pearsall)b-Redford
                                    d-June 28, 1893 age 22 of drowning
                                    res. Walled Lake
                                    (Albert Bristol)b-Mi. res. Fowl.
                                    d-Dec. 13, 1909 age 73
                                    (Ruhama Bristol)female, b-Mi.
                                    d- 11-19-1914 age 70 res. Fowl.
109 BURGESS--VAN RIPER
     Emma L M Burgess   b- Putnam
     died Feb. 6, 1862 aged 13ys, 4ms   d-of typhoid
     Samuel Burgess   b-N. Y.
     died Apr. 29, 1881(?) ag'd 54ys, 10ms & 11ds   d-1861
     Lucy A, dau. of Samuel Burgess b-N. Y.   res. Brighton
     and widow of Hiel Perry
     died Jan. 1, 1891 aged 78ys, 1m, 11d (record shows d-1890, bur. 1-3-90)
     Daniel Van Riper   res. Webberville (listed on lot 110)
     1845-1926   d-Feb. 10, 1928 age 83
     Lucy Van Riper   "Lucy A" b-Mi. res. Fowlerville
     1845-1926   d-Nov. 19, 1920 age 75
110 DREW
     Emerald D Drew   b-N. Y.
     died Sept. 12, 1887 aged 50yrs, 11ms   d- of consumption
                                    removed from vault, burial Oct. 26.
     Saran M Drew-Stowe   b-Mi. res. Holly, Mi.
     Jan. 17, 1838-Jan. 29, 1926

Section "B"   Greenwood cemetery
lot #
110 continued
    our baby, son of E D & S M Drew   removed from old cem.
    died J___ (illegible)   d-1879? stillborn, bur. May 23, 1888
    D M Hughes "mother"   "Delia M" b-N. Y. res. Fowl.
    1819-1906   d-July 6, 1906 age 87
    J D Hughes "father"   "John D" b-Trenton, N. J.
    1808-1889   d-Sept. 20, 1889 age 81
    on monument-Drew
        Emerald D and "baby" at rest
111 MILETT
    John P, "son"   b-Mi. res. Daytona Beach, Florida
    1871-1957   d- 2-16-1957 age 85
    Patrick "father"   b-Ireland, res. Perry
    1842-1920   d-Dec. 23, 1920 age 78
    Margaret A, "mother"   res. Handy
    1852-1903   d-April 27, 1903 age 51y, 9m, 16d
    Sarah E, "sister"   (Sarah Elizabeth Milet)b-Howell
    1884-1888   d-Dec. 3, 1888, age 14, typhoid
    on monument-Milett
112 FARRELL
    Patrick D Farrell   res. Fowlerville
    1867-1938   d-age 71, burial June 4, 1938
    Eugene B Farrell   "Eugene Bert" b-Mi. res. Fowl.
    1885-1907   d-June 7, 1907 age 22, heart trouble
    double stone-Farrell
    Patrick O, 1838-1893   b-America
                                   d-Sept. 22, 1893 age 55 of poisoning
    Nancy, 1846-1914   (Nancy Spade)b-Pa. res. Fowlerville
                                   d- 3-3-1914 age 68

113 DICKINSON
    double stone;
    Carrol J, 1819-1878   b-N. Y.   removed from old cem.
                                   d-March 14, 1878 age 57
    Sarah J, 1835-1916   (Sarah J Stoddard)b-Mi. res. Fowl.
                                   d- 8-24-1916 age 80
    on monument-Dickinson
        Carroll J,
        born Jan. 4, 1819, died Mar. 14, 1878
        Elizebeth C,   no record
        born Apr. 1, 1824, died Aug. 10, 1854
        Sarah J,   no record
        born Oct. 15, 1885, died
        Rolla A,   no record
        born Mar. 27, 1837, died Oct. 6, 1900
        Edward C,   no record
        born Jan. 20, 1859, died
        Catherine R,   no record
        born Feb. 15, 1868, died Sept. 10, 1902
        Lewis R,   no record
        born Mar. 25, 1847, died
        Chloe I,   no record
        born Aug. 27, 1848, died
        Elizabeth J,   no record
        born June 9, 1853, died June 22, 1903

Section "B"   Greenwood cemetery
lot #
113 continued

                                    (Mrs. F Ingersol)
                                    d-May 6, 1906
                                    (Kitty Robbins)b-Farmington
                                    d-Sept. 10, 1893 age 24 res. Saginaw

114 BRADLEY--PERRAY
     Rachel P Bradley   res. Cavallas, Oregon
     1848-1923   d-Oct. 30, 1923 age 74
     William E Bradley   (Edward Bradley)b-Mi. res. California
     1833-1909   d-Feb. 2, 1909 age 74, bur. May 1.
     on monument-Bradley-GAR

                                    (Rosanna M Perray)
                                    burial June 10, 1888
                                    removed to lot B-15, Nov. 26, 1901
                                    (Lorence Perray)b-Bernon
                                    d-Sept. 23, 1888 age 3 months
                                    removed to lot B-15, Nov. 26, 1901

115 WINEGAR
     multiple stone;-Winegar
     John M, "father"   b-N. Y.
     1809-1888   d-Oct. 20, 1888 age 79
     Lydia M, dau. of J M
     1849-1863   burial 1878, removed from old cem.
     Frederick J, son of J M   b-Mi.   res. Handy
     1854-1903   d-Oct. 7, 1903 age 49
     Arristeen, wife of F J   b-Mi.
     1852-1920   d-Feb. 21, 1920 age 67
     Ell, dau. of F J & A   "Ella"
     1879-1879   d-1878 age 5 weeks, bur. 1878
                                 removed from old cemetery

     on monument-Winegar
                                    (Edwin Westmoreland) res. Milford
                                    d-1872, burial 1872 -from old cem.

116 OWEN
     Eva M, daughter of R D & C J Owen   b-Fowlerville
     died May 28, 1874 aged 8ms, 14ds   removed from old cem.
                           (Robert Doll Owen)b-Mi.
                           d-Oct. 26, 1911 age 65
                           res. Missoula, Montana
                           (Carrie Kenyon)b-Mi. res. Detroit
                           d-Jan. 26, 1912 age 35, heart failure

117 DYKE
     no stones   (Ruel Van Dyke)b-Mi. res. Lansing
                             d- 12-22-1912 age 56, fractured skull
                             (Mary Elizabeth Vandyke)b-N. Y.
                             d-Jan. 27, 1923 age 72, res. Ingham Co.

Section "B"   Greenwood cemetery
lot #
118 Glover
     Garland S Glover   res. Williamston
     Tec. 5, U S Army, World War II
     1916-1979   d- 9-11-1979 age 63, carbon monoxide
                                   burial from Williamston

     large double stone;-Glover
     Roy J, 1874-1920   b-Mi. res. Fowlerville
                                   d-Feb. 6, 1920 age 43, pnuemonia
     Lillian M, 1873-1959   "Lillian May"b-Mi. res. Ingham Co.
                                   d- 9-29-1959 age 85
119 CRAIG
     Harold M Craig   no record
     Capt. Med. Corps, U S A
     1888-1918
     Elizabeth A Craig   res. Detroit
     1917-1930   d-April 11, 1930 age 12
                                   (Mary Craig)b-Mi. res. Livingston Co.
                                   d- 7-4-1961 age 79

119½ SMITH
     double stone;-Smith
     Homer W, 1867-1949   res. Fowlerville
                                   d-Aug. 18, 1949 age 82
     Harriet E, 1870-1953   b-Mi. res. Fowlerville
                                   d-March 10, 1953 age 82

120 SWITS--WEISS
     Peter R Swits   res. Detroit
     1848-1935   d-July 22, 1935 age 77
     Martha A Swits   res. Fowlerville
     1853-1932   Burial 11-19-1932 age 79
     Lydia E, 1881-1968   (Lydia E Gotts) res. Wayne Co.
                                   d- 10-4-1968 age 87
     Chancy E Weiss   b-Livingston Co. res. Fowl.
     1875-1912   d- 12-1-1912 age 37, peritonitis
     on monument-Weiss
121 FOWLER--CARPENTER
     Alonzo Fowler   "Lon" b-Mi. res. Howell twp.
     1830-1918   d- 3-22-1918 age 86
     Polly Fowler   b-N. Y. res. Fowlerville
     1840-1915   d- 10-5-1915 age 74
     Susan I Carpenter "mother"   no record
     born July 3, 1848, died Feb. 6, 1920
     Martin L Carpenter "father"   b-Mi.   res. Lansing
     born Apr. 13, 1848, died Apr. 11, 1917
122 SMITH
     Robert Smith   "Robert B"b-Handy, res. Flint
     Jan. 2, 1864, Feb. 28, 1939   d-age 75
     Millie, wife of Robert Smith res. Owasso? or Flint?
     July 14, 1871, May 14, 1936 age 64, cancer
     Lahbelle dau. of Robert & Millie Smith   "Ila" b-Mi. res. Flint
     June 15, 1893, Aug. 8, 1912   d-age 19 of T B.

Section "B"   Greenwood cemetery
lot #
122½ SAYLOR
     double stone;-Saylor
     Robert J, "beloved father"   res. Livingston Co.
     Dec. 20, 1936-Feb. 15, 1977   d-age 40, suicide
     Joyce A, "beloved mother"   res. Livingston Co.
     Aug. 12, 1941-Feb. 15, 1977   d-age 35, murdered
123 NEWTON
     William F Newton   res. Howell
     1875-1967   d- 11-18-1967 age 92, pnuemonia
     Rev. Newell Newton "father"   no record
     1824-1904
     Thurza M Dailey Newton "mother" "Thirza", b-Farmington, res. Fowl.
     1840-1899   d-March 30, 1898 age 58, bur. 4-1-98
124 McDANIELS
     Albert McDaniels (FLT emblem)   "Bert" b-Mi. res. Fowlerville
     1873-1925   d-May 27, 1925
     Dora T McDaniels (ROG emblem)   (Cora Ling McDaniels) res. Handy
     1876-1948   d-Aug. 23, 1948 age 72
                                      (Alma J "Mc" Daniels)b-Mi. res. Handy
                                      d- 6-24-1916 age 3 months
                                      (Earl McDaniels) res. Iosco twp.
                                      d-Dec. 23, 1927 age 10 hours

125 LOREE
     double stone;-Loree
     John, 1856-1940   res. Williamston
                                      d-age 84   burial June 17, 1940
     Elizabeth S, 1856-1928   res. Williamston
                                      d-March 10, 1928 age 71

     double stone;-Loree
     Harrison G, 1892-1969   (Harrison Laree) res. Delta twp.
                                      d- 5-2-1969 age 76
     Murriel F, 1903-1965   res. Ingham Co.
                                      d- 10-21-1965 age 62
     Eileen Loree   res. Lansing
     Jan. 31, 1934   d-Jan. 31, 1934 stillborn
126 STRAWS
     Lulu Straws Hall   res. Jackson
     1846-1930   d-April 23, 1930 age 68
     Charles, 1845-1899   b-Kentucky, res. Fowlerville
                                      d-July 31, 1899 age 54

     on monument-Straws
126½ JOHNSON
     double stone;-Johnson
     Norton E, 1914-1965   "Norton Earl" b-Mi. res. Grand Traverse
                                      d- 9-23-1965 age 51

     Gladys I, 1914-
127 BERRY
     double stone;-Berry
     Jacob E, "father"   res. Eaton Rapids
     June 28, 1854-June 4, 1934   d-age 79
     Emma A Stout "mother"   res. Eaton Rapids
     Sept. 25, 1856-March 9, 1931   d-age 75

Section "B"   Greenwood cemetery
lot #
127 continued
    Orson J Berry   b-Mi.   res. Fowlerville
    1884-1920   d-April 19, 1920 of T B.
                    (J D Berry)b-Mi. res. Howell twp.
                    d- 4-13-1915 age 1 month, pnue.

128 READ
    Loothda, wife of James Read   no record
    died July 29, 1877 aged 55ys, 6ms & 9ds
                    (Amanda Jone) no information
                    (Lucinda Reed) no information
                    (James Reed) no information

129 BERRY
    father and
    Serrilla Berry "mother"   b-N. Y. res. Handy
    1833-1906   d-July 1, 1906 age 75
    Chamberlain Berry "father"   b-N. Y. res. Handy
    born June 25, 1819, died Jan. 10, 1895
                    d-1896 age 76, burial 1-14-1896

    Jason T, infant son   no record
    Lucy Ann,   b-Handy   (listed on lot 132
                    d-age 2, removed from old cemetery
                    (Herbert Berry)b-Handy
                    burial ?, removed from old cemetery
                    (Josie Berry)b-Handy
                    burial ?, removed from old cemetery

130 BERRY
    Olive M Berry   b-Handy
    July 6, 1894-Sept. 16, 1894   d-age 2 months
    Julia A Berry   "Julia E" res. Handy
    Jan. 11, 1861-Mar. 15, 1928   d-age 72
    Chester Berry   res. Handy
    Aug. 15, 1857-Oct. 1936   d-Oct. 18, 1936 age 79
130½ BERRY
    double stone;-Berry
    Chester A, 1882-1942   "Chester Avery" res. Howell
                    d-Nov. 16, 1942 age 60
    Caroline E, 1886-1960   b-Mi. res. Livingston Co.
                    d- 7-30-1960 age 74
131 NEWMAN
    D R Newman, Co. L, 3rd Mich. Cav.
    on monument-Newman
        D R Newman   no record
        1830-1895
        Sarah, his wife   b-Handy, res. Jackson
        1844-   d-Nov. 18, 1940 age 96
        Lilla, their dau. aged 1yr & 5mos   no record
                    (Elwin E Newman)res. Farmington twp.
                    d- 3-26-1970 age 97
                    (Olive Berry)b-Handy
                    d-Sept. 16, 1894 age 2 months
                    (Eunice Iocla Emerson)b-Handy
                    d- 8-16-1968 age 83, bur. from Jackson

Section "B"   Greenwood cemetery
lot #
131½ NEWMAN
     double stone-Newman
     Elwin E, 1877-1970   res. Farmington twp. (listed-lot 131)
                                     d- 3-26-1970 age 97
     Annie E, 1882-1942   res. Lansing
                                     d- April 26, 1942 age 60
132 SHAW
     Thomas R, "father"   "Thomas B" b-Mi. res. Lansing
     Dec. 12, 1843-Jan. 13, 1914   d-age 64
     Susan Gott Shaw "mother"   b-Mi.   res. Lansing
     Oct. 9, 1856-June 4, 1924   d-age 74
     Elkanah E Shaw "our son"   "Ellsworth A" b-Mi. res. Lansing
     died Mar. 29, 1905 aged 18yrs, 10ms & 21 days d-heart failure
     on monument-Shaw
                                    (Thomas Berry)b-Handy
                                    burial 9-1874 age 3-from old cemetery
133 DICKINSON--COLLINS
     William C, "fatner"   (Wm. Dickson)b-N. Y. res. Fowlerville
     1833-1912   d- 8-7-1912 age 79, pnuemonia
     Betsey "mother   b-Mi.   res. Fowlerville
     1850-1917   d- 7-13-1917 age 67
     Frank D, 1871-1945   (Frank D Collins) res. Lansing
                                    d-July 21, 1945 age 73
     Nancy E, 1877-1944   (Nancy E Collins) res. Lansing
                                    d-Feb. 2, 1944 age 66
     Amos C, "son"   (Amos C Collins)b-Mi. res. Lansing
     1898-1912   d-May 31, 1912 age 14 of drowning
134 ELLIOTT
     H C Elliott   "Hiram C" b-N. Y.
     Co. E, 26 Mich. Inf.   d-Jan. 29, 1903 age 84 res. Handy
     Henry J Elliott   b-Mi.   res. Fowlerville
     Co. E, 30 M Vol. Inf.
     1845-1920   d-April 8, 1920 age 74
     Minnie E Elliott   res. Fowlerville
     1868-1934   d-April 8, 1934 age 66
     Cornelius Cadwell   b-Mi.
     Co. A, 1 M Vol. Inf.
     1880-1917   d- 12-9-1917 age 87
                                    (Amanda Elliott)b-Lockport, N. Y.
                                    burial ?, removed from old cemetery
135 MURRAY
     enpty
135½ HALL
     George S Hall "beloved father"   res. Wayne
     Jan. 16, 1906-Jan. 10, 1972   d-age 65
136 PALMERTON--BRISTOL
     double stone;-Palmerton
     Hugh O, 1918-   not listed
     Adeline, 1922-   not listed
     Frances Palmerton "mother"   b-Mi.   res. Lansing
     1882-1925   d-March 11, 1925 age 42, weak heart
     Garth Bristol   b-Mi.   res. Fowlerville
     1902-1903   d-Feb. 12, 1903 age 8mo & 10 days

{176}

Section "B"   Greenwood cemetery
lot #
137 ROFF--PALMERTON
     R W Roff   "Richard W" b-England
     Co. K, 9th Mich. Inf.   d-July 21, 1867 age 23, sunstroke
                                       removed from old cemetery
     Sarah Roff   no record
     1822-1897
     R W Roff, Co. K, 9th Mich. Inf.
     Sarah A Palmerton   res. Webberville
     1845-1931   d-Dec. 22, 1931 age 86
     Z M Palmerton   "Zeenis" res. Fowlerville
     Co. K, 9th Mich. Inf.   d-Jan. 12, 1909 age 68
                                       (Richard N Roff)d-July 21, 1867 age 23
                                       removed from old cemetery (see above)
                                       (Richard F Roff)b-London, England
                                       d-Nov. 10, 1863 age 45, pnuemonia
                                       burial 11-12-1873--from old cem.

138 COPELAND
     triple stone;-Copeland
     Esther S, 1869-1948   "Esther Susan" res. Fowlerville
                                       d-Sept. 19, 1948 age 78
     Joseph, 1857-1942   res. Fowlerville
                                       d-Feb. 2, 1942 age 87
     Ida M, 1862-1889   "Mrs."
     on monument-Copeland
         Ida M, wife of Joseph Copeland
         died May 18, 1889 aged 27yrs & 9ds
138½ COPELAND
     double stone;-Copeland
     Cleve, 1886-1947 (masonic)   res. Fowlerville
                                       d-age 61 burial 12-9-1947
     E Blanche, 1885-1945 (star)   "Ethel Blanche" res. Fowlerville
                                       d-July 2, 1945 age 60

139 CHAPMAN
     no stones   (Richard Chapman)b-N. Y.
                                       d-Aug. 25, 1859 age 42--from old cem.
                                       (Emily Chapman) burial 5-17-1915
                                       (John A Chapman)b-N. Y. res. Fowl.
                                       d-July 8, 1912 age 76
                                       (Clark E Lowell)b-N. Y.
                                       d-1876 age 79, removed from old cem.
                                       (Sarah Lowell)b-N. Y.
                                       d-1865 age 58, from old cemetery
                                       (Caroline Lowell)
                                       d-1860 age 18, removed from old cem.
                                       (Eliza Burgh)
                                       d-1885 age 43, from old cemetery

139½ ST. CHARLES--STOCK
     Evelyn St. Charles "beloved wife & mother" b-Mi. res. Wayne Co.
     1923-1960   d- 10-29-1960 age 36
     Grace E Stock "wife"   not listed
     1904-19-

Section "B"   Greenwood cemetery
lot #
140 NORTHRUP
     no stones   (Mrs. Northrup)b-N. Y.
                                        d-Dec. 25, 1884 age 53
141
     no stones   (Lizzie Tinax)b-Mi.   res. Handy
                                        d-July 13, 1906 age 24
142 TANNER
     Nancy M, wife of John A Tanner
     died Nov. 27, 1866 aged 44yrs, 3ms & 21ds   d-of consumption
                                        removed from old cemetery
                                        (John A Tanner)b-N. Y. res. Fowl.
                                        d-May 11, 1908 age 88
                                        (John Tanner)b-Mi. res. Royal Oak, Mi.
                                        d- 1-7-1913 age 58
142½ HALL
     double stone;-Hall
     John H, 1884-1951   res. Detroit
                                        d-May 26, 1951 age 72
     Blanche M, 1885-1948   "Blanche May" res. Conway
                                        d-Aug. 18, 1948 age 62
143 PARKER
     Sarah, wife of Alanson Parker b-N. Y.   (stone broke, laying flat)
     died April 6, 1882(?) aged 65(?)yrs, 1ms & 29 days
                                        removed from old cemetery
                                        (Lansing Parker)bur. ?-from old cem.
                                        (Charles Parker)bur. ?-from old cem.
                                        (Armond Billings)b-N. Y. res. Handy
                                        d-Sept. 18, 1903 age 69
                                        (Jane Anna Perrish) res. Webberville
                                        burial April 1, 1926
                                        (George W Gibson) res. Fowlerville
                                        d-March 30, 1929 age 78
                                        (see stone on lot A-143)
143½ BOYCE
     Earl F Boyce "father"   res. Howell
     1873-1949   d-July 12, 1949 age 76
     Mary E Boyce "mother"   (Mary Ellen Peters)b-Mi. res. Ingham Co.
     1881-1961   d- 2-7-1961 age 79
144
     no stones   (Ira Wade)b-Mi. res. Iosco twp.
                                        d-Dec. 13, 1921 age 46
                                        (Junior P Waid) res. Morrice, Mi.
                                        d-June 21, 1922 stollborn
145 COPELAND
     Charles W Copeland (FLT emblem)b-Mi.   res. Fowlerville
     1866-1922   d-March 11, 1922 age 55
     Nettie B Copeland   res. Fowlerville
     1877-1966   d- 4-30-1966 age 88
     Hazel I Copeland   not listed
     1909-19-

Section "B"   Greenwood cemetery
lot #
146 HARMON
     Henry Harmon "father"   res. Ann Arbor
     1879-1931   d-June 7, 1931
     Henry S Harmon "brother"   res. Pontiac
     1910-1963   d- 11-20-1963 age 53, pnuemonia
     Dorothy V Harmon   res. Detroit
     1916-1943   d-Aug. 6, 1943 age 27
                                        (Julia Harmon)b-Mi. res. Iosco twp.
                                        d-Aug. 18, 1921 age 2, dysentery

147 PRICE--CROCKETT
     Iva Davis Price   b-Mi.   res. Livingston Co.
     April 24, 1961   d-Apr. 24, 1961 age 84
     double stone;-Crockett
     Frank W, 1889-1972   res. Washtenaw Co.
                                        d- 3-26-1972 age 83
     Alberta M, 1891-1962   b-Mi.   res. Cheboygan, Mi.
                                        d- 2-15-1962 age 71
                                        (Charles W Manning)res. Handy
                                        d-Mar. 22, 1928 age 55(stone on A-147)
                                        (Emma Doane)b-Mi. res. Livingston Co.
                                        d- 8-21-1961 age 68

148 SHEPPARD
     Samuel T Sheppard   res. Detroit
     Feb. 5, 1930   d-Feb. 5, 1930 age 41
     Clara Davis Sheppard   res. Detroit
     Nov. 30, 1934   d-Nov. 30, 1934 age 54
153 WESTMORELAND
     Galen J Westmoreland "in memory"   no record
     1919-1945, killed in action on Kyushu, Japan
     Bertha C Westmoreland Oesterle res. Livingston Co.
     1892-1972   d- 2-29-1972 age 79
     Walter T Westmoreland   res. Washtenaw Co.
     1916-1977   d- 9-17-1977 age 61, bur. from Howell
     John W Westmoreland   b-Norway, res. Fowlerville
     1880-1924   d-Aug. 6, 1924 age 43
     Ruth A Westmoreland   res. Fowlerville (listed on lot A-356)
     1914-1922   d-July 19, 1922 age 7
     James Earle Westmoreland   res. Ingham Co.
     Apr. 15-Nov. 27, 1957   d-age 7 months
154 BRISTOL
     double stone;-Bristol
     Asa,   no record
     Everett,   "Everett Edward" res. Fowlerville
                                        d-Nov. 24, 1950 age 75

154½ COFFEY
     double stone;-Coffey
     Joseph C,   res. Howell twp.
     Jan. 20, 1918-June 30, 1975   d-age 57
     Violet D,   not listed
     Jan. 13, 1928-

Section "B"   Greenwood cemetery
lot #
155 FRENCH--BENNETT
     Alta B Moody   res. Ingham Co.
     1908-1981   d- 1-31-1981 age 72, bur. from Lansing
     Signa B French   b-Mi.   res. Fowlerville
     1900-1921   d-Oct. 15, 1921 age 21 in childbirth
                                   (Letha Odomia French) res. Fowl.
                                   d-Oct. 15, 1921 age 3 hours
                                   buried at foot of grave above

     double stone;-Bennett
     Clyde L, 1875-1936   res. Lansing
                                   d-March 30, 1936 age 60
     Lena A, 1878-1953   res. Lansing
                                   d-June 22, 1953 age 75

156 BARRY
     double stone;-Barry
     George W, 1881-1927   res. Lansing
                                   d-Dec. 15, 1927 age 46
     Elsie B, 1889-1976   res. Ingham Co.
                                   d- 1-25-1976 age 86
     Doris A Barry   b-Virginia, res. Lansing
     1919-1923   d-Aug. 23, 1923 age 3
157
     enpty
158 HUSCHKE
     John F Huschke   res. Handy
     1879-1934   d-Nov. 9, 1934 age 55
     Mille M, wife of John Huschke b-Mi.   res. Conway twp.
     1885-1920   d-March 20, 1920 age 34
                                   (Mary Huschke) res. Webberville
                                   d-Nov. 15, 1952 stillborn

159 EMONS
     double stone;-Emons
     Eugene E, 1892-1933   res. Handy
                                   d-Jan. 3, 1933 age 40, pnuemonia
     Pearl C White   res. Ingham Co.
     1898-1958   d- 5-12-1958 age 59
160 ROSE
     Oscar D Rose   no record
     1893-1920, Co. A, 125th Inf.
     Orson A Rose   b-Mi.   res. Fowlerville
     1890-1918   d-Oct. 10, 1918 age 27
     killed in action, Co. A, 125th Inf.   (killed in France)
                                   burial Aug. 1921
     Luther Rose   res. Lansing
     1855-1941   d-Aug. 9, 1941 age 85
     Eliza Ann Rose   res. Conway twp.
     1857-1927   d-Jan. 18, 1927 age 69
                                   (Daniel Rose)b-Mi. res. Howell
                                   d-March 5, 1920 age 27, pnuemonia

{180}

Section "B"   Greenwood cemetery
lot #
161 HARRIS--GOTT
     Edw'd Harris   "Edward" b-N. Y. res. Handy
     Co. E, 106 N Y Inf.   d-Oct. 5, 1902 age 80
                                     (Sarah M Harris) res. Fowlerville
                                     d-April 22, 1926 age 89

     Ellen L Gott (womens relief Corp. emblem) res. Fowlerville
     1849-1929   d-April 20, 1929 age 79 in accident
     Wm. Gott   b-Mi. res. Fowlerville
     Co.B, 1 Mich. SS   d- 6-20-1917 age 73
162 VREELAND
     Lorinda, wife of E Vreeland   res. Handy twp.
     Apr. 27, 1817-Mar. 27, 1899   d-age 81
     Emory Vreeland (GAR emblem)   "Emra" b-N. Y.
     Co. M, 1st N. Y. LA   d-July 9, 1893 age 79
                                     (Lyman Stewart) res. Howell, Mi.
                                     d- 7-10-1913 age 78

163 GOTT
     mother
     father
     Eliza Sawyer   res. Locke
     1855-1931   d-Dec. 10, 1930 age 75, bur. Dec. 13,1930
     Hector   (Hector Shaw)b-N. Y. res. Fowlerville
     (part of inscription-"children & wife")   d-age 28
     on monument-Gott
        Hector S Shaw
     died Nov. 25, 1884 aged 28ys, 1mo, 22ds
        Wm. Gott Sr.   b-England
        born April 20, 1813, died Feb. 7, 1892 d-age 78
        Elizabeth, wife of Wm. Gott   b-England, res. Fowl.
        born Apr. 28, 1817, died Apr. 5, 1888 d-age 70
164 VEALEY
     mother   (Lydia Vealey)b-Canada, res. Detroit
     1835-1916   d- 6-21-1916 age 80
     father   (Benjamin P Vealey)res. Webberville
     1812-1881   d-March 1, 1881 age 67-from old cem.
     Eva A Tye   res. Vevey twp. Ingham Co.
     1851-1943   d-May 30, 1943
     on monument-Vealey
                                     (Lysbe Vealey)male, b-Handy
                                     d-age 3, diptheria, burial 1882
                                     removed from old cemetery
                                     (Lenard Vealey)b-Handy
                                     d-age 1, bur. ? -from old cemetery
                                     (H F Vealey)
                                     d-age 4-removed from old cemetery
                                     (Hulda Sly) res. Handy
                                     d-Sept. 18, 1858 age 44-from old cem.
                                     (Margarett Pitts)b-N. Y, res. Handy
                                     d-Sept. 18, 1860 age 83

165 DEY
     Geo. A Dey (masonic)   "George Augusta" b-Mi. res. Fowl.
     1850-1924   d-March 5, 1924 age 73
     Nettie Dey (OES)   res. Fowlerville
     1858-1928   d-July 28, 1928 age 69

Section "B"
lot #
165 continued

    A Eugene Dey (masonic)   res. Detroit
    1860-1946   d-Jan. 16, 1946 age 65
    Lida May Dey Levett   res. Grand Rapids
    1880-1948   d-Feb. 22, 1948 age 67
                                  (Fred Wainwright) res. Handy
                                  d-March 11, 1899

166 KIRKLAND
    Joe Kirkland   "Joseph" b-Mi. res. Handy
    1893-1914   d- 7-27-1914 age 21 by drowning
    Frances Kirkland   res. Farmington
    1850-1932   d-March 24, 1932 age 81 of flu
    Frank Kirkland   res. Fowlerville
    1852-1926   d-Dec. 14, 1926 age 74, pnuemonia
    Lemira Kirkland   (Lemira Gott Kirkland)b-Handy
    1872-1900   d-March 2, 1900 age 28   res. Handy

167 DEZESS
    no stones   (Mabel Dezess)b-Mi. res. Fowlerville
                                  d-Oct. 2, 1905 age 25, typhoid
                                  (Helen Shaw) burial 1864 to 1888(?)

167½ CHRISTENSEN
    double stone;-Christensen
    Florence M, 1908-   not listed
    William W, 1901-1975
    William W Christensen   res. Livingston Co.
    Pvt. U S Army
    Jul. 28, 1901-Jan. 18, 1975   d-age 73

168 BENTLEY
    double stone;-Bentley
    Nelson E, 1865-1938   "Nelson B" res. Langsbueg
                                  d-age 73, burial Apr. 16, 1938
    Mable E, 1881-1942   res. Bancroft
                                  d-Aug. 29, 1942 age 61
                                  (Flora Bentley)b-Mi. res. Cohoctah
                                  d-March 7, 1907 age 10
                                  (Lida A Bentley)b-Mi. res. Bennington
                                  d-May 13, 1907 age 8
                                  (Howard Bentley)b-Mi. res. Fowl.
                                  d- 12-18-1913 age 3, appendacitis

169 ROWE--PEEK
    double stone;-Rowe
    John E, 1873-1962   "John Edward" b-Mi. res. Wayne Co.
                                  d- 12-14-1962 age 89, bur. from Dearborn
    Winifred M, 1872-1965   res. Wayne
                                  d- 10-15-1965 age 92, bur. from Dearborn
    double stone;-Peek
    William H, 1869-1945   res. Linden
                                  d-Jan. 15, 1945 age 75
    Claudia M, 1874-1958   b-Mi.   res. Linden
                                  d- 7-28-1958 age 84
    Almira Hatch "mother"   b-Ohio, res. Mason, Mi.
    1840-1923   d-Oct. 28, 1923 age 83

Section "B"   Greenwood cemetery
lot #
170 SMITH
     Ruth R Smith "mother"   b-Mi.   res. Fowlerville
     1861-1921   d-Dec. 12, 1921 age 60
                                    (Frank H Smith) res. Livingston Co.
                                    d-Jan. 12, 1941 age 83
                                    (Emeline Taylor)b-N. Y. res. Fowl.
                                    d-Nov. 23, 1908 age 73
                                    (Isaih Gott)b-England, res. Fowl.
                                    d- 3-2-1913 age 65 of T B.

171 FOSTER
     no stones   (Leona Foster)b-Mi. res. Detroit
                                    d-Aug. 17, 1922 age 1 month
                                    (Dortha V Foster)b-Mi. res. Detroit
                                    d-Aug. 30, 1922 age 22 months, paralysis
                                    (Daniel Newman) res. Handy
                                    d-Sept. 9, 1895 age 65-from old cem.
                                    (Wesley Ray Bradfield)b-Mi. res. Leroy
                                    d-Jan. 4, 1904 age 6 months

171½ BERRY
     double stone;-Berry
     William L, 1891-1979   "Will" res. Livingston Co.
                                    d- 7-5-1979 age 87
            married June 3, 1914
     Clara E, 1894-1974   res. Ingham
                                    d- 10-21-1974 age 80

172 SMITH
     double stone;-Smith
     Ola A, 1870-1918   b-Pa.   res. Conway
                                    d- 12-3-1918 age 48, paralysis
     Bessie L, 1879-1942   res. Ingham Co.
                                    d-July 1, 1942 age 62
                                    (Herbert A Smith) res. Ingham Co.
                                    d- 11-2-1979 age 81
                                    (Myrtle Mae Smith) res. Lansing
                                    d-Oct. 15, 1951 age 51

173 WILLIAMS
     double stone;-Williams
     Andrew L, 1870-1951   res. Fowlerville
                                    d-April 3, 1951 age 81
     Prudence A, 1874-1911   b-Mi.   res. Handy
                                    d-April 4, 1912 age 37, bur-1912
     Geneva M Williams   no record
     born Nov. 18, 1907, died Mar. 19, 1908
                                    (Fredrick Williams) res. Pontiac
                                    d-June 12, 1929 age 2 days
                                    (Eunice Williams)b-Mi. res. Handy
                                    d-March 19, 1908 age 4 months, pnue.
                                    (Evelyn Barteg) res. Handy
                                    d-July 22, 1932 age 2mo, 2 days

Section "B"   Greenwood cemetery
lot #
174 GARDENHOUSE
     John Gardenhouse "father"   b-Germany, res. Conway
     1840-1914   d- 9-10-1914 age 74
     Mary Gardenhouse "mother"   b-Germany, res. Conway
     1845-1915   d- 4-13-1915 age 69
     J Gardenhouse "husband"   "John" b-Mi. res. Conway
     1877-1907   d-April 24, 1907 age 30
     Vern,   "Verne" res. Conway
     Feb. 1-Apr. 23, 1907   d-age 2 months, pnuemonia
     on monument-Gardenhouse
175 MacKENZIE
     Newton W Mac Kenzie   res. Fowlerville
     1890-1946   d-April 3, 1946 age 56
     Thomas H MacKenzie   res. Jackson IOOF home
     1874-1941   d-May 5, 1941 age 67
     Thomas MacKenzie   b-Chicago, Ill. res. Conway
     1850-1922   d-Feb. 18, 1922 age 71
     Dinah, "mother"   b-Canada, res. Conway twp.
     July 25, 1849-Dec. 24, 1904   d-age 55
     on monument-MacKenzie
176 GRINDLING
     Charles, "father"   b-Germany, res. Handy
     1837-1911   d-Jan. 14, 1911 age 64
     Laura, "mother"   b-Germany, res. Handy
     1843-1919   d-Dec. 30, 1919 age 76
     Mary K, 1873-1909   no information
     Keneth, 1904   (Kenneth Grinland)b-Mi. res. Marion
                                      d-Oct. 24, 1905 age 6 months

     infant, 1907   (daughter of Brooks)? res. Fowlerville
                                      d-July 23, 1907 stillborn

     on monument-Grindling
177 FIELDS
     Waldon S, 1871-1951   "Waldon Seth" b-Iosco, res. Ypsilanti
                                      d-Nov. 14, 1951 age 80

     Anna, 1879-1906   "Anna A" b-Mi. res. Fowlerville
                                      d-Dec. 8, 1906

     Ethel B Yerkes   res. Howell
     1904-1938   burial 5-19-1938 age 34
     on monument-Fields

                                      (Gladys Alberta Shamka)res. Ingham Co.
                                      d- 4-15-1982 age 79,
                                      burial from Williamston

178 McMANUS
     J Henry McManus   "John Henry" res. Lansing
     1853-1936   d-Nov. 17, 1936 age 83, skull fracture
     Emily Sutherland, wife of J H McManus   res. Lansing
     1857-1944   d-Dec. 9, 1944 age 87
     Susan A Sutherland, wife of G W McManus   (Susan McManus Cornell)b-Mi.
     1849-19-   d-Feb. 15, 1924   res. Lansing
     George W McManus   b-Mi. res. Lansing
     1846-1904   d-Aug. 27, 1904 age 58

Section "B"   Greenwood cemetery
lot #
178½ McDANIELS
    double stone;-McDaniels
    Merrill J, 1895-1947   res. Howell
                                      d-Dec. 7, 1947 age 52
    Anna M, 1897-1970   no record
                                      (Nina May Biard) res. Shiawassee Co.
                                      d- 1-31-1970 age 72

179 GRIEVE
    double stone;-Grieve
    John J, 1870-1964   "John James" res. Iosco twp.
                                      d- 10-26-1964 age 94
    Charlotte A, 1903-1978   res. Livingston Co.
                                      d- 9-28-1978 age 75
    Lillie E Grieve   b-Mi.   res. Handy
    1875-1920   d-Dec. 18, 1920 age 45
    on monument-Grieve (west side)
180 JOY
    Mary A Joy   b-N. Y.   res. Handy
    Sept. 10, 1831-Aug. 24, 1915   d-age 85
    Charles Joy   b-N. Y.   res. Iosco
    Aug. 8, 1833-March 30, 1900   d-age 66, suicide by hanging
    on monument-Joy (east side)
181 BIRD
    Iva,   (Iva Bird)b-Mi.   res. Iosco
                                      d-April 22, 1906
    mother
    father
    on monument-Bird
        Robert J Bird   res. Bancroft
        July 15, 1863-Oct. 3, 1934   d-age 71
        Nora Bird   "Nora Jane" b-Howell, res. Iosco
        b-Oct. 4, 1864, d-Feb. 25, 1906
        Iva Bird   (listed as buried on lot B-61)
        b-Jan. 27, 1898, d-Aug. 26, 1898
182 EMMONS
    Willard Emmons   "Wm. E" res. LeRoy
    1869-1937   d-Dec. 3, 1937 age 68
    Emma Emons   "Emma E" res. Ingham Co.
    1877-1934   d-March 6, 1934 age 57 of cancer
                                      (Roland C Emens)b-Handy
                                      d-Feb. 6, 1903 age 17 months, 6 days
183 DEY
    P W Dey, Co. K, 9th Mich. Inf.
    mother
    Charles O Dey   b-Mi.   res. Marion
    1863-1926   d-Feb. 25, 1926 age 62
    on monument-Dey
        Pierson W Dey   b-N. Y.   res. Handy
        died Sept. 15, 1882 aged 75 years, 8mo, 3ds
        Anna, wife of P W Dey   res. Handy
        died Feb. 19, 1891 aged 61 years, 3mo, 6ds
                                      burial July 3, 1903, removed from
                                      Munsell cemetery

Section "B"   Greenwood cemetery
lot #
183 continued
    Olive Dey Wakefield   "Olive M" res. Howell
    1871-1933   d-July 19, 1933 age 63, stroke
    Deo Dey   b-Mi.   res. Livingston Co.
    1897-1913   d- 9-25-1913 age 15
184 WELLER
    Leah,
    mother
    Elmer D Weller "father"   b-Mi.   res. Handy
    1852-1917   d- 4-8-1917 age 65
    on monument-Weller
        Elizabeth Dickinson, wife of E D Weller
        June 9, 1858-June 22, 1893 (Jane Elizabeth Weller)b-N. Y.res. Fowl.
                                 d-June 22, 1903 age 50, consumption
        Leah A Weller, wife of C E Cole   no record
        Dec. 15, 1875-Dec. 1, 1903
185 NICHOLS--Scott
    Seth A Nichols   res. Lansing
    1848-1931   d-May 4, 1931 age 82
    Louise F Nichols   (Florence Nichols)res. Lansing
    1853-1936   d-March 12, 1936 age 82
    Rollin C Nichols   res. East Lansing
    1889-1933   d-June 13, 1933 age 44, heart trouble
    Hannah, "mother"   (Mrs. Benj. Scott)b-N. Y. res. Lansing
    1825-1917   d- 7-23-1917 age 92
    Benjamin "father"   (Benj. Scott) res. Handy
    1816-1899   d-March 2, 1899 age 82
    on monument-Scott
185½ SHARPE
    double stone;-Sharpe
    Clifford E, 1882-1914   res. Lansing
                               d-Nov. 24, 1944 age 62, bur. Nov. 27, 1944
    Ruth I, 1884-19-   (Ruth Imogene Sherwood) res. Adrian
                               d- 7-23-1969 age 84
186 MOSHER
    Benjamine Mosher   "Ben" res. Bemedji, Minn.
    Sept. 11, 1873, Feb. 12, 1901 d-age 27, pnuemonia
187 COX
    E Cox "father"   (Ebenezer Cox)b-England, res. Handy
    1823-1895   d-April 30, 1895 age 73
    Martha Cox "mother"   b-England, res. Handy
    1827-1904   d-May 8, 1904 age 76
    double stone;-Cox
    Joseph, 1866-1944   res. Charlotte
                               d-Feb. 19, 1944 age 78
    Rose, 1864-1952   "Rose Marie" b-Mi. res. Charlotte
                               d-June 22, 1952 age 91
188 JONES--DAVIS
    Orville H Jones "father"   b-N. Y.   res. Handy
    1817-1896   d- 7-10-1896
    Elizabeth Jones "mother"   b-N. Y.   res. Fowlerville
    1828-1899   d-Dec. 27, 1899 age 71

Section "B"   Greenwood cemetery
lot #
188 continued
        Robert M Davis "husband"   b-Unadilla, res. Handy
        1847-1895   d-Feb. 9, 1895 age 47
        Co. H, first Mich. Inf.
        (behind stone above) R M Davis, Co. H, 1st Mich. Inf.
        on monument-Jones-Davis
                                        (Lucy A Davis)b-Unadilla, res. Handy
                                        d-May 16, 1894 age 39, insanity
189 SMITH
        Anna B Kyser   "Anna Bell" b-Clinton, res. Handy
        born Aug. 3, 1871, died Sept. 7, 1895   d-age 24 in childbirtn
                                        removed from old cemetery(?)
        G T Smith   no record
        Thomas Smith   b-Staffordshire, England
        born Jan. 18, 1819, died Aug. 18, 1894   d-age 75
                                        (d-Nov. 18, 1894, bur. Nov. 21, 1894
        father   (?)
                                        (Alfred Smith) res. Howell
                                        d-Feb. 7, 1941 age 70
                                        (C F Smith)male, b-Mi. res. Handy
                                        d-Dec. 29, 1902 age 3y, 6m or 36 years (?)
                                        was burned to death
                                        (Dorothy Smith)b-England, res. Handy
                                        d- 1-24-1915 age 82
                                        (Harry Kyser)b-Mi. res. Handy
                                        d-March 13, 1909 age 13, accident

189½ COLEMAN
        double stone;-Coleman
        Clifford W, 1889-1962   "Clifford Walcott"b-Mi. res. Liv. Co.
                                        d- 1-26-1962 age 72
        Dora B, 1900-1983   (Dora Blanche Curtis) res. Livingston Co.
                                        d- 2-4-1983 age 82
190 WESTMORELAND
        Thomas, 1844-1917   b-Mi.   res.Fowlerville
                                        d- 7-11-1917 age 73
        Mary L, 1853-1922   no record
        E W   (Edwin Westmoreland)b-Handy, res. Milford
                                        d-1872 of consumption, bur. 1872
                                        removed from old cemetery

        on monument-Westmoreland
                                        (Nora Armstrong)b-Mi. res. Fowlerville
                                        d-Nov. 2, 1922 age 69-from old cem.
191 JEFFERY
        mother
        father
        on monument-Jeffery
            Thomas Jeffery   b-N. Y.   res. Bath, Mi.
            1827-1915   d-age 87
            Mary, his wife   b-Wayne Co.Mi.res. Iosco
            1833-1893   d-July 6, 1893 age 61.

Section "B"   Greenwood cemetery
lot #
191 continued
     double stone;-Jeffrey
     Eddie E, 1869-1950   "Eddie Emerson" res. Howell
                                  d-June 8, 1950 age 81
     Pearl C, 1879-1947   res. Handy
                                  d-Dec. 31, 1947 age 68
192 CRAIG
     Arthur W, 1877-1936   res. Fowlerville
                                  d-March 24, 1936 age 58
     Mattie R, wife of Wm. Craig   b-Mi. res. Fowl.
                                  d-Jan. 19, 1923 age 62
     Irene L, 1880-1903   b-Mi.   res. Fowlerville
                                  d-April 6, 1903 age 22y, 1om
                                       from a operation
     Mary C, wife of Wm. Craig   b-New Jersey
     1849-1893   d-April 20, 1893 age 44
     William, 1847-1935   res. Fowlerville
                                  d-Dec. 9, 1935 age 88
     on monument-Craig
                                  (Harold Craig)b-Mi. res. Oregon
                                  d- of pnuemonia
193 HALE
     (name broke off)son of E R & R A Hale
     died Jan'y 1, 1866 aged 22yrs, 5mo & 19ds
                                  (Sanford S Hale)b-Liv. Co.
                                  d-of typoid   res. Lenewee Co.
                                  removed from old cemetery
     Rachel A Hale   b-Ohio, res. Fowlerville
     died Oct. 21, 1893 aged 81yrs, 1mo, 26ds d-age 71
     Eliza D Hale   "Elisha B"
     died(rest of stone broke off) d-1863 age 54
                                  burial 1--26-1893-from old cem.
                                  (George Hale)b-Handy
                                  d-age 2 weeks, burial ?
                                  removed from old cemetery
                                  (Carrie E Hale)b-N. Y. res. Fowl.
                                  d-Feb. 5, 1909 age 64
                                  (Ellis Hale)b-Ohio, res. Fowl.
                                  d-Sept. 23, 1910 age 75
194 FISHER
     Alma L Fisher "mother"   res. Fowlerville
     1851-   d-Oct. 27, 1932 age 81
     Mabell I, dau. of G M & A L Fisher   b-Fowlerville
     died Oct. 28, 1879 aged 3ys, 4m & 9d d-of diptheria
     John D Fisher   b-Mi.   res. Fowlerville
     1869-1918   d- 7-8-1918 age 46
                                  (infant dau. of C D Fisher)
                                  d-Nov. 10, 1904 stillborn
                                  (Hattie Fisher)b-Marion
                                  d-Mar. 5, 1905 age 37, consump.
                                  res. Chilson

Section "B"   Greenwood cemetery
lot #
195 GOULD
     no stones   (Jerome Gould)
                                      d-May 30, 1893 age 47, consump.
                                      (John Gould)b-Mi. res. Bell Oak
                                      d-Oct. 11, 1905, a infant
                                      (Otis Gould) res. Howell
                                      d-March 6, 1849 age 67, accident
                                      (John G Gould)b-Conway,
                                      d-May 15, 190 age 23 res. Handy
                                      (Mary A Way)res. Mecosta Co.
                                      d-Sept. 14, 1942 age 90
195½ BOWERS
     empty
196 GRAHAM
     double stone;
     Ellen E Gould   (Ellen Graham)b-Hartland
                                      d-Jan. 25, 1893 age 46 res. Howell
     Miller Graham   no record
     1846-1893
     Flossie Smelser Kinghorn res. Buffalo, N. Y.
     1899-1975   d- 6-25-1975 age 75
                                      (body shipped from Albany, N. Y)
     Lester Gould   res. Livingston Co.
     tec. 5, U S Army, World War II
     Feb. 5, 1917-Feb. 14, 1982   burial 4-29-1982 ashes
196½ COADY--MARK
     no stones   (Harold Edward Coady)
                                      d- 6-29-1979 age 66,bur.-ashes
                                      res. Sacremento, Cal.
197 CHAPLIN
     Willie   "William H"b-Lapeer Co.res. Fowl.
     born Aug. 3, 1876, died May 21, 1893   d-age 16, drowned
     Betsy, wife of G W Chaplin "mother"   no record
     May 2, 1838-Jan. 19, 1882
     G W Chaplin   "George W" res. Saginaw
     Co. B, 7 Mich. Inf.   d-Nov. 8, 1904
     on monument-Chaplin
198 SHOWERS
     Oliver P Showers   b-N. Y. res. Plymouth, Mi.
     1845-1922   d-June 18, 1922 age 77
     Keturah Showers   b-Mi. res. Plymouth
     1847-1913   d- 1-19-1913 age 66
     Herbert Showers   "Herbert J" b-Redford, res. Fowl.
     1870-1895   d-April 6, 1895 age 28, consump.
     on monument-Showers
199 NICKLOY--FASSETT--REECE
     Irene T Nickloy   b-Mi. res. Ingham Co.
     1875-1962   d- 10-26-1962 age 86
     Martin D Nickloy   b-Mi.   res. Fowlerville
     1865-1921   d-June 20, 1921 age 56
                                      (Carolina Cook)b-N. Y.
                                      d-Mar. 25, 1888 age 54

{189}

Section "B"   Greenwood cemetery
lot #
199 continued
    double stone;-Fassett
    Philo, 1824-1896   (Philo Fawcet)b-Black river
                                 d-Jan. 16, 1896 age 72
    Elizabeth, 1832-1905   (Elizabeth Tobin) res. Conway
                                 d-Sept. 4, 1905 age 82
                                 (infant son of James Harrison)
                                 d-Aug. 24, 1923, stillborn
                                 res. Fowlerville
                                 (Lillian M Harrison)res. Fowl.
                                 d-Dec. 23, 1930 age 5 months
                                 (Clarence Harrison)res. Fowl.
                                 d-Jan. 11, 1932 age 1
                                 (baby Harrison)res. Fowl.
                                 d-Oct. 15, 1936 stillborn
                                 (Wm. Henry Meader)b-Ingham Co.
                                 d-Nov. 2, 1901 age 2y, 5m, 18d
                                 burial on H Rau lot, res. Handy

200 PECKENS
    Lewis H Peckens   "Louis H" b-Cohoctah
    1874-1887   d-Jan. 7, 1887 age 13
                                 killed by busted millstone
    Carrie Peckens Horton   "Carrie R" b-Mi. res. Howell
    1876-1953   d-March 19, 1953 age 76
    Miranda Peckens "mother"   res. Fowlerville
    1842-1926   d-Nov. 10, 1926 age 84
    Alton Peckens "father"   res. Fowlerville
    1845-1932   d-Aug. 3, 1932 age 87
                                 (infant son of Geo. Peckens)
                                 d-Sept. 23, 1911 stillborn
                                 res. Fowlerville

200½ SMITH
    double stone;-Smith
    Robert W, 1915-   not listed
    Dorothy M, 1913-1970   res. Livingston Co.
                                 d- 12-5-1970 age 57

201 CARR
    Eldorus W Carr   b-Fowlerville, res. Fowl.
    1854-1898   d-Dec. 19, age 44, consumption
    mother
    father
    on monument-Carr
        Thomas N Carr   b-N. Y.   res. Fowlerville
        1828-1900   d-Nov. 14,1900 age 42y, 7 days
        Cordelia J, his wife   b-N. Y.   res. Fowlerville
        1829-1902   d-Sept. 11, 1902 age 72y, 8m, 28d
                                 (Albert B Carr)b-Mi. res. Lansing
                                 d- 12-7-1912 age 54, pnuemonia

201½ LAMB
    double stone;-Lamb
    James D, 1875-1938   res. Fowl. listed on lot B-100
                                 burial Aug. 20, 1938 age 63
    Bertha V, 1885-1945   (Bertha Lamb Johnson)res. Ionia
                                 d-Aug. 14, 1947 age 62

Section "B"   Greenwood cemetery
lot #
202   WOOD--SCHLAAK
      Geo. A, 1857-1904   (Geo. A Wood)b-N. Y. res. Oak Grove
                                 d-Jan. 4, 1904 age 47
      Gustie, 1858-1933   (Augusta B Wood)res. Birmingham
                                 d-Feb. 17, 1933 age 73
      Hal M Schlaak   res. Eloise, Wayne Co.
      Sgt. U S Army, World War 1
      July 2, 1896-Feb. 24, 1967 d-age 70, bur. from Dearborn
      on monument-Wood
                                 (Vera Schlaak)res. Riverview, Mi.
                                 d- 8-24-1979 age 73, bur. from Warren

203   MINER
      Marion E Hebert "mother"(OES) "Marion Elizabeth"
                                 d- 1-26-1976 age 69(found Jan. 26?)
                                 d-Oceanside, Cal. Listed lot 204
      double stone,-Miner
      Oral W, 1881-1963 (masonic) b-Mi.   res. Livingston Co.
                                 d- 1-3-1963 age 81
            married June 10, 1903
      Helen B, 1881-1966 (OES)   (Helen Bates Miner)res. Lansing
                                 d- 12-8-1966 age 85
                                 (John C Miner)res. Plymouth
                                 d-May 2, 1937 age 25 days
                                 (Ronald David Miner)b-Fowlerville
                                 d-July 11, 1948 age 0, res. Lansing

204   MINER
      no stones   (Oral Miner) res. Fowlerville
                                 d-Sept. 12, 1911 stillborn
                                 (Seth Miner)b-N. Y. res. Pontiac
                                 d- 1-20-1913 age 83
                                 (Nellie C Miner) res. Fowlerville
                                 d-June 30, 1933 age 76
                                 (A R Miner) res. Fowlerville
                                 d-April 2, 1937 age 78

204½ ROSE
      double stone;-Rose
      mother of Wm. Roben, 1941-   no record
              Penna A, 1943-
              Chris R, 1950-
      Mary Carr Rose, dau. of Goldie & Robin Carr   not listed
      1915-
205   Thompson
      Alvin, son of S W & E Thompson   no record
      born March 5, 1893, died April 13, 1893
      Ray Thompson   b-Mi.   res. Fowlerville
      28 Inf. 1st Div.   killed in war in France
      1894-1918   d-Oct. 12, 1918 age 24
      Orlo, 1837-1907   b-Mi.   res. Fowlerville
                                 d-Oct. 4, 1907 age 10, appendacitis
      Euphemia Hoyt Thompson   b-Mi.   res. Fowlerville
      1868-1925   d-Oct. 13, 1925 age 58
      Samuel W, 1860-19-   res. Grand Rapids
                                 d-March 8, 1939 age 78
      on monument-Thompson

Section "B"   Greenwood cemetery
lot #
205½ LaROWE
    no stones   (Harry J LaRowe) res. Florida
                                  d- 3-8-1972 age 71

206   ZEEB
    Christian Zeeb   b-Mi. res. Iosco twp.
    1858-1917   d- 4-24-1917 age 58
    Florence, his wife   b-Mi. res. Iosco
    1856-1915   d- 3-17-1915 age 59, pnuemonia
    John B Knoop   b-Mi. res. Cohoctah
    1894-1921   d-Jan. 5, 1921 age 26(listed-A 206)
    Lucy E Viehweger   (Lucia Viahweger) res. Cohoctah
    1895-1929   d-June 2, 1929 age 34 of T B.
    on monument-Zeeb

207   ARMSTRONG
    Thomas E Armstrong   b-Livingston Co. res. Handy
    1877-1952   d-May 6, 1952 age 75
    Anna E Armstrong   no record
    1880-1970
    M Alleen Armstrong   no record
    1911-
    Willis P Armstrong   "Willis Padley" b-Mi. res. Fowl.
    1912-1959   d- 7-25-1959 age 46
                                  (William H Armstrong)res. Iosco
                                  d-June 2, 1927 age 54
                                  (Mary J Armstrong) res. Iosco
                                  d-Feb. 23, 1947 age 72.

208   ARMSTRONG
    Zaccheus L Armstrong   "Zack" b-N. Y. res. Handy
    1838-1912   d-Feb. 26, 1912 age 87
    Martha M Armstrong   no record
    1842-1924
    William H Armstrong   listed lot 207
    1872-1927   burial 6-5-1911(?) age 54
    Mary J Armstrong   listed lot 207
    1874-1947   burial 2-25-1947 age 72
    on monument-Armstrong

                                  (Anne E Armstrong) res. Howell
                                  d- 6-7-1970 age 89

209   CHURCH
    Sylvia, wife of Daniel Church no record
    died (rest of stone broke off)1859(?)
    Orson Church   no record
    died Jan. 30, 1869 aged 66yrs.
    Sally, wife of Orson Church   no record
    died Feb. 11, 1886 aged 81yrs, 3ms, 11ds
    footstone-S C and O C

210   BESSERT
    Amalie Bessert "mother"   "Amalie C" res. Hartland
    Sept. 7, 1860-Feb. 22, 1941   d-age 80
    Carl H Bessert "father"   b-Germany, res. Handy
    July 13, 1839-Sept. 16, 1906   d-age 67
    on monument-Bessert

Section "B"
lot #
210 continued

(Ruth Ann Cole) res. Fowlerville
d-Oct. 29, 1952 age 2 days
(Douglas Richard Cole)b-Mi.
d- 9-19-1960 stillborn, res. Ingham Co.

210 VAN CAMP
    Earl J Vancamp   res. Ingham Co.
    1893-1973   d- 6-29-1973 age 79
211 CANFIELD
    Judson L Canfield   no record
    Aug. 5, 1852-Oct. 12, 1855
    Abigail, his wife   no record
    Dec. 28, 1832-
    J A Canfield   "Judson A" b-N. Y. res. Fowl.
    Oct. 5, 1827-Oct. 10, 1907 d-age 80
    on monument-Canfield

                               (female Canfield)
                               d-April 12, 1919
                               (Louis J Canfield) res. Handy
                               d-July 21, 1942 age 85
                               burial Dec. 10, 1948-from Coffey cem.

211½ VAN CAMP
    triple stone;-Van Camp
    James W Sr. 1923-   not listed
    James W Jr. 1965   "James Wm." res. Gregory
                               d- 3-8-1965 stillborn
    Irene E, 1931-   not listed
212 COLES
    Benjamin Coles   b-England, res. Fowlerville
    1843-1923   d-June 22, 1923 age 75
    Louise Coles   res. Fowlerville
    1845-1929   d-July 19, 1929 age 84
    Lawrence B Coles   no record
    1873-1891
    Sarah L Coles   no records
    1876-1880
    Katie Jones   no record
    1873-1879
    Henry Coles   b-England
    1861-1906   d-Feb. 23, 1906 age 43
    on monument-Coles
212½ MacDONALD
    no stones   (Anna B MacDonald) res. Livingston Co.
                                 d- 12-16-1976 age 82
                               (Eben G MacDonald) res. Genesee Co.
                               d- 1-31-1969 age 70

213 PALMERTON
    empty
214 PALMERTON
    empty

Section "B"   Greenwood cemetery
lot #
214½ HARRISON
      James F Harrison
      1898-1976   burial 4-6-1976, ashes, from Howell
      Ethel D Harrison   res. Lansing
      1900-1973   d-4-26-1973 age 72
215   WORTHINGTON
      Lucy E.
      on monument-Worthington
          Robert C, 1839-   no record
          Lucy D, his wife   res. Lansing
          1831-1909   d-Jan. 13, 1909 age 68
215½ FASSETT
      Philo A Fassett   res. Howell
      1875-1946   d-April 5, 1946 age 71
                                    (Capitan J Davenport)res. Lansing
                                    d-Jan. 6, 1949 age 54

216   KENT-WORTHINGTON
      Frank Kent   no record
      Oct. 28, 1846-Mar. 11, 1903
      Anna E Kent   b-Mi.   Res. Howell
      1872-1921   d-Nov. 15, 1921 age 49 of cancer
      double stone;-Worthington
      Gaylon O, 1921-1976   "Garfon O" res. North Carolina
      Cpl. U S Army   d-11-11-1976
      Laura K, 1922-   not listed
                                    (M Kent) res. Fowlerville
                                    burial 2-9-1906

217   OSBORNE
      Myrtle, dau. of W J & A D Osborne   "Myrtle Maria"b-Liv. Co.
      1886-1901   d-Feb. 24, 1901 age 14y, 9m, 28d
                                    died of pnuemonia, res. Fowlerville
                                    (Irving Osborne) res. Lansing
                                    d-Oct. 29, 1929 age 35
                                    (Divida D Smith) res. Howell
                                    d-Dec. 21, 1929 age 63
                                    (D Martha Dehart)? b-Canada
                                    d-Sept. 19, 1908 age 74, res. Looma?

218   HEAD
      Frank Head   b-Mi.   res. Fowlerville
      1853-1924   d-Jan. 5, 1924 age 70
      Emma Head   b-Mi.   res. Fowlerville
      1853-1919   d-Oct. 25, 1919 age 66(listed lot A-239)
      on monument-Head
218½ LANG
      double stone-Lang
      Floyd D, 1907-1978   res. Livingston Co.
                                    d-9-21-1978 age 70 (listed as lot 281½)
          married June 19, 1935
      Orpha H, 1913-   not listed
219   FISHER
      no stones   (Bill Fisher) res. Fowlerville
                                    d-of consumption-from old cemetery
                                    (Andrew Fisher)res. Fowlerville
                                    (no other information)

Section "B"   Greenwood cemetery
lot #
219½ HICKS
      double stone-Hicks
      John, 1894-1978   "John S" res. Livingston Co.
                                   d-10-20-1978 age 84

              married Sept. 16, 1916
      Geraldine, 1895-1976   res. Livingston Co.
                                   d-6-11-1976 age 80
220   WORDEN
      William J, 1853-1925   b-Mi. res. Fowlerville
                                   d-Sept. 30, 1925 age 72
      Florence, dau. of W J & L A Worden   no record
      1889-1909
      Laura A, 1855-1949   "Laura Abigal" res. Fowlerville
                                   d-Nov. 2, 1949 age 94
221   WICKMAN
      Perry B, 1871-1921   b-Mi. res. Fowlerville
                                   d-July 21, 1921 age 50

      Carrie E, 1874-1967   (Carrie E Snell)res. Fowlerville
                                   d-12-1-1967 age 92

      Lura M Tuttle   "Laura" b-Mi. res. Fowlerville
      1837-1909   d-Dec. 9, 1909 age 72
      on monument-Wickman
222   SMITH
      George B,   b-Mi.   res. Handy
      May 1, 1888-Feb. 18, 1903 age 14, pnuemonia
      on monument-Smith

                                   (Hallie C Smith) res. Fowlerville
                                   d-age 75, burial May 3, 1940
                                   (Freeman Smith) res. Fowlerville
                                   d-Dec. 8, 1950 age 91
                                   (Ralph Burke) b-Mi. res. Fowl.
                                   d-Feb. 11, 1920 age 15 mo. of measles
                                   (Bessie Dora Woll)res. Fowlerville
                                   d-2-7-1966 age 82

222½ SMITH
      double stone-Smith
      Grover C, 1885-1965   "Grover Cleveland"res. Charlotte
                                   d-4-30-1965 age 79

      Mabel L, 1892-1968   "Mabel D"
                                   d-8-6-1968 age 76
223   MARTIN
      Sophia, his wife   b-Germany   res. Howell
      1842-1904   d-Oct. 1, 1904 age 66 of typhoid
      John D Martin   "John" b-Germany, res. Howell
      1840-1906   d-July 10, 1908 age 86
      Amelia K Milett "daughter"   b-Mi.   res. Livingston Co.
      1880-1960   d-3-3-1960 age 79
      Katherine M Melendy "daughter" res. Meridian twp. Ingham Co.
      1885-1966   d-4-12-1966 age 80
      on monument-Martin

Section "B"   Greenwood cemetery
lot #
224 MALTBY
     Agnes Maltby "mother"   b-Handy, res. Fowlerville
     1878-1951   d-March 26, 1951 age 72
                                    (infant of G Maltby) res. Grand Ledge
                                    d-May 4, 1906
                                    (Sarah S Spencer)b-N. Y. res. Fowl.
                                    d- 9-30-1913 age 71
                                    (Charles E Spencer)b-Mi. res. Fowl.
                                    d- 4-12-1917 age 74

225 BIRD
     Ellen Bird "mother"   b-Ireland, res. Fowlerville
     1833-1906   d-June 11, 1906 age 74
     on monument-Bird
                                    (Robert Bird) res. Mecosta, Mi.
                                    d-Aug. 16, 1908 age 85
                                    (William Bird)b-Mi. res. Fowl.
                                    d-Nov. 15, 1925 age 74

226 BOWERS
     Anna M Bowers   (Mrs. Joseph Bowers)b-Mi. res. Handy
     1831-1906   d-May 14, 1906 age 74
                                    (Joseph Bowers)b-N. Y. res. Handy
                                    (Alice M Edwards)b-Mi. res. Handy
                                    d-Sept. 6, 1910 age 55
                                    (Cyrus Gould)b-Mi. res. Handy
                                    d- 4-6-1913 age 72
                                    (Florence Odell) res. Handy
                                    d-Aug. 29, 1931 age 66, diebetis

227 BOWEN
     double stone;-Bowen
     William H, 1855-1922   b-Mi. res. White Oak twp.
                                    d-Jan. 17, 1922 age 67
     Rose C, 1872-1932   (Rose C Johnson) res. White Oak twp.
                                    d-Sept. 5, 1932 age 60
     T D Bowen   (no name)b-Mi. res. White Oak twp.
                                    d- 5-2-1918 age 18, diptheria
                                    (Edward Bowen)b-Mi. res. Fowl.
                                    d-Jan. 8, 1909 age 52

228 LEE
     no stones   (Floyd Eugene Lee)b-Mi. res. Rives
                                    d-Sept. 3, 1906 age 6 months

229 FERGUSON
     Joseph, husband of C Ferguson res. Detroit
     Nov. 22, 1862-Nov. 25, 1938   d-age 76
     Carrie, wife of J Ferguson   b-Mi. res. Fowlerville
     Sept. 10, 1862-Feb. 5, 1907   d-age 44
     Zoe, wife of G Ferguson   "Zoe E" b-Mi. res. Livingston Co.
     Mar. 2, 1888-Apr. 17, 1962 age 74
     Glenn, husband of Zoe Ferguson
     Nov. 11, 1892-Mar. 1, 1966   d-age 73, burial 3-3-66 from Brighton
     on monument-Ferguson

Section "B"   Greenwood cemetery
lot #
230 MILLER
    Newton V Miller   "N M" b-Mi. res. Conway
    1864-1910   d-March 19, 1910 age 45, consumption
    Nellie I, wife of N V Miller "Nellie J" b-Mi. res. Linfield
    1868-1907   d-Oct. 17, 1907 age 38 of T B.
230½ DONALD
    double stone;-Donald
    Edward E, 1888-1970   res. Chelsea
                                 d- 12-27-1970 age 82
    Myrtle A, 1891-1957   b-Mi. res. Livingston Co.
                                 d- 3-22-1957 age 66
231 SMITH
    on monument-
        Sidney Smith   b-Mi. res. Langsburg
        1862-1906   d-Nov. 22, 1904 age 44, typhoid
    George E Dibble   res. Lansing
    1879-1927   d-Oct. 27, 1927 age 47, appendacitis
                                 (Theo. Bentley) res. Owasso
                                 d-Dec. 9, 1927 age 68

231½ SCHNEEBERGER
    Carrie R Schneeberger   b-Mi. res. Lansing
    1871-1954   ·   d- 8-1-1954 age 83
    Fred C Schneeberger   res. Mason, Mi.
    1876-1966   d- 4-13-1966 age 89
232 SIMPSON
    Susan D Simpson   b-N. Y. res. Fowlerville
    Nov. 24, 1851-Dec. 13, 1922
    Anna J Franks   b-Mi. res. Fowlerville
    Mar. 8, 1873-July 24, 1911   d-age 38, concer
    Villa M Simpson   b-Mi. res. Fowlerville
    Feb. 15, 1886-Nov. 4, 1916   d-age 29, epilepsy
    George H Parsons   b-Mi. res. Fowlerville
    June 30, 1848-Dec. 16, 1922 d-age 74 from gas
233 CALKINS--FARMER
    double stone;-CALKINS
    Freely, 1865-1934 (masonic) "Freely E" res. Fowlerville
                                 d-July 16, 1934
    Sarah, 1869-1939   res. Fowlerville
                                 d-April 24, 1939 age 70
    Lula Mae Calkins, wife of Frank D Farmer b-Mi. res. Detroit
    1887-1908   d-June 20, 1908 age 20
                                 (infant of HARRY Calkins)res. Handy
                                 d-Dec. 13, 1923 stillborn
234 BENNETT
    Francis Bennett "father"   b-N. Y. res. Handy
    1839-1908   d-Dec. 22, 1908 age 70
    Adelia V Bennett "mother"   res. Howell
    1845-1917   d- 1-23-1917
    Asa W Bennett   b-Mi. res. Handy
    1885-1907   d-Nov. 8, 1907 age 22 of poisoning
    Freddie Bennett   no record
    May 1887-Dec. 1888
    Alice L Davis   res. Charlotte
    1880-1967   d- 10-27-1967 age 87

Section "B"   Greenwood cemetery
lot #
234 continued
    Albert L Bennett "infant"   no record
    died 1880
    Johnie H Bennett   no record
    Dec. 1872-Apr. 1874
    on monument-Bennett
234½ WILEY
    double stone;-Wiley
    Clarence E, 1885-1946   res. Livingston Co.
                                     d-April 4, 1946 age 60
    Myrtle J, 1895-1973   (Myrtle J Thompson) res. Royal Oak
                                     d- 2-4-1973 age 77
235 FIELDS
    Jennie L Crittenden   b-Mi.   res. Ann Arbor
    1861-1907   d-Sept. 11, 1907 age 46
    Mary A Fields   "Mary Ann" b-Mi. res. Iosco twp.
    1840-1920   d-April 29, 1920 age 79
    Seth W Fields   b-Mi.   res. Handy
    1833-1910   d-May 14, 1910 age 76
    on monument-Fields
235½ HOWE--GROVER
    double stone,-Howe
    Ida Mae, 1921-1970 (Aux. emblem)   res. Ingham Co.
                                     d- 10-12-1970 age 48
    Lorin D, 1919-   not listed
                                     (baby Grover) res. Howell
                                     d- 5-16-1946, premature female
236 JONES
    no stones   (David Jones)b-Ohio, res. Fowl.
                                     d-May 19, 1912 age 80
                                     (Mary Jones) res. Lansing
                                     d-Jan. 4, 1923 age 73
                                     (John F Jones) res. Fowlerville
                                     d-May 25, 1947 age 83
237 MEADER
    double stone;-Johnston
    Fred Chas. 1885-1960   b-Mi.   res. Ingham Co.
                                     d- 10-9-1960 age 75
    Lila Meader, 1890-1966   "Lila G" res. Williamston
                                     d- 1-6-1966 age 75
    double stone;-Meader
    Harry J, 1858-1940   "Harry John" res. Williamston
                                     d-age 81
    Adella J, 1866-1944   res. Lansing twp.
                                     d-March 17, 1944 age 77
    David McCraner   "David William" res. Lansing
    Dec. 16, 1942-Jan.29, 1943   d-age 1 month
238 McENTIRE--MEADER
    double stone-McEntire
    James, 1839-1908   "James H" b-Kentucky, res. Fowl.
                                     d-Aug. 8, 1908 age 72
    Nannie, 1846-1928   no record

Section "B"   Greenwood cemetery
lot #
238 continued
    double stone;-Meader
    William, 1871-1950   res. Fowlerville
                               d-Sept. 7, 1950 age 79
    Nina, 1871-1946   res. Fowlerville
                               d-March 16, 1946 age 75
239 WEST
    no stones   (George West)b-Mi. res. Locke twp.
                               d- 10-27-1918 stillborn
                               (Archie W West)b-Mi. res. Locke twp.
                               d-Feb. 20, 1923 age 41, appendecitis
                               (Helen J West)b-Mi. res. Locke twp.
                               d-April 12, 1923 age 3, diabetis

239½ RICHARDSON
    Lewis Andrew Richardson   res. Livingston Co.
    S2 U S Coast Guard, World War II
    1921-1977   d- 10-11-1977 age 56, bur. from Howell
240 COLE
    double stone;-
    Herbert M, 1882-1960   b-Mi.   res. Perry, Mi.
                               d- 3-11-1960 age 77
    Maud L, 1881-1909   "Maud Lida" b-Mi. res. Handy
                               d-March 11, 1909 age 28
    Harold F Cole   "Harold Frank" b-Mi. res. Ingham Co.
    1905-1959   d- 5-4-1959 age 54
    on monument-Cole
241 TRUHN
    Charles Truhn   "Chas. H" b-Mi. res. Livingston Co.
    1882-1962   d- 5-1-1962 age 79
    Glen Truhn   b-Mi.   res. Handy
    1892-1910   d-Aug. 16, 1910 age 19, internal injury
    double stone-
    Charles "father"   "Charles Sr." res. Handy
    1848-1934   d-Jan. 14, 1934 age 86
    Catherine "mother"   "Catherine M" res. Handy
    1863-1943   d-Dec. 20, 1943 age 79
    on large monument-Truhn
242 HACKETT
    James D Hackett   b-Mi.   res. Owasso
    1859-1921   d-Dec. 4, 1921 age 62, heart trouble
    Cora L Hackett   "Cora Luella" b-Mi. res. Ovid, Mi.
    1868-1957   d- 6-17-1957 age 88
    Bertha E Fuhr   (Mrs. Bertha Fahr)b-Mi. res. Brooklyn, N. Y
    1889-1918   d- 9-29-1918 age 29
    Orpha L Lindsey   res. Royal Oak
    1903-1937   d-April 25, 1937 age 33
                               (Lorenzo Gue) res. Kingston, Mi.
                               d-Dec. 23, 1944 age 76

Section "B"   Greenwood cemetery
lot #
243 BENJAMIN
     George W Benjamin   b-Mi.   res. Fowlerville
     1844-1925   d-Dec. 2, 1925 age 81
     Laura Jane, his wife   "Laura F" b-Mi. res. Conway twp.
     1849-1910   d-Sept. 18, 1910 age 62
     double stone;-Benjamin
     Cecil L, 1913-1980   res. Livingston Co.
                                     d- 11-4-1980 age 66
     Ellen I, 1918-   not listed
     on monument-Benjamin
                                     (Joseph Franks)b-England, res. Fowl.
                                     d- 4-28-1914 age 69

244 BENJAMIN
     double stone-Benjamin
     Roy F, 1877-1948   "Roy E" res. Conway
                                     d-Feb. 5, 1948 age 70
     Erdine, 1877-1957   b-Mi.   res. Livingston Co.
                                     d- 5-2-1957 age 79
     double stone-Benjamin
     Roger L, 1878-1966   res. Mt. Pleasant (listed lot 244½)
                                     d- 12-28-1966 age 88
     Helen May, 1878-1964   res. Midland
                                     d-May 24, 1964 age 86
244½ JENSEN
     Roger G Jensen   "Roger Clifford" res. Howell
     U S Navy, World War II
     1925-1981   d- 12-9-1981 age 56, heart trouble
245 SMALLEY
     a slab   no information
245½ DOUGLAS
     James K Douglas "father"   b-Mi.   res. Detroit
     1892-1956   d- 1-26-1956 age 65
     Lucy V Douglas   res. Handy
     1890-1948   d-Feb. 7, 1948 age 58
246 GLOVER
     Romaines P, "father"   b-N. Y.   res. Fowlerville
     1845-1919   d-March 2, 1919 age 74
     Ann, "mother"   b-England, res. Fowlerville
     1842-1911   d-Oct. 13, 1911 age 69
     Kevin J Glover   "Kevin James" b-Mi. res. Fowl.
     July 9-Sept. 19, 1958   d-age 9 weeks
     on monument-Glover
                                     (infant of W Y Glover) res. Fowl.
                                     d- 1-9-1913 stillborn

247 DEZESS
     John Dezess   res. Fowlerville
     1852-1927   d-March 8, 1926 age 74, bur. 3-11-26
     Velma C Dezess   b-Mi.
     1903-1913
                                     (Claude E Dezess) res. Ingham Co.
                                     d- 6-15-1970 age 92

Section "B"   Greenwood cemetery
lot #
247½
    no stones   (Leslie Leo Mead) res. Ingnam Co.
                              d- 3-5-1969 age 68
248 GOTT
    no stones   (Laura June Gott)b-Mi. res. Fowl.
                              d-Feb. 26, 1907 age 1, pneumonia
                              Ardella Springer) res. Flint
                              d-April 21, 1926 age 63

249 HOYT
    Zella R, wife of Theodore S   "Estella" b-Fowl. res. Iosco twp.
    born Jan. 22, 1867, died Oct. 26, 1895   d- of blood poisoning
    Theodore   res. Iosco twp.
    born Oct. 2, 1868, died Mar. 2, 1896   d-age 29
    on monument-Hoyt

                              (Curtis C Hoyt)b-N. Y. res. Marion
                              d- 12-27-1912 age 77, suicide

249½ WOLLENHAUPT
    double stone;-Wollenhaupt
    Fred, 1870-1949   res. Genoa twp.
                              d-May 3, 1949 age 79

    Mattie, 1877-1955   "Mattie Elizabeth" b-Mi. res. Genoa
                              d- 10-6-1955 age 78

250 BROWER
    Elizebeth, 1863-1946   res. Fowlerville
                              d-Aug. 27, 1946 age 78

    Edwin r, 1850-1946   no record
    Alice A, 1849-1916   b-N. Y.   res. Fowlerville
                              d- 9-24-1916 age 66, cancer

    on monument-Brower
251 BOWMAN
    Victor E Bowman   "V Eugene" b-N. Y. res. Williamston
    1878-1924   d-Sept. 17, 1924 age 46, blood poison
    Minnie M Bowman   res. Lansing
    1883-1927   d-July 30, 1927, cancer
                              (Dell Clara Hall)b-Mi. res. Detroit
                              d- 10-23-1918 age 36, pnuemonia

252 HUFF--GOTT
    double stone;-Huff
    Joseph S, 1884-1972   res. Charlotte, Mi.
                              d- 3-21-1972 age 87
    Arvilla S, 1884-1971   res. Ingham Co.
                              d- 4-4-1971 age 87
    mother
    Richard Gott, Co. F, 6 Mich Inf.
    on monument-
       Richard Gott   b-England, res. Handy
       1839-1914   d- 3-31-1914 age 74
       Martha A, his wife   b-Vermont, res. Fowlerville
       1848-1918   d- 10-20-1918 age 70

Section "B"
lot #
252½ SCHNEIDER
    double stone;-Schneider
    Fred H, 1905-1975   res. Lansing
                          d- 7-9-1975 age 75
    Ruth L, 1912-   not listed
    Marilyn R Lantis   res. Ingham Co.
    1944-1969   d- 10-7-1969 age 24
252 PIPER
    Ione, 1916-1916   no record
    Lewis, 1863-1920   res. Lansing
                          d-Feb. 26, 1920 age 60
    on monument-Piper
253½ WISE
    double stone;-Wise
    Joseph V, 1909-1975   res. Licingston Co.
                          d- 6-23-1975 age 66
    Martha J, 1915-   not listed
254 CAMERON
    Herbert Cameron   no record
    1884-1981
    Tressa L Cameron   b-Mi.   res. Wayne
    1891-1963   d- 1-31-1963 age 72
                          (John H Cameron) res. Howell
                          d-Oct. 27, 1931 age 46, of burns
                          (Claude Cameron)b-Mi. res. Howell
                          d-Feb. 7, 1920 age 29, pnuemonia
                          (Ruth M Cameron) res. Howell
                          d- 3-6-1965 age 48
255 DEVINE
    James Devine   b-Mi.   res. Howell
    1861-1952   d-June 14, 1952 age 90
    Mary Josephine Devine res. Green Oak twp.
    1880-1965   d- 8-19-1965 age 84
    Patrick Devine   res. Pinckney
    1864-1945   d-April 24, 1945 age 80
                          (Gladys Devine)b-Mi. res. Fowl.
                          d-Sept. 19, 1921 age 2mo, 9d
255½ DEVINE
    no stones   (William Devine) res. Liv. Co.
                          d- 10-13-1970 age 56
                          (Dorothy Devine) res. Brighton
                          d- 8-7-1981 age 66
256 DEVINE
    no stones   (Minnie Pfeier?) res. Lansing
                          d-May 27, 1936 age 55
257 LEONARD--WENDELL
    Fred Force   res. Fowlerville
    (on metal tag-Fred Force, 1875-1936)
                          d-March 28, 1932 age 61, bur. 1932
    Malcolm T Leonard   res. Lansing
    1865-1928   d-Dec. 22, 1928 age 63

Section "B"   Greenwood cemetery
lot #
257 continued
    Ella R Wendell   res. Lansing
    1866-1947   d-Jan. 18, 1947 age 80
    J Jerome Wendell   res. Williamston
    1865-1937   d-March 14, 1937 age 72
258 POLLACK--GRISWALD
    double stone;-Pollack
    Leslie H, 1875-1951   res. Fowlerville
                                  d-April 16, 1951 age 75
    Norah D, 1878-1960   (Norah D Tucker)b-Mi. res. Liv. Co.
                                  d- 9-23-1960 age 82
    William Force   b-Mi.   res. Fowlerville
    Feb. 11, 1864-May 21, 1923 age 59
                                  (baby Griswald) res. Fowlerville
                                  d-age 24 hours, bur. June 4, 1927
                                  (infant girl Brookland) res. Handy
                                  d-age 2 hours, bur. June 13, 1938

259 GRISWOLD
    Roger A Griswold   (Roger Griswold Campo) res. Ingham Co.
    1952-1971   d- 8-30-1971 age 19, fractured spine
260 ROBERTS
    double stone;-Roberts
    Clemence G, 1874-1947   res. Fowlerville
                                  d-Dec. 8, 1947 age 73
    Edith, 1888-1963   b-Mi.   res. Fowlerville
                                  d- 10-11-1963 age 74
    Andrew B Roberts
    Michigan Sgt. 379 AAF Bomb Sq, World War II   d-overseas
    March 5, 1917-April 29, 1944 burial Dec. 1, 1948
    Clemence G Roberts   res. Livingston Co.
    July 15, 1921-Dec. 27, 1972   d-age 51
    Virginia Marie Vermillion   res. Perry
    Jan. 5, 1957-Jan. 10   d-Jan. 10, 1957 age 5 days
262 BARNARD
    double stone-Finch
    Joseph, 1891-   res. Handy
                                  d-age 75, burial 6-4-1926
                                  removed from home
    Susan, 1894-   res. Handy
                                  burial 6-4-1926, removed from home
    double stone-Barnard
    Edward C, 1859-1945   res. Lansing
                                  d-April 12, 1945 age 85
    Lucy A, 1856-1936   res. Fowlerville
                                  d-March 3, 1936 age 79
262½ GRISWOLD
    double stone-Griswold
    Jerold R, 1922-1971   res. Ingham Co.
                                  d- 4-6-1971 age 49, electic shock
    Esther L, 1929-   not listed
                                  (Robert Lester Griswold)b-Mi.
                                  d- 11-20-1954 age 3 res. Fowl.

Section "B"   Greenwood cemetery
lot #
263 ELLIOTT
     Harrison A, 1859-1930   res. Owasso
                                     d-Aug. 29, 1930 age 71
     Kate E, 1852-1923   b-Mi.   res. Owasso
                                     d-Jan. 8, 1923 age 70
     J C Elliott   res. Owasso
     1890-1930   d-Aug. 31, 1930 age 40
     Ellen, wife of J C   (Ellen Jane Sillman)res. Shiawasee
     1891-1973   d- 1-16-1978 age 86 from Owasso
     on monument-Elliott
264 YAHN
     double stone-Yahn
     Clarence M, 1900-   not listed
     Roy H, 1898-1982   "Roy Henry" res. Livingston Co.
                                     d- 1-18-1982 age 83

265 DONAL
     Lloyd R Donal   b-LeRoy   res. LeRoy
     1916-1918   d- 6-3-1918 age 1
     Wilna Donal Titmus   "Wilma Mary" res. Webberville, Mi.
     1887-1965   d- 5-22-1965 age 77
     Fred Donal   (Fred Donald)b-Mi. res. Williamston
     1885-1919   d- 1-12-1919 age 33, flu
     on monument-Donal
266 SLEAFORD--JOSLIN
     Minnie, 1868-1940   res. Bell Oak
                                     d-age 71, burial Aug. 17, 1940
     John E, 1864-1937   res. Locke
                                     d-Aug. 19, 1937 age 72
     Neva B Fichtenberg   "Neva Bell" res. Ingham Co.
     1900-1982   d- 7-26-1982 age 81 from Williamston
     on monument-Sleaford
     double stone;-Joslin
     Grant H, 1901-1969   res. Kalamazoo
                                     d- 1-24-1969 age 67, pnuemonia
     Neva B, 1900-19-   (see other above)
266½ CAMERON
     double stone;-Cameron
     Leo V, 1918-1982   res. Livingston Co.
                                     d- 7-12-1982 age 64
     Ruth M, 1916-1965   no record
267 ROBERTS
     Elva G Roberts   "Mrs." b-Mi. res. Howell twp.
     1897-1922   d-May 19, 1922 age 24
     Bruce W Roberts (masonic)   b-Mi. res. Pontiac
     1887-1950   d- 10-20-1956 age 69
     Anna S Roberts   (Mrs. Bruce Roberts)b-Mi. res. Howell
     1897-1918   d- 12-19-1918 age 22, pnuemonia
267½ WRIGHT
     Effie Jane Wright   res. Fowlerville
     July 30, 1887-Jan. 13, 1966   d-age 78
     Earl D Wright   b-Mi.   res. Handy
     Michigan Pfc, 16 Cavalry, World War 1
     July 14, 1892-July 4, 1952   d-age 59

Section "B"   Greenwood cemetery
lot #
268 YAHN
     John K Yahn   res. Conway
     1857-1934   d-March 26, 1934 age 77
     Mary Yahn   res. Conway
     1868-1943   d-April 2, 1943 age 75
     Frank Yahn   res. Howell twp.
     1867-1934   d-May 27, 1934 age 67
                                    (Catherine Bowen)b-Mi. res. Detroit
                                    d- 5-21-1918 age 65

269 SCHNEIDER
     John, 1873-1913   b-Germany, res. Lansing
                                    d- 6-18-1913 age 40
     Geo. H "father"   (Geo. H Schneider)b-Germany,
     1833-1915   d- 9-8-1915 age 82 res. Conway twp.
     Elisabeth Schneider   res. Ingham Co.
     1881-1983   d- 2-4-1983 age 101, bur. 2-19-83
     Albert Schneider   b-Mi. res. Leroy, Ingham Co.
     1898-1915   d- 11-6-1915 age 16, auto accident
     on monument-Schneider
270 SCHNEIDER
     Martha Schneider "mother"   "Mrs. Conrad" b-Germany, res. Leroy
     1876-1916   d- 7-12-1916 age 49
     Conrad Schneider "father"   res. LeRoy
     1860-1935   d-March 20, 1935 age 74
270½ MacMILLAN
     Alta M MacMillan   b-Mi.   res. Adrian twp.
     Aug. 8, 1879-June 3, 1963   d-age 83
     Hugh A MacMillan   res. Detroit
     Michigan Sgt. Qm. Corps, World War II
     Aug. 17, 1890-Nov. 27, 1948   d-age 58
271
     no stones   (Raymond Glenn)b-Mi. res. Fowlerville
                                    d- 3-13-1913 age 13 days, pnuemonia
                                    (Wayne Glenn) res. Handy
                                    d-2-11-1915 age 3 months, heart cond.
                                    (Ryland M Glenn)b-Mi. res. Handy
                                    d-Jan. 7, 1921 age 2 weeks
                                    (Arthur Glenn) res. Greenville
                                    d-May 5, 1929 age 1

271½ MEAD
     Leo L Mead   no record
     1900-1969
     Mabel P Mead   no record
     1902-19-   not listed
272 MEYER
     Adam, "father   res. Fowlerville
     1858-1934   d- 1-11-1934 age 75
     Louisa, "mother"   res. Fowlerville
     1858-1929   d- 5-1-1929 age 70
     Louisa Wilker   (Louisa M Wilkes)b-Canada, res. Handy
     1876-1912   d- 2-2-1912 age 36
     on monument-Meyer

Section "B"   Greenwood cemetery
lot #
273 Sprague
     Truman A Sprague   b-Mi.   res. Fowlerville
     1845-1922   d-Jan. 15, 1922 age 76
     Lucinda Sprague   res. Fowlerville
     1847-1938   d-age 91, burial 11-28-1938
     Myra L, dau. of T & L Sprague res. Handy
     born Jan. 28, 1883, died Sept. 16, 1884
                                   (d-1889? age 3? of spinal mengitis)
                                   burial Sept. 18, 1909 (listed Lot 34)
     Ada E Cole, wife of Roy T Sprague   res. Livingston Co/
     1880-1968   d- 12-25-1968 age 88
     on monument-Sprague (lot 273-274)
274 SPRAGUE
     Roy T Sprague   res. Fowlerville
     1877-1964   d- 1-15-1964 age 86
     Lee C Sprague   res. Wayne Co.
     1885-1969   d- 6-5-1969
     Mabel C Benjamin, wife of Lee C Sprague   b-Arkansas, res. Arkansas
     1884-1960   d-age 76, burial 9-26-1960
     Marion M Sprague, wife of Joseph Klimkowski
     1909-   not listed
274½ KLIMKOWSKI--SPRAGUE
     Joseph Klimkowski   res. Jackson
     1909-   d- 11-14-1983 age 74,
                                   burial from Brooklyn, Mi.
275 SMITH
     Estella C Smith   b-Mi. res. Rives twp, Jackson Co.
     1870-1957   d- 11-2-1957 age 87
     Francelia E, wife of A H Smith   b-N. Y. res. Fowl.
     1841-1916   (WRC emblem) d- 4-8-1916 age 75
     Alfred H,   (GAR emblem)   res. Fowlerville
     1841-1935   d-Aug. 4, 1935 age 94
     on monument-Smith

                                   (Lydia W Spencer)b-Mi. res. Marquette
                                   d-March 26, 1909 age 85
275½ EDDY
     Lawrence O Eddy
     Michigan Pfc. 112 Inf. 28 Inf. Div. World War II
     August 30, 1915-August 10, 1944   d-a war casualty
                                   burial Oct. 22, 1948
276 STOWE--SNYDER
     double stone;-Stowe
     Claud I, 1890-1967 (masonic) res. Jackson
                                   d- 10-17-1967 age 77
     Louise M, 1893-19- (star)   res. Grand Rapids
                                   d- 7-11-1983 age 90
     Hazel B Snyder (OES)   res. Livingston Co.
     1886-1983   d- 1-25-1983 age 96
     Roy J Snyder   res. Charlotte, Mi.
     1890-1931 (masonic)   d-Sept. 29, 1931 age 41

Section "B"   Greenwood cemetery
lot #
277 NICHOLS
     Adreannie, 1869-1932   "Adre Anna" res. Handy
                                 d-June 12, 1932 age 63
                                 (Oscar Nichols) res. White Oak twp.
                                 d-Oct. 7, 1932 age 81
                                 (Wm. Frederick Sheppard) b-Mi.
                                 d- 12-11-1959 age 75   res. Wayne

278 NICHOLS
     Hillyard, 1856-1939   res. Handy
                                 d-age 82, burial Jan. 9, 1939
     Rhoda Jane, 1867-1924   b-Mi. res. Handy (listed lot 211)
                                 d- April 10, 1924 age 62
     mother   (Sarah Nichols)b-N. J. res. Handy
     1830-1907   d-May 13, 1907 age 76
     Mary, "wife"   "Mary E" res. Howell
                                 d-Dec. 4, 1943 age 86(listed lot B278½)

278½ NICHOLS
     Jeremiah Nichols   res. Howell
     1853-1947   d-Jan. 30, 1947 age 93
     Charles E, "son"   res. Lansing
     1883-1945   d-March 11, 1945 age 61
279 JENSEN
     triple stone;-Jensen
     Frank R, 1886-1967   res. Williamston, Mi.
                                 d- 7-3-1967 age 81
     Gladys I, 1910-1911   "Gladys Irene" res. Cohoctan
                                 d-Sept. 30. 1911 age 10 months
     Bessie M, 1891-1976   "Bessie Melvina" res. Ingham Co.
                                 d- 11-25-1976 age 85
                                 burial from Williamston
     Alice I Jensen   "Isabell Alice" res. Williamston
     1916-1966   d- 5-20-1966 age 50
279½ HACKETT
     Loy B Hackett   not listed
     1888-19-
280 PETERSON
     John M, 1887-1908   b-Mi.   res. Handy
                                 d-June 21, 1908 age 24, drowning
     Louis J, "father"   res. Fowlerville
     1859-1933   d-Dec. 29, 1933 age 74, cancer
     Emma J, "mother"   res. Handy
     1862-1937   d-Sept. 2, 1937 age 74
     on monument-Peterson
281 MONROE
     Marion J Monroe   res. Fowlerville
     1874-1926   d-June 11, 1926 age 52, blow on head
     Arthur C Monroe   res. Milwaukee
     1872-1947   d-Aug. 13, 1947 age 75
     Mary H Monroe   "Mrs. Arthur" b-Mi. res. Handy
     1870-1908   d-Sept. 5, 1908
     Hue A Monroe   "Hugh A" b-Mi.
     May 27, 1907-Oct. 4, 1907   d- age 4
     on monument-Monroe

Section "B"   Greenwood cemetery
lot #
282 CONVERSE
     George D, (GAR emblem)   b-Mi.   res. Fowlerville
     1846-1911   d-April 1, 1911, bur. <u>5-6-1911</u>
     Charlotte, 1849-1932   res. Fowlerville
                                 d-Dec. 21, 1932 age 83

     on monument-Converse
     double stone;-Hart
     Lewis, 1873-1964   res. Fowlerville
                                 d- 10-29-1964 age 91
                                 (Ilah G House Hart)res. Liv. Co.
     Ilah, 1892-19-   d- 11-5-1983 age 90

282½ MEIRNDORF
     double stone;-Meirndorf
     Frank, 1892-1966   res. Williamston
                                 d- 12-17-1966 age 74
                                 res. Ingham Co.
     Hazel Meader, 1897-1979   d- 9-27-1979 age 82,
                                 burial from Lansing
                                 (baby boy, McGowan) res. Ingham Co.
                                 d-April 19, 1947 stillborn

283 CONVERSE
     Eva M Reilly   "Mildred Eva" res. Palm Beach, Fla.
     1893-1979   d- 11-22-1979
     double stone-Converse
     Clyde E, 1882-1954   b-Mi.   res. Lansing
                                 d- 12-14-1954 age 72
                                 res. Lansing
     Leona B, 1888-1971   d- 3-1-1971 age 82
                                 (Ira W Calkins) res. South Bend, Ind.
                                 d-June 27, 1927 age 67

284 GEORGE
     John E, 1873-1949   res. Detroit
                                 d-Jan. 22, 1948 age 74, bur. 1948
     Nora B, 1877-1965   b-Mi.   res. Wayne
                                 d- 10-1-1965 age 88
     Marion Gue "mother"   "Hanna H" res. Detroit
     1847-1932   d-Feb. 26, 1932 age 84
                                 (Eliza S Torry)b-Litchfield, Conn.
                                 d-April 11, 1895 age 90

285 ESCH
     double stone;-Esch
     Robert C,   "Robert Carl" b-Mi. res. Liv. Co.
     Oct. 4, 1899-Dec. 14, 1962 d-age 63
     Lucy L,   b-Mi.   res. Livingston Co.
     Apr. 13, 1901-Mar. 7, 1961 d-age 59
                                 (Herman C Spencer)b-Mi. res. River Rouge
                                 d- 8-3-1955 age 77
                                 (Lillie M Spencer) res. River Rouge,Mi.
                                 d-age 67, bur. Sept. 26, 1938

286 NEWSOME
     double stone;-Newsome
     George H, 1851-1925   res. Fowlerville
                                 d-?   no information
     Ida May, 1857-1929   res. Fowlerville
                                 d-July 13, 1929 age 71

Section "B"   Greenwood cemetery
lot #
287 ROBINS
     double stone-Robins
     Carson E, 1876-1945   res. Fowlerville
                                   d-Oct. 18, 1945 age 69
     Pearl A, 1880-1966   res. Meza, Arizona
                                   d- 7-31-1966 age 86
     Marian, dau. of C E & P A Robins   b-Mi. res. Handy
     1904-1908   d-April 27, 1908 age 3, whooping cough
     Wayne L Robins "son"   res. Marion twp.
     1909-1929   d-Sept. 2, 1929 age 20
287½ FENN
     Genevieve R Fenn   b-Mi. res. Wayne
     1880-1959   d- 11-2-1959 age 78
288 KLEIN
     August Klein "father"   "Augusta F" res. Fowlerville
     1857-1926   d-July 16, 1926 age 69
     Line Klein "mother"   "Lina" res. Fowlerville
     1859-1933   d-May 11, 1933 age 74
289 TEACHWORTH
     Laverne E, son of W H & H O Teachworth   res. Fowlerville
     1906-1907   d-April 21, 1907 age 5 months, pnue.
                                   (Wm. Harry Teachworth) res. Ann Arbor
                                   d-July 1, 1939 age 73
                                   (Hattie Teachworth) res. Ann Arbor
                                   d-March 9, 1947 age 70
                                   (Catherine Teachworth)b-Mi.
                                   d- 2-7-1917 age 7, croup, res. Ann Arbor

290 FENN
     Eva G Fenn "daughter"   b-Mi. res. Detroit
     1907-1957   d- 6-12-1957 age 49
     George S Fenn   res. Wayne
     1876-1942   d-Oct. 31, 1942 age 65
     Eva M Fenn   b-Mi. res. Detroit
     1879-1907   d-Oct. 24, 1907 age 28, typhoid
     on monument-Fenn
290½
     no stones   (L Joyce Smith) female, res. Detroit
                                   d-May 22, 1946 age 1

291 KRAUSE
     Harold, 1898   b-Mi. res. Handy
                                   burial Dec. 12, 1907
                                   transferred from Barnard yard
     Arthur B, 1892-1942   res. Lansing
                                   d-June 17, 1942 age 50

     on monument-Krause
                                   (infant son of E Krause)
                                   bur. Dec. 12, 1907 from Barnard yard
                                   (Ruel Randall) burial ? (old records)

292 KRAUSE
     Ernest, 1867-1944   res. Fowlerville
                                   d-June 8, 1944 age 76
     Rose D, 1867-1950   "Rose Delina" res. Fowlerville
                                   d-March 11, 1950 age 82

Section "B"   Greenwood cemetery
lot #
292 continued
    Claude, 1890-1906   b-Mi.   res. Fowlerville
                                       d-Dec. 1, 1906 age 16

    Viola, 1906-1907   "Viola Eunice" b-Mi. res. Fowl.
                                       d-April 9, 1907 age 6 months, pnue.

293 McINTOSH
    L D McIntosh "father"   "Lorenzo D" b-N. Y. res. Fowl.
    1821-1903   d-June 16, 1903 age 82
    Mary A McIntosh "mother"   b-Conn. res. Howell twp.
    1823-1903   d-Nov. 30, 1903 age 80
    Albert N McIntosh   res. Fowlerville
    1846-1930   d-Nov. 17, 1930 age 84
    Edgar N McIntosh "brother"   b-Canadeas, N. Y. res. Byron, Mi.
    1849-1872   d-March 24, 1872 age 23
                                       removed from Byron 10-30-1900
    Wallace F McIntosh "brother"   b-Mi.   res. Fowlerville
    1855-1900   d-July 23, 1900 age 44,consumption
                                       (Mamme? McIntosh)female
                                       d-Dec. 14, 1928 age 72, pnuemonia
                                       res. Williamston (no lot number)

294 RICHMOND
    Jay T Richmond "father"   b-Mi.   res. Fowl.
    1858-1914   d- 1-24-1914 age 55
    Celia A Richmond "mother"   res. Fowlerville
    1861-1933   d-Aug. 3, 1933 age 71
    Eva Richmond Foster   b-Mi.   res. Iosco
    1888-1915   d- 3-30-1915 age 26 of T B.
    baby Foster   no record
    on monument-Richmond
                                       (Patience C Green)b-N. Y.
                                       d-Dec. 9, 1903 res. Lansing

294½ BORST
    double stone;-
    William M Borst (vet)   res. Oakland Co.
    1895-1979   WW-I   d- 6-12-1979 age 84
    Mary Jane Borst   b-Mi.   res. Livingston Co.
    1883-1961   d- 5-5-1961 age 78
295 GROVER
    "baby" infant son of B D & E H Grover   res. Fowlerville
    June 16, 1911   d-June 16, 1911 stillborn
    Ella, wife of B D Grover   no record
    1874-1941
    Elsa May Watters   res. Fowlerville
    1912-1931   d-Nov. 25, 1931 age 19, accident
    on monument-B D Grover (east side)
                                       (Betty Grover)b-Mi. res. Handy
                                       d-March 22, 1921 age 3 days
                                       (Zedoc Grover)male, b-N. Y.
                                       d-Feb. 3, 1907 age 70 res. Fowl.
                                       (Charles Wm. Hyne)
                                       burial 4-21-1900, age 5 months
                                       transfered from lot B-298, 11-1-1901

Section "B"   Greenwood cemetery
lot #
295½ KUNDE
      double stone;-Kunde
      Fritz F, 1897-1964   res. Fowlerville
                                       d- 8-14-1964 age 67

      Pauline E, 1898-19-   res. Saginaw Co.
                                       d- 6-13-1983 age 85
296 FEAGLES--GROVER
      Sylvester, 1846-1928 (vet)   "S L" res. Fowlerville
                                       d-Oct. 5, 1928 age 85
      Ellen, 1847-1926   (Ellen Feagles) res. Fowlerville
                                       d-Nov. 6, 1926 age 78(listed on lot 295)
      Katie E, wife of B D Grover   b-Mi.   res. Handy
      1874-1906   d-Nov. 22, 1906 age 32
      Burr D Grover   "Burr Dey" b-Mi. res. Daytona Beach,fla.
      1874-1963   d- 6-4-1963 age 89
      (monument on lot 295-west seide-Feagles)
297 GRISWOLD
      Joseph R, 1836-1915   res. Handy
                                       d- 1-16-1915 age 76
      Laura L, 1837-1909   b-N. Y.   res. Handy
                                       d-June 25, 1909 age 73
      Laura V, 1902-1923   b-Mi.   res. Detroit
                                       d-April 16, 1923 age 20

      on monument-Griswold
298 BEAN
      James, 1842-1899   b-England, res. Detroit
                                       d-July 18, 1899 age 57
      Chloe, 1842-1898   b-N. Y.   res. Fowlerville
                                       d-April 25, 1898 age 56, consumption

      on monument-Bean
                                       (Anne S Hyne)b-N. Y.   res. Fowl.
                                       d- 8-15-1913 age 52
298½ SEYMOUR
      double stone;-Seymour
      Fred J, 1884-1959   "Frederick Joseph" b-Mi. res. Liv. Co.
                                       d- 9-17-1959 age 75
      Eda L, 1889-19-   no record
299 WALTON
      on monument-Walton   no burials
299½ JOHNSTON
      triple stone;-Johnston
      Charles F, 1902-1966 (masonic)   "Charles Flynn" res. Lansing
                                       d- 9-10-1966 age 64
      Frida C, 1906-1982   res. Livingston Co.
                                       d- 2-19-1982 age 75
      Charlotte B Bohmert   res. Lansing
      1903-1978   d- 3-4-1978, bur. 3-29-78 ashes
300 WALTON
      Floyd E, "father"   res. Fowlerville
      1873-1929   d-Aug. 2, 1929 age 56, bur. 8-12-29
      Myrtle B, "mother"   b-Mi.   res. Tecumpseh
      1875-1961   d- 7-29-1961 age 85

Section "B"   Greenwood cemetery
lot #
300 continued
    Guy L, 1904-1937   d-May 15, 1937 age 33
    Jay E, 1896-1941 (vet)   res. Handy
                                d-Jan. 20, 1941 age 44
    on monument-Walton (on lot 299-300)
301 COOK
    Jared L Cook "father"   b-N. Y.   res. Fowlerville
    1829-1906   d-Jan. 17, 1906 age 76
    (stone behind above)Com. Sgt. J L Cook, Co. O, 6 Mich Cav.
    Sarah M Cook "mother"   b-Adrian, Mi. (listed on lot 300)
    1837-1897   d-Dec. 25, 1897 age 60
                                burial 3-24-97(?) (was in vault)
    Sophie P Swinburne, dau. of Jared L & Sarah M Cook
    Aug. 2, 1859-Mar. 22, 1939 d-Mar. 26, 1939 age 79
                                burial April 4, 1939, res. Washington
    Frank J Cook   b-Mi. res. Tacoma, Washington
    1878-1922   d-Nov. 7, 1922 age 49
    on monument-Cook
302 COOK
    Fred Jared Cook, son of Jared L & Sarah M Cook
    June 11, 1868-Apr. 4, 1929 d-age 60   res. Howell
302½ BENJAMIN
    no stones   (Charles Coon) res. Cohoctah
                                d-Feb. 19, 1946 age 69
                                (Hazel Y Coon)b-Mi. res. Ingham Co.
                                d- 6-4-1957 age 76
                                (both are Mrs. L. Benjamin's parents)

303 COOK
    Joseph L,   res. Florida
                                d-April 2, 1937 age 43, drowning

    Sarah E,
    on monument-Cook
        Joseph L, 1837-1897   b-Calhoun Co. res. Handy
                                d- 2-8-1897 age 60
        Sarah E, his wife   res. Fowlerville
        1840-1926   d-Dec. 4, 1926 age 86
    Fred A,   (son of Jos. & Eliz. Cook)
                                d-age 2, removed from Vanness? cem.
                                res. Cohoctah
    Bradford   (Bradford E Cook)b-Mi. res. Ottowa,Ill.
                                d-Sept. 16, 1904 age 39, drowning
303½ CARUSI
    John Carusi Jr. "beloved husband"   b-Mi. res. Ingham Co.
    1932-1959   d- 7-20-1959 age 27
304 DICKERSON
    no stones   (Kate Dickerson) res. Florida
                                d-April 28, 1941 age 77

Section "B"   Greenwood cemetery
lot #
305 SOWDERS
     A E Sowders   "Alonzo" b-Mi. res. Fowlerville
     1852-1908   d-Oct. 28, 1908 age 55
     on monument-Sowders
                                    (Cora Souders) res. Fowlerville
                                    d-Aug. 17, 1936 age 74
                                    (Jamus Lockwood) res. Jackson
                                    d-Jan. 10, 1928 age 51

305½ BYRD
     double stone-Byrd
     Frank M, 1902-1970   "Frank Martin" res. Livingston Co.
                                    d- 6-30-1970 age 68
     Hettie, 1899-19-   not listed
307 ELLIOTT
     Emmett Elliott "husband"   res. Handy
     1886-1924   d-Aug. 21, 1924 age 38 of tumor
     Hazel Elliott "baby"   b-Mi. res. Handy
     1914-1916   d- 6-26-1916 age 1y, 6m
                                    (Inez Elliott Mitchell)
                                    d- 5-8-1978 age 82 res. San Diego, Cal.

308 RAY
     on monument-Ray
        John Ray, 1853-   "John R" res. Grand Rap9ds,Mi.
                                    d-June 4, 1929 age 76
        Emily Ray   1855-1906   "Mrs. John" b-Mi. res. Conway twp.
                                    d-Feb. 24, 1906, bur. April 26, 1906
308½ MacDONALD
     Eben G MacDonald   no record
     1898-1969
     Anna B MacDonald   no record
     1894-1976
309 CHILDS
     Marcus B Childs   res. East Lansing
     1847-1930   d-June 26, 1930 age 83
     Harriett E Childs   "Harriett Elizabeth" res. Lansing
     1857-1940   d-Feb. 23, 1940 age 83
     Maude Childs   res. Ingham Co.
     1878-1965   d- 1-4-1965 age 86
     Mabel C Aldrich   res. Delhi twp. Ingham Co.
     1879-1966   d- 9-9-1966 age 86
     on monument-Aldrich-Childs
309½ ALDRICH
     Hugh G Aldrich   res. Ingham Co.
     1880-1979   d- 7-26-1979 age 99
     Henry Russoll   res. Livingston Co.
     1884-1970   d- 7-9-1970 age 86
310 VAN RIPER
     O J Van Riper "father"   "Oren" b-Mi. res. Handy
     1852-1918   d- 7-26-1918 age 66 of T B.
     Helen Van Nest, Van Riper "mother"   (Helen Smith)b-Mi.
     1849-1908   d-Aug. 21, 1908 age 59, res. Handy

Section "B"   Greenwood cemetery
lot #
310 continued
    Maud E, 1874-1965   (Maud E Cook) res. Fowlerville
                                  d- 2-2-1965 age 90
    Charles I Cook (masonic)   "Charles Ives" b-Mi. res. Liv. Co.
    1878-1960   d- 11-5-1960 age 82
311 HOWELL
    triple stone;-Howell
    F Emmet, 1888-1960   "Floyd Emmet" b-Mi. res. Liv. Co.
                                  d- 11-25-1960 age 72
    Carrie, 1891-1980   "Carrie C" res. Mason, Mi.
                                  d- 12-20-1980 age 89
    Maxine, 1913-1920   b-Mi.   res. Fowlerville
                                  d-July 20, 1920 age 7
                                  burial 12-23-1981(?)

312 BAKER--LADD
    Lamont L Baker   b-Mi.   res. Iosco twp.
    1866-1910   d-Oct. 31, 1910 age 44
    Nettie Armstrong   "Jeanette E" res. Belleville,Mi.
    1868-1949   d-Dec. 15, 1949 age 81
    on monument-Baker(reverse side -Ladd)
                                  (Martha M Armstrong)b-Mi. res. Iosco
                                  d-Aug. 28, 1924 age 82

312½ HUSCHKE
    Roy H Huschke   b-Mi.   res. Scio twp.
    1918-1953   d-Jan. 16, 1953 age 34, fractured skull
313 HUSCHKE
    double stone;-Huschke
    Louis H, 1887-1962   b-Mi.   res. Montmorency
                                  d- 10-9-1962 age 75(listed lot 384½)
    Anna E, 1881-1969   res. Genesee Co.
                                  d- 11-8-1969 age 88(listed lot 384½)
    Margaret "mother"   b-Germany, res. Ingham Co.
    1856-1912   d- 8-24-1912 age 56
    Rudolph "father"   b-Germany, res. LeRoy, Ingham Co.
    1845-1915   d- 8-21-1915 age 70
    on monument-Huschke
313½ HUSCHKE
    double stone;-
    Carl A, 1881-1947   "Carl August" res. Locke twp.
                                  d-May 14, 1947 age 65
    Katherine A, 1885-1963   b-Mi.   res. Montcalm
                                  d- 9-5-1963 age 78

314 CROFOOT
    Edward Crofoot   "James Edward" b-New Brunswick
    1843-1922   d-June 16, 1922 age 79   res. Iosco
    Louisa A Crofoot   b-N. Y.   res. Iosco twp.
    1853-1909   d-Nov. 23, 1909 age 56, pnuemonia
    Bess L Crofoot   "Bess Luella"
    1887-1964   d- 12-29-1964 age 77(listed lot 314½)
    on monument-Crofoot
                                  (Marvin Wesley Crofoot)b-Iosco
                                  d-Sept. 6, 1941 age 14, accident
                                  res. Iosco

Section "B"
lot #
315 WAKEFIELD
     Myrtie,   no record
     1879-1946
     Guy,   no record
     1880-1952
     Sarah A, (star emblem)   b-Mi.   res. Fowlerville
     1854-1916   d- 3-12-1916 age 61
     Robert R, (masonic)   b-Mi.   res. Fowlerville
     1854-1917   d- 8-1-1917 age 63
     on monument-Wakefield
315¼ WAKEFIELD
     double stone;-Wakefield
     Roland R "father"   res. Howell
     1861-1943   d-June 9, 1943 age 81
     Alice J, "mother"   "Alice Julia" b-Mi.   res. Howell
     1869-1952   d-Dec. 31, 1952 age 83
330 SHARP
     double stone;-Sharp
     John Sr. 1864-1939   res. Handy
                                          d-Sept. 10, 1939 age 75
     Hattie W, 1864-1935   res. Conway twp.
                                          d-July 27, 1935 age 71, pnuemonia
330½
     empty
331 PEARSON
     Roy E Pearson "father"   b-Mi.   res. Lansing
     1886-1952   d-July 18, 1952 age 65
     Bessie B Pearson "mother"   res. Lansing
     1889-1935   d-Aug. 4, 1935 age 46
332 SHARPE
     Tracy Sharpe   no record
     1890-1959
     Florence A Sharp   b-Mi.   res. Lansing
     1890-1954   d- 4-4-1954 age 64
     Alphonso Waterer   res. Lansing
     1861-1950   d-April 14, 1950 age 89
333 SHARPE
     double stone;-Sharpe
     Russell W, 1896-1962   "Russell Walker" b-Mi. res. Liv. Co.
                                          d- 11-4-1962 age 66
     Lucy E, 1898-19-   not listed
     Thomas Leroy Sharp   b-Mi.   res. Oak Grove
     1917-1919   d- 2-6-1919 age 2, diptheria
333½ HUFF
     double stone;-Huff
     Raymond D, 1924-   not listed
     Charlotte, 1922-1963(Amer. Leg. Aux.)   res. Fowlerville
                                          d- 11-3-1963 age 41

Section "B"   Greenwood cemetery
lot #
334 KETCHUM
     Lawrence Ketchum   res. Albion, Mi.
     June 22, 1888-July 23, 1926   d-age 38 in accident
     Delilah "mother"   res. Fowlerville
     1858-1930   d-Oct. 5, 1930 age 73
     Theodore N, "father"   b-Mi. res. Amatilla, Fla.
     1852-1919   d- 1-18-1919 age 67
                                    (Mary Herron) res. Jackson Co.
                                    d- 4-12-1975 age 92, bur. from Jackson

335 KETCHUM
     Alexander Herron   res. Jackson
     May 6, 1882-May 6, 1946   d-age 63
     Mary Ketchum, wife of James Guy Lockwood   no record
     April 13, 1882-April 12, 1975
     Lillian Ketchum, wife of Ethan L Cowie   res. Jackson
     October 7, 1880-December 2, 1945   d-age 65
     Helen Ketchum, wife of Leslie A Simpson   no record
     April 19, 1893-January 17, 1942
     on monument-Ketchum
336 WILKINSON
     Floyd George, 1871-1954   b-Mi. res. Conway
                                    d- 7-16-1954 age 82
     Lois Ellen, 1871-1929   res. Conway twp.
                                    d-Feb. 23, 1929

     on monument-Wilkinson
338 WILKINSON (and village)
     no stones   (Wayne E Wilkinson) res. Liv. Co.
                                    d- 10-6-1983 age 66,
                                    burial 10-26-1983 ashes

339 WILKINSON
     Charles, 1833-1916 (vet)   b-England, res. Fowlerville
                                    d- 12-5-1916 ahe 83
     Anna T, 1844-1918   b-England, res. Conway twp.
                                    d- 10-7-1918 age 74
     C Wesley, 1877-1908 (masonic) "Charles Wesley"
                                    removed from Cofferin cemetery
     Emily H Wilkinson   b-England, res. Fowlerville
     1842-1915   d- 4-24-1915 age 72
     on monument-Wilkinson

                                    (Alma Dorothy Wilkinson) res. Liv. Co.
                                    d- 7-21-1972 age 89

340 WILKINSON
     James H Wilkinson (masonic)   res. Conway twp.
     1869-1942   d-July 22, 1942 age 72
     Alma D Wilkinson   "Alma Lucina" res. Conway
     1876-1951   d-Oct. 17, 1951 age 74
     Catherine Ann Wilkinson "our daughter"   b-Mi. res. Fowl.
     Feb. 17, 1953-Feb. 19, 1953   (d-Feb. 12, 1953 age 2 days)
                                    burial Feb. 15, 1953
                                    (George W Wilkinson)res. Presque Isle
                                    d- 5-16-1983 age 66

Section "B"   Greenwood cemetery
lot #
341 GRANT
     Floyd E, 1874-1887   b-Mi.   res. Conway twp.
                               d- 9-14-1887 age 13
                               burial 3-19-1915 from Benjamin cem.

     Sarah, 1852-1926   b-Mi.   res. Fowlerville
                               d-Jan. 14, 1926 age 72
     James B, 1848-1915   b-Mi.   res. Conway
                               d- 3-19-1915 age 67, bur. from Conway
     on monument-Grant
342 HOYT--GUE
     double stone;-
     Lorenzo Gue   no record
     1868-1944
     Zaida Gue   no record
     1876-1973
     double stone;-
     Thomas J Hoyt   b-Mi.   res. Conway
     1851-1914   d- 1-20-1914 age 63
     Hannah L Hoyt   b-Mi. Res. Caro, Mi.
     1854-1925   d-Dec. 18, 1925 age 70
343 WARDEN
     empty
344 WAID
     double stone;-Waid
     Orrin, 1878-1936 (FLT emblem) res. Ingham Co.
                               d-March 3, 1936 age 57, menengitis
     Bessie, 1884-1978   "Bessie M" res. Howell
                               d- 5-4-1978 age 94
     Orval Waid   (baby Waid)b-Mi.   res. Handy
     born Mar. 9, 1912, died Feb. 28, 1915   d-age 3, heart trouble
                               (Howard J Waid) res. Ingham Co.
                               d- 11-8-1983 age 78
                               burial from Williamston

345 TITMUS
     double stone;-
     Wade G, 1896-1965   res. Fowlerville
                               d- 1-23-1965 age 68, pnuemonia
     Vivian L, 1900-   not listed
     Edith S, 1871-1947   res. Webberville
                               d-Feb. 2, 1947 age 75
     David W, 1863-1914   b-Mi.   res. Iosco twp.
                               d- 7-11-1914 age 51 of operation

     on monument-Titmus
346 MATTIESEN
     double stone;-
     Herman Matthiesen   res. Fowlerville
     1847-1928   d-April 4, 1928 age 80
     Cathrina Mattheisen   res. Fowlerville
     1849-1932   d-Jan. 24, 1932 age 84
     John H Wolter   b-Mi.   res. Kalamazoo
     1869-1955   d- 8-30-1955 age 86

Section "B"
lot #   Greenwood cemetery
347 RATHBUN
     mother   no record
     1818-1885
     Ada, wife of E L Rathbun   "Ada Olive" b-Mi. res. Fowl.
     1837-1913   d- 9-19-1913 age 76
     Edgar L Rathbun   "Edgar Lucas" b-Mi. res. Fowl.
     1837-1918   d- 6-21-1918 age 67
     on monument-Rathbun
                                       (Unice Cooper)b-N. Y. res. Corunna,Mi.
                                       d- 12-?-1885 age 68 (may be "mother")
                                       removed from Benjamin cemetery

348 SOPP
     Charles G Sopp   b-Mi. res. Pontiac
     1872-1959   d- 2-11-1959 age 84
     Mabel V Sopp   res. Lansing
     1882-1933   d-Aug. 30, 1933 age 51, cancer
     C G Sopp "husband"   "George" res. Flint
     1902-1939   d-Aug. 8, 1939 age 36
     George, 1846-1876   b-Mi. res. Conway twp.
                                       d-July 25, 1876, heart failure
                                       burial May 4, 1910
     Millie, 1874-1876   b-Mi. res. Conway
                                       d-Sept. 1, 1876, bur. May 4, 1910
                                       (William Faulke)b-Germany, res. Fowl.
                                       d-Nov. 5, 1910 age 89

349 WOLTER
     Fred Wolter   b-Germany, res. Fowlerville
     1865-1920   d-July 9, 1920 age 54 of T B.
     Mary G Wolter   res. Fowlerville
     1876-1943   d- Sept. 2, 1943 age 67
     Clara A Wolter   "Clara Ann" b-Mi. res. Leroy
     1899-1913   d- 11-26-1913 age 14,typhoid
350 ROBINS
     on monument-Robins
         Calvin, 1837-1913   b-Canada
                                       d- 1-6-1913 age 76 at Williamston
         Grace, 1836-1927   res. Perry
                                       d-Jan. 30, 1927 age 91
         Ella M Price   b-Mi. res. Alma
         1869-1955   d- 8-20-1955 age 85
                                       (infant dau. of Lewis Price)
                                       d- about 1913 stillborn, res. Fowl.
                                       (removed from "a private lot")

351 SOULE
     Sibyl Stiles   res. Port Huron
     1868-1936   d-April 1, 1936 age 67
     Charles C, "father"   res. Fowlerville
     1851-1926   d-Sept. 3, 1926 age 74
     Sarah J, "mother"   b-Mi. res. Conway
     1854-1909   d-Dec. 23, 1910 age 55
                                       burial Apr. 1, 1910(listed lot A-192)
     on monument-Soule

Section "B"   Greenwood cemetery
lot #
352 CONRAD
     Selden D Conrad   b-Mi.   res. Iosco twp.
     1881-1898   (two entries-burial Nov. 6, 1911
                                       d- of heart failure
                                       burial July 24, 1913
                                       d-1901 age 17, gun shot)
                           removed from Iosco cemetery

     Charlotte M Conrad
     1873-1971   d- 9-4-1971 age 98
     Anna A Conrad   res. Lansing
     1850-1934   d-May 20, 1934 age 84
     Charles Conrad   b-N. Y.   res. Iosco twp.
     1839-1911   d-May 18, 1911 age 71,
                           burial May 20 from Lansing
353
     no stones   (Hannah M Place)b-Ohio, res. Fowl.
                           d-July 20, 1911 age 74
                           (infant son of Addison Fry)b-Mi.
                           d- 7-4-1916 stillborn, res. Ann Arbor
                           (William Frey)b-Mi.   res, Fowlerville

353½ COLE
     no stones   (Carol V Cole) res. Lansing
                           d- 3-8-1967 age 34

355 O'DELL--GRAHAM
     Claude L O'Dell "brother"   b-Mi.   res. Conway
     1895-1915   d- 8-5-1915 age 22, appendecitis
     double stone;-O'Dell
     Miles S, "father"   b-Mi.   res. Genesee Co.
     1872-1957   d- 11-29-1956 age 85
     Cora B, "mother"   "Cora Bell" b̄-Mi. res. Oakland Co.
     1872-1959   d- 1-1--1959 age 86
                                  (all above listed on lot 343)
                                  (Magie Graham)b-Mi.   res. Iosco
                                  d-Jan. 3, 1911, heart failure
                                  burial Jan. 20, 1911

356 LOCKWOOD
     little Rex, 1902-1905   b-Mi.   res. Fowlerville
                                  d-Dec. 6, 1909 age 3, diptheria
                                  (listed on lot B-297)bur. May 26,1909
     John G, "father"   b-N. Y.   res. Handy
     1836-1909   d-Sept. 10, 1909 age 73
     Mary A, "mother"   (Mary A Benton) res. Webberville
                                 d-July 12, 1930 age 84
     Harold R Lockwood   not listed
     1924-
     on monument-Lockwood
357 LOCKWOOD
     Ezra J, 1868-1954   b-Mi.   res. Fowlerville
                                 d- 8-1-1954 age 85
     Emma Jean, 1875-1924   b-Mi.   res. Williamston
                                 d-Aug. 5, 1924 age 49 in accident
     double stone;-Lockwood
     J D, 1895-19-   not listed
     Zella, 1899-19-   not listed

Greenwood cemetery
Section "B"
lot #
358 MEE--HOAGLAND
     double stone;-Mee
     Glenn F, 1916-1979 (masonic)   res. Livingston Co/
                                     d- 1-4-1979 age 62

     Joanna M, 1917-   mot listed
     Ella M, 1882-1968   (Ella M Hoagland) res. Liv. Co.
                                     d- 5-22-1968 age 83
     Fred C, 1874-1943   (Fred C Hoagland) res. Fowl.
                                     d-Nov. 7, 1943 age 69

     on monument-Hoagland
359 COPELAND-HOAGLAND
     James H, 1849-1938 (KOTM emblem)   res. Fowlerville
                                     burial 1-17-1938 age 89
         Emily O, 1853-1933 (Star emblem)   res. Fowlerville
                                     d-Nov. 13, 1933

     on monument-Hoagland
     Zula E,   (Zula H Copeland)b-Mi. res. Fowl.
     Aug. 5, 1886-Mar. 19, 1910   d-age 23
     Lawrence   b-Mi.   res. Fowlerville
     June 8, 1881-Sept. 28, 1910   d-age 24, of epilepsy
     on monument-Copeland
360 FRANKS--WOLL
     double stone-Franks
     G D, 1889-1973   res. Livingston Co.
                                     d- 10-26-1973 age 84, bur. from Howell
     Myrtie A, 1891-1978   res. Livingston Co.
                                     d- 3-22-1978 age 86, bur. from Howell
     on monument-Woll (lot 360 & 361)
                                     (infant male, Shannon)b-Mi.

361 WOLL
     Charles W Woll   b-Mi.   res. Handy
     1867-1896   (d & Bur. listed as Nov. 8, 1909)
     Electa Woll   b-Mi.
     1849-1872   (d & bur. listed as Nov. 8, 1909)
     Andrew Woll, GAR (& emblem)   res. Fowlerville
     1844-1929   d-April 1, 1929 age 85
     Rose Woll "mother" WRC   (Rose Sheperd Woll) res. Handy
     1862-1938   d-age 75, burial June 20, 1938
                                     (Gean E Franks)female, res. Handy
                                     d-July 14, 1931, premature

361½
     no stones   (Thomas J Burke) res. Liv. Co.
                                     d- 7-6-1972 age 91

362 CEPHELUS
     Gustave "father"   b-Mi.   res. Iosco twp.
     1853-1918   d- 11-21-1918 age 64, cancer
     Ernestine "mother"   (Ernetine Supheylus) res. Iosco
     1852-1929   d-March 12, 1929 age 78, diabetis
     Olga F Gehringer   b-Germany, res. Iosco twp.
     1879-1924   d-Feb. 20, 1924 age 45
     on monument-Cephelus

Section "B"   Greenwood cemetery
lot #
363 CARDOTT--HERBERT
     Martha, "mother"   (Martha Cardott)b-N. Y. res. Fowl.
     1849-1924   d-Dec. 6, 1924 age 75
     double stone;-Herbert
     Perry K, 1875-1924   b-Mi. res. Fowlerville
                                       d-Jan. 5, 1924 age 48, pnuemonia

     Cora M, 1875-1935   (Cora Arnold) res. Fowlerville
                                       d-July 30, 1935 age 61

     on monument-Cardott
364 REYHL
     Frank A,   no record
     Jan. 27, 1892-Aug. 9, 1909
     Christian F,   "Christian Frank" b-Mi. res. Howell
     Apr. 17, 1886-Jan. 9, 1909   d-age 22, typhoid
     Selma, "mother"   (Semma Rediger) res. Howell
     Apr. 14, 1861-June 11, 1936   d-age 75
     Richard, "father"   no record
     Oct. 10, 1857-May 20, 1910
365 REYHL
     Donald E Reyhl   res. Howell twp.
     1921-1948   d-March 26, 1948 age 27
     Arden D Reyhl (vet emblem)?   res. Fowlerville
     1930-1963   d- 11-10-1963 age 33
     Ruth M Reyhl   res. Livingston Co.
     1893-1974   d- 7-7-1974 age 81
     Ernest C Reyhl   res. Howell twp. b-Iosco
     1888-1951   d-Jan. 12, 1951 age 62, gun shot
     on monument-Reyhl
366 GIBSON
     double stone;-Gibson
     William C, 1877-1932   res. Conway twp.
                                       d-Feb. 25, 1932 age 55
     Lottie M, 1881-1969   res. Oakland
                                       d- 4-1-1969 age 87
     George William Gibson   "Jr." b-Mi. res. Handy
     1909-1910   d-May 1, 1910 age 6 mo. menengitis
     Hazel Irene Gibson   b-Mi. res. Handy
     2 mo.-1919   d- 11-7-1918 age 8 weeks
     Laura Ada Gibson
     1911-1928   d- April 12, 1928 age 16, peritonitis
                                       d-in Lansing hospital
367 STRAITH
     father
     mother
     on monument-Straith
         Andrew T Straith   res. Detroit
         born Aug. 1, 1855, died July 24, 1934   d-age 78
         Alida L, his wife   b-Mi. res. Handy
         born Oct. 24, 1857, died Oct. 7, 1908   d-age 51
     John Todosciuk   res. Fowlerville
     Michigan, S2, U S Navy, World War II
     Dec. 25, 1923-March 29, 1964   d-age 40
                                    (male Straith) res. Detroit
                                    d- 5-14-1914 age 1 day, premature

Section "B"   Greenwood cemetery
lot #
368 WORTHINGTON
     Gertrude M, 1885-1908   b-Mi.   res. Fowlerville
                                    d-Sept. 1, 1908 age 22, typhoid

     James R Worthington   b-Mi.   res. Williamston
     1883-1952   d-Oct. 16, 1952 age 69
     on monument-Worthington
369 BROWN
     J S Brown   "Jacob Seymour" res. Howell twp.
     Nov. 3, 1899-Nov. 3, 1908   d-age 9
     double stone-Brown
     Royal G, 1875-1966   res. Northville
                                    d- 1-18-1966 age 90
     Luella B, 1874-1960   "Luella Belle" b-Mi. res. Northville
                                    d- 3-9-1960 age 85

370 MASTIC
     Marie Amstutz Mastic   "Marie L" b-Mi.   res. Plymouth
     1895-1956   d- 3-31-1956 age 60
     John R Mastic (FLT emblem)   "John Richard" b-Mi.   res. Wayne
     1881-1960   d- 5-30-1960 age 78
     Agnes M Mastic   res. Plymouth
     Aug. 2, 1881-Nov. 22, 1935   d-age 53
                                    ("she was the sunshine of our home")
                                    (Lavern Richard Mastic)b-Mi.
                                    d-Oct. 14, 1920 age 20 months
                                    d- of infintale paralysis, res. Plymouth

371 WINT--BRISTOL
     double stone-Bristol
     Charles H, 1865-1930   res. Fowlerville
                                    d-Nov. 3, 1930 age 64
     Mary M, 1869-1958   b-Mi.   res. Phoenix, Arizona
                                    d- 12-6-1958 age 89
     Alice A Wint   b-Mi.   res. Fowlerville
     1878-1908   d-Sept. 12, 1908 of consumption
     Alice Wint   no record
     1848-1893
     Joseph Wint   b-N. Y.   res. Fowlerville
     1846-1925   d-June 3, 1925 age 79
372 DEAN
     Michael B Lillard   "Michael Burnett" b-Howell
     Oct. 6, 1951-Nov. 26, 1951   d-age 1 month, res. Lansing
     Helen A Dean "mother"   res. Mason, Mi.
     Oct. 13, 1859-Dec. 17, 1949   d- age 90
     James O Dean   (Rev. J O Dean) res. Fowlerville
     1857-1908   d-Aug. 4, 1908 age 56
373 HUSS
     Elizebeth, wife of D J Huss   b-Indiana, res. Handy
     May 11, 1855-May 15, 1909   d-age 54
     David J Huss   res. Fowlerville
     1853-1940   d-of heart trouble, bur. Sept. 20, 1940
     Melinda Mastic Huss   res. Fowlerville
     June 24, 1849-Jan. 12, 1934   d-age 84
                                    (Daisy Bullis) res. Ingham Co.
                                    d-March 13, 1936 age 52

Section "B"   Greenwood cemetery
lot #
374 BOWEN
     no stones   (Caroline Bowen) res. Ann Arbor
                                            (d-July 23, 1926 age 65

375 GAGE
     Carrie Gage Stuart   res. Lansing
     1884-1968   d- 3-6-1968 age 83
     Virginia Gage   res. Los Angeles, Cal.
     1906-1928   d-Dec. 25, 1929 age 22
     Clay W Gage   b-Mi.   res. Lansing
     1884-1923   d- April 22, 1923 age 40
     Ellen M Gage   res. Fowlerville
     1846-1932   d-Nov. 13, 1932 age 85
     Wm. Gage (vet emblem)   res. Fowlerville
     1841-1933   d-March 8, 1933 age 92, broken leg
376 FISCHER
     Julia May Fischer   (Mary Fisher)b-Mi. res. Saginaw
     1858-1909   d-March 23, 1909 age 50, pnuemonia
     Fred W Fischer   b-Germany, res. Fowlerville
     1855-1908   d-June 5, 1908 age 53
     on monument-Fischer
377 ROBERTS
     Antonett Kinney   b-Mi.   res. Handy
     1838-1916   d- 1-28-1916 age 80
     Rosa E Colby   (Rose C Woll) res. Mason, Mi.
     1861-1926   d-Sept. 22, 1926 age 65
     David P Colby   b-Mi.   res. Handy
     1857-1916   d- 5-8-1916 age 58 of T B.
     Margarett, wife of Riley Roberts   b-Mi. res. Cohoctah
     1885-1908   d-Sept. 13, 1908 age 23
     on monument-Roberts
378 WHITE
     Howard W White   b-Mi.   res. GrAYLING, Mi.
     1887- 1955   d- 9-3-1955 age 67
     Anna M White "mother"   res. Fowlerville
     1863-1934   d-April 20, 1934 age 70, pnue.
     Henry White "father" (vet)   b-Mi.   res. Fowlerville
     1835-1922   d-Nov. 8, 1922 age 87
                                            (infant son of Fred Dillingham)
                                            d- 10-19-1916 stillborn, res. Conway

379 BARNARD
     double stone-Barnard
     Harry L, 1885-1967   res. Charlotte
                                            d- 9-17-1967 age 82
     Irene M, 1905-1976   res. Eaton Co.
                                            d- 7-30-1976 age 71,
                                            burial from Charlotte
     Ida May, wife of H L Barnard   b-Mi.   res. Handy
     1888-1911   d-Sept. 19, 1911 age 24
                                            (female Barnard) res. Fowlerville
                                            d-Sept. 1, 1912 stillborn
                                            transferred from ?

Section "B"   Greenwood cemetery
lot #
379½ WAKEFIELD
     multiple stone- Wakefield
     George Sr. 1907-   not listed
     Anna M, 1907-   not listed
     George, 1927-   not listed
     Betty A, 1928-   not listed
380 HUCK
     Leonard Huck "father"   no record
     1837-1901
     Mary Ann, wife of Leonard   no record
     1842-1927 "mother"
     Charles D Huck "son"   res. Fowlerville
     1874-1944   d-June 27, 1944 age 70
     on monument-Huck
        Leonard Huck, 1837-
        Mary Huck, 1843   "Mary A" b-Germany, res. Fowl.
                                      d-June 8, 1923 age 80

        Frank Huck Sr. 1791-1861   no record
        Catherine Huck, 1797-1877   no record
380½ MERIGNAC
     double stone-Merignac
     Harold P, 1904-19-   not listed
     Eleanor A, 1907-1969   res. Livingston Co.
                                      d- 8-24-1969 age 62
                                      (Myrtie Wakefield) res. Howell twp.
                                      d-Sept. 9, 1946 age 67
                                      (Guy Wakefield)b-Mi. res. Fowl.
                                      d-Oct. 29, 1952 age 72

381 HUCK
     Wm. H Huck "father"   b-N. Y.(?) res. Meridian
     1860-1910   d-Nov. 29, 1910
     Barbara E Huck "mother"   "Barbara Elizabeth" res. Lansing
     1864-1939   d-Feb. 28, 1939 age 74
     double stone;-
     William L, 1888-1956 (masonic)   (Wm. L Huck)b-Mi. res. Detroit
                                      d- 12-10-1956 age 68
     Mabel V, 1886-1961 (Star)   b-Mi. res. Oakland Co.
                                      d- 7-13-1961 age 75
382 ROUNSVILLE
     no stones   (Helen Roundsville)
                                      burial 5-20-1893

383 MILLER--COFFEY
     double stone;-Miller
     Albert, 1864-1950   res. Conway
                                      d-Jan. 4, 1950 age 85
     Isabelle, 1860-1932   "Luella" res. Handy
                                      d-Feb. 26, 1932 age 71, pnuemonia
     double stone;-Coffey
     John, 1888-1957   b-Mi. res. Pontiac
                                      d- 10-17-1957 age 68
     Lena I, 1890-1964   "Lena Ida" res. Fowlerville
                                      d- 4-1-1964 age 73

Section "B"   Greenwood cemetery
lot #
383½ CHRISTIAN
     double stone;-
     George A Christian   "George Alva" b-Mi. res. Fowl.
     1886-1958   d- 12-4-1958 age 72
     Elizabeth M Christian   res. Livingston Co.
     1888-1975   d- 4-3-1975 age 89
384 KESKE--BAKER
     double stone;-Keske
     August, 1848-1922 (vet)   (August Kaske)b-Germany,
                                 d-Jan. 22, 1920 age 72
                                 res. Ingham Co.

     Wilhimena, 1838-1912   b-Germany, res. Fowlerville
                                 d- 11-13-1912 age 74

     double stone;-Baker
     William, 1867-1936   "Wm. W" res. Howell twp.
                                 d-Dec. 17, 1936 age 69, pnue.
     Alvena, 1881-1958   (Alvena W Glenn) res. Ingham Co.
                                 d- 7-11-1958 age 16
     Mae Schneider   (Mae Alvena Fredricka Schneider)b-Mi.
     1911-1912   d- 12-18-1912 age 1y, 8mo.
                                 res. Leroy, Ingham Co.

384½ HUSCHKE
     double stone;-Huschke
     Fred, 1885-1968   "Fred R" res. Fowlerville
                                 d- 3-3-1968 age 82
     Grace, 1891-1981   "Hazel Grace" res. Stockbridge
                                 d- 12-26-1981 age 90

385 FOWLER
     W H H Fowler "husband"   "Harrison H" b-Mi. res. St. Johns
     1859-1923   d-Feb. 13, 1923 age 65
     Polley, "wife"   b-Mi. res. Fowlerville
     1855-1914   d- 3-12-1914 age 59, cancer
     Floss Fowler Coffey   (Myrtle F Coffey) res. Fowlerville
     1883-1928   d-Jan. 10, 1928 age 44, pnuemonia
     Vern Coffey   res. Corpus Christi, Texas
     1885-1960   d- 1-8-1960 age 75
     on monument-W H H Fowler
386 MITCHELL
     Arthur, 1882-1963   "Arthur B" b-Mi. res. Liv. Co.
                                 d- 9-2-1963 age 80
     EllA, 1856-1914   b-Mi. res. Fowlerville
                                 d- 5-2-1914 age 58, cancer

     on monument-Mitchell
387 WALKER
     Wm. B Walker   res. Handy
     Co. F, 31st Reg. Vol. Inf.
     1869-1944   d-May 29, 1944 age 75
     Ellen Matilda Walker   res. Handy
     1862-1946   d-Jan. 11, 1946 age 82
     Mary Walker "mother"   (Mrs. David Walker) res. Handy
     1836-1915   d- 4-7-1915
     David Walker "father"   b-England, res. Handy
     1828-1917   d- 11-22-1917 age 89(listed lot 388)

Section "B"   Greenwood cemetery
lot #
388 RUGGLES
     George A, 1853-1913   b-Mi.   res. Handy
                                      d- 4-23-1913 age 60
     Elizabeth J, 1860-1939   "Eliz. Jane" res. Handy
                                      d-April 29, 1939 age 79
     on monument-Ruggles (masonic emblem)
388½ MORRISON
     Walter Leroy, 1902   not listed
     Helen L, 1909-1983   "Helen May" res. Dearborn, Mi.
                                      d- 2-28-1983 age 73
                                      burial from Allen Park, Mi.
     Elizabeth D, 1941-   not listed
     on monument-Morrison
389 DICKINSON--HART
     Anna Dickinson "mother"   no record
     1857-1913
     Patricia Brown   res. Howell
     1935-1941   d-June 15, 1941 age 5
                                      (John A Rex) res. Lansing
                                      d-Sept. 14, 1930 stillborn

389½ HETCHLER
     Helen Hetchler "wife"   "Helen B" res. Handy
     1855-1942.   d-March 1, 1942 age 86
     Henry Hetchler Sr. "husband"   res. Handy
     1853-1945   d-Aug. 10, 1945 age 92
     on monument-Hetchler
390 COOPER
     Agnes E Cooper   b-Pontiac, res. Pontiac
     1886-1952   d-Feb. 6, 1952 age 65
     Albert E Cooper   res. Pontiac
     1876-1935   d-April 29, 1935 age 58
     (behind stone above)Albert E Cooper
                    Oregon, Captain 139 Inf. 35 Div.
                    April 29, 1935
     Nora Wallace Cooper   res. Fowlerville
     1874-1949   d-Dec. 2, 1949 age 75
     Lewis H Cooper   res. Lansing
     1875-1939   d-July 22, 1939 age 64
390½ ALLEN
     double stone;-Allen
     William E, 1878-1955   "Wm. Edward" res. Green Oak twp.
                                      d- 12-17-1955 age 77
     Bertha V, 1878-1962   "Bertha Viola"
                                      d- 2-7-1962 age 83
391 COOPER
     Joseph Cooper Jr.   b-Mi.   res. Pontiac
     1884-1960   d- 4-13-1960 age 76(listed on lot 390)
     Amy B Cooper Miner   b-Mi.   res. Birmingham
     1882-1925   d-Nov. 24, 1925 age 43(listed lot 390)
     Mary S Cooper   res. Fowlerville
     1850-1931   d-Feb. 5, 1931 age 81
     Joseph L Cooper   b-Canada, res. Fowlerville
     1844-1913   d- 2-22-1913 age 69
     on monument-Cooper

Section "B"
lot #
391½ TAYLOR
        double stone;-Taylor
        Ralph L, 1900-1967   res. Brighton
                                            d- 7-1-1967 age 67

        Laura A, 1905-1980   res. Livingston Co.
                                            d- 2-6-1980 age 74, bur. from Howell

392 FARRELL--GROVE
        Grace A Grove   "Grace Dell" res. Washtenaw Co.
        1886-1948   d-Sept. 13, 1948 age 62
        infant dau. of J & P Farrell   res. Handy
        "our darling baby"   d-Jan. 8, 1929 stillborn
        double stone;-Farrell
        John H, 1882-1940   b-Handy, res. Ingham Co.
                                            d-Dec. 9, 1940 age 58
        Pearl S, 1892-19-   (Pearl S Welton) res. Hamburg, Mi.
                                            d- 4-14-1976 age 83
                                            (female Farrell) res. Handy
                                            d-stillborn (may be same as above)
                                            removed from ? to lot B-392

392½ RISCH
        double stone;-Risch
        Herman L, 1883-1948   "Herman Louis" res. Howell twp.
                                            d-July 8, 1948 age 65
        Ida G, 1884-1962   "Ida Augusta" b-Mi. res. Liv.Co.
                                            d- 10-5-1962 age 77

393 SIMPSON
        triple stone;-
        Bert H, 1875-1968   "Bert R" res. Fowlerville
                                            d- 2-17-1968 age 92
        Ruth E, 1884-1975   res. Bloomfield twp. Oakland Co.
                                            d- 5-20-1975 age 91(list lot 393½)
        Edith M, 1915-1919   "Edith Marion" b-Mi. res. Handy
                                            d-Oct. 28, 1919 age 3
        William B McAfee   (Wm. B McCoffee) res. Conway
        1871-1913   d- 6-1-1913 age 41
394 ABBOTT
        Fred K Abbott   res. Howell
        1869-1948   d-April 21, 1948 age 79
        Clara Abbott   res. Howell
        1871-1946   d-Dec. 28, 1946 age 75
        Ruth E Abbott   b-Mi.   res. Livingston Co.
        1908-1913   d- 10-4-1913 age 5,Appendicitis(?)
        on monument-F K Abbott
                                            (Claude J Foster) res. Iosco twp.
                                            d-March 8, 1909 age 3½ months

394½ GIBSON
        double stone;-Gibson
        Gale H, 1904-1960   b-Mi.   res. Ingham Co.
                                            d- 12-29-1960 age 56
        Ruth L, 1909-1977   res. Middlesex, N. J.
                                            d- 8-14-1977 age 68, bur. from Lansing

Section "B"   Greenwood cemetery
lot #
395 ABBOTT
     Matilda M, 1848-1916   (Mrs. Frank Abbott)b-Mi. res. Handy
                                   d- 6-28-1916 age 68

     Franklin B, 1844-1923   b-N. Y.   res. Handy
     Co. i, 16th Mich.   d-April 28, 1923 age 78
396 KUNDE
     Herman L, 1866-1916   b-Germany, res. Handy twp.
                                   d- 12-8-1916 age 51
     Pauline C, 1860-1912   b-Germany, res. Handy
                                   d- Jan. 7, 1912 age 50, bur. Jan. 19.

     on monument-Kunde
                                   (Fran Louise Seymour)b-Mi.
                                   d-May 31, 1924 age 3, pnuemonia
                                   res. Cohoctah twp.

396½ KUNDE
     double stone;-
     Otto B Kunde   res. Fowlerville
     1900-1965   d- 8-11-1965 age 65
     Inez M Kunde   res. Livingston Co.
     1907-1980   d- 3-25-1980 age 72
                                   (infant male, Kunde) res. Fowl.
                                   d-Feb. 17, 1945 stillborn

397 HOYT--GUE
     Rex F, 1915-1918   (Rex F Hoyt)b-Mi. res. Conway twp.
                                   d- 3-23-1917 age 1, bur. 3-25-1917
     Leila H, 1910-1914   (Leah Lilah Hoyt)b-Mi. res. Conway
                                   d- 3-17-1914 age 2, pnuemonia
     Sadie McNee   "Sadie L" b-Mi. res. Livingston Co.
     1881-1962   d- 9-30-1962 age 81
     Charles H Hoyt   res. Fowlerville
     1869-1944   d-July 28, 1944 age 74
                                   (Zaida Savella Gue) res. Washtenaw Co.
                                   d- 7-1-1973 age 97, bur from Ann Arbor

397½ DYE
     double stone;-
     Harold B Dye   b-Mi.   res. Howell
     1887-1954   d- 6-7-1954(listed lot 392½)
     Marian M Dye   not listed
     1899-19-
398 SMOCK
     Lawrence W, 1893-1939   res. Ann Arbor, Mi.
                                   d-July 21, 1939 age 45, pnuemonia

     double stone;-
     Norman C, 1868-1914 (masonic) b-Marion twp. res. Handy
                                   d- 5-27-1914 age 45
     Cora E, 1868-1951 (Star)   res. Lansing
                                   d-April 9, 1951 age 82

     on monument-Smock
                                   (baby Smock) res. Ann Arbor, Mi.
                                   d- 4-20-1918 age 3 days

Section "B"   Greenwood cemetery
lot #
399   HYNE
        Charles W Hyne   no record
        1850-1914
        Josephine Hyne
        1847-   burial Feb. 13, 1924
        on monument-Hyne
400   WHITBECK
        Marcus Whitbeck   "Mark" b-Mi. res. Bancroft, Mi.
        1848-1914   d- 3-14-1914 age 65, pnuemonia
                                            (Emma Whitbeck) res. Handy
                                            d-Aug. 8, 1932 age 79
400½ LINT
        double stone;-Lint
        Glen, 1888-1943 (masonic)   res. Fowlerville
                                            d-Sept. 25, 1943 age 55
        Jessie, 1891-1963 (Star)   (Jessie Lint Reed) res. Mecosta Co.
                                            d- 10-24-1961
                                            burial 8-2--1980, moved from Coloma,Mi.
401   MINER
        Georgiann Barchus "mother"   res. Flint
        1863-1940   d-age 77, burial Oct. 7, 1940
        double stone-Miner
        William H, 1878-1972   res. Livingston Co.
                                            d- 4-4-1972 age 94
        Evelyn N, 1883-1973   "Nellie E"
                                            d- 3-29-1973 at Fowlerville
401½ COLE
        Carol V Cole   no record
        1932-1967
402   McCALL
        George   "George E Sr." b-Canada, res. Iosco
        born 1862, died 1913   d- 12-17-1913
        Emma, 1870-1956   b-Mi. res. Dearborn, Mi.
                                            d- 5-25-1956 age 88
        Robert Bruce McCall   res. Bay City, Mi.
        Michigan Mach. Mate, 1 cl. U S Navy
        March 31, 1930   d-March 31, 1930 afe 31
        Henry Leon McCall   res. Saginaw
        Michigan Pvt. 2481 Qm. Truck Co. AVN, World War II
        Oct. 20, 1897-March 29, 1966   d-age 68
        George E   "George Jr."
        born 1904, died 1910   d- 7-13-1910, accident
                                            burial 12-19-1913
        Lloid   no record
        born 1895, died 1896
        on monument-McCall
402½ MORAN
        double stone;-Moran
        John L, 1878-1943   res. White Oak twp.
                                            d-June 29, 1943 age 64
        Myra M, 1884-1979   "Myra Mae" res. Ingham Co.
                                            d- 9-18-1979 age 94
                                            burial from Williamston

Section "B"   Greenwood cemetery
lot #
403 O'GRADY
     double-double stone-O'Grady
     Bernard, 1882-1925 (masonic)   b-Mi.   res. Fenton, Mi.
                                    d-June 9, 1925 age 43
     Leroy   "Leroy C" b-Mi. res. Flint
     Mar. 24-1914-Sept. 17   d-age 6 months
     Lena N Crawford   res. Ann Arbor
     1891-1974   d- 9-13-1974 age 83
     Sherman G Crawford   res. Flint
     1882-1958   d- 12-21-1958 age 66
403½ WILLIAMS
     double stone;-Williams
     Willard J, 1899-1959   b-Mi.   res. Ingham Co.
                                    d- 1-24-1959 age 59
     Mollie M, 1910-1953   b-Mi.
                                    d- 10-6-1953
404 COLL--BENEDICT
     double stone;-Benedict
     Chester Omar, 1896-1955 (vet) b-Mi.   res. Calhoun Co.
                                    d- 10-4-1955 age 58
     Gertrude Coll, 1897-1973   b-Canada, res. Fowlerville
             (Amer. Legion Aux)   d- 4-8-1973 age 76
     double stone;-Coll
     Samuel, 1852-1940   d-Nov. 3, 1940 age 88
     Laura E, 1858-1915   b-Canada, res. Fowlerville
                                    d- 2-26-1915 age 57
404½ RIES
     triple stone;-Ries
     Wayland C, 1914-   not listed
     Vetha M, 1913-1977   res. Livingston Co.
                                    d- 9-8-1977 age 63, pnuemonia
     Ozonna Lou,   female baby, res. Fowlerville
     Apr.-July-1941   d- July 21, 1941 age 3 months
405 LUCE
     Luella B Luce   (Luella B Ling Luce)b-Mi.
     1874-1922   d-Sept. 24, 1922 age 49, res. Fowl.
     Moses Luce (FLT emblem)   res. Fowlerville
     1846-1927   d- Feb. 7, 1927 age 80
     on monument-Luce
                                    (Erwin Luce) res. Detroit
                                    d-Jan. 18, 1942 age 37
405½ DUNSMORE
     no stones   (Mary E Dunsmore)
                                    d- Nov. 1, 1946 age 23 in Lansing
406 WHITE
     Mary L White   "Mary Louisa" res. Fowlerville
     1878-1947   d-April 16, 1947 age 69
     Charles H White   b-Mi.   res. Williamston
     1864-1953   d- 12-8-1953 age 89
     Jennie B White   b-Mi.   res. Howell
     1864-1915   d- 11-12-1915 age 51
     on monument- C H White

Section "B"   Greenwood cemetery
lot #
406½ MALEITZKE
     Clare A Maleitzke   res. Howell twp.
     1913-1944   d-Nov. 4, 1944 age 31
     Helen Maleitzke Armstrong   b-Mi.   res. Fowlerville
     1916-1959   d- 10-8-1959 age 43
407 TITMUS
     Martha A Titmus "daughter"   b-Mi.   res. Fowlerville
     1910-1918
     Ezra J Titmus "father"   b-Mi.   res. Locke twp.
     1875-1953   d-July 13, 1953 age 78
     Martha E Titmus "mother"   "Martha Estella" res. Williamston
     1876-1940   d-age 65, burial July 15, 1940
     baby,   (dau. of Ezra Titmus) res. Iosco
     Mar. 6, 1900-Mar. 15, 1900   (d-Mar. 5, 1900, burial May 23, 1900)
                                  removed from Wrights cemetery

408
     double stone;-Allen (in memory of)
     Raymond A, (masonic)   "Raymond Albert" b-Mi. res. Liv. Co.
     1890-1963   d- 3-8-1963 age 72
     Ruth E, (Star)   "Ruth Emily" res. Conway twp.
     1893-1948   d- Dec. 30, 1948, bur. Jan. 2, 1949
408½
     no stones   (Wm. Ronald Porter) res. Fowl.
                                  d- 7-9-1966 premature
                                  (Lena Anne Porter) res. Fowl.
                                  d- 4-22-1967 age 1 day

409 WILKINSON
     double stone;-Wilkinson
     Marshall T, 1868-1950   res. Conway twp.
                                  d- March 14, 1950 age 82
     Blanche A, 1873-1948   "Blanch R" res. Fowlerville
                                  d- Oct. 15, 1948 age 75

409½ WILKINSON
     Heber G Wilkinson (masonic) res. Livingston Co.
     1883-1969   d- 6-9-1969 age 85
     Dorothy Wilkinson (OES)   no record
     1883-1972
410 LEWIS
     no stones   (Mrs. Frank Lewis)b-Mi. res. Fowl.
                                  d- 11-28-1918 of cancer
                                  (Frank Lewis) res. Putnam twp.
                                  d- Feb. 14, 1937 age 79
                                  (Mrs. E Malcour)b-Mi. res. Lowell, Mi.
                                  d- 1-24-1919 age 17, blood poison

410½ LEWIS
     double stone;-Lewis
     Ernest, 1890-1963   res. Fowlerville
                                  d- 12-14-1963 age 73
     Bessie, 1890-1942   res. Putnam twp.
                                  d- Sept. 27, 1942 age 52

Section "B"   Greenwood cemetery
lot #
411 TOBIN
     Mary S Tobin, wife of William   b-Fowlerville, res. Fowl.
     1867-1922   d-June 24, 1922 age 52, cancer
     Elva M Tobin, dau. of W & M S   b-Mi.   res. Fowlerville
     1905-1919   d-March 4, 1919 age 14, consumption
                                     burial July 30, removed from Howell
                                     (William Tobin) res. Fowlerville
                                     d-April 12, 1943 age 71

412 PETERSON-ALLEN
     Fae L Peterson   res. Clinton
     Feb. 26, 1900-Mar. 18, 1971   d-age 71
     Frank R Joslin   b-Mi.   res. Fowlerville
     Aug. 2, 1902-Feb. 8, 1920   d-age 18, pnuemonia
413 BATRAM--DRIVER
     double stone;-Driver
     Lyall W, 1903-1976   res. Isabella Co.
                                     d- 11-26-1976 age 73

     Olga J, 1905-1976   res. Lakeland, Florida
                                     d- 3-29-1976 age 70

     Emily A, 1860-1947   (Emily B Batram) res. Handy
                                     d-Sept. 30, 1947 age 87

     Mark W, 1856-1921   (Mark W Batram)b-England, res. Handy
                                     d- Nov. 29, 1921

     on monument-Batram
                    - - - -- - - - - -
                      end

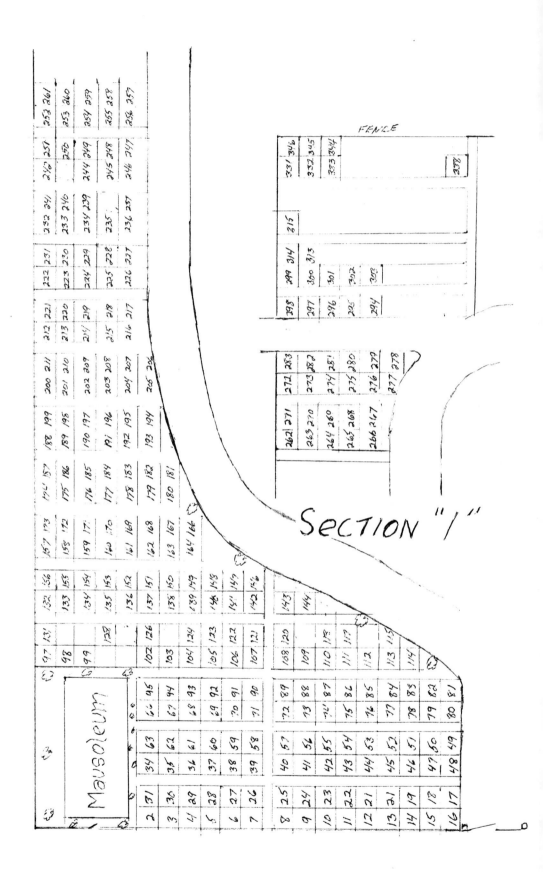

FENCE

Mausoleum

SECTION "I"

Section "One"   Greenwood cemetery
lot #
2   BAILEY--SUMNER
     Jessie Bailey "mother"   (Jessie Bailey Giltrap)
     185801925   d-age 67
     on monument-Bailey-Sumner
3   FOWLER--RISDON
     double stone-Fowler
     Wilbur, 1885-1957   "Lewis Wilber" b-Mi. res. Ingham Co.
                                   d- 6-12-1957 age 70
     Elvie L, 1886-1946   (Elvia Wooden Fowler) res. Iosco
                                   d-May 30, 1946 age 60
     Treva Risdon   not listed
     1914-
     Russell L Risdon   res. Fowlerville
     Michigan EM3, U S Navy, World War II
     July 6, 1916-July 24, 1970   d-age 54
4   KUNZELMAN--FOWLER
     J C Kunzelman   "John George" res. Williamston, Mi.
     1873-1941   d- Dec. 20, 1941 age 68
     Minnie Kunzelman   (Minnie Berryhill) res. Shepherd, Mi.
     1874-1947   d- March 24, 1947 age 72,
                                   burial May 29, 1947
     Vera M Kronk   (Vera M Fowler Kronk) res. Dewitt
     1890-1943   d- Oct. 16, 1943 age 52
     double stone;-Head
     Cyril J, 1886-1962   res. Ingham Co.
                                   d- 4-9-1962 age 75 (listed lot one-3)
     Verna F, 1890-19-   res. Ingham Co.
                                   d- 10-24, 1977 age 86
5   RICHMOND--RADINOVICH
     Melvin Richmond   "Jr." res. Howell
     Michigan Pvt. III Field Arty. Bn. World War II
     Feb. 25, 1926-April 7, 1947   d-age 22 of T B.
     Norman F Roberts   b-Mi. res. Dearborn
     Michigan Sgt. Co. A, 125 Infantry, 32 Div. World War 11
     Dec. 4, 1895-March 3, 1955   d-age 59
     Julia Radinovich   b-Mi. res. Livingston Co.
     1890-1955   d- 4-2-1955 age 64
6   DENDEL
     Lyle C Mackenzie   res. Livingston Co.
     1915-1983   d- 1-16-1983 age 67
     double stone;-Dendel
     Donald B, 1914-1955   b-Mi. res. Howell
                                   d- 12-8-1955 age 41
7   ATWELL--DAMMAN
     double stone;-Atwell
     William J, 1892-1979 (vet)   res. Livingston Co.
                                   d- 3-21-1979 age 86
     Vida M, 1895-1974   "Vida Marie" res. Livingston Co.
                                   d- 12-4-1974 age 79
     double stone;-Damman
     Henry C, 1905-1966   d- 6-14-1966 age 61
                                   burial 6-17-1966 from Houghton Lake,Mi.
     Gladys A, 1907-1957   b-Mi. res. Livingston Co.
                                   d- 8-26-1957 age 50

Section "One"   Greenwood cemetery
lot #
8   BOLTON--SNYDER
     double stone;-Bolton
     Frederick, 1884-1953   b-England, res. Howell
                                   d- 8-23-1953 age 69
     Ida Mae, 1888-1955   b-Mi. res. Howell
                                   d- 11-17-1955 age 67

     double stone;-Snyder
     Thorne W, 1892-1951   "Thorne Wilse" res. Conway twp.
                                   d-Aug. 5, 1951 age 59
     Evelyn M, 1893-1960   b-Mi. res. Livingston Co.
                                   d- 4-29-1960 age 66
9
     empty
10   MORGAN--EPLEY
     double stone;-Morgan
     Lawton F, 1883-1956   burial 2-2-1956
     Christine A E, 1885-1974   res. Berrion Co.
                                   d- 5-15-1974 age 88 (listed lot 13)

     triple stone;-Epley
     Samuel F, 1896-1973   res. Fowlerville
                                   d- 4-7-1973 age 77
     Clara J, 1897-1978   res. Ingham Co.
                                   d- 2-9-1978 age 81
     Alice I, 1920-1921   b-Mi. res. Handy
                                   d-Feb. 1, 1921 age 40 days
                                   (burial Feb. 2, 1921 Lot A-22
                                   of potters field)?

11   SOBER
     Charles W Sober (masonic)   b-Mi. res. Roosevelt Game Park, Ohio
     1918-1956   d- 5-18-1956 age 38, carbon monoxide
                                   (may have died in Scioto Co. Ohio)

     double stone;-Sober
     Sylvester, 1897-1965 (masonic) "Sy. Manuel" res. Handy
                                   d- 3-19-1965 age 67, gunshot-suicide
     Reta M, 1897-19-   not listed
12   RUTTMAN--JENSEN
     double stone-Ruttman
     John, 1876-1960 (masonic)   b-Mi. res. Livingston Co.
                                   d- 8-22-1960 age 84
     Laurens, 1893-1981 (OES)   "Laurena J" res. Handy
                                   d- 6-6-1981 age 87

     double stone;-Jensen
     Eli F, 1903-1979 "brother"   "Eli Frank" res. Riverside, Cal.
                 (masonic)   d- 6-22-1979 age 76
                                   burial 7-3-1979 ashes
     Alice Marie, 1906-   "sister"   not listed
13   KEENY--MORGAN
     Adah W Keeny, 1914-   not listed
     double stone-Morgan
     Cecil, 1893-1963   res. Brighton, Mi.
                                   d- 8-18-1963 age 70
     Alice G, 1906-1956   b-Mi. res. Brighton
                                   d- 7-15-1956 age 48 (listed lot one-138)

Section "One"   Greenwood cemetery
lot #
14   HARMON
     double stone;-Harmon
     Edgar B, 1912-1964   res. Fowlerville
                                      d- 1-8-1964 age 51

     Ruth M, 1915-   not listed
     Colleen S Harmon "daughter"   res. Lansing
     1934-1967   d- 6-23-1967 age 33
15   JONES
     Leon L Jones Jr.   "Leon Leroy" res. Ingham Co.
     1956-1971   d- 5-4-1971 ag 14, train wreck
     double stone-Jones
     Earl, 1896-1971   res. Lansing
                                      d- 2-20-1971 age 75,
                                      burial from Williamston
     Annabell, 1893-1952   b-Howell twp. res. Ingham Co.
                                      d- Feb. 10, 1952 age 59, heart

16   REYHL
     double stone;-Reyhl
     William R, 1901-1979   res. Royal Oak, Mi.
                                      d- 1-1-1979 age 77
     Irene, 1906-   not listed
     double stone;-Reyhl
     Fred C, 1882-1960   b-Mi. res. Oakland Co.
                                      d- 8-8-1960 age 77

     Ida E, 1883-1961   "Ida Eva" b-Mi. res. Wayne Co.
                                      d- 9-8-1961 age 77

17   SOUTHWELL
     double stone;-Southwell
     Harold E, 1915-1975 (vet)   res. Ingham Co.
                                      d- 11-3-1975 age 60

     Mabel V, 1925-   not listed
     Andrew Bernard Haley   res. Lansing
     Michigan cook, U S Army, World War 1
     July 28, 1892-Nov. 1, 1965   d-age 73
     Ezra A Neely "uncle"   b-Mi. res. Mason, Mi.
     1872-1957   d- 10-30-1957 age 85
18   SOUTHWELL
     double stone;-Southwell
     Howard A, 1915-1975   res. Lansing
                                      d- 9-30-1975 age 60, bur.from Lansing
     Victoria P, 1918-1973   res. Ingham Co.
                                      d- 4-11-1973 age 55, bur. from Lansing
     Howard L Southwell "son"   b-Mi. res. Ingham Co.
     1936-1956   d- 9-6-1956 age 20
19   DIETERLE
     double stone-Dieterle
     William A, 1870-1957   b-Mi. res. Livingston Co.
                                      d- 12-19-1957 age 87
     Ruby S, 1888-1975   res. Livingston Co.
                                      d- 3-26-1975 age 86

     Gust Radke   "Gustave" b-Mi. res. Genessee Co.
                                      d- 5-9-1960 age 78

Section "One"   Greenwood cemetery
lot #
20   SMALLEY
      triple stone;-Smalley
      Guy, 1882-1956   b-Mi.   res. Wayne Co.
                                      d- 9-26-1956 age 74

      Milton, 1905-1907   res. Iosco
                                      d-April 9, 1907 age 16 months, pnue.
                                      burial May 10, 1907(listed lot B-245)
      Edna, 1878-1956   res. Livingston Co.   b-Mi.
                                      d- 12-6-1956 age 77
21   HUSCHKE
      Edith F Huschke "mother"   b-Mi.   res. Handy
      1885-1954   d- 9-8-1954 age 69
      on monument-Huschke

                                      (Henry Huschke)b-Mi.   res. Ingham Co.
                                      d- 3-23-1961 age 8-

22   PARDEE
      Charles D Pardee   "Charles Duane" b-Mi. res. Liv. Co.
      1890-1955   d- 9-23-1955 age 65
                                      (Alice Pardee) res. Iosco twp.
                                      d- 10-6-1982, age 84

23   EVERS--BARTLETT
      double stone;-Evers
      Harry B, 1905-1955 (vet)   "Harry Bernard" b-Mi. res. Unadilla
                                      d- 12-24-1955 age 50
      Loretta A, 1909-1983   (Loretta A Paetsch) res. Liv. Co.
                                      d- 4-18-1983 age 73

      double stone;-Bartlett
      Robert J, 1889-1964   "Robt. James" res. Howell twp.
                                      d- 1-3-1964 age 74 of shock
      Julia P, 1890-19-   not listed
24   VAN GORDER
      Robert L Van Gorder
      Michigan Pfc. E3, Hq. Co. 1st Bg, 28th U S Inf.
      1935-1972   d- 12-28-1972 age 37
      double stone;-Van Gorder
      Krause, 1892-1963 (masonic)   "Krause E" res. Fowlerville
                                      d- 7-2-1963 age 70

      Margaret, 1897-   not listed
25   VAN GORDER
      double stone;-Van Gorder
      Glenn, 1886-19-   (masonic)   "George Glenn" res. Liv. Co.
                                      d- 12-1-1983 age 97

      Mamie, 1886-1973   "Mamie Agnes" res. Howell
                                      d- 10-11-1973 age 86
      Edna M Van Gorder   "Edna Mae" b-Mi. res. Iosco twp.
      Aug. 7, 1889-July 4, 1948   d-age 68
      Clyde Van Gorder   "Lavern Clyde" b-Mi. res. Liv. Co.
      Michigan Pfc. Co. E, 168 Infantry, World War 1, PH
      June 6, 1894-Nov. 16, 1955   d-age 61

Section "One"   Greenwood cemetery
lot #
26   WORDEN--KENT
     Wesley Worden "father"   b-Mi.   res. Livingston Co.
     1873-1955   d- 7-10-1955 age 81
     Annie Worden "mother"   res. Fowlerville
     1883-1967   d- 1-10-1967 age 83
     double stone-Kent
     Earl C, 1880-1955 (FLO emblem) "Earl Clarence" b-Mi. res. Liv. Co.
                                   d- 11-13-1955 age 75
     Maude W, 1885-1956 (IOOF)   b-Mi.   res. Livingston Co.
                                   d- 12-4-1956 age 71
27   STEARNS
     Howard L Stearns   "Howard Livingston" b-Mi. res. Liv. Co.
     1886-1955   d- 8-26-1955 age 69
                                   (Bertha May Sterns) res. Oakland Co.
                                   d- 10-14-1973 age 79
28   STRONG--SHAFER
     double stone;-Strong
     Hubert C, 1900-1955 (vet)   b-Mi.   res. Mio, Oscoda Co. Mi.
                                   d- 11-20-1955 age 54
     Lulu C, 1904-   not listed
     double stone-Shafer
     Wm. Franklin, 1887-1955   b-Mi.   res. Livingston Co.
                                   d- 6-30-1955 age 67
     Edna, 1894-   not listed
29   DRIVER
     Trudy K Driver "our daughter" b-Mi.   res. Iosco twp.
     Aug. 18, 1955-Nov. 26, 1955 age 3 months
30   ELLIOTT
     double stone;-Elliott
     Mac G, 1895-1955   "Mac George, b-Mi. res. Howell,Mi.
                                   d- Jan. 10, 1955 age 59
     Christine J, 1900-1958   b-Iosco, res. Howell
                                   d- 3-31-1958 age 57
     Kenneth N Thompson   b-Mi.   res. Livingston Co.
     1953-1958   d- 1-31-1958 age 4
31   RATHBUN
     Walter J Rathbun   "Walter John" res. St. Charles twp.
     1934-1962   d- 10-6-1962 age 28, crushed chest
     double stone;-Rathbun
     John A, 1902-19-   not listed
     Thelma G, 1904-1950   res. Ann Arbor, Mi.
                                   d-June 7, 1950 age 45
     Mary C Rathbun   not listed
     1911-
34   COLL
     double stone-Coll
     Charles H, 1893-1956 (vet)   b-Mi.   res. Howell
                                   d- 5-15-1956 age 62
     Agnes M,   not listed

Section "One"   Greenwood cemetery
lot #
35   HOTCHKISS
     Anita Lee Hotchkiss   res. Fowlerville
     1880-1945   d-March 17, 1945 age 65
36   WALLACE--CROFOOT
     Willard A Wallace   res. Handy
     1872-1944   d-Dec. 10, 1944 age 71 in Howell
     Lottie E Wallace   res. Livingston Co.
     1880-1975   d- 2-26-1975 age 93
     Coreen Marie Crofoot "our baby"   res. Fowlerville
     Nov. 29, 1967-Nov. 18, 1968   d-age 1
     on monument-Wallace
37   WHITE
     Charles Chandler White   res. Montana
     April 28, 1918-Nov. 13, 1945   d-age 27, burial Nov. 22, 1945
     on mon8ment-White

                                      (Everett C White) res. Mobile, Ala.
                                      d- 11-14-1978 age 83(stone- lot one-60)
                                      (Walter Wilson Donaldson) res. Howell
                                      d-April 2, 1947 age 68

38   DIBBLE
     double stone;-Dibble
     William J, 1869-1950   res. Handy twp.
                                      d-Sept. 20, 1950 age 81
     Harriet E, 1875-1961   b-Livingston Co. res. Liv. Co.
                                      d- 10-19-1961 age 86
     Lavern Dibble   "Lavern K" res. Livingston Co.
     1914-1969   d- 5-17-1969 age 54
     double stone;-Dibble
     William Harold, 1911-1982   res. Fowlerville
                                      d- 12-24-1983 age 71,
                                      burial 12-27-1983
     Elizabeth Grace, 1909-   not listed
                                      (baby Dibble) res. Fowlerville
                                      d-Jan. 30, 1947 stillborn
                                      (baby twins Dibble)male & female
                                      d-Dec. 26, 1944 premature
                                      (Jennie Adaith Sharpo) res. Oakland Co.
                                      d- 10-17-1968 age 71
39   LIVERANCE
     on monument-Liverance
     (no burials)
40   JOSLIN
     Edward C, "father"   res. Fowlerville
     Apr. 6, 1859-Sept. 19, 1929   d- age 70
     Eugene M,   b-Mi.   res. Ingham Co.
     Mar. 21, 1887-Nov. 11, 1957   d-age 70
     Edward E,   res. Fowlerville
     Dec. 7, 1910-Jan. 8, 1942   d-age 30
     on monument-Joslin

Section "one"   Greenwood cemetery
lot #
41 WALLACE
    Lottie B, 1904-1947 (Star)   no record
    Colin K, 1903-1973 (masonic)   "Colin Kemp" res. Handy
                                    d- 12-18-1973 age 69
    double stone-Denton
    Charles A, 1925-   (masonic) not listed
    Colleen B, 1928-1966 (Star)   "Colleen Bernice" res. Howell
                                    d- 10-22-1966 age 37,fractured skull
    baby Wallace   res. Handy twp.
    Aug. 30, 1943   (d-Aug. 12, 1943 stillborn)
                                    burial Aug. 12, 1943
    on monument-Wallace
                                    (Ernest Hayward)b-Mi. res. Liv. Co.
                                    d- 12-16-1957 age 72
42 UTTER-HILLMAN
    double stone;-Utter
    Frank C, 1934-   not listed
    Anna B, 1937-   not listed
    double stone-Hillman
    Frederick, 1904-1966   "Fred. C" res. Fowlerville
                                    d- 11-29-1966 age 62, heart trouble
    Inez B, 1907-   not listed
43 CALKINS--BUCKLEY
    double stone;-Calkins
    Orvill A, 1866-1950   "Orville" res. Palm Beach
                                    d-Dec. 24, 1950 age 84
    Alice M, 1867-1947   no record
    double stone;-Buckley
    Merrell, 1909-   not listed
    Katherine, 1907-   not listed
44 RUDNICKI
    Kate Ann Rudnicki   res. Livingston Co.
    Nov. 7, 1959   d- stillborn
    Jane Lena Rudnicki   res. Howell
    January 26, 1949   d-stillborn
    double stone;-Rudnicki
    Andrew, 1908-1954 (masonic)   b-Mi.   res. Fowlerville
                                    d- 10-4-1954 age 45, cancer
    Lena I, 1910-19-   (Star)   not listed
45 ELLIOTT
    double stone;-Elliott
    Earl, 1888-1968 (masonic)   burial 6-10-1968
    Bessie, 1883-1980   Bur. 4-12-1980 age 97 from Livonia
    Beverly E Lane   (Beverly Elaine Murphy)b-Mi.
    1918-1954   d-Nov. 25, 1954 age 36, fractured skull
    dear mother of Richard, Terry and Sharon Haist
46 ALLEN
    Burr D Allen "fatner"   res. Fowlerville
    1888-1951   d-Sept. 13, 1951 age 63
    Mabel M Allen "mother"   res. Howell
    1884-1949   d-May 18, 1949 age 65
    on monument-Allen

Section "one"   Greenwood cemetery
lot #
47   FERGUSON
     Bernice Ferguson   res. Howell
     1903-1949   d-Aug. 2, 1949 age 44
48   SMITH--DEWAR
     double stone;-Dewar
     William, 1883-1948   "Wm. Wylie" b-Scotland, res. Fowl.
                                   d-Dec. 21, 1948 age 65
     Mary, 1888-1951   b-Scotland, res. Springport, Mi.
                                   d-Nov. 27, 1951 age 62
     double stone;-Smith
     Flex B, 1891-1948 (vet)   d-Dec. 14, 1948 age 57, accident
     Florence A, 1890-1967   "Florence Agnes" res. Mason, Mi.
                                   d- 6-17-1967 age 76
     Morris E Sherwood (masonic)   b-Mi.   res. Ingham Co.
     1882-1958   d- 8-30-1958 age 76
49   VEITH--McMANUS
     triple stone;-
     Floyd H McManus   b-Mi.   res. Lansing
     July 21, 1884-Feb. 27, 1955   d-age 70
     Retta J Emich   (Retta J Emigh)b-Mi. res. Lansing
     Mar. 1, 1876-Jan. 23, 1959   d-age 82
     Ethel M Simpkins   no record
     Jan. 16, 1887
     double stone;-Veith
     William B, 1860-1952   b-Germany
                                   d- 8-7-1952 age 92
     Hattie A, 1881-1967   "Hattie Amalia" res. Lansing
                                   d- 2-8-1967 age 86, bur. from Lansing
50   SIMPSON
     double stone;-Simpson
     John, 1897-1981   res. Washtenaw Co.
                                   d- 10-31-1981 age 84
     Marie, 1897-1962   b-Wayne, res. Wayne city, Mi.
                                   d- 1-8-1962 age 64
51   RICH
     Bernard C Rich (masonic)   b-Mi.   res. Livingston Co.
     1886-1960   d- 2-13-1960 age 73
     Jessie S Rich   res. Fowlerville
     1882-1964   d- 5-8-1964 age 82
     Robert E Rich   b-Livingston Co. Res. Liv. Co.
     1942-1961   d- 12-22-1961 age 19, auto accident
     double stone;-Rich
     Elden B, 1909-1982   res. Hastings, Mi.
                                   burial 11-24-1982 age 72 ashes
                                   bur. from Hastings
     Leona L, 1914-   not listed
52   ELLIOTT--ARMSTRONG
     double stone;-Elliott
     Ova V, 1884-1948 (masonic)   "Ova Vern" res. Handy
                                   d-Feb. 27, 1948 age 63
     Anna M, 1885-1980 (Star)   "Anna Mae"
                                   Burial 2-27-1980 age 94

Section "One"   Greenwood cemetery
lot #
52 continued
      double stone;-Armstrong
      Glenn O, 1908-1967 (masonic)   "Glenn Opelt" res. Fowl.
                                     d- 4-14-1967 age 58
      Mildred I, 1913-   not listed
      Donna Sue Armstrong, dau. of Dale & Jewel res. Detroit
      May 8, 1967-May 9, 1967   d-age 1 day, bur. 5-15-1967
53   STEVENS--NELSON
      double stone;-Stevens
      Harvey M, 1892-1976   res. Livingston Co.
                                   d- 11-18-1976 age 84
      Edith M, 1893-1960   b-Mi. res. Livingston Co.
                                   d- 5-23-1960 age 67, operation

      double stone;-Nelson
      John J, 1901-19-   not listed
      Helen M, 1912-19-   not listed
54   CARSON-ALLEN
      Anna L, 1891-1957   (Anna L Allen)b-Mi. res. Liv. Co.
                                   d- 12-10-1957 age 66
      Ray W, 1891-1956   (Ray W Allen)b-Mi. res. Lansing
                                   d- 8-4-1956 age 64
55   ALLEN
      Leona M, 1910-1981   (Leona May Ferguson) res. San Antonia
                                   d- 2-20-1981 age 70
      Clesson S, 1908-1960 (masonic) "Clesson Silas" b-Mi. res. Liv. Co.
                                   d- 2-2-1960 age 51
      Minnie E, 1884-1957   b-Mi. res. Livingston Co.
                                   d- 7-16-1957 age 72
      Coye T, 1881-1956   b-Mi. res. Livingston Co.
                                   d- 7-18-1956 age 75
      on monument;-Allen
56
      empty
57   LUCAS--WENNIER
      double stone;-Lucas
      Glenn D, 1892-1967 (masonic) res. Fowlerville
                                   d- 12-10-1967 age 75
      Alice R, 1902-1979   res. Livingston Co.
                                   d- 6-11-1979 age 77
      John Wennier   b-Mi. res. Howell
      1886-1955   d- 12-15-1955 age 69
      Catherine E Coree Crofoot Wennier   res. Howell twp.
      1889-1963   d- 10-11-1963 age 74
58   LIVERANCE
      Lorrain C, "father" (masonic) res. Livingston Co.
      1907-1977   d- 1-19-1977 age 69
      Irene L, "mother" (OES)   not listed
      1916-
      Pearl G, "mother"   res. Fowlerville
      1887-1966   d- 3-12-1966 age 79
      Lloyd D, "father" (masonic) res. Livingston Co.
      1884-1970   d- 12-20-1970 age 86
      on monument-Liverance

Section "One"   Greenwood cemetery
lot #
59   WRIGHT
     Gary Stuart Wright   res. Ingham Co.
     May 13-18, 1972   burial 5-20-1972
60   WHITE
     double stone;-White
     Everett C,   res. Mobile, alabama
     Sept. 25, 1895-Nov. 14, 1978 d-age 83
     Bertha F,   "Bertha Frances" res. Lansing
     Nov. 11, 1897-Nov. 12, 1970 d- age 73
     on monument-White
61   CROFOOT
     Marvin Wesley Crofoot, son of A B & Iva   no record
     1927-1941
     Iva Irene Crofoot   res. Ingham Co.
     1900-1969   d- 3-13-1969 age 68
     Arthur Budd Crofoot   res. Handy
     Michigan Pvt. Co. I, 340 Inf. 85 Div. World War 1
     May 7, 1894-Nov. 30, 1965
     John A Crofoot
     Michigan staff Sgt. 720 AAF Bomb Sq. World War II
     June 17, 1923-Sept. 4, 1944   burial 3-18-1949 from overseas
     on monument-Crofoot
62   CROFOOT
     double stone;-Crofoot
     Robert,   not listed
     Virginia,   res. Livingston Co.
     Feb. 26, 1976   d-age 58, burial 2-28-1976
63   MACUT
     Patricia Kay Macut "our baby" b-Mi.   res. Lansing
     Mar. 25, 1953-July 30   d-age 4 months(listed lot 34)
66   WEBB
     double stone:-Webb
     Otis Watts, 1876-1954   b-Mi.   res. California
                                  d- Nov. 20, 1954 age 78

     Georgia, 1879-1965   res. California
                                  d- 5-19-1965
67   OLIVER
     Roy H Oliver "father"   res. Oakland Co.
     1894-1976   d- 12-23-1976 age 82
     Mary I Oliver "mother"   not listed
     1892-19-
     Robert J Oliver "son" (vet) res. Lansing
     1921-1946   d-March 21, 1946 age 24
     Ivan E Oliver   res. Howell
     1915-1970   d- 5-22-1970 age 55
     on monument-Oliver
68   SHARPE
     double stone;-Sharpe
     William, 1894-1970 (masonic) res. Clarkston, Mi.
                                  d- 1-7-1970 age 75
     Jennie A, 1896-1968   no record

{243}

Section "One"   Greenwood cemetery
lot #
69   HOAG
     Charles Hoag
     Michigan Pfc 165 Inf. 27 Div. World War ll
     Nov. 18, 1921-May 17, 1945   burial 3-18-1949 from overseas
                                     (Arvin Nelson Hoag) res. Iosco twp.
                                     d- 3-11-1973 age 90
                                     (Juanita Sue Adams)
                                     d- 2-20-1941 stillborn
                                     bur. 9-26-1973 from Evergreen cem.
                                     (Irene M Adams) res. Ingham Co.
                                     d- 10-21-1972 age 72, pnuemonia

70   CHENEY
     Clarissa F Pond   "Clarissa Fanny" res. Liv. Co.
                                     d- 8-31-1962 age 88
     Pfc. Ronald G Cheney "in memory of"   d-age 20
     killed in France, Dec. 11, 1944 while serving his country
                                     bur. 1-10-1949, returned by army
     double stone;-Cheney
     Glenn D, 1891-1974   res. Howell
                                     d- 4-27-1974 age 82

     Chloe B, 1897-1961   "Chloe Belle" b-Mi. res. Liv. Co.
                                     d- 1-4-1961 age 63

71   KUEHN
     William C, "father"
     1870-1943   burial 3-13-1943
     Mary E, "mother"   res. Fowlerville
     1881-1963   d- 6-17-1963 age 82
     on monument-Kuehn

72   FOSTER
     Leon G H, 1905-1970   res. Livingston Co.
                                     d- 9-17-1970 age 64

     Myra M, 1894-1970   res. Livingston Co.
                                     d- 1-14-1970 age 75

     Mary M Foster "mother"   res. Iosco twp.
     1873-1947   d-Feb. 4, 1947 age 73
     Ira E Foster "father"   res. Iosco
     1869-1948   d-Jan. 20, 1948 age 78

73   LIDDICOATT
     double stone;-Liddicoatt
     Roger C,   (masonic   res. Howell
     Oct. 12, 1894-Dec. 12, 1978   d-age 84
     Eunice E,   (OES)   res. Fowlerville
     Nov. 3, 1902-Oct. 13, 1968   (d-10-17-1968 age 65)

74   BECKER
     double stone-Becker
     Roy I, 1888-1970 "father"   "Roy L" res. Livingston Co.
                                     d- 11-22-1970 age 82

     Lessie M, 1892-1979 "mother"   res. Livingston Co.
                                     d- 10-10-1979 age 87

Section "One"   Greenwood cemetery
lot #
75   COPELAND
      Clifford H, 1875-1963   res. Conway twp.
                                     d- 1-28-1963 age 87
      Mary, 1875-1948   b-Conway twp. res. Fowlerville
                                     d-June 22, 1948 age 72
      double stone;-Copeland
      Claude L, 1903   not listed
      Lucille, 1905-   not listed
      on monument-Copeland
76   PALMER
      Pvt. Ernest J Palmer
      killed in France, Jan. 23, 1945
      1920-1945   bur. 12-30-1948, returned by army
      double stone;-Palmer
      Fred, 1884-1966   res. Fowlerville
                                     d- 3-21-1966 age 81
      Laura, 1890-1974   res. Okemos, Mi.
                                     d- 6-8-1974 age 83
77   PALMER
      empty
78   HENDRYX
      double stone;-Hendryx
      Paul L, 1904-1946   res. Conway twp.
                                     d-Dec. 11, 1946 age 42
      Myrtle C, 1906-19-   not listed
79   SMOCK--HEINRICH
      Dale L Smock   not listed
      1922-
      Vivian L Smock   res. Fowlerville
      1913-1964   d- 12-14-1964 age 52
      Velma, 1913-1971   (Velma Ione Heinrich) res. Liv. Co.
                                     d- 10-23-1971 age 58
      Harold, 1910-1972   (Harold Heinrich) res. Liv. Co.
                                     d- 7-27-1972 age 62, plane crash
                                     (body brought from Whitehorse, Yukon)
      Linda Mae, 1942-1950   (Linda Mae Heinrich) res. Howell
                                     d-Aug. 22, 1950 age 7, accident
      on monument-Heinrich
80   DeWATERS
      Richard K DeWaters (FFA)   "Richard Keith" b-Mi. res. Fowl.
                                     d- 6-9-1955 age 17, shock
      Sophia A Hall   res. Orlando, Florida
      1866-1950   d-April 27, 1950 age 84
      David R DeWaters (masonic)   res. Fowlerville
      1908-1949   d-Nov. 16, 1949 age 41, gun shot
81   DeWATERS
      empty
82   BURNS
      double stone-Burns
      Horace G, ;891-1969   res. Livingston Co.
                                     d- 12-20-1969 age 78
      L Ruth, 1890-1953   "Laura Ruth" b-Mi. res. Iosco.
                                     d- 4-19-1953 age 62, tumor

Section "One"   Greenwood cemetery
lot #
83   THOMAS
      Lemuel C, "father"   b-Mi.   res. Handy
      1874-1958   d- 8-24-1958 age 84
      May M, "mother"   b-Mi.   res. Fowlerville
      1876-1952   d- 10-1-1952 age 76
      Russell F, 1898-1972   res. Livingston Co.
                                      d- 11-30-1972 age 74

      Ivah C, 1903-19-   not listed
      on monument- Thomas
84   RICHMOND
      empty
85   MEYER
      Merrie
      William
      on monument-Meyer
          William L, 1882-1951(masonic)   res. Handy
                                      d- Aug. 25, 1951 age 69

          Merrie E, 18-   19-   no record
86   COPELAND
      double stone;-Copeland
      F Harold, 1904-1982   res. Livingston Co.
                                      d- 6-23-1982 age 77

      Cleo M, 1905-   not listed
87   ROCHE
      double stone;-Roche
      George,   "Geo. G" res. Livingston Co.
      July 6, 1890-May 6, 1963   d-age 72
      Ella,   "Ella J" res. Livingston Co.
      June 23, 1894-Feb. 4, 1973   d- age 78
      James W Roche   b-Pinckney, res. Conway twp.
      Aug. 23, 1916-Jan. 15, 1952   d-age 35, carbon monoxide
                                      (Ida H Anderson) res. Fowl.
                                      d- 8-10-1967 age 85

88   McGALLIARD
      Clyde T McGalliard Jr.   res. Livingston Co.
      Apr. 26, 1929-Dec. 21, 1976   d-age 47, pnuemonia
      Clyde T McGalliard Sr.   res. Howell
      Aug. 29, 1896-Aug. 15, 1973   d- age 76
      Grace L Cole   "Grace Laverne" res. Detroit
      July 15, 1906-Feb. 3, 1952   d-age 45, peritonitis
89   ROBERTS-CRAMER
      Joseph D Roberts   res. Roscommon, Mi.
      1873-1956   d- 10-25-1956 age 83
      Tina I Roberts   "Tina Irene" b-Mi. res. Liv. Co.
                                      d- 11-2-1962 age 85

      double stone-Cramer
      Jester M, 1895-1952 (masonic)   b-Iosco, res. Webberville
                                      d-March 6, 1952 age 57, heart
      Gladys M, 1898-1969   res. Howell twp.
                                      d- 7-7-1969 age 70

Section "One"   Greenwood cemetery
lot #
90   CANFIELD
     Howard A, 1902-19-   not listed
     Hazel M, 1904-1948   "Hazel May" res. Handy
                                    d-Aug. 24, 1948 age 44

     on monument-Canfield
91   BLAIR
     double stone;-Blair
     Guy S, 1884-1971   res. Livingston Co.
                                    d- 5-15-1971 age 86
     Edna G, 1888-1953   res. Conway
                                    d- 3-12-1954 age 65, bur. 5-15-1954

92   WESTMORELAND--DILLINGHAM
     George K Westmoreland "son"   no record
     1946-1968
     double stone;-Dillingham
     Roy C, 1886-1971   res. Howell
                                    d- 2-11-1971 age 84
     Lulo A, 1888-1966   res. Howell
                                    d- 11-29-1966 age 81

93   HOWARD--BARTIG
     double stone;-Howard
     Ernest B, 1880-1952   b-Mi.   res. Howell twp.
                                    d- 8-11-1952 age 71
     Agnes B, 1895-1977   (Agnes B Howard DeAngelo)res. Liv. Co.
                                    d- 6-7-1977 age 82
     double stone;-Bartig
     Charles A, 1876-1968 "father" res. Fowlerville
                                    d- 4-3, 1968 age 93
                                    burial 3-5-1968
     Luella J, 1882-1960 "mother"   "Luella Jane" b-Mi. res. Oakland Co.
                                    d- 1-20-1960 age 77

94   GLOVER--CARSON
     double stone;-Glover
     Walter Z, 1883-1965 (vet)   "Walter S" res. Fowlerville
                                    d- 10-14-1965 age 84
     Maude A, 1889-1980   (Maud Glover Bessert)
                                    burial 3-19-1980
     double stone;OCarson
     Percy E, 1881-1964   (Percy Monroe Carson) res. Fowl.
                                    d- 11-28-1964 age 83
     Jessie A, 1880-1954   no record
95
     empty
97   COOPER--HASKELL
     Carolyn Furbush
     1920-   not listed
     Wallace W Cooper   b-Mi.   res. Lenewee city, Mi.
     1889-1960   d- 5-5-1960 age 70
     Cathryn Cooper   not listed
     1900-19-

                                    (Mary Cooper Haskell) res. Wayne
                                    d- 11-30-1977 age 92

Section "One"   Greenwood cemetery
lot #
98   GRANGROSSO-FOSTER
     Alma Grangrosso St. Charles   res. Livingston Co.
     Oct. 4, 1897-May 26, 1977   d-age 79
     Cecil Bruno Grangrosso (vet)   res. Fowlerville
     Oct. 22, 1914-Sept. 9, 1968   burial 9-13-1968 age 53
     Guiseppe Grangrosso   (Guiseppe Giangrosso)
     Michigan Cpl. Co. A, 2 development Bn. World War 1
     April 15, 1887-Dec. 18, 1963   d-age 76
     Richard A Foster   "Richard Alfred" res. Washtenaw Co.
     Michigan Pvt. Co. A, 302 Bn. Tank Corps, World War 1
     Nov. 23, 1893-Jan. 16, 1962   d-age 69
99   DeTROYER-BOWERS-HUBBARD
     Laurence R DeTroyer Sr.   "Laurence Robert"
     1910-1964   d- 2-22-1964 age 54, auto accident
                                      (Ernest Henry Swarthwood)
                                      burial 11-22-1968
                                      (Martha J Hubbard) res. Wash. Co.
                                      d- 3-27-1972 age 55, heart failure
                                      (Finley Allen Hubbard) res. Fowl.
                                      d- 11-9-1968 age 64

102 VAN GILDER
     Frederick O, 1858-1949   "Fred Orley" res. Ingham Co.
                                      d-July 13, 1949 age 90

     Catherine E, 1864-1937   res. Mason, Mi.
                                      d-July 8, 1937 age 73

     Grace Hanson   res. Grand Rapids
     1894-1943   d- Dec. 28, 1943 age 49
     Hugh Jr. 1922-1977   (Hugh Van Gilder) res. Liv. Co.
                                      d- 12-3-1977 age 55

     on monument-Van Gilder
103 ECKHART
     George S, 1878-1947 "father"   res. Handy
                                      d-Dec. 13, 1947 age 69

     Ora M, 1878-1958 "mother"   "Ora Mae" b-Mi. res. Liv. Co.
                                      d- 6-21-1958 age 79

     Edgar W, 1908-1971   res. Livingston Co.
                                      d- 5-11-1971 age 63

     Ella M, 1913-19-   not listed
     on monument-Eckhart
104 DILLINGHAM
     double stone;-Dillingham
     Fred H, 1880-1968 (FLT emblem) res. Fowlerville
                                      d- 6-30-1968 age 88

     Leona A, 1885-1943   "Leona Agnus" res. Fowl.
                                      d-June 1, 1943 age 58

     S/Sgt Frederick H Dillingham
     1919-1943   d-Sept. 14, 1943 age 24
     in a glider accident at SPAAF, Lubbock, Texas
     September 15, 1943 while in the service of his country
     on monument-Dillingham

Section "One"   Greenwood cemetery
lot #
105 FOWLER
     double stone;-Fowler
     Frank, 1866-1947   "Franklin" res. Fowlerville
                                   d- Aug. 17, 1947 age 81
          Effie, 1887-1940   b-Croswell. res.Howell twp.
                                   d-Nov. 25, 1940 age 53, cancer
106 KNOOP--FOWLER
     Guy E Knoop   res. Livingston Co.
     1896-1981   d- 10-26-1981 age 85
     Ruth F Knoop   (Ruth Fowler Knoop) res. Wash. Co.
     1891-19-   d- 9-15-1983 age 92
     Ina Fowler   no record
     1866-1954
     William Fowler   res. Howell twp.
     1864-1936   d-Sept. 9, 1936 age 72
     on monument-Fowler-Knoop (lot 106-107)
107 BOICE-FOWLER-KNOOP
     double stone-Boice
     William, 1867-1937   "Wm. H" res. Fowlerville
     Prudence   res. Lansing
     1873-1948   d-Aug. 21, 1948 age 74
     Robert M Gates (vet)   "Robert Marshall" b-Guilford, N. C.
     1917-1958   d- 12-21-1958 age 41,
                                   res. Greensboro, N. C.
108 DUNCAN
     James Duncan   res. Conway
     1854-1943   d-Oct. 26, 1943 age 88
     Eunice M Duncan,"ever faithful and true"   res. Conway
     June 22, 1899-Jan. 17, 1933   d-age 33
     Emma C Duncan   b-Mi.   res. Washtenaw Co.
     1868-1957   d- 2-14-1957 age 88
     on monument-Duncan
109 KEENMON
     Frank, "father"   res. Howell, Mi.
     1872-1966   d- 5-3--1966 age 93
     May Louise, "mother"   res. Howell twp.
     1879-1942   d-March 15, 1942 age 62
     Arthur A, "son"   res. Livingston Co.
     1907-1969   d- 2-7-1969 age 61
     Ruby O, wife of Arthur   "Ruby Octavia
     1913-1977   d- 3-1-1977 age 63, bur. from Howell
     on monument-Keenmon
110 GALLUP
     double stone;-Gallup
     Merrilla, 1872-1944   res. Fowlerville
     1872-1944   d-April 14, 1944 age 70
     Edith, 1880-1968   "Edith D" res. Milford twp.
                                   d- 2-11-1968 age 87

Section "One"   Greenwood cemetery
lot #
111 STOW
     Clyde S, 1889-1974   res. Blue Island, Illinois
                                 d-1-3-1974 age 84, bur. from Chicago
     Edith, 1880-1968   no record
                                 (Florence Stow) res. Blue Island, Ill.
                                 d- 5-18-1974 age 84, bur. from there

112 HOLMES
     Cpl. Ralph A Holmes
     1916-1944   burial July 4, 1948 from Europe
     Co. M, 313 Inf. -died in France
     double stone-Holmes
     Orra H, 1886-1947   res. Howell (listed lot One-17)
                                 d-March 18, 1947 age 60
     Mae E, 1891-1969   "Mae Edna" res. Livingston Co.
                                 d- 11-3-1969 age 78

113 MUNSELL
     "our baby daughter"   no record
     Nov. 7, 1946
114 DEVINE--PASKEURIC
     double stone;-Devine
     Fred J, 1911-1975   "Fred John" res. Livingston Co.
                                 d- 5-10-1975 age 63

     Edna R, 1918-   not listed
     double stone;-Paskeuric
     Francis J, 1907-1973   "Francis Joseph" res. Livingston Co.
                                 d- 7-4-1973 age 60 in Kent Co.

     Winifred M, 1911-   not listed
115 KELLEY
     double stone;-Kelley
     William H, "husband"   res. Ingham Co.
     1891-1963   d- 5-10-1963 age 71
     Ruth L, "wife"   b-Mi.   res. Shiawassee Co.
     1896-1958   d- 2-7-1958 age 61
116
     empty
117 HOLMES
     triple stone;-Holmes
     Warren S, 1885-1950   res. Arizona
                                 d-March 15, 1950 age 64
     Genevieve B, 1908-1949   res. Handy
                                 d-Sept. 1, 1946 age 70
118 STOWE--CAREY
     double stone;-Stowe
     Merle Bliss, 1884-1951 (masonic)   res. Iosco twp.
                                 d-March 2, 1951 age 66
     Louise Mae, 1883-1970 (Star)   (Louisa Mae Rollins) res. Muskegon Co.
                                 d- 9-15-1970 age 87
     double stone;-Carey
     Frank L, 1874-1949   res. Fowlerville
                                 d-Jan. 24, 1949 age 74
     Lyda A, 1886-1975   res. Livingston Co.
                                 d- 2-5-1975 age 88

Section "One"   Greenwood cemetery
lot #
119
      empty
120   DUNCAN
      double stone;-Duncan
      Willis J, 1881-1959   b-Mi.   res. Liv. Co.
                                     d- 11-28-1959 age 78
      Jessie A, 1882-1965   res. Fowlerville
                                     d- 4-29-1965 age 82

      on monument-Duncan

                                     (Diane K Duncan) res. Durand, Mi.
                                     d-Jan. 5, 1946 age 3 days

121   NEILSON--KOCH
      double stone;-Neilson
      Helmar, 1882-1969   res. Wayne
                                     d- 2-22-1969 age 87
      Minnie H, 1875-1951   b-Greenville, res. Fowl.
                                     d-Feb. 15, 1951 age 75
      double stone;-Koch
      John F, 1907-1952   res. Livingston Co.
                                     d-Jan. 21, 1952 age 44, fractured skull
      Lucie E, 1916-   not listed
122   TABER--FORD
      double stone;-Taber
      Eathel H, 1883-1951   res. Howell twp.
                                     d-Jan. 17, 1951 age 67, auto accident
      Tressa M, 1887-1963   res. Fowlerville
                                     d- 4-10-1963 age 80
      Buell D Ford   no record
      1903-1960
123   FORD--LAWSON
      Bernice D Ford   "Bernice Lawrence" b-St. Ignace
      1905-1950   d-Dec. 13, 1950 age 45, res. Detroit
      Richard B Ford   b-Mi.   res. Howell
      1937-1953   d- 11-16-1953 age 16, pnuemonia
      Lenore E Lathrop   res. Dade
      1904-1969   d- 4-21-1969 age 65
      Bertha Lawson   no record
      1883-1966
      Edwin J Lawson   b-Mi.   res. Howell
      1875-1954   d- 9-15-1954 age 79
124   BELL--REYNOLDS
      Louise M Bell   res. Detroit
      1879-1950   d-Aug. 28, 1950 age 70
      Bert J Bell   "Herbert" b-Mi. res. Handy
      1878-1959   d- 5-30-1959 age 81
      Ileta Reynolds   not listed
      1904-19-
      Raymond R Reynolds
      Michigan Tec. 4, 167 Ord. Tire Rep. Co. World War 11
      April 4, 1907-July 13, 1965   d-age 58, carbon monoxide
                                     burial from Detroit
125
      empty

{251}

Section "One"   greenwood cemetery
lot #
126 VAN GILDER
     Hugh, 1887-1951 (vet)   b-Ingham Co. res. Lansing
                                      d-Feb. 16, 1951 age 63
     Clara R, 1890-1970   res. Livingston Co.
                                      d- 1-25-1970 age 79
     on monument-Van Gilder
127
     empty
128 HART
     double stone-Hart
     George R, 1903-1971   res. Genoa twp.
                                      d- 1--13-1971 age 68
     NaVorna M, 1902-19-   not listed
     Edward L Stacy "son"   res. Livingston Co.
     1949-1976   d- 8-13-1976 age 26
129-130
     empty
131 WORTHINGTON
     double stone-Worthington
     Gordon L, 1915-1979   res. Livingston Co.
                                      d- 2-2-1979 age 63
     Hazel L, 1927-   not listed
(in love and memories "husband and father" rest in peace)
132 HAAS
     triple stone;-Haas
     Glen O, 1899-1978   res. Pt. Orange, Florida
                                      d- 4-29-1978
                                      burial 5-19-78 ashes from Florida
     Flossie E, 1903-1956   (Flossie E Haas Toutnier)b-Mi.
                                      d- 3-20-1956 age 52
                                      res. Highland Park, Mi.
     Earl Glen, 1932   b-Mi.   res. Livonia city, Mi.
                                      d- 8-2-1932 age 26 days, pnue.
                                      bur. at Detroit, trans. 4-4-1956
     John O Worthington"father"   "John Oscar" res. Kalamazoo
     1885-1969   d- 9-6-1969 age 84
     Wanetta DeLine "mother   "Wanetta M" b-Mi. res. Liv. Co.
     1889-1957   d- 11-26-1957 age 68
133 RUGGLES
     Archie E, "father" (masonic)   "Archie Edward" res. Fowl.
     1882-1966   d- 6-10-1966 age 83
     Hannah S, "mother"   b-Mi.   res. Handy
     1885-1956   d- 6-12-1956 age 70
     K Donald, "son"   not listed
     1913-
     on monument-Ruggles
134 KUNDE
     double stone;-Kunde
     Carl A, 1892-1958 (vet)   "Carl August" b-Mi.   res. Handy
                                      d- 7-18-1958 age 65
     Minnie E, 1896-1978   burial 2-8-1978

Section "One"   Greenwood cemetery
lot #
135 BETTERLY
     double stone;-Betterly
     Lester R, 1869-1947   res. Fowlerville
                                  d-Feb. 26, 1947 age 77

     Linnie I, 1867-1961   b-Liv. Co. res. Liv. Co.
                                  d- 12-13-1961 age 94

136
     Merrit K Cook   b-Mi.   res. Auburn Heights
     Michigan Pvt. 317 Tech. Sch. Sq. AAF, World War 11
     March 8, 1902-Aug. 9, 1960   d-age 58
137 DONALDSON
     double stone;-Donaldson
     Walter W, 1879-1947   no record
     Nellie L, 1885-1967   res. Fowlerville
                                  d- 9-28-1967 age 82

138 LORD--POLMAN
     Emma Lord Polman, "wife"   "Emma J" res. Columbus, Ohio
     1882-1951   d- May 23, 1931 age 46
                                  burial 5-27-1931

     William Lord   b-Mi.   res. Fowlerville
     1886-1953   d- 10-25-1953 age 68
     Charley H Lord   res. Onaway, Mi.
     1872-1946   d-April 5, 1946 age 73
139 BELL
     Clyde Bell   res. Detroit
     1882-1942   d-Jan. 2, 1942 age 59
     Amelia Bell   res. Ann Arbor, Mi.
     1884-1931   d-Aug. 15, 1931 age 46
     Philip A Bell   "Phillip C" res. Handy
     1880-1934   d-Sept. 3, 1934 age 54, cancer
     Eliza A Bell   res. Handy
     1855-1941   d-Feb. 24, 1941 age 86
     John C Bell   res. Handy
     1850-1931   d-Sept. 14, 1931 age 81
140 SIMPSON
     Chas. W Simpson "father"   res. Williamston
     1884-1929   d-Jan. 29, 1929 age 45, pnuemonia
141 MARLING
     Lucius H, 1859-1931   (Lucius H Marling) res. Ypsilanti
                                  d-Dec. 18, 1931 age 72
     Mary L, 1863-1928   (Mary L Marling) res. Jackson
                                  d-March 19, 1928 age 63

142 DEY
     Henry N, 1858-1929   res. Fowlerville
                                  d-Oct. 23, 1929 age 71
     Clementina, 1858-1926   b-Mi.   res. Detroit
                                  d-July 9, 1926 age 68

     on monument-Dey

Section "One"   Greenwood cemetery
lot #
143 LANE--WRIGHT
     Kathleen Loop Lane   no record
     Emmett Dinturff Lane (vet)   res. Wayne
     1895-1975   d- 10-11-1975 age 80
     on monument-Lane
144 GLENN--SMYTH
     Mirtie Glenn Gardner   b-Mi.   res. Ypsilanti, Mi.
     1864-1958   d- 9-4-1958 age 81
     Mable E Smyth   no record
     1897-1969
     Dorothy V Glenn   not listed
     1920-
     Sammie L Glenn   res. Howell
     1909-1952   d- 11-8-1952 age 43, plane crash
     Freda J Smyth   not listed
     1919-
     William E Smyth   b-Mi.   res. Howell
     1915-1952   d- 11-8-1952 age 37, plane crash
     on monument-Smyth
146 BOYCE-EGLESTON-HAYWARD
     Earnest Hayward
     1885-1957   burial 12-12-1957
     Stella F Robertson   res. Ingham Co.
     1881-1972   d- 3-30-1972 age 90
     Olin W Hayward   res. Ingham Co.
     1916-1980   d- 6-14-1980 age 63
     Harry O Egleston
     1882-1964   d- 7-29-1964 age 82
                                     burial 8-1-1964 from Livonia
     Louis E Boyce   b-Mi.   res. Fowlerville
     Michigan Pfc. 1299 Mil. Police Co. AVN, Waorld War 11 BSM
     Jan. 22, 1918-April 14, 1956   d-age 38
                                     (Lottie B Wallace)b-Mi. res. Liv. Co.
                                     d- 12-17-1957 age 53
                                     (baby girl, Smyth) res. Liv. Co.
                                     d- 3-1-1959 age 2 hours, premature
                                     (Cynthis Hayward) res. Ingham Co.
                                     d- 12-23-1979 stillborn
                                     buried at head of Stella Robertson)
147 MUNSELL
     double stone;-Munsell
     Floyd W, 1882-1967   res. Fowlerville
                                     d- 1-24-1967 age 85
     Ida E, 1876-1945   res. Iosco twp.
                                     d-June 28, 1945 age 68
148 BUNN
     Clayton W, 1886-1953   res. Fowlerville
                                     d- 8-31-1953 age 66
     Isabel E Bunn   res. Florida
     1889-1977   d- 11-4-1977
     Kenneth C, 1914-1933   d-May 11, 1933 age 20, accident
     on monument-Bunn

Section "One"   Greenwood cemetery
lot #
149 DALIUS--ALLEN
     double stone;-Dalius
     Wilson S, 1876-1955 (FLT emblem)   b-Mi. res. Liv. Co.
                                               d- 9-9-1955 age 78
     Mina L, 1879-1954   b-Mi. res. Fowlerville
                                               d-Oct. 18, 1954 age 76
     Maude Allen   "Maude M" res. Bell Oak
     1876-1939   d-Oct. 15, 1939 age62, heart dis.
     Joel B Allen   res. Livingston Co.
     1874-1962   d- 8-20-1962 age 88
     Cressa Newman Allen   res. Bell Oak
     1883-1950   d- Oct. 11, 1950 age 67
     on monument-Allen-Newman
150 NEWMAN--HAGERMAN
     Leah H Newman   "Philemon" res. Fowlerville
     1875-1932   d-May 22, 1932 age 57
     mother
     father
     on monument-Hagerman
         Maria Maud, wife of John B Hagerman   res. Alpena
         Aug. 2, 1865-July 4, 1904   burial here 7-20-1932 from Alphena
         John B,   (John B Hagman) res. Fowlerville
         Apr. 28, 1855-Apr. 21, 1932 d-age 70
151 GRILL--SOBER
     doible stone-Grill
     Loraine H, 1914-   (masonic) not listed
     Louisa M, 1916-   (Star)   not listed
     double stone;-Sober
     Wayne H, 1907-   not listed
     Marian I, 1909-   not listed
152 PHILLIPS
     Ethel E, "mother"   b-Mi.   res. Livingston Co.
     1891-1957   d- 4-26-1957 age 66
     Roy W, "father"   res. Livingston Co.
     1889-1970   d- 6-3-1970 age 80(listed lot 153)
     on monument-Phillips

                                               (Lester E Raymer) res. Genessee Co.
                                               d-Jan. 14, 1952 age 76

153 HOUSE--PHILLIPS
     double stone-House
     Archie G, 1888-1959   burial 3-24-1959
     Ruth L, 1894-19-   "Ruth Lorena" res. Novi. Mi.
                                               d- 1-15-1984 age 89

154 WILCOX
     Melvin D Wilcox "Pete"   b-Mi.   res. Livingston Co.
     Apr. 11, 1944-Jan. 5, 1958   d-age 13, accident
     Russell J Benjamin   res. Livingston Co.
     Michigan Cpl. U S Army, world War 11
     May 28, 1906-April 2, 1972   d-age 65

Section "One"   Greenwood cemetery
lot #
155 BREWBAKER
     Maude Zella Peck "mother"   b-Mi.   res. Livingston Co.
     1883-1958   d- 2-8-1958 age 74
     Vinna O Brewbaker "mother"   res. Fowlerville
     1902-1967 (Ladies Aux.)   d- 1-10-1967 age 64, heart trouble
     Iral Amos Brewbaker   res. Fowlerville
     Michigan Pvt. U S Marine Corps
     Aug. 22, 1893-Dec. 5, 1965   d-age 72
156 BREWBAKER--SULKOWSKI
     double stone;-Brewbaker
     Adelbert H, 1923-1972   res. Livingston Co.
                                       d- 8-12-1972 age 48, pnuemonia
     Pearl V, 1926-1976   res. Howell   (listed lot 155)
                                       d-6-17-1976 age 49, pnuemonia

     double stone;-Sulkowski
     Casmer, 1905-   not listed
     Lola M, 1918-   not listed
157 STRAITH--TITUS
     Ovid H Straith "husband"   b-Mi.   res. Wayne
     1884-1956   d- 9-13-1956 age 81
     Hazel C Straith "wife"   (Hazel C Sidell) res. Livingston Co.
     1889-1963   d- 1-26-1963 age 73
     on monument-Straith
     double stone;-Titus
     Hugh E, 1876-1965   res. Fowlerville
                                       d- 4-20-1965 age 89
     Laura A, 1876-1965   res. Livingston Co.
                                       d- 9-24-1965 age 89

158 BURKHART--JACKSON
     Ivah Rudolph Burkhart   b-Mi.   res. Liv. Co.
                                       d- 10-31-1959 age 67
     Claude A Burkhart   b-Mi.   res. Cohoctah
     1879-1955   d- 12-19-1955 age 76
     on monument-Burkhart-Jackson
159 THUMSER
     double stone;-Thumser
     Charles A, 1889-1967 (vet)   "Charles Andrew" res. Howell
                                       d- 5-14-1967 age 77
     Ruth M, 1896-1971   "Ruth May" res. Howell
                                       d- 12-16-1971 age 76
     double stone;-Thumser
     Charles F, 1924-1976 (vet)   res. Oakland Co.
                                       d- 4-24-1976 age 51
     Dorothy B, 1926-   not listed
160 BERGLUND--REXIN
     double stone;-Berglund
     Carl Oscar, 1890-1948   res. Fowlerville
                                       d-Aug. 31, 1948 age 58
     Emma O, 1893-1982   res. Ingham Co.
                                       d- 1-15-1982 age 88
     double stone-Rexin
     Floyd, 1918-   not listed
     Caroline, 1923-1968   "Ida Caroline" res. Farmington, Mi.
                                       d- 1-10-1968 age 44,carbon monoxide

Section "One"   Greenwood cemetery
lot #
161 GRIFFIN
     Donald Wesley, 1876-1951   res. Fowlerville
                                     d-July 6, 1951 age 74
     Julia Ellsworth, 1881-1946   res. East Lansing
                                     d-May 30, 1946 age 65

     on monument-Griffin
162 HERRON
     no stones   (Glen G Herron) res. Detroit
                                     d- 10-15-1967 age 82
                                     (Waldo E Herron) res. Detroit
                                     d-March 16, 1938 age 56
                                     (Jane V Herron) res. Detroit
                                     d- 11-25-1981 age 68, heart trouble

163 BURKHART
     Eugene W, 1856-1938 (masonic)   res. Fowlerville
                                     d-age 82, burial 11-20-1938

     Ettie Pulver   (EttA Burkhart)
     1857-1936   d- Dec. 9, 1936 age 79
     Lelah Grace, 1884-1965   res. Howell
                                     d- 6-19-1965 age 80

     Glenn Pulver Burkhart   res. Fowlerville
     1886-1943   d-April 7, 1943 age 56
     Florence L Fowle, wife of Glenn Burkhart   res. Livingston Co.
     1893-1970   ·   d- 4-17-1970 age 76
     on monument-Burkhart
164 BOHM--CHAPMAN
     Nicholas M Bohm "father"   Nicholas Marlin"
     Mar. 1, 1852-Mar. 15, 1937   burial 4-3-1939 from mauseleum
     Elizabeth M Bohn Janner "mother" (Tanner)? res. Fowlerville
     May 26, 1861-Apr. 2, 1939   d-age 77
     Myrtle B Chapman   res. Lansing
     Jan. 3, 1881-Apr. 6, 1951   d-age 70
     Charles W Chapman (vet)   res. Vicksburg
     Sept. 10, 1874-Mar. 11, 1965   d-age 90
     Harold Chapman   no record
     Jan. 3, 1904-Jan. 4, 1904
     on monument-Chapman-Bohm
165 ADAMS
     empty
166 UTTER
     double stone-Utter
     Frank, 1878-19-   no record
     Mertie, 1883-197-   b-Mi. res. Coldwater, Mi.
                                     d- 1-22-1957 age 73

167 MOORE
     double stone-Moore
     Floyd R, 1897-1953 (masonic-vet)   b-Mi. res. Fowl.
                                     d- 2-12-1953 age 55
     Eliza E, 1903-1971 (OES)   res. Fowlerville
                                     d- 12-1-1971 age 68
     (behind stone above) Floyd R Moore, Michigan Pvt. Stu. Army
                     tng. Corps, World War 1
                     Mar. 10, 1897-Feb. 12, 1953

Section "One"   Greenwood cemetery
lot #
168 SOULE
     double stone;-Soule
     Howard C, 1883-1948   res. Conway
                                  d-Jan. 26, 1948 age 64

     Bessie, 1891-1963   res. Howell
                                  d- 5-25-1963 age 79

     Howard Soule Jr.   b-Mi. res. Monroe, Mi.
     Michigan EM 2, USNR, World War 11
     Nov. 4, 1920-Dec. 6, 1952   d-age 32, fractured skull
169 LASHER
     Daisy A Lasher   res. Howell
     1882-1967   d- 5-11-1967 age 85
     Ione D Weller   "Ione Daisy" res. Liv. Co.
     1909-1971   d- 10-8-1971 age 61(listed lot 170)
170 LASHER
     Carl F Weller   not listed
     1901-
     Virginia E Lasher   not listed
     1920-
     Ford A Lasher   no record
         "1907"
     Orel J Lasher   "Oral" b-Mi. res. Howelltwp.
     1882-1954   d- 6-16-1954, railroad accident
     on monument-Lasher
                                  (Agnes Kleinschmidt)
                                  d- 10-15-1964 age 88, bur. from Dexter

171 KEENMAN--ANDREWS
     double stone;-Keenman
     Fred B, 1886-1974   res. Eaton Co.
                                  d- 10-13-1974 age 88

     Myrtie M, 1891-1974   res. Ingham Co.
                                  d- 7-15-1974 age 83

     double stone;-Andrews
     Thad. C, 1862-1960   b-Mi. res. Liv. Co.
                                  d- 2-2-1960 age 97

     Ida K, 1869-1958   b-Mi. res. Ingham Co.
                                  d- 3-5-1958 age 88

172 CURTIS--McDONALD
     double stone;-Curtis
     Louis F, 1923   not listed
     Marie A, 1925-   not listed
     Bruce R Curtis "son"   "Bruce Randolph" b-Mi. res. Liv. Co.
     1956-1960   d- 1-5-1960 age 3, fractured skull
     double stone;-McDonald
     Roy T, 1902-1959   "Roy Thomas" b-Mi. res. Liv. Co.
                                  d- 11-17-1959 age 57
     Ida M Inez, 1909-   not listed
173 HANSON--GRISWOLD
     double stone;-Hanson
     Henry V, 1894-1978   res. Ingham Co.
                                  d- 10-28, 1978 age 84

     Margaret A, 1898-19-   not listed

Section "One"   Greenwood cemetery
lot #
173 continued
    double stone;-Griswold
    Ford C, 1876-1964   res. Ingham Co.
                                     d- 9-15-1964 age 88
    Catherine M, 1872-1951   b-Howell twp, res. Detroit
                                     d- Dec. 21, 1951 age 79
174 HANSON
Charles A, 1862-1930   res. Howell
                                     d-July 24, 1930 age 67
    Flora May, 1861-1934   res. Howell
                                     d-Nov. 15, 1934 age 73
    William E Hanson   "Wm. Edward" res. Liv. Co.
    Michigan Pvt. U S Army, World War 1
    March 22, 1892-April 29, 1970 d-age 78
    on monument-Hanson
175 ALEXANDER
    double stone;-Alexander
    William, 1885-1951 (masonic)   "Wm. L" res. Iosco twp.
                                     d-April 2, 1951 age 66
    Alzina, 1891-1981   res. Livingston Co.
                                     d- 5-16-1981 age 89
176 REDFIELD
    L Redfield (masonic)   "Lysander" b-Liv. Co. res. Liv. Co.
    1881-1961   d- 11-8-1961 age 80
    Bessie M Redfield (Star)   res. Livingston Co.
    1882-1980   d- 6-18-1980 age 98
    Gladys I Redfield (Star)   res. Fowlerville
    1919-1976   d- 7-30-1976 age 57
    J B Redfield (masonic)   no record
    on monument-Redfield
177 VOGT--MILLER
    Joseph Miller (FLT emblem)   res. Bennington
    1865-1935   d-Dec. 27, 1935 age 70
    Emma Kunde Miller   res. Bennington twp. Shia. Co.
    1868-1944   d-Oct. 15, 1944 age 76
    Anna M Ball   (Anna M Bell) res. Eaton Co.
    1888-1979   d- 11-16-1979 age 91
    Clara E Vogt   res. Barry Co.
    1889-1974   d- 11-27, 1974 age 74
    on monument-Vogt-Miller

                                     (George Vogt) res. Baltimore, Mi.
                                     d- 6-23-1980 age 95
                                     burial from Nashville, Mi.
178 STEWART
    double stone;-Stewart
    Henry F, 1892-19- (Amer Leg.)   no record
    Ivah G, 1890-1956   "Ivah Grace" b-Mi. res. Detroit
                                     d- 4-22-1956 age 66

Section "One"   Greenwood Cemetery
lot #
179 HOLMES
     Lorenzo D, 1862-1945   res. Perry, Mi.
                                   d-Dec. 10, 1945 age 83
     Ida B Holmes   b-Mi.   res. Conway twp.
                                   d-March 11, 1927 age 35 of T B.
     Otilla Holmes   "Ottilla May" res. Ingham Co.
     1870-1952   d-Jan. 29, 1952 age 81
     Norman Holmes   res. Conway
     1865-1940   d-May 4, 1940 age 74
     on monument-Holmes

                                   (Lester P Burbank) res. Pinckney
                                   d-May 5, 1940 age 61
                                   (his stone in Sec. 2, lot 31)

180 DAMMAN
     John Junior, 1926-1932   res. Handy
                                   d-Feb. 27, 1932 age 5
     Ellen V, 1885-1969   res. Livingston Co.
                                   d- 1-26-1969 age 83
     John, 1876-1946   res. Handy
                                   d-July 5, 1946 age 70

     on monument-Damman
181 MAPES
     Merta Ball Mapes   "Myrite C" res. Wayland, Mi.
     1867-1933   d-Oct. 20, 1933 age 66
182 MILLER
     Walter, "father"   b-Iosco twp. res. Iosco
     1868-1939   d-Sept. 1, 1939 age 72
     Fannie, "mother"   burial 4-6-1938
     1865-1938   d-age 72, killed by husband
     on monument-Miller
183 HUNT
     Lester, 1864-1946   res. Iosco twp.
                                   d-May 17, 1946 age 82
     Eliza, 1862-1927   b-Mi.   res. Iosco
                                   d-March March 15, 1927 age 64

     triple stone;-
     Nellie, 1900   (all removed from Munsell cem.
     Wesley, 1901   June 7, 1927)
     Stanley, 1902
     Jessie Hunt   (Jessie Brown Hunt) res. Liv. Co.
     1870-1959   d- 7-9-1959 age 89
     on monument-Hunt
184 KLEIN
     Theodore C Klein   b-Mi.   res. Howell
     1875-1954   d- 5-7-1954 age 81
     Salone Klein   res. Fowlerville
     1872-1947   d-May 29, 1947 age 74
     Ruth L Klein   b-Mi.   res. Fowlerville
     1909-1927   d-Feb. 10, 1927

Section "One"   Greenwood cemetery
lot #
185 REDFIELD
     Jay Redfield "father   res. Handy twp.
     1845-1931   d-July 2, 1931 age 86
     Betsey Redfield "mother"   "Betsey B" res. Handy
     1845-1927   d-Sept. 26, 1927 age 82
     William Redfield
     1877-1885   d-age 8, burial 1885
     Carrie Redfield
     1873-1876   d-age 3, burial 1876
     (fresh grave)   (Ivan W Redfield) res. Iosco twp.
                                          d- 11-11-1982 age 67

186 ALEXANDER
     William, 1843-1927   "Sr." b-Mi.   res. Fowlerville
                                          burial 2-18-1927
     Eva E, 1857-1938   res. Fowlerville
                                          d- age 86, burial 10-24-1938
     Robert T, 1879-1956   b-Mi.   res. Livingston Co.
                                          d- 5-12-1956 age 76
     Minnie, 1875-1955   b-Mi.   res. Leroy, Ingham Co.
                                          d- 9-27-1955 age 80

     on monument-Alexander
187 McPHERSON
     Linda Louise McPherson   res. Fowlerville
     Mar. 14, 1948-Feb. 11, 1949   (d-Feb. 8, 1949 age 11 months)
                                          burial 2-9-1949

     double stone;-McPherson
     Wilfred, 1903-1982   res. Oakland Co.
                                          d-age 82, burial 8-6-1982
     Jessie, 1907-1974   res. Livingston Co.
                                          d- 1-28-1974 age 67
     Marian D Nichols "our loving mother"   res. Lansing
     1927-1975   d- 7-15, 1975 age 48
188 DAMMAN
     father
     mother
     on monument-Damman
         John H, 1857-1923   b-Germany, res. Howell twp.
                                          d-Oct. 28, 1923 age 73
         Augusta S, his wife   b-Mi.   res. Howell twp.
         1860-1923   d-June 9, 1923 age 63
189 SHALLER
     John H, 1865-1923   res. Cohoctah
                                          burial ?
     R Magdalena, 1870-1955   "Rebecca Magdelena" b-Mi.
                                          d-Jan. 10, 1955 age 84
                                          res. Howell, Mi.
     "our " Ralph,   res. Cohoctah
                                          d-Dec. 27, 1927 age 2, pnuemonia

Section "One"   Greenwood cemetery
lot #
189 continued
    triple stone;-Shaller
    Lloyd Adam, 1892-1972   res. Livingston Co.
                                   d- 8-5-1972 age 72

    Ruth M, 1897-19-   not listed
    Ralph Lloyd, 1925-1927   burial 12-30-1927
    on monument-Shaller
190 HOLMES
    Marion L Holmes   "Marion Louise" b-Mi. res. Conway
    1914-1924   d-April 19, 1924 age 8, mengitis
    double stone;-Holmes
    Orville T, 1893-1957   res. Fowlerville
                                  d- March 29, 1951 age 57, bur 1951
    Nina C, 1894-1960   b-Livingston Co. res. Liv. Co.
                                  d- 7-4-1960 age 65
                                  (Jessie A Carson) b-Mi. res. Iosco
                                  d-Dec. 27, 1954 age 74

191 LONG
    double stone-Long
    John W, "father"   no record
    1858-1937
    Emma, "mother"   res. Dearborn, Mi.
    1853-1941   d-May 9, 1941 age 88(listed lot 192)
    William C Lee   b-Mi.   res. Howell twp.
                                  (d-May 3 or 9, pnuemonia)
                                  (burial May 11 or June 3, 1924)?

192 EMMONS--SCOTT
    Reginald Scott "father"   "Reginald Fredrick" res. Illinois
    1888-1972   d- 5-22-1972 age 82
                                  cremated, burial from Freeport, Ill.
    (behind stone above) Alice Long Scott   no record
                    1887-1939
    Alfred Emmons Scott   res. Howell
    1919-1934   d-July 16, 1934 age 14, appendecitis
    Abraham H Emmons   b-Mi.   res. Chicago, Illinois
    1849-1925   d-Dec. 2, 1925, pnuemonia
                                  burial, Sept. 9, 1926
    Alice Ayling Emmons   res. Wayne Co.
    1857-1947   d-Sept. 29, 1947 age 89
                                  (John Long) res. Howell
                                  d-March 3, 1937 age 78

193 COOK--HENDRYX
    double stone;-Cook
    Clifton G, 1892-1974   res. Livingston Co.
                                  d- 12-28, 1974 age 82
    Lucy L, 1897-19-   not listed
    double stone--Hendryx
    Frank M, 1868-1954   b-Mi.   res. Howell
    d- 1-14-1954 age 85
    Celia, 1870-1945   res. Cohoctah
                                  d-May 15, 1945 age 75
    John Swailes   b-Mi.   res. Conway
    1908-1924   d-July 10, 1924 age 15 by drowning

Section "One"   Greenwood cemetery
lot #
194 BENNETT
     small double stone;-Bennett
     Dell, 1869-1951   "Adelbert D" b-Mi. res. Shiawassee
                                        d- 5-15-1952 age 87, bur. 1952
     Julia L, 1870-1946   res. Perry
                                        d-Dec. 26, 1945 age 75, bur. 1945
     Norman Bennett   "Norman B"
     1891-1904   burial April 14, 1928, removed from ?
     Edna R Wright   b-Livingston Co res. Detroit
     1879-1952   d-March 19, 1952 age 73
195 HAARER
     John G Haarer   b-Livingston Co. res. Kent Co.
     1894-1961   d- 12-11-1961 age 67
     Beulah N Haarer "baby"   "Beulah Norine"b-Mi. res. Iosco
                                        d-Dec. 10, 1924 age 22 months, pnue.

196 KLEIN
     double stone;-Klein
     Charles, 1841-1927   b-Mi.   res. Conway twp.
                                        d-May 9, 1927 age 83
     Leah, 1858-1931   res. Conway
                                        d-March 16, 1931 age 72
     double stone;-Klein
     George L, 1885-1951   res. Conway twp.
                                        d-March 31, 1951 age 66
     Gertrude E, 1886-1965   res. Fowlerville
                                        d- 9-4-1965 age 79
                                        (baby, Chappel) res. Detroit
                                        d-Dec. 6, 1931, premature

197 KEEBLE
     George J Keeble   res. Atlanta, Georgia
     1895-1974   d- 6-21-1974 age 79
     double stone;-
     Sylvia A Keeble   b-Mi.   res. Fowlerville
     1896-1926   d-Sept. 9, 1926 age 30
     baby, 1926   d-Sept. 9, 1926 stillborn
     Violet M Keeble   res. Leslie, Mi.
     1893-1968   d- 1-18-1968 age 74
198 SABIN
     double stone;-Sabin
     Devillo, 1885-1961(FLT emblem)   "Devillo H" b-Mi. res. Liv. Co.
                                        d- 1-25-1961 age 75
     Ellen, 1889-19-   no record
     Ernest D Sabin   "Ernest Devillo" b-Mi. res. Fowl.
     Feb. 8, 1925-Oct. 31   burial 11-3-1925 age 8mo. 23 days
     double stone;-Sabin
     Harold D, 1913-1973   res. East Grand Rapids, Mi.
                                        d- 2-5-1973 age 59
                                        cremated, bur. from Grand Rapids
     Virginia D, 1915-   not listed

Section "One"   Greenwood cemetery
lot #
198 continued

                        (Roy Arlington Wilson)res. Wash. Co.
                        d- 8-12-1970 age 72, bur from Ypsi.
                        (baby, Harren) res. Howell twp.
                        d-Jan. 11, 1943, premature

199 IRELAND
    large double stone;-Ireland
    Ridgeley P, 1864-19-   "Ridgeley Porter" b-Ohio, res. Handy
                        d-Feb. 16, 1924 age 60
    Edith C, 1867-1923   b-Mi.   res. Fowlerville
                        d-Jan. 20, 1923 age 59, cancer

200 FOSTER--MUNSELL
    Martin R Foster (vet)   b-Iosco, res. Ann Arbor, Mi.
    1888-1940   d-May 17, 1940 age 52, cancer
    Viola Foster   b-Mi.   res. Eaton Rapids, Mi.
    1894-1952   d- 11-14-1952 age 59
    Emma J, 1862-1925   b-Mi.   res. Fowlerville
                        d-Sept. 26, 1925
    Jonathan B, 1853-1923   b-Mi.   res. Fowlerville
                        d-Jan. 3, 1923 age 69
    on monument-Munsell(lot 200-201)

201 MUNSELL
    Eva M, 1917-   not listed
    Silas E, 1916-   not listed
    David Elwin Munsell "our dear son"   no information
       1954
    J B Jr. 1888-1957 (masonic)   b-Mi.   res. Livingston Co.
                        d- 1-29-1957 age 69
    Greta E, 1889-1948   b-Detroit, res. Fowlerville
                        d-June 16, 1948 age 58

202 WARD
    Delcie W, "mother"   "Delcie Whitney" res. California
    1895-1977   d- 10-26-1977 age 82
    Bertha, "mother"   b-Mi.   res. Iosco twp.
    1877-1924   d-Jan. 9, 1924 age 46
    Hugh F, "father"   "Hugh Freeman" b-Mi. res. Jackson
    1878-1956   d- 4-20-1956 age 78
    on monument-Ward

203 MOHRLE--MacKENZIE
    Andrew E MacKenzie   res. Fowlerville
    1877-1947   d-May 21, 1947 age 69
    Emma R MacKenzie   "Emma Rebecca" res. Fowl.
    1886-1949   d-Feb. 12, 1949 age 63
    Lydia Mohrle   b-Canada, res. Conway twp.
    1862-1923   d-age 62, burial 5-13-1923
                        (listed on lot 198)

204 PALMERTON
    Willie H Palmerton "father"   "Wm. H" b-Conway, res. Howell
    1862-1936   d-age 76, burial 12-24-1938
    Delanie Palmerton "mother"   "Deline" b-Mi.   res. Howell
    1867-1924   d-Sept. 7, 1924 age 65

Section "One"   Greenwood cemetery
lot #
204 continued
    Vern Palmerton   b-Mi.   res. Livingston Co.
    1887-1961   d- 5-1-1961 age 73
    Lowello E Dittmar   "Louella" res. Clare, Mi.
    1911-1968   d- 4-21-1968 age 57
    Ralph A Dittmar   not listed
    1902-19-
205 GARDNER
    Jas. Romine, 1851-1933   (James R Gardner) res. Fowl.
                              d-Nov. 11, 1933 age 82

    Emma K, 1850-1926   (Emma Kinsman Gardner)b-Milford
                              d-Oct. 18, 1926 age 79, res. Fowl.

    Helen Kinsman Beach   res. Fenton, Mi.
    1853-1931   d-March 21, 1931 age 77
    Frank Beach   (Benjamin Frank Beach) res. Dearborn
    1853-1939   d-Nov. 27, 1939 age 86
    on monument-Gardner
206 FAUNCE
    Clifford W Faunce   res. Lansing
    1888-1931   d-June 22, 1931 age 43
    Jessie D Faunce   "Jessie P" res. Lansing
    1887-1927   d-Dec. 23, 1927 age 40, pnuemonia
    Betty J Faunce   res. Handy
    1924-1941   d-Feb. 16, 1941 age 17
207 COFFEY
    Kenneth R Coffey   b-Mi.   res. Lansing
    1920-1924   d-Nov. 10, 1924 age 4
                              (Bruce A Coffey) res. Liv. Co.
                              d- 10-17-1978 age 83

208 PARSONS
    J Frank Parsons   "Julius Frank" b-Conway, res. Conway
    1872-1940   d-Oct. 4, 1940 age 68, cancer
    Alma S Parsons   res. Oakland Co.
    1891-1973   d- 8-21-1973 age 82
    on monument-Parsons (south side)
209 DEFOREST
    Elmer Deforest   b-Conway, res. Conway twp.
    1884-1939   d-Feb. 21, 1939 age 54
    William Deforest   "Wm. N" b-Mi. res. Handy twp.
    1856-1924   d-Dec. 24, 1924 age 68
    Jane Deforest   (Jane Fewlass Deforest)b-Mi.
    1861-1923   d-Oct. 14, 1923 age 62   res. Handy
210 MUNSELL
    Elwin B, 1890-1958 (masonic)   (Elwin Bert Munsell)b-Mi.
                              d- 3-28-1958 age 67, cancer
                              res. Eaton Co.
    Rachel M, 1892-1937   res. Fowlerville
                              d-Dec. 29, 1937 age 47

Section "One"   Greenwood cemetery
lot #
211 MUNSELL
     Hazel A Munsel   not listed
     1899-19-
     Lavern J Munsel   res Fowlerville
     1899-1968   d- 4-15-1968 age 68 (listed lot 210)
     Carl Munsell   "Carl Westly" b-Mi. res. Handy
     1925-1926   d-Feb. 27, 1926 age 4 months, pnue.
212 BUNTING
     George H Bunting "father" b-Mi. res. Flint
     1883-1923   d-Feb. 6, 1923 age 39, accident
     Laura I Bunting Taylor "mother"   res. Flint
     1885-1967   d- 8-6-1967 age 81
     Ford H Bunting "son"
     1911-1932   burial 5-30-1932
     Rodger W Bunting "son"   b-Fowlerville, res. Flint
     1904-1925   d-Sept. 13, 1925 age 20
213 HEMSTED--LANG
     Frederick G Lang "father" res. Howell
     1871-1950   d-May 6, 1950 age 79
     Sarah Jane Lang Sherwood "wife"   b-Canada, res. Conway
     1869-1952   d- 8-19-1952 age 83
     Elizebeth Lang Hemsted "mother"   b-Mi. res. Conway
     1844-1926   d-Jan. 12, 1926 age 81
214 WICKMAN
     Roy D Wickman   b-Mi. res. Webberville
     1869-1925   d-Nov. 21, 1925 age 56
     Agnes L Wickman   b-Mi. res. Ingham Co.
     1873-1960   d- 2-18, 1960 age 87
     double stone-West
     Merrill G, 1900-1978   "Merrill Guy" res. Ingham Co.
                                d- 9-28, 1978 age 77
     Marie E, 1900-   not listed
215 CHALKER
     Llewellyn Chalker (vet)   b-Mi. res. Fowlerville
     1847-1925   d-Nov. 12, 1925 age 79
     Co. H, 1st Mich. Reg. Lt. Art.
     Mary Chalker   res. Jackson
     1855-1935   d-Jan. 7, 1935 age 79
     Etta Hopkins   res. Jackson
     1871-1947   d-Oct. 14, 1947 age 75
216 ELLIOTT (wide lot)
     Elmer D Elliott   res. Ingham Co.
     1899-1975   d- 8-13-1975 age 76, bur from Lansing
     Marna May Elliott   "Mona M" res. Lansing
       "1928"   d-April 25, 1928
     Shirley June Elliott   b-Mi. res. Lansing
     1924-1926   d-June 9, 1926 age 2, broncitis
     Floyd A Elliott   res. Iosco
     1902-1927   d-Sept. 8, 1927, accident
     Eva Elliot   no record
     1903-
     Harry C Elliot   res. Ingham Co.
     1906-1977   d- 11-27-1977 age 70
                                (baby girl, Elliot)res. Liv. Co.
                                d- 3-4-1958 stillborn

Section "One"   Greenwood cemetery
lot #
217 BIGELOW (wide lot)
     Wayne H Bigelow   "Wayne Wilbur" b-Conway, res. Howell
     1904-1938   burial Aug. 12, 1938
     Arlene Clark Bigelow   (Edna A Bigelow) res. Ypsilanti
     1904-1928   d-April 1, 1928 age 23, heart
     double stone;-
     Rollin C Bigelow   "Rollin Clayton" b-Conway, res. Byron
     1883-1951   d-Jan. 31, 1951 age 67
     Sarah C Bigelow   res. Livingston Co.
     1883-1970   d- 12-25-1970 age 87
     double stone;-
     Burr Bigelow   "Wilbur C" res. Livingston Co.
     1898-1970   d- 5-25-1970 age 71
     Marion Bigelow   not listed
     1901-
     Hollis C Bigelow   res. Livingston Co.
     Michigan Pfc. Infantry USAR, Korea
     March 6, 1929-June 15, 1971   d-age 42

218 BARTON
     no stones   (Catherine Smith) res. Bay Co.
                                      d-5-26-1972 age 90
                                      burial from Bay City, Mi.
                                      (Emmett J Barton) res. Conway twp.
                                      d-Nov. 30, 1928 age 64

219 WOODARD
     Frank E Woodard   res. Howell
     1859-1927   d-Nov. 26, 1927 age 73, auto accident
     Sarah E Woodard   (Sava Vines Woodard) res. Howell
     1879-1943   burial Aug. 29, 1943 age 64
                                      (d-Aug. 26, listed-S. Woodard Vines)
                                      (Robert James Woodard) res. Fowl.
                                      d-March 13, 1932 age 2 months, pnue.

220 PERKINS
     Arthur C Perkins (FLT emblem)   b-Mi.   res. Lansing
     1877-1926   d-Jan. 16, 1926 age 48
     Bertha C Perkins   b-Handy, res. Lansing
     1880-1938   d-age 58, burial 12-9-1938
     (new grave)   (Ruby Clarissa Perkins)
                                      d- 12-16-1982 age 101
                                      burial 2-8-1983 ashes

221 BENSON
     Joyce Ann Benson "our darling"   b-Cass City, Mi. res. Cass city
     Dec. 23, 1951   d-age 4½ months, convulsions
     Mattis, 1890-1925   b-Sweden, res. Ingham Co.
                                      d-Jan. 6, 1925 age 34
     Ellen B, 1895-1966   res. Fowlerville
                                      d- 3-21-1966 age 71
     Jonas, 1880-1976   d- 4-19-1976
     on monument-Benson
222 GRILL
     Ira D Grill   res. Conway twp.
     1884-1965   d- 2-10-1965 age 80
     Alice M Grill   res. Fowlerville
     1888-1967   d- 8-26-1967 age 79
     Thelma L Grill   b-Mi.   res. Locke twp.
     1915-1923   d-March 6, 1923 age 8, pnue.

Section "One"   Greenwood Cemetery
lot #
223 ALLISON
     Marcus B Allison   res. Conway
     1857-1934   d-Dec. 18, 1934 age 77
     Viola A Allison   b-Mi.   res. Lansing
     1856-1926   d-May 22, 1926 age 69, appendecitis
     Maude M Martin   res. Wayne
     1882-1969   d- 5-14-1969 age 82
     Florence E Snyder   res. Dallas, Texas
     1891-1979   d- 12-9-1979 age 88
224 OPELT--DeFOREST
     Frank, 1842-1916   no record
     Maggie, 1845-1927   (Magdalen H Opelt)b-Mi. res. Handy
     on monument-Opelt
     double stone;-DeForest
     William N, 1889-1965   res. Handy twp.
                               d- 1-18-1965 age 75
     Martie F, 1882-1977   "Matie"
                               d- 4-3-1977 age 94

225 WILLIAMS
     double stone;-Williams
     Fred A, 1872-1941   res. Handy
                               d-Jan. 4, 1941 age 68
     Erma E, 1877-1924   b-Mi.   res. Locke twp.
                               d-Sept. 7, 1924 age 47
                               (Gordon E Smith)b-Mi. res. Leroy
                               d-Nov. 21, 1925 age 2 months

226 BELEC--HOLT (wide lot)
     double stone;-Belec
     Joseph H, 1895-1964   res. Livingston Co.
                               d- 1-14-1964 age 68
     Garnet M, 1901-1981   "Garnet Mabel" b-Mi. res. Dearborn
                               d- 8-26-1981 age 80
     double stone;-Holt
     Laverne G, 1906-1980   "Laverne Gibbson" res. Westland, Mi.
                               d- 1-30-1982 age 76, bur. 2-2-1982
     Gertrude L, 1905-1954   b-Mi.   res. Dearborn, Mi.
                               d-Nov. 27, 1954 age 49
     double stone;-Holt
     Roy J, 1884-1947   res. Handy
                               d-Oct. 22, 1947 age 63
     Myrtie B, 1885-1957   b-Mi.   res. Livingston Co.
                               d- 10-14-1957 age 71
227 GROVER
     double stone;-Grover
     Shirley L, 1898-1977 (masonic) res. Livingston Co.
                               d- 8-9-1977 age 78
     Ella B, 1899-   (OES)   not listed
                               ("baby" Betty Grover)
                               d-Feb. 21, 1941, from B D Grover lot

228 THOMAS
     George E Thomas
     Michigan Pvt. Infantry, World War ll PH
     April 10, 1915-Aug. 17, 1944   burial 11-16-1948, from U S Army
                                     (John Thomas) res. Marion twp.
                                     d-Jan. 29, 1930 age 75
                                     (Maria D Thomas) res. Ann Arbor
                                     d-Jan. 10, 1929 age 49, pnuemonia
                                     (Bobbie L Maciezenski)res. Lansing
                                     d-April 20, 1935, premature

229 FLURIA
     C H Fluria "father" GAR   "Columbus" res. Fowlerville
     1840-1928   d-Nov. 6, 1929. bir. 1929
     Emily Fluria "mother"   (Emily Fleuria) res. Jackson
     1846-1928   d-April 3, 1928 age 82
     Ella M Leaich "daughter"   (Ella M Leach) res. Fowl.
     1867-1929   d-Aug. 25, 1929 age 61 of T B.
     Joseph D Fleury   res. Oceola twp.
     1871-19-   d-Jan. 17, 1946

230 KAIN-ROLFE-MILLER
     Fred Michael Kain   res. Livingston Co.
     Jan. 24, 1885-Oct. 27, 1973   d-age 88, burial from Williamston
     Ada May Kain   (Ada M Cain) res. Howell
     July 25, 1872-Sept. 29, 1927   d-age 53
     Julia Elizabeth Rolfe   "Lizzie" b-Mi. res. Lapeer
     Dec. 1, 1893-Jan. 20, 1954   d-age 60, heart trouble
     double stone;-Miller
     William, 1899-1974   res. Lansing
                                     d- 3-6-1974 age 74 bur. from Lansing
     Alice W, 1906-   not listed
     Roderick P Laird   res. Howell
          1932   d-April 29, 1932, blue baby
     Richard D Pearson   res. Conway
     1930-1933   d-May 29, 1933 age 2½
231 SHIREY
     double stone;-Shirey
     Reed C, 1879-1962   res. Livingston Co.
                                     d- 5-21-1962 age 83
     Wealthy E, 1882-1962   res. Livingston Co.
                                     d- 4-12-1962 age 80
     Adelbert D Shirey   res. Conway twp.
     1921-1932   d-March 5, 1932 age 10, pnue.
     Nellie E Shirey   res. Ann Arbor, Mi.
     1910-1928   d-April 19, 1928 age 17
                                     (Mary P Shannon)
                                     d-June 8, 1939 age 75
                                     (James H Shannon)res. Hamburg
                                     d-Aug. 23, 1934 age 72

232 GRINDLING
     double stone;-
     Loyce M Nelson   "Loca M Nelson) res. Dansville
     1931-1932   d-Aug. 22, 1932 age 1, pnue.
     Patricia L Grindling   b-Mi.   res. Ingham Co.
          1927   d-Aug. 15, 1927 age 8 days,mengitis

Section "One"   Greenwood cemetery
lot #
232 continued
    Ephriam Hanigan   (Joseph H Hannagan)res. Windsor twp.
    1864-1932   d- 12-12-1932 age 69
    Mae B Grindling   b-Mi.   res. Dansville
    1886-1923   d-March 23, 1923 age 38, flu
    Gusta H Grindling   "Augustus" res. Shiawassee Co.
    1879-1968   d- 12-20-1968 age 89
233 GROSTIC
    Margaret Carol Grostic   "Margrette" res. Webberville
    1927-1928   d-Feb. 24, 1928 age 1
    double stone;-Grostic
    L Ford, 1903-1964   "Lewis Ford" res. Handy
                             d- 1-18-1964 age 61, shotgun to head
    Agnes M, 1904-1983   "Agnes Mae" res. Orlando, Florida
                             d- 3-15-1983

234 COPELAND
    multi stone;-Copeland
    Lloyd E, 1895-1956 (vet)   "Lloyd Edwin" b-Mi. res. Fowl.
                             d- 6-1-1956 age 61
    Ruth A, 1897-1980   res. Livingston Co.
                             d- 12-24-1980 age 83
    Arthur Joe, 1930-1938   b-Fowlerville, res. Fowl.
                             d-age 8, lockjaw, bur. 10-2-1938
    Marjorie E, 1925-1928   res. Fowlerville
                             d-Jan. 6, 1928 age 2
235 BRADLEY
    Milton J Bradley   b-Mi.   res. Iosco twp.
    October 10, 1871-December 1, 1955   d-age 84
    Mary Conrad Bradley   b-Mi.   res. Iosco
    April 10, 1871-September 7, 1907   d-age 36
                             (removed from lot A-285)
    Charlotte M Walker Bradley   res. Iosco
    June 25, 1883-November 27, 1934   d-age 51
    Ione Weaver Bradley   "Ione Mae" res. Webberville
    December 9, 1886-June 21, 1971   d-age 84
236 BRADLEY
    Maggie R Bradley   (Margaret Martin) res. Iosco
    September 3, 1873-May 2, 1949 d-age 75
    Guy C Bradley   b-Mi.   res. Iosco twp.
    August 22, 1875-October 22, 1954   d-age 79
                             (Edward Elliotte)
                             burial 3-21-1938 stillborn
237 BRADLEY--UREN
    Marie A Bradley (OES)   res. Livingston Co.
    1901-1979   d- 8-27-1979 age 78
    Ralph C Bradley (masonic)   res. Livingston Co.
    1899-19-   d- 10-26-1983 age 84
238 BRADLEY
    empty

Section "One"   Greenwood cemetery
lot #
239 CHURCH--VOSS
     large stone-Voss
        Mary Church   "Mary Jane" res. Handy
        1857-1929   d-Feb. 1, 1929 age 71, pnue.
        Sadie, 1879-19-   "Sarah M" b-Mi. res. Ingham Co.
                                   d- 12-9-1956 age 78
        John, 1875-19-   "John Henry" res. Ingham Co.
                                   d-Aug. 3, 1951 age 75

240 GROSTICK
     double stone;-Grostick
        Sylvia M, 1911-   not listed
        Charles H, 1911-   not listed
        double stone;-Grostick
        Ida A, 1882-1976   res. Washtenaw Co.
                                   d- 5-28-1976 age 93
        Henry C, 1878-1958   b-Mi. res. Handy twp.
                                   d- 8-25-1958 age 80

241 BIRDSALL
        Louis E Birdsall (masonic)
        1881-1971   d- 9-5-1971 age 89
        Fern Birdsall (OES)   res. Midland, Mi.
        1888-1974   d- 3-17-1974 age 90
        Kathryn Birdsall   "Catherine F"
        1917-1931   d-Aug. 1, 1931 age 14
                                   (Betty Fern Birdsall)b-Mi. res. Fowl.
                                   d-July 16, 1923 age 10 months, pnue.

242 BAYES--PAMMENT
        Wm. D Pamment "husband"   res. Lansing
        1888-1930   (FLT emblem)   d-April 28, 1930 age 41
        Edna P Pamment   b-Canada, res. Leroy twp.
        1886-1923   d-Feb. 9, 1923 age 36
        Leta Blasick Bayes "mother" b-Mi. res. Ingham Co.
        1918-1961   d- 6-11-1961 age 43
        Phyllis M Bayes   res. Ingham Co.
        1950-1975   d- 12-29-1975 age 25, gunshot wounds
243 REILLY
     empty
244 HOLLOWAY
        Carrie Holloway   res. Fowlerville
        1874-1950   d-Feb. 6, 1950 age 75
                                   (Peter Halloway) res. Fowl.
                                   d-June 28, 1929 age 61, cancer
        Chas. F Van Hyning   res. Lansing
        1873-1932   d-Sept. 13, 1932 age 55
                                   (Edwin Baker) res. Howell
                                   d-Jan. 8, 1946 age 84
                                   (Frank H Opelt)
                                   burial July 3, 1927 from Lake cem.

Section "One"   Greenwood cemetery
lot #
245 SMITH--RADDATZ
     double stone;-Raddatz
     William, 1860-1938   "Wm. Carol" res. Fowlerville
                                     burial 4-18-1938 age 77

     Bertha, 1863-1940   "Bertha C" res. Fowlerville
                                     burial 5-16-1940 age 77

     double stone;-Smith
     Flex, 1891-19-   no record
     Edith, 1889-1944   res. Fowlerville
                                     d-March 15, 1944 age 54, cancer

     Johanna Balfanz   res. Fowlerville
     1842-1929   d-July 22, 1929 age 87
246 COOK--SCHNEIDER
     Gladys M Cook, wife of Roy Schneider   res. Detroit
     1905-1930   d-Dec. 6, 1930 age 24 of operation
     double stone;-Cook
     G Dewitt, 1867-1960   "Grove Dewitt" b-Mi. res. Shiawassee
                                     d- 7-21-1960 age 93

     Ida B, 1868-1937   "Ida Bell" res. Cohoctah
                                     d-Jan. 14, 1937 age 68

247 JOYS
     double stone;-Joys
     John A, 1905-1982   res. Reed City, Mi.
                                     d- 5-19-1982 age 76

     Muriel E, 1915-   not listed
     double stone;-Joys
     George, 1862-1946   res. Iosco twp.
                                     d-March 20, 1946 age 83

     Mary, 1879-1952   "Mary Lena" b-Mi. res. Iosco
                                     d- 11-8-1952 age 73
                                     (baby, Joys) res. Iosco
                                     d-March 20, 1932 stillborn
                                     (baby, Joys)
                                     d-March 24, 1940 stillborn

248 LINE
     double stone;-Line
     James, 1866-1939   res. Handy
                                     d-Dec. 7, 1939 age 73

     Bertha, 1872-1974   res. Fowlerville
                                     d- 11-16-1974 age 102

     Debra K U-Ren   res. Fowlerville
     1964-1964   d- 1-5-1964, premature
     Lester Line "husband"   res. Fowlerville
     1890-1964   d- 12-23-1964 age 74
     Florence Line "wife"   res. Fowlerville
     1896-1931   d-Dec. 24, 1931 age 35 of T B.
     Anna M Line   res. Handy twp.
     1928-1930   d-June 1, 1930 age 1 y & 8mo.
249 ANDERSON
     Carl J, "father"   res. Fowlerville
     1873-1929   d-July 29, 1929 age 56, heart
     Anna S, "mother"   b-Mi.   res. Ingham Co.
     1877-1957   d- 12-14-1957 age 80
     on monument-Anderson

Section "One"   Greenwood cemetery
lot #

250 LEIGHTON
     Anthony A Rohr   res. Detroit
     Michigan Cpl. 20 Aero Sq. World War 1
     Aug. 18, 1898-Sept. 21, 1966   d-age 68, burial from Detroit
                                     (Wm. V Leighton) res. Detroit
                                     d-Aug. 2, 1937 age 22, appendecitis
                                     (Garna Pearl Minkley) res. Eloise
                                     d- 9-29-1963 age 77, bur. from Detroit

251 VAUGHN--POWELL
     double stone;-Vaughn
     Morgan E, 1874-1958   b-Mi. res. Livingston Co.
                                     d- 2-25-1958 age 83

     Ada A, 1878-1958 (Amer. Leg. Aux.)   no record
     Marguerite E Vaughn
     1907-   not listed
     double stone;-Powell
     Ronald N, 1908-1979   res. Lansing
                                     d- 9-15-1979 age 71

     Maurine, 1909-   not listed
     Ronald Novak   res. Chicago, Illinois
     May 8-12, 1950   d-May 12, 1950 age 4 days
252 SPRAGUE
     Newlon L Sprague   b-Mi. res. Elington, Mi.
     1857-1907   d-June 11, 1907 age 48
                                     burial Nov. 24, 1923, removed from ?
     E Leola Sprague   b-Indiana, res. Muskegon Heights
     1863-1923   d-Jan. 27, 1923 age 59, cancer
     Julia A Sprague "daughter"   b-Mi. res. Livingston Co.
     1888-1960   d- 4-3-1960 age 72
253 FLANIGAN--DAILEY
     Edna M Dailey   res. Lansing
     1889-1929   d-Feb. 14, 1929 age 40
     John J Dailey   "John Jones" res. Howell
     1889-1949   d-Oct. 5, 1949 age 60
     Emma Flanigan   res. Fowlerville
     1859-1933   d-June 14, 1933 age 73
     William Flanigan   res. Detroit
     1862-1949   d-March 26, 1949 age 87
254 MELVIN
     Roy C Melvin (FLT emblem)   res. Fowlerville
     1878-1929   d-Feb. 21, 1929, bronchitas
     Elnora I Melvin   res. Handy
     1897-1934   d-Aug 29, 1934, age 38, diabetis
     double stone;-Melvin
     Clarence D, 1917-   "husband" not listed
     Doris A, "wife"   res. Washtenaw Co.
     1924-1981   d- 6-15-1981 age 56
255 LATHROP--CLACK
     Walter E Lathrop   res. Fowlerville
     1853-1929   d-Jan. 5, 1929 age 75. bur. Feb. 28.
     Louise D Lathrop   (Lewis D Lathrop) male, res. Fowl.
     1858-1929   d-Feb. 25, 1929 age 72

Section "One"   Greenwood cemetery
lot #
255 continued
    double stone;-Clack
    Edward J, 1863-1931   res. Fowlerville
                                    d-Oct. 3, 1931 age 68
    Lillian A, 1887-1958   (Lillian A LaCroix)b-Mi.
                                    d- 9-28-1953 age 70
                                    burial 10-1-1953, res. Lansing

256 LOCKWOOD--VAINISI
    double stone;-Lockwood
    Frank R, 1867-1957 (FLT emblem)b-Mi.   res. Ingham Co.
                                    d- 8-29-1957 age 90
    Winnifred E, 1873-1937   res. Webberville
                                    d-March 26, 1937 age 63
    Bernice Lockwood Vainisi   res. Chicago, Illinois
    1902-1929   d-June 4, 1929
257 KEENY
    Ralph Keeny   res. Iosco twp.
    1929-1931   d-March 10, 1931 age 3, scarlet fever
    Rose A Keeny   res. Howell
    1891-1967   d- 3-21-1967 age 75
258 SMITH
    triple stone;-Smith
    William H, 1901-19-   not listed
    Alma B, 1902-19-   not listed
    Dolores E, 1928-1931   res. Fowlerville
                                    d- Aug. 5, 1931 age 2

259 BOARDWAY
    double stone;-Boardway
    James V, 1859-1929   res. Conway twp.
                                    d-June 23, 1929 age 70
    Anna M, 1872-1955   b-Mi.   res. Fowlerville
                                    d- 5-19-1955 age 82
    triple stone;-BOARDWAY
    Rollin E, 1897-1981   res. Ingham Co.
                                    d- 7-5-1981 age 83
    Suzanne, July 27, 1935   res. Fowlerville
                                    d-Oct. 1, 1935 age 3 months
    Gay 1, 1900-1970   res. Livingston Co.
                                    d- 6-13-1970 age 70
                                    (male baby, Boardway)res. Conway
                                    d-May 14, 1931 stillborn

260 DIETRICH
    double stone;-Dietrich
    Anson, 1895-1961   "Anson D" b-Mi. res. Liv. Co.
                                    d- 3-20-1961 age 65
    Ruth, 1898-1975   "Ruth E" res. Livingston Co.
                                    d- 1-30-1975 age 76

261 DEAN
    Chester B,   res. Conway twp.
    Feb. 24, 1957-Feb. 16, 1935   d-age 71, auto accident
    Laura E,   b-Mi.   res. Conway
    Nov. 8, 1866-July 1, 1927   d-age 60, heart failure

Section "One"   Greenwood cemetery
lot #
261 continued
    double stone;-Dean
    Glen W, 1896-1976   res. Livingston Co.
                              d- 12-24-1976 age 80

    Vance, 1901-1974   res. Lansing
                              d- 6-26-1974 age 73

    on monument-Dean
262 DAVIDSON--BURLEY
    double stone-Burley
    Gasper, 1877-1954   b-Mi. res. Webberville
                              d- 9-8-1954 age 76, bur. 9-16.

    Ada H, 1880-1952   b-Mi. res. Handy twp.
                              d- 4-19-1952 age 71

    Benjamin F Andrews "father" res. Fowlerville
    1870-1949   d-May 27, 1949 age 78
    Laura L Andrews "sister" res. Ovid, Mi.
    1908-1930   d-April 14, 1930 age 47, flu
    Amelia M Davidson   res. Perry, Mi.
    1881-1929   d-Aug. 3, 1929 age 47, lockjaw
263 GRANT
    double stone;-Grant
    Sumner, 1858-1939   res. Fowlerville
                              burial 7-28-1939 age 80

    Emma, 1868-1944   res. Fowlerville
                              d-Sept. 20, 1944 age 76

    double stone;-Grant
    Alton B, 1869-1952   b-Mi. res. Fowlerville
                              d- 7-14-1952 age 82

    Rosella, 1872-1938   res. Conway
                              d-age 65, bur. 5-14-1938,suicide

264 RATHBUN-VENASKA
    double stone;-Rathbun
    Fred A, 1872-1958 (masonic) b-Mi. res. Oakland Co.
                              d- 6-19-1958 age 86

    Luella, 1872-1963 (OES) res. Livingston Co.
                              d- 2-19-1963 age 90

    double stone;-Venaska
    Charles E, 1896-1978 (vet) res. Livingston Co.
                              d- 10-1-1978 age 82

    Ada E, 1900-   not listed
265 DAVIS
    double stone-Davis
    Howard F, 1903-1965   "Howard Franklin"
                              d- 10-31-1965, bur. from Lake Odessa

    Georgia R, 1903-1980   res. Hastings, Mi.
                              d- 7-28-1980 age 77

    Howard F Davis Jr. "son" res. Fowlerville
                              d-Oct. 1, 1929 age 4, accident

Section "One"   Greenwood cemetery
lot #
266 MALEITZKE
     Lewis E Maleitzke   res. Howell
     1882-1929   d-Feb. 10, 1929 of operation
     Merle I Maleitzke Bobier
     1889-1980   burial 1-12-1980 age 90
     double stone-Maleitzke
     Fred W, 1905-1975   "Fred Wm." res. Ingham Co.
                                    d- 2-3-1975 age 69

     Josephine M, 1907-   not listed
     double stone;-Maleitzke
     Henry G, 1879-1962   "Henry George" res. Livingston Co.
                                    d- 6-6-1962 age 82

     Anna C, 1884-1965   res. Fowlerville
                                    d- 10-13-1965 age 81
267 WRONS- (part is Handy twp. lot)
     Ellison G Ebert   res. Webberville
     1918-1934   d-Aug. 21, 1934 age 16, killed by truck
     Marise Paulette Wrons "our beloved baby"   (Matica Pacoletta Wrons)
     daughter of Richard and Zoya Wrons   res. Handy
     born June 26, 1933, died Nov. 11, 1933   (d-Nov. 13, 1933 age 4 mo.)
                                    (Fredrick J Doebck) res. Fowl.
                                    d-March 17, 1932 age 67
                                    (Ernest A Mitchell)b-Arkansas
                                    d-Aug. 9, 1941 age 29, res. Handy
                                    (Allen DeForest)b-Conway
                                    d-Nov. 13, 1941 age 53, res. Ann Arbor
                                    (Anthony L LaPratt) res. Fowl.
                                    d-Sept. 23, 1947 age 75
                                    (Roger Dale Galarneaw) res. Howell
                                    d-Sept. 3, 1948
                                    (Henry F Smith) res. Howell
                                    d-April i, 1951 age 84
                                    (Elmer King)b-Mi. res. Fowl.
                                    d- 6-26-1952 age 76
                                    (Albert D Crawford)b-Cohoctah
                                    d-Feb. 12, 1951 age 58, res. Handy
268 SHIREY
     Frederick C Shirey   b-Mi. res. Brownstown twp. Wayne Co.
     Nov. 21, 1899-Oct. 6, 1956   d-age 56 by drowning
     Dorothy L Shirey   res. Detroit
     Jan. 11, 1908-Nov. 8, 1938   d-age 30, blood poison
     Lucille D Shirey "our dream baby"   res. Lansing
     1930-1931   d-July 17, 1931 age 1, auto accident
269 COMER
     John H Comer   res. Fowlerville
     1859-1930   d-Sept. 3, 1930 age 71
     Dema Riace Comer   (Demarice V Comer) res. Fowl.
     1865-1943   d-Oct. 31, 1943 age 78
     Myrtle Comer   res. Ingham Co.
     1888-1968   d- 2-13-1968 age 79

Section "One"   Greenwood cemetery
lot #
270 KLEINSCHMIDT--ALLEN
     Frank H Allen   "Frank Henry" res. Lansing
     March 31, 1950   d-stillborn
     Lambert H Kleinschmidt   "Henry L" res. Iosco twp.
     1870-1930   (masonic)   d-July 27, 1930 age 60
     Agnes Kleinschmidt (Star)   no record
     1876-1964
     Stanley K Allen   res. Ann Arbor, Mi.
     Mar. 22, 1948   d-stillborn
     on monument-Kleinschmidt
271 WINEGAR
     triple stone;-Winegar
     John H Kerney   res. Handy
     1863-1934   d-June 20, 1934 age 71, killed by auto
     Elizabeth, "wife"   res. Handy
     1856-1933   d-March 19, 1933 age 76
     William H, "husband"   res. Handy
     1857-1933   d-April 1, 1933 age 77
272 BENJAMIN
     John M Benjamin   b-Mi. res. Fowlerville
     1844-1922   d-Dec. 4, 1922
     Lauretta Benjamin   "Luretta B" res. Fowlerville
     1845-1927   d-Sept. 22, 1927 age 83
     Andrew J Benjamin   b-Mi. res. Conway twp.
     1865-1972   d-age 6,
                                      burial Nov. 30, 1923, removed
                                      from Caugfer cem.(Coffin cem.?)
     mother   (Charity Benjamin) res. Conway
                                      d-age 89, removed from Coughin cem.
273 SEYMOUR
     Ed Seymour (Spanish-Amer.)   "edward" res. Fowlerville
     Michigan Pvt. U S Army
     December 2, 1935   d-age 60
     Lillie Seymoure   "Lilly Smith Seymour)b-Mi. res. Fowl.
     1884-1923   d-Feb. 19, 1923, bur. Mar. 3, 1923
274 WORDEN
     Wellie A Worden   male, b-Mi. res. Webberville
     Sept. 12, 1873-Jan 8, 1920   (d-Jan. 18, 1921) age 47, pnue.
                                      burial Jan. 22, 1921 from lot A-259
     Ida E Worden   b-Mi. res. Toledo, Ohio
     Mar. 27, 1872-May 15, 1953   d-age 81
     Josephine White   res. Detroit
     1901-1929   d-April 18, 1929
     on monument-Worden
275 VANDEVENNE
     August J Vandevenne   "August Joseph" b-Mi. res. Ingham Co.
     Michigan Sgt. U S Army, World War 1
     Aug. 10, 1890-Aug. 2, 1961   d-age 70
     Gertrude M Vandevenne
     June 4, 1898-Sept. 29, 1971   d-age 73, bur. from Portland, Mi.
     Arthur Vandevenne "baby"   "Arthur G" b-South Lyon, Mi.
     1924-1925   d-Aug. 19, 1925 age 1, res. Fowl.

Section "One"   Greenwood cemetery
lot #
276 CAVANAUGH
     double stone;-Cavanaugh
     Basil, 1896-1973   res. Fenton, Mi.
                                   d- 9-19-1973 age 77
     Fern S, 1896-1964   res. Fowlerville
                                   d- 5-1-1964 age 67
     Rose Mary Cavanaugh   b-Mi. res. Fowlerville
                                   d-May 23, 1926 age 34, pnue.
277 SMITH--BARBER
     double stone;-Barber
     John D, 1867-1943   res. Handy
                                   d- Jan. 23, 1943 age 75
     Minnie L, 1872-1955   b-Mi. res. Howell
                                   d- 6-15-1955 age 82
     Clara J Smith   (Clara S Hill) res. Pontiac
     1863-1930   d-March 17, 1930 age 66
278 CHENEY
     Albert H, (FLT emblem)   Al. Howard" b-Mi. res. Liv. Co.
     1872-1961   d- 1-3-1961 age 88
     Valeva W, 1876-1926   b-Mi. res. Lansing
                                   d-June 25, 1926 age 49
     Ethel M, 1880-1966   res. Ypsilanti, Mi.
                                   d- 10-17-1966 age 84
279 SMITH--RIDER
     double stone;-Smith
     Charles F, 1912-   (masonic) not listed
     Jean A, 1919-   (OES)   not listed
     double stone;-Rider
     Fred P, 1885-1958   b-Mi. res. Howell
                                   d- 5-17-1958 age 73
     Viola B, 1888-1956   "Viola Belle" b-Mi. res. Liv. Co.
                                   d- 10-4-1956 age 67
     Goldie May Rider   b-Mi. res. Howell
     1923-1926   d-Oct. 20, 1926 age 3
280 MANN--YELLAND
     double stone;-Mann
     Frank E, 1867-1950   b-Handy, res. Handy twp.
                                   d-Oct. 7, 1950 age 83
     Lucinda, 1871-1936   res. Handy
                                   d-Oct. 9, 1936 age 65
     double stone;-Yelland
     Clyde, 1894-1975 (masonic)   res. Livingston Co.
                                   d- 5-20-1975 age 81
     Effie, 1899-   (OES)   not listed
281 SLEEPER
     Merle F Sleeper "husband"   b-Mi. res. White Oak twp.
     Sept. 3, 1892-March 11, 1927 d-age 35 of T B.
                                   (Lillian A Sleeper)res. Detroit
                                   d-Oct. 17, 1949 age 60
282 DIETRICH
     George K Dietrich   b-Mi. res. Conway
     1852-1927   d-March 15, 1927 age 75
     Caroline E Dietrich   b-Canada, res. Conway
     1859-1938   burial 10-20-1938 age 79

Section "One"   Greenwood cemetery
lot #
282 continued
     Matilda S Gallop   res. Conway
     1881-1946   d-May 26, 1946 age 64
     double stone-Dietrich
     Allen F, 1894-1966   res. Fowlerville
                                   d- 3-21-1966 age 72

     Leah S, 1897-1977   res. Livingston Co.
                                   d- 1-3-1977 age 79
283 CRANE
     Rozell F, 1875-19-   no record
     Mae L, 1869-1927   "Mary" b-Mi. res. Leroy
                                   d- Aug. 1, 1927 age 57

     on monument-Crane (IOOG)
284 to 290
     (used as roadway to connect the new and old sections)
291 to 293
     empty
294 LANE
     John A Lane   res. Madison Heights
     Illinois S Sgt. U S Army, World War 11
     Oct. 28, 1912-Mar. 5, 1973   d-age 60, burial from Royal Oak, Mi.
295 BALL
     double stone-Ball
     Charles E, 1863-1924   "Chas. Edward" res. Iosco twp.
                                   d-May 17, 1929 age 66
     Lydia M, 1870-1949   "Tillie" res. Fowlerville
                                   d-Dec. 13, 1949 age 79
                                   (Walter Spadlin)res. Liv. Co.
                                   d- 10-20-1958, age 0, suffication

296 BUTTON
     Cora, wife of Oren Button   "Cora Bell" res. Fowlerville
     1876-1932   d-Aug. 21, 1932 age 56
                                   (Shirley A Rowley)res. Howell
                                   d-Aug. 17, 1932 age 6 months
                                   (baby Rowley) res. Fowlerville
                                   d-Oct. 16, 1928 stillborn
                                   (Willis M Rowley) res. Howell
                                   d-Sept. burial 9-4-1937 age 3 mo.
                                   (Darrell Duane Rowley) b-Mi.
                                   d-11-10-1955 age 1mo. 14 days
                                   res. Genoa twp.
                                   (Laurence Rowley) res. Liv. Co.
                                   d- 9-17-1972 age 71
                                   (Lilah D Rowley) res. Howell
                                   d- 10-11-1973 age 62

297 RAY
     Kenneth T Hall   "Ken Truhan" res. Royal Oak, Mi.
     1904-1969   d- 7-7-1969 age 64
     double stone-Ray
     Sidney Jr.   "Sidney M" res. Detroit
     1927-1928   d-May 9, 1928 age 5, measles
     Charles E,   res. Royal Oak, Mi.
       1934   d-March 17, 1934 age 8 days
     Betty Jane Winchell   res. Lansing
     1925-1966   d- 3-15-1966 age 41

Section "One"   Greenwood cemetery
lot #
298 WILSON
     double stone;-Wilson
     Roy A, 1898-1970   "Roy Arlington"
                                         burial 8-15-1970 age 72
                                         not listed

     Winnieferd,   (Thomas Wilson) res. Ypsilanti, Mi.
     1902-   d-Dec. 12, 1927 age 6 hours, heart
                                         (John & Nellie Wilson)twins
                                         d-Aug. 26, 1928 stillborn
                                         res. Ypsilanti, Mi.

299 WRIGHT
     Lawrence B Wright "our son"   res. Ingham Co.
     Dec. 16, 1968-Feb. 24, 1970   d-age 1
300 TOMLIN
     Marvin R Tomlin   "Marvin Rex" res. Washtenaw Co.
     SP 3, U S Army
     Nov. 25, 1930-Sep. 21, 1974   d-age 43, pnuemonia
     double stone;-Tomlin
     Alvin A, 1896-1967   "Alvin Armo" res. Fowlerville
                                         d- 6-6-1967 age 71
     Blanche, 1898-1979   res. Livingston Co.
                                         d- 2-26-1979 age 81
     Emmette Tomlin   res. Conway twp.
     1917-1935   d-June 2, 1935 age 17, auto accident
                                         (baby, Tomlin) res. Conway twp.
                                         d-March 23, 1943 stillborn

301 CURTIS
     Gertrude Curtis   "Gertrude L" res. Washtenaw Co.
     1877-1970   d- 6-18-1970 age 92
     (on stone above) baby-
     Fred B Curtis   no record
     1878-1938
     Grace L Curtis
     1881-1911   d-age 20, burial 4-13-1939,childbirth
302 PARSONS
     double stone;-Parsons
     Cecil D, 1885-1968   "Cecil Dwight" res. Fowlerville
                                         d- 3-11-1968 age 82
     Nellie M, 1885-1960   b-Mi.   res. Livingston Co.
                                         d- 3-15-1960 age 74

303 BESSERT--GALLOP
     double stone;-Gallop
     Leslie H, 1914   not listed
     Coralbell, 1915-   not listed
303 to 312
     empty

Section "One"   Greenwood cemetery
lot #
313 TOMLIN
     Lisa Ann Gilboe   (listed on lot 300)
     April 15, 1968   burial 4-19-1968
     Mildred E Heller "our mother"   res. Livingston Co.
     June 21, 1915-Dec. 16, 1977   d-age 62
     Tracey Lynn Tomlin "our daughter"   res. Washtenaw Co.
     June 7, 1970-Dec. 3, 1974   d-age 4, snowmobile accident
314 TOMLIN
     double stone;-Tomlin
     Melva E, 1925-   not listed
     Alvin Jr. 1920-1978   res. Livingston Co.
                                d- 8-3-1978 age 58, pnuemonia

315 O'DELL--REDINGER
     Wayne K Redinger   res. Pontiac
     1909-1965   d- 3-25-1965 age 55
     Susie D O'Dell "mother"   b-Mi.   res. Livingston Co.
     1885-1957   d- 7-2-1957 age 71
316 to 330
     empty
331 HANNA-(Handy twp.)
     William M Hanna   "Wm. Melvin" res. Oakland Co.
     1938-1979   d- 1-16-1979 age 40
                                (baby, Truss Of Gerald M Truss)
                                d- 3-16-1976, premature,
                                res. Ann Arbor, Mi.
                                (baby girl, Smith) res. Cook Co. Ill.
                                d- 12-25-1973, burial from Chicago

332 HANNA-(Handy twp.)
     Esther M Hanna   b-Mi.   res. Fowlerville
     1905-1953   d- 1-6-1953 age 47
     Claude H Hanna   res. Livingston Co.
     1905-1972   d- 9-16-1972 age 66
                                (baby girl, Brissaud) res. Liv. Co.
                                d- 10-19-1957, age 0
                                (David Allen Ramsey)
                                d- 9-5-1971 age 1 (on county lot)
                                (Walter Willard)res. Liv. Co.
                                d- 1-25-1972 age 71 (on county lot)

333 HUDSON
     Jan Hudson   b-Mi.   res. Lansing
     May 21, 1953-Jan. 1, 1954 d- 12-30-1953 age 7 months, bur 1954
334 to 337
     empty
338 ARNOLD
     no stones   (Joyce M Arnold)res. Lansing
                                d- 4-22-1982 age 50, heart trouble

339 to 343
     empty

Section "One"   Greenwood cemetery
lot #
344 PLUMMER
     Ralph Plummer   b-Mi.   res. Wayne
     Michigan Pvt. Tank Corps, World War 1
     Dec. 20, 1896-June 4, 1954   d-age 57
                                       (Harvey L Orrdley? or Buadsley?)
                                       d-Jan. 3, 1934 age 26, fractured skull
                                       removed from lot 274, July, 1953

345 (Handy township)
     no stones   (Floyd Earl Dieterle)b-Mi.
                                       d- 1-11-1956 age 60,res. Liv. Co.
                                       (Lewis Woll)
                                       burial 2-20-1956 age 73
                                       (Genevieve B Cunningham)res. Handy
                                       d- 1-19-1965 age 67, pnuemonia

346 (Handy township)
     no stones   (John Dee) res. Livingston Co.
                                       d-Sept. 1971, murdered
                                       burial 2-18-1975
                                       (Carl Hartwick)
                                       burial 2-18-1975, murdered
                  - - - - - - - - - - - -
                        end

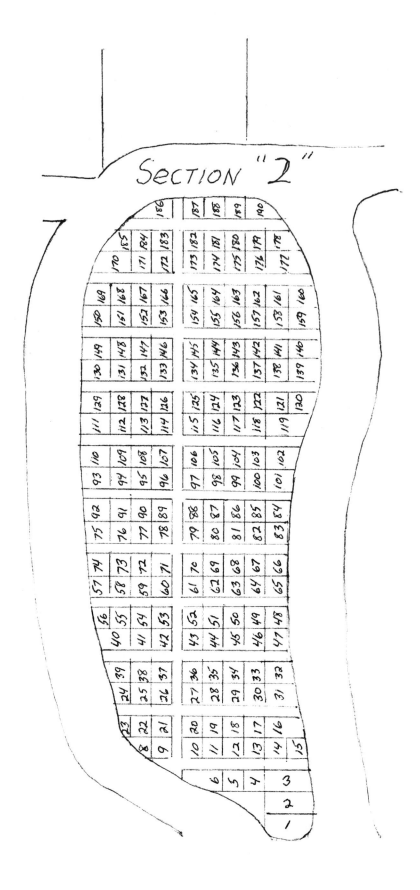

Section "2"

Section "Two"   Greenwood cemetery
lot #
1   MILLER --WEGIENKA (wide lot)
     Charles Miller   b-Detroit, res. Handy
     1870-1938   d-age 68, stroke. bur. 6-23-1938
     Hattie Miller   b-Mi. res. Livingston Co.
     1875-1959   d- 11-10-1959 age 84
     double stone;-Wegienka
     Lawrence B,   res. Southgate, Mi.
     July 25, 1901-Nov. 26, 1972   d-age 71
     Hattie M,   res. Wayne
     Oct. 19, 1906-June 30, 1978
2   CARLSON-SMITH-McKENZIE (wide lot)
     Bonnie Lee Carlson   res. Howell
     Sept. 2, 1940   d-Sept. 3, 1940 stillborn
     double stone;-Smith
     Floyd J, 1870-1964   res. Fowlerville
                                     d- 9-10-1964 age 93
     Maude M, 1877-1966   res. Fowlerville
                                     d- 3-16-1966 age 88

     double stone;-McKenzie
     Admiral "Mac" 1899-1976   res. Livingston Co.
                                     d- 5-15-1976 age 77

            married Aug. 9, 1924
     Irene L, 1903-1981   res. Livingston Co.
                                     d- 7-23-1981 age 77

3   KREBS-WEGIENKA- (wide lot)
     double stone;-Krebs
     Frederick, 1895-1982   res. Livingston Co.
                                     d- 8-8-1982 age 87
     Lena, 1900-19-   not listed
     Vincent V Wegienka   "Vincent Victor" res. Oakland Co.
     1870-1962   d- 3-21-1962 age 91
     Martha F Wegienka   res. Fowlerville
     1885-1951   d-March 5, 1951 age 65
     Henry Tiedman   (vet)   res. Fowlerville
     1891-1941   d-May 4, 1941 age 49
4   LEEDLE   (wide lot)
     Maggie
     George
     Catherine
     on monument-Leedle
        Geo. W Leedle   res. Marshall, Mi.
        June 17, 1871-Sept. 17, 1929   d-age 58
        Maggie, his wife   "Margaret"b-Mi. res. Conwau
        Nov. 20, 1872-March 24, 1895 d-in childbirth, bur. 6-4-1923 (?)
        Catherine   res. Ingham Co.
        Dec. 19, 1871-Sept. 15, 1970   d-age 98
     John Leedle "father   b-England, res. Conway
     1848-1900   d-Oct. 12, 1900 age 52 of T B.
                                     burial June 4, 1923
     Alvira Leedle   "Alvira R"
     1848-1931   burial 12-18-1931 age 83
     on monument-Leedle

Section "Two"   Greenwood cemetery
lot #
5   LEEDLE (wide lot)
     Clement H, 1882-1944   res. Homer, Mi.
                                     d-March 5, 1944 age 61
     Lucy C, 1882-1956   "Lucy Caroline" b-Mi.
                                     d- 7-14-1956 age 73, res. Albion, Mi.
     Barbara Jean Leedle   (infant, Leedle) res. Albion
     May 20, 1942   D-May 20, 1942
     on monument-Leedle
6   GORDON
     double stone;-Gordon
     Clay W, 1883-1970   res. Howell
                                     d- 8-15-1970 age 87
     Hermoine, 1884-1944   res. Howell
                                     d-Jan. 30, 1944 age 59
7
     empty
8   DENSMORE
     double stone;-Densmore
     William C, (masonic)   res. Howell
     1892-1933   d-July 7, 1933 age 40, accident
     Mary L, (Star)   not listed
     1890-19-
9   RICHMOND
     large double stone;-Richmond
     Dr. Ray W, (masonic)   b-Howell twp. res. Lansing
     1887-1951   d-Feb. 28, 1951 age 64
     Bertha A, (Star)   b-Mi. res. Livingston Co.
     1891-1957   d- 5-3-1957 age 65
                                     (Mary E Franklin) res. Howell
                                     d-May 17, 1945 age 81
10   BURDEN--CURTIS
     Cort B, 1877-1959   b-Mi. res. Perry, Mi.
                                     d- 5-25, 1959 age 82
     Iva G, 1875-1928   "iva Grace" res. Locke
                                     d-Oct. 19, 1928 age 53
     Lillie, wife of James Burden   res. Chaelsea, Mi.
     1862-1945   d-July 30, 1945 age 82
     James Burden
     185801904   burial ? removed from ?
     on monument-Burden-Curtis
11   WELLER
     double stone;-Weller
     Merritt P, (FTL emblem)   b-Mi. res. Howell, Mi.
     1870-1956   d- 11-19-1956 age 86
     Carlie M,   b-Plainfied, res. Fowl.
     1872-1950   d-Nov. 26, 1950 age 79
                                     (Lewis Wilson) res. Lansing
                                     d-June 13, 1928 age 41
12   DOYLE--KUTTLER
     Paul Doyle "husband"   res. Chicago, Ill.
     1886-1929   d-Jan. 1, 1929 age 42
     Mabel Doyle "wife"   (Mabel Doyle Brausch)res. Howell twp.
     1892-1982   d- 6-29-1982 age 90

Section "Two"   Greenwood cemetery
lot #
12 continued
    Herbert Brausch   res. Howell
    1898-1967   d- 4-2-1967 age 68, heart trouble
    double stone;-Kuttler
    Arthur W, 1899-   not listed
    Mabel P, 1898-1980   burial 2-7-1980 age 81
13 MUNSELL--SATTERLA
    double stone;-Munsell
    Silas H, 1860-1930   res. Howell
                                   d-March 9, 1930 age 69, bronchitis
    Viola, 1864-1940   res. Howell twp.
                                   d-Dec. 10, 1940 age 76
    double stone;-Satterla
    Glen H, 1891-1967   res. Williamston
                                   d- 1-30-1967 age 75,
                                   burial from Williamston
    Ina, 1895-1976   res. Ingham Co.
                                   d- 6-1-1976 age 81
                                   (baby, Munsell) res. Fowlerville
                                   d-Nov. 6, 1946 stillborn

14 DRAPER--ACKER
    James H Draper   res. Howell
    1869-1930   d-July 8, 1930 age 61
    double stone;-Acker
    Eugene M, 1873-1953   b-Mi.   res. Oxford, Mi.
                                   d- 6-22-1953 age 80
    Margaret A, 1876-1953   b-Mi.   res. Fowlerville
                                   d- 4-22-1953 age 76

15 MANNING
    double stone;-Manning
    John H, 1863-1933   res. Fowlerville
                                   d-June 4, 1933
    Laura E, 1865-1944   "Libbie" res. Fowlerville
                                   d-June 12, 1944 age 79

16 GALE--CADWELL
    Harrison Thayer Gale   b-Wisconcin, res. Green Bay,Wis.
    1873-1951   d-May 9, 1951 age 77
    Amrille B Gale   "Arville" res. Cleveland, Ohio
    1885-1940   d-Dec. 12, 1940 age 52
    Una Ruf Zerbe   (Ana Sophia Zerbe) res. Fowl.
                                   died Aug. 18, 1940 age 75
                                   (William Zerbe)b-Mi. res. Wayne
                                   d- 4-26-1952 age 86

17 ECKERT
    double stone;-Eckert
    Joseph P, 1940   res. Howell
                                   d-Sept. 1, 1940 stillborn
    Dianne E, 1945   "Dian Elaine" res. Conway
                                   d-Feb. 13, 1945 age 0
    (recent grave)   (Helen Irene Eckert)
                                   d- 11-24-1982, res. Dade City, Fla.
    (recent grave)   (Otto Geo. Eckert)
                                   d- 8-7-1983 res. Zephrhills, Fla.

lot #
18   PALMER
      double stone;-Palmer
      George H, (vet)   b-Leroy, res. Brighton
      1886-1939   d-Oct. 28, 1939 age 53, accident
      Susan M, 1889-1979   "Susan May" res. Liv. Co.
                                        d- 9-24-1979 age 90

19   WILCOX--WARD
      (grave?)
      Norman E Wilcox (FLT emblem)   res. Lansing
      1878-1950   d-Sept. 25, 1950 age 73
                                        (Charles Ward) res. Fowl.
                                        d-Sept. 23, 1939 age 72
                                        (Mary Louise Ward)
                                        d- 7-17-1963 age 90
                                        (Matilda Peltier)b-Mi.
                                        d- 10-19-1956 age 88
                                        res. Meridian twp. Ingham Co.

20   MORLOCK
      double stone;-Morlock
      Ezra H, 1866-1943   res. Conway twp.
                                        d-Jan. 27, 1943 age 75
      Margaret E, 1877-1955 (Star)   b-Mi.   res. Howell
                                        d-Jan. 11, 1955 age 77
      George E Morlock (masonic)   res. Howell
      1897-1971   d- 12-27-1971 age 74
      triple stone;-Morlock
      Harry, "father" (masonic)   res. Florida
      1900-1979   burial 4-30-1979 ashes
      Edith, "mother" (OES)   not listed
      1913-
      Janett F, "daughter"   "Janett Florence" res. Conway
      1939-   d-April 3, 1939 age 22 days, pnue.
21   RATHBUN
      Marion L, 1905-1974   res. Livingston Co.
                                        d- 1-23-1974 age 68
      G Ray, 1896-1970   res. Livingston Co.
                                        d- 6-28-1970 age 73
      Anna B, 1875-1953   b-Mi.   res. Conway twp.
                                        d- 1-18-1953 age 82
      Walter B, 1850-1938   res. Conway
                                        d-age 87, burial June 22, 1938

      on monument-Rathbun
22   EATON
      double stone;-Eaton
      Wayne G, "husband" (masonic)   "Wayne Garwood"
      1908-1975   d- 7-6-1975 age 67(ashes)
      Alice Nelson "wofe" (OES)   "Veena Alice"
      1916-1971   d- 8-24-1971 age 55
                                        ashes bur. 7-20-1975 (?)

      Double stone;-Eaton
      Frank, 1874-1959   "Frank J" b-Mi. res. Ingham Co.
                                        d- 4-7-1959 age 84
      Bena, 1877-1953   b-Mi.   res. Lansing
                                        d- 6-8-1953 age 75

Section "Two"   Greenwood cemetery
lot #
22 continued
    Leona M Eaton   no information-listed lot 23
    1902-1913
    Patricia L Eaton   not listed
    1948-
    Frank G Eaton   not listed
     1948
23 EATON
    empty
24 GRILL
    double stone;-Grill (Maccabees emblem)
    Chris H, 1874-1953   b-Canada, res. Fowlerville
                                    d- 1-28-1953 age 78
    Carrie D, 1877-1941   res. Fowlerville
                                    d-Oct. 2, 1941 age 64
    infant daughter of L A & R M Grill   res. Fowlerville
      1929   d- Nov. 20, 1929 stillborn
                                    (Ruth Grill) res. Liv. Co.
                                    d- 9-12-1983 age 80
25 FULLER
    Clarence J Fuller (masonic)   b-Mi.   res. Fowlerville
    1876-1954   d-Oct. 15, 1954 age 77
    Elizabeth R Fuller   b-Mi.   res. Fowlerville
    1875-1952   d- 8-31-1952 age 77(listed lot 26)
26 FULLER
    Clara M Fuller "mother"   b-Mi.   res. Conway twp.
    1854-1924   d-Sept. 1, 1924
    Wells Fuller "father"   res. Ann Arbor, Mi.
    1850-1932   d-April 9, 1932 age 82
    on monument-Fuller
27 BETTS
    Russell Forest Betts   b-Mi.   res. Washtenaw Co.
    1884-1958   d- 4-12-1958 age 73
    Duane Fuller Betts   res. Ann Arbor
    1912-1938   d-age 25, pnue. bur. 5-19-1938
    Mabel Mehan Betts   res. Washtenaw Co.
    1884-1973   d- 6-1-1973 age 89
28 HUCK
    double stone;-Huck
    Harry J, 1895-1971   res. Howell
                                      d- 12-9-1971 age 76
    Eddie Lee, 1909-   not listed
    Alta Ruth Huck "mother"   b-Mi.   res. Livingston Co.
    1891-1959   d- 12-12-1959 age 68
    Countise M Huck   (listed as buried on lot A-126)see
    1925-1925
    Leonard A Huck   Buried ?
    1924-1925

                                      (Wilbur E Huck)
                                      burial 10-15-1956 (listed as lot 268)
29 VOGT
    Mary Ellen Vogt "daughter "   b-Mi.   res. Bay co. Mi.
    November 15, 1954-June 14, 1955   d-age 7mo. accident

Section "Two"   Greenwood cemetery
lot #
30   VOGT
        Levi S Vogt   b-Mi. res. Fowl. (or Conway)?
        1863-1925   d-Nov. 3, 1925 age 62
        Louisa Vogt   res. Fowlerville
        1863-1933   d-July 9, 1933 age 69
        Louisa S Vogt   not listed
        1899-19-
        John S Vogt (masonic)   "John Sebastian" b-Mi. res. Fowl.
        1888-1956   d- 5-15-1956 age 68
        Edith L Vogt (Star)   res. Livingston Co.
        1889-1973   d- 4-30-1973 age 83
        on monument-Vogt
           Theodore J, 1903-1911   res. Fowlerville(or Conway)?
                                        d-Aug. 17, 1911 age 14
                                        burial Nov. 7, 1925, removed from ?

31   BURBANK--HALE
        double stone-Hale
        Orman Bennett, 1866-1941   (Arman B Hale) res. Fowlerville
                                        d-Feb. 16, 1941 age 74
        Iva May, 1879-1965   res. Wayne
                                        d- 9-21-1965 age 86

        double stone;-Burbank
        Bester P, "father"   (listed on lot One-179) see
        1879-1940
        Carrie E, "mother"   b-Mi. res. Wayne city, Mi.
        1883-1960   d- 3-1-1960 age 76
32   HAMBURGER--HOPKINS
        double stone;-Hamburger
        Fred J, 1895-1971 (vet)   "Fred Jacob" res. Howell
                                        d- 12-19-1971 age 76
        Mary L, 1891-1949   res. Handy
                                        d-Dec. 29, 1949 age 58
        Wm. J Hopkins "father"   res. Brighton, Mi.
        1862-1934   d-Aug. 24, 1934 age 71
33   VOGT
        Julian B Vogt   res. Conway twp.
        1916-1936   d-June 20, 1936 age 19, fractured skul
                                        (Simon D Vogt) res. Liv. Co.
                                        d- 12-16-1983 age 92

34   VOGT--SEXTON
        double stone-Vogt
        William H, 1893-1982   res. Livingston Co.
                                        d- 12-6-1982 age 89

                married May 8, 1915
        Alma I, 1895-19-   not listed
        James A Sexton   "Sr." res. Detroit
        1913-1978   d- 4-4-1978 age 64
                                        burial from Lincoln Park

35   BERRY
        Anson Berry   res. Handy twp.
        1859-1927   d- 8-30-1927 age 68
        Mary E Berry   res. Handy
        1864-1930   d-July 6, 1930 age 66(listed lot 32)

Section "Two"   Greenwood cemetery
lot #
35 continued
        Eugene Berry   res. Handy twp.
        1885-1947   d-Aug. 22, 1947 age 61
        Clyde A Berry
        Michigan Pvt. Sup. Co. 340 Inf. 85 Div, World War 1
        Jan. 20, 1889-Dec. 30, 1961   d-age 72
36   CALKINS
        Harry G Calkins (masonic)   res. Handy
        1889-1936   d-Oct. 31, 1936 age 48,frac. skull
        Ima H Calkins   (OES)   res. Livingston Co.
        1885-1981   d- 3-10-1981 age 96
        on monument-Calkins

                                        (Margaret L West) res. Lansing
                                        d-June 26? 1947 age 1½ days
37   BOYD
        Frank J Boyd   b-Conway twp. res. Detroit
        June 19, 1873-Sept. 1, 1939   d-age 66
        Maud Maxfield Boyd   res. Detroit
        March 13, 1874-Sept. 22, 1936   d-age 62
        on monument-Boyd
38   HENDRYX
        double stone;-Hendryx
        Jesse J, 1874-1956   d- 9-8-1956 age 82 (listed lot 54)
        Nettie I, 1879-1960   b-Mi.   res. Kent city
                                        d- 5-28-1960 age 80

        Marene L Heil   no record
        1903-1928
39   WARNER
        triple stone;-Warner
        Florence E, (Star)   res. Byron, Mi.
        1886-1943   d-Dec. 7, 1943 age 57
        Ira B,   (masonic)   b-Liv. CO. res. Byron, Mi.
        1874-1952   d-April 6, 1952 age 77
        Julia A, 1879-1936   res. Pasadena, California
                                        d-Dec. 1936 age 57
                                        bur. Apr. 20, 1944, removed
                                        from Oak Hill cem.-California
40   PECKENS
        Laura Verre Polite, wife of Geo. A Peckens
        1891-1925   d-March 27, 1925
        George A Peckens (FLT emblem)"Geo. Alton" res. Fowlerville
        1881-1963   d- 9-12-1963 age 82
        Mabel Warren, wife of Geo. A Peckens   res. Brighton, Mi.
        1881-1940   d-Jan. 3, 1940 age 58
        Edith, wife of Pierre V Warren "mother"   res. Fowlerville
        1859-1934   d-Dec. 27, 1934 age 75
                                        (Wm. Peckens)
                                        d- March 27, 1925 stillborn
                                        (Lu-Ann A Roy) res. Fowl.
                                        d-June 12, 1945 age 2 months

Section "Two"   Greenwood cemetery
lot #
41   KINGSLEY
     Leila L Kingsley
     1896-19-   not listed
     Archie C Kingsley (masonic)   b-Mi.   res. Livingston CO.
     1890-1959   d- 6-18-1959 age 69 (listed lot 42)
     June Evelyn Kingsley   b-Fowlerville, res. Owasso, Mi.
     1924-1925   d-Aug. 19, 1925 age 2 months
     Calvin E Kingsley   res. Fowlerville
     1860-1930   d-Aug. 14, 1930 age 70
     Sarah F Kingsley   res. Fowlerville
     1861-1942   d-Jan. 1, 1942 age 80
42
     no stones   (Bernie Harris)
                                          burial 8-15-1972

43   ROGERS
     W J Rogers   "Willard J" b-Mi. res. Liv. Co.
     1873-1961   d- 4-29-1961 age 87
     Emma J Rogers   res. Locke twp. Ingham Co.
     1876-1948   d-July 30, 1948 age 71(bur. July? 2.)
     Don C Rogers   res. Williamston
     1911-1941   d-June 25, 1941 age 30
     double stone-Rogers
     Leo. W, 1906-   not listed
     Marjorie G, 1919-1977   res. Lansing
                                          d- 11-16-1977 age 58

44   PIERSON
     Hannah A Pierson   "Hannah Ann" res. Locke
     1866-1939   d-May 27, 1939 age 73
     George Pierson   b-Mi.   res. Fowlerville
     1860-1926   d-Nov. 10, 1926 age 66, pnue.
     Otto E Pierson   res. Livingston Co.
     1898-1976   d- 9-5-1976 age 78
     Florence E Pierson   not listed
     1901-19-
     Junior E,   "Juniro Emerson" res. Conway twp.
     June, 1935   d-June 15, 1935
45   NORDMAN--PIERSON
     double stone;-Nordman
     Frank Z, 1898-1982   res. St. Johns, Mi.
                                          d- 1-13-1982 age 83,
                                          burial from St. Johns

     Laura C, 1924-   not listed
     double stone;-Pierson (FLT emblem)
     Alfred, 1891-1963   b-Livingston Co. res. Fowl.
                                          d- 5-11-1963 age 72
     Sarah Ann, 1896-1947   res. Fowlerville
                                          d-Oct. 12, 1947 age 51

     On large vase-Pierson

Section "Two"   Greenwood cemetery
lot #
46   RATHBUN
     Frank A Rathbun "father" (vet)res. Wayne
     Sept. 14, 1856-Apr. 30, 1938   d-age 81
     Addie H Rathbun "mother"   res. Nankin twp. Wayne Co.
     Nov. 7, 1866-   d-Oct. 25, 1944 age 77
                                    (Monnie J Rathburn)b-Mi. res. Wayne
                                    d- 10-23-1960 age 74
47   CIMONS-CONNOR-JOHNSON (wide lot)
     double stone;-Cimons
     Lydia, 1882-1965   "Lydia L" res. Ingham Co.
                                    d- 9-2-1965 age 83

     Arthur, 1885-1958   b-Mi.   res. Ingham Co.
                                    d- 1-12-1958 age 72

     Mollie Connor   res. Fowlerville
     1854-1948   d-Jan. 2, 1948 age 93
     double stone;-Johnson
     Frank H, 1878-1950   res. Fowlerville
                                    d-Aug. 30, 1950 age 72

     Nancy J, 1880-1944   res. Fowlerville
                                    d-Aug. 18, 1944 age 64
                                    (Ruth E Johnson)b-Mi. res. Liv. Co.
                                    d- 10-16, 1955 age 83
48   WITT
     John H Witt   res. Fowlerville
     1857-1934   d-Jan. 3, 1934 age 76
     Grace Witt   "Grace M" res. Fowlerville
                                    d-Jan. 11,1948 age 81

49   CURTIS
     Joyce Ellis Curtis   no record
     S 2/c USN lost at sea
     Dec. 15, 1921-Dec. 11, 1942
     double stone;-Curtis
     Freeman L,   res. Livingston Co.
     June 14, 1900-Feb. 11, 1976   d-age 75
     Carrie A, (ladies Aux, VFW)   b-Mi.   res. Liv. Co.
     Apr. 16, 1899-June 15, 1960   d-age 61
50   WORSFOLD--MILLER
     double stone;-Worsfold
     Alfred C, 1891-1966   res. Farmington
                                    d- 11-24, 1966 age 75
                                    cremated in Detroit, bur. 1966
     Ida E, 1890-1964   burial 1964
     Bobbie W Miller   (Robert Worsford Miller)b-Mi.
     1946-1954   d-Dec. 12, 1954 age 8, res. Lansing
     baby Miller, 1944   (Mary P Miller) res. Lansing
                                    d-Feb. 25, 1944, bur. Mar. 21, 1944
51   FRANSON
     triple stone;-Franson
     Carl E, 1880-1941 (masonic)   (Charles E Franson)b-Sweden
                                    d-Aug. 22, 1941 age 60, res. Handy
     Helga, 1888-1973   res. Detroit
                                    d- 9-9-1973 age 85
     Thomas C,   "Thomas Charles" res. Detroit
        1932   d-April 14, 1932 age 2 weeks

Section "Two"   Greenwood cemetery
lot #
51 continued

                                  (Lois E Tomion)b-Mi. res. Liv. Co.
                                  d- 7-4-1957 age 81

52   SHOOTER--MONROE
      Irene E Voigt   res. Owasso
      1883-1941   d-Feb. 13, 1941 age 57
      double stone;-Shooter
      Benjamin, 1879-1945   "Wm. Benj." res. Fowlerville
                         d-Sept. 1, 1945 age 66
      Mae, 1881-1974   "Addie May" res. Liv. Co.
                         d- 12-1-1974 age 93
      double stone;-Monroe
      William E, 1902-19-   not listed
      Estella J, 1904-1979   res. Livingston Co.
                         d- 9-17-1979 age 74
      Cynthia Ann Monroe   b-Mi. res. Wayne
      Oct. 8, 1959-Jan. 23, 1960   d-age 3 months
53   SEYFRIED
      double stone;-Seyfried
      William F, 1889-1941   res. Tyrone twp.
                         d-Jan. 19, 1941 age 51
      Sopha U, 1892-1979   res. Genessee Co.
                         d- 12-25-1979 age 87

54   HILLMAN--SOULE
      double stone;-Hillman
      Ray M, 1896-1939   burial 12-19-1939
      Sarah C, 1891-1960   (Sarah G Manning)b-Mi. res. Liv. Co.
                         d- 3-21-1960 age 68, pnue.
      Jay W Manning   "J W" res. Fowlerville
      1888-1950   d-Nov. 29, 1950 age 62
      double stone;-Soule
      Bertha B, 1894-1967   res. Fowlerville
                         d- 9-16-1967 age 72
      (on footstone)wife, Bertha B
      Alger, 1893-1954   b-Mi. res. Fowlerville
                         d- 9, 1954 age 54, bur. 9-20-1954
      (on footstone)husband, Alger
55   MILLER
      Levi, "father"   res. Fowlerville
      1873-1948   d-March 9, 1948 age 74
      Emma, "mother"   "Emma Mary" b-Mi. res. Fowl.
      1865-1952   d- 5-25-1952 age 86 (listed lot 52)
      Brenda Lee Smith "our baby"   res. Ingham Co.
      Nov. 30, 1958 age 7 hours
      Richard D Smith "our baby"   res. Livingston Co.
      Jan. 3, 1956-Jan. 5, 1956
      on monument-Miller   (Wm. Allen Field) res. Liv. Co.
                         d- 3-8-1963 age 57
                         burial 3-11-1963 on L Miller lot

lot #
56   SHERWOOD (wide lot)
     double stone;-Sherwood
     Fred E, 1860-1943   res. Lansing
                                      d-May 5, 1943 age 82
     Emma L, 1865-19-   res. Lansing
                                      d-Dec. 16, 1949 age 84

     triple stone;-Sherwood
     Cleil V, "daughter"   not listed
     F Alta "mother"   "Flora A" res. Detroit
     1863-1940   d-Jan. 8, 1940 age 76
     Frank D, 1860-1958 "father"   res. Charlotte, Florida
                                      d- 6-14-1958 age 97

57   SISSON   (wide lot)
     Frank C, 1860-1927   res. Lansing
                                      d-Dec. 28, 1927 age 67
     Daisy B, 1876-1949   res. Lansing
                                      d-Dec. 8, 1949 age 79
     Dollie Fowler   res. Saginaw
     1868-1931   d-March 6, 1931 age 62
     Michael H McManus "father"   res. Howell
     Aug. 27, 1878-June 22, 1965   d-age 86
58   WESTMORELAND
     double stone;-Westmoreland
     George W, 1883-1947   res. Handy
                                      d-June 30, 1947 age 64
     Katherine H, 1892-1965   res. Handy
                                      d- 9-18, 1965 age 73
     Duane G Westmoreland   res. Livingston Co.
     F 2, U S Navy, World War 11
     Sep. 8, 1918-Dec. 17, 1980   d-age 62
59   DORNER
     double stone;-Dormer
     Charles, 1878-1953   b-Mi. res. Fowlerville
                                     d- 8-31-1953 age 75
     Emma M, 1881-1946   res. Fowlerville
                                     d-May 3, 1946 age 65

60   COTTON
     Claude E Cotton "father   "Claude Elliot" b-Mi. res. Detroit
     June 20, 1885-Nov. 3, 1958   d-age 73
     Hettie E Cotton "mother"   res. Detroit
     Nov. 14, 1884-Dec. 3, 1946   d-age 62
61   MOORE
     Frank J Moore   res. Detroit
     Co. m, 35 Mich. Vol.
     1873-1928   d-July 9, 1928, appendecitis
     Cadda E Moore   b-Mi. res. Wisconcin
     1882-1953   d- 8-23-1953 age 70(listed lot B-61)
     Elizabeth Jean, "daughter   (Eliz. J Moore) res. Detroit
     1829 -1943   d-Feb. 21, 1943 age 14
                                     (stone should read 1929-1943)
     Dorothy Mae, 1912-1913   (Dorothy Moore)
                                     burial ?, removed from Chelsea
     (has a big square pot with large base)

Section "Two"   Greenwood cemetery
lot #
62   NELSON
     Henry Eugene Nelson   res. Williamston
     1881-1929   d-July 19, 1929 age 48
     Carrie M Nelson Chase   not listed
     1888-19-
63   BOHN
     Lulu B Bohm   res. Fowlerville
     1883-1930   d-Jan. 8, 1930 age 46
     Howard E Bohm   b-Mi.   lived in Fowlerville
     1883-1961   d- 12-14-1961 age 78 in Florida
     Ollie L Bohm   b-Mi.   res. Howell
     1885-1957   d- 5-17-1957 age 71
     on monument-Bohm
64   SNELL
     triple stone;-Snell
     Ruby, 1882-1930   res. Ionia
                                     d-July 9, 1930 age 48
     John, 1879-1954   b-Mi.   res. Fowlerville
                                     d- 1-6-1954 age 75
     Ethel, 1889-1956   "Ethel Grace" b-Mi. res. Owasso
                                     d- 6-29, 1956 age 67
65   BROWN
     double stone;-Brown
     George T, 1868-1940 (masonic)   res. Detroit
                                     d-age 70, burial 1-18-1938
     Eliza B, 1868-1933 (OES)   res. Detroit
                                     d-Dec. 20, 1933 age 65,cancer
     Harold G Brown   (masonic)   b-Mi.   res. Wayne
     1893-1960   d- 4-11-1960 age 66
66   DREHER--FERRIN
     Jacob Dreher   res. Fowlerville
     1854-1940   d-March 14, 1940 age 85
     Ida B Dreher   "Ida F" res. Detroit
     1863-1942   d-April 26, 1942 age 78
     Winafred E Faunce   "Wineford
     1884-1934   d-Feb. 6, 1934 age 50
     double stone;-Ferrin
     Harry S   (FLT emblem)   res. Fowlerville
     1881-1949   d-May 19, 1949 age 68
     Grace L,   res. Fowlerville
     1879-1948   d-April 27, 1948 age 68
67   FERRIN
     Ronald D Ferrin (vet)   res. Lansing
                                     d- 2-26-1982 age 35

68   FERRIN--PECK
     double stone;-Ferrin
     Edmund M, 1916-1973 (vet)   "Edmund Milton" res. Eaton Co.
                                     d- 8-4-1973 age 57
                                     burial from Lansing

             married Sept. 4, 1936
     Dorothy E, 1917-   not listed

Section "Two"   Greenwood cemetery
lot #
68 continued
    double stone;-Peck
    Ida E, 1895-19-   not listed
    Joshua, 1891-1949 (vet)   res. Iosco twp.
                                       d-March 25, 1949 age 58
69 HETRICK
    double stone;-Hetrick
    Paul, 1898   not listed
         married April 7, 1920
    Madge, 1894-1980   "Madge V"
                                       d-age 85, burial 1-17-1980
    Paul H Hetrick Sr.
    M Sgt. U S Air Force, World War 11, Vietnam
    Jan. 29, 1923-Sep. 27, 1978   d-age 55
    Gordon Hetrick "son"   "Gordon L" res. Iosco twp.
    1927-1945   d-Sept. 30, 1945 age 18
                                  (baby, Hetrick) res. Ingham Co.
                                  d- 8-23-1963 stillborn
70 MOORE
    Sara C Moore, wife of Hubert S,   "Sarah" res. Merten, Wis.
    1901-1943   d-Aug. 8, 1943 age 41, bur. Aug. 13.
71 WRIGHT
    Sidney Wright "husband" (vet) res. Fowlerville
    1887-1963   d- 9-4-1963 age 76
    Earl Porter "father"
    1896-1973   res. Owasso, Mi.
                                  d- 3-4-1973 age 76
    Edith F Porter "mother"   b-Mi.   res. Livingston Co.
    1872-1956   d- 12-11-1956 age 84
    Sidney J Wright   res. Fowlerville
    1926-1945   d-Dec. 20, 1945 age 19
72 DALY--HILL
    double stone;-Daly
    Eleazer C, 1882-1962   res. Livingston Co.
                                  d- 5-24-1962 age 80
    Clara M, 1888-1969   res. Fowlerville
                                  d- 1-21-1969 age 80
    double stone;-Hill
    Mabel, 1910-   not listed
    Samuel, 1886-1972   res. Livingston Co.
                                  d- 3-10-1972 age 85
73 CHASE
    Dorothy B Chase   res. Ingham Co.
    1911-1982   d- 11-15-1982 age 71,bur. from Owasso
    Warren K Chase   res. Howell twp.
    1903-1944   d-Oct. 25, 1944 age 40
    Lydia E Chase   "Lydia Ann Eliz."b-Liv. Co.
    188--1961   d- 12-18-1961 age 80, res. Liv. Co.
    J Burr Chase   "James Burr" b-Cohoctah
    1864-1942   d-May 5, 1942 age 77
    on monument-Chase

Section "Two"   Greenwood cemetery
lot #
74   RUSSELL--MORLOCK (wide lot)
     double stone;-Russell
     Henry D, 1890-1946   res. Genoa twp.
                                     d-Nov. 16, 1946 age 56

     Mayme C, 1891-1970   res. Washtenaw Co.
                                     d- 4-30-1970 age 78

     double stone-Morlock
     Ralph W, "husband"   res. Livingston Co.
     1917-1981   d- 11-30-1981 age 64
     Lorene A, "wife"   (new grave?) no record
     1922-
75   COLE (wide lot)
     Arthur E Cole   res. Fowlerville
     1853-1937   d-Feb. 13, 1937, flu
     Ruth E Stanfield, wife of Arthur E Cole   res. Fowlerville
     1850-1933   d-Feb. 17, 1933 age 81
     Inez E, daughter of A E & Ruth E Cole   res. Fowlerville
     1877-1964   d- 8-3-1964 age 87
     Rollin E Cole (masonic)   res. Conway tpw.
     1895-1946   d-Sept. 23, 1946 age 51
     Mildred Hoffman, wife of Rollin E Cole   "Mildred L" res. Liv. Co.
     1900-1982   d- 2-15-1982 age 81
     on monument-Cole
76   LOREE
     Floyd W Loree   res. Williamston
     1880-1929   d-Nov. 4, 1929 age 48, appendecitis
     Flora Loree   (Flora Loree Wheeler) res. Liv. Co.
     1891-1973   d- 2-6-1973 age 81
                                     burial from Williamston
     Amelia Hacker   res. Williamston
     1859-1950   d-Nov. 30, 1950 age 91
     Henry C Hacker   res. Williamston
     1859-1930   d-Nov. 22, 1930 age 72
77   BENJAMIN
     double stone-Benjamin
     Clarence W, 1870-1958   b-Mi. res. Livingston Co.
                                     d- 3-18-1958 age 87
     Florence M, 1877-1970   res. Fenton, Mi.
                                     d- 8-5-1970 age 93
78   RICHMOND
     double stone-Richmond
     Deak Daniel, 1896-1948 (FLT)   "Daniel D" res. Williamston
                                     d-Jan. 26, 1948 age 51
     Addie Meader, 1895-1949   no record
     double stone;-Richmond
     Russell L, 1875-1946   res. Fowlerville
                                     d-Jan. 6, 1946 age 71
     Millie, 1878-1954   b-Mi. res. Fowlerville
                                     d-Oct. 16, 1954 age 76

Section "Two"   Greenwood cemetery
lot #
79   GARDENHOUSE--PAMMENT
     double stone;-Gardenhouse
     Charles, 1886-1938   b-Conway, res. Lansing
                                  d-age 52, cancer, bur. 9-20-1938
     Hazel M, 1892-1976   res. Ingham Co.
                                  d- 9-27-1976 age 76
80   LEMUNYON
     double stone;-Lemunyon
     Floyd, 1874-1955 "father"   b-Mi.   res. Leroy, Ingham Co.
                                  d- 10-14-1955 age 81
     Matie, 1876-1974 "mother"   d- 6-29-1974 age 98
81   BURRELL--MILLER
     Joseph Burrell
     Illinois Cpl. SVC Co. 2, Inf. 19 Div. World War 1
     Oct. 23, 1898-April 18, 1949 (d-April 14?, bur. Aug. 12, 1949)
                                  removed from Elmwood cem, Flora, Ill.
     Beulah Burrell (ladies Aux. VFW)"Beulah Hellen" b-Mi. res. Liv. Co.
     July 31, 1908-Oct. 26, 1958 d-age 50
     Herman T Miller   res. Livingston Co.
     1904-1941   d-March 31, 1941 age 36
82   OLSON
     Fred F, 1876-1953   b-Mi.   res. Lansing
                                  d- 5-21-1953 age 76
     Sarah C, 1877-1953   b-Mi.   res. Lansing
                                  d- 6-21-1953 age 75

     on monument-Olsen
                                  (Crystal J Baker) res. Ingham Co.
                                  d- 1-24-1982 age 58

83   HOLMES
     double stone;-Holmes
     Samuel R, 1863-1934   res. Conway
                                  d-Feb. 14, 1934 age 70
     Jennie, 1865-1944   res. Conway
                                  d- June 29, 1944 age 78
84   SCHAADT
     Larry L Schaadt   res. Dowagiac, Mi.
          1934   d-April 6, 1934 age 5 days
85   OLSEN
     Carl C Olsen "father"   res. Fowlerville
     1884-1932   d-Dec. 26, 1932 age 48,menengitis
86   DARE
     no stones   (Fredrick M Dare) res. Detroit
                                  d-Oct. 22, 1942 age 35
                                  (Harry E Coley) res. Howell
                                  d-Feb. 7, 1950 age 66
                                  (Cornelia Coley) res. Fowlerville
                                  d- 6-16-1963 age 80

87   MUNRO
     double stone;-Munro
     Harold, 1897-1968 "father"   "Harold B" res. Howell
                                  d- 1-21-1968 age 71
                                  (had amputated leg buried 11-15-67)
     Bethel, 1906   "mother" not listed
     Stanley Munro "son"   "Harold" res. Howell twp.
     1927-1942   d-Oct. 18, 1942 age 15

Section "Two"   Greenwood cemetery
lot #
88   JACKSON--HEINEMAN
      Alfred J Jackson "father"   "Alfred R" res. Fowlerville
      1857-1939   d-Aig. 30, 1939 age 84
      Effie C Jackson "mother"   "Effie Cornelia" res. Fowl.
      1868-1939   d-July 16, 1939 age 70
      Charles D Heineman   b-Mi. res. Blissfield, Lenawee Co.
      1887-1956   d- 5-11-1956 age 69
      Blanche A Heineman   res. Livingston Co.
      1886-1975   d- 8-19-1975 age 88
89   YERKS
      double stone-Yerks
      Louise A, 1903-19-   not listed
      Marion L, 1892-1944   res. Handy twp.
                                       d-Aug. 30, 1944 age 51

      (behind stone above)Marion L Yerks
                     Michigan Pvt. 107 Engrs. 32 Div.
                     Nov. 21, 1892-Aug. 30, 1944
90   DANIELS
      Leroy C Daniels   res. Howell
      Jan. 10, 1939-Aug. 18, 1944   d-age 5
      double stone;-Daniels
      Lelain B, 1910-1958   "Lelain Bruckner" b-Mi. res. Liv. Co.
                                       d- 3-15-1958 ahe 47, heart trouble

      Goldie L, 1914-   not listed
      Elmer C Pearson (masonic)   not listed
      1910-
91   VON RICHTER
      Naretta E Von Richter "mother" res. Lansing
      1912-1967   d- 11-10-1967 age 55
      multi stone;-Von Richter
      Floyd, 1868-1945   "Floyd W" res. Lansing, Mi.
                                       d-March 20, 1945 age 77

      Harriet, 1880-1965   res. Lansing
                                       d- 11-2-1965 age 85
      Gladys, 1905-   not listed
      Selden, 1907-1950   res. Pontiac
                                       d-July 9, 1950 age 43, accident
92   SMALLEY-FRANKS-MURPHY (wide lot)
      double stone-Smalley
      William, 1860-1936   "Wm. H" res. Ingham Co.
                                       d-June 29, 1936 age 76
      Kate, 1864-1951   "Katherine" res. Lansing
                                       d-Sept. 4, 1951 age 86
      Addie M Franks   res. Conway twp.
      1870-1936   d-July 4, 1936 age 66, heart
      George D FRanks   res. Conway
      1864-1937   d-July 20, 1937 age 73
      double stone;-Murphy
      Mayme K, 1878-1957   "Mayme Katherine" b-Mi. res. Eloise
                                       d- 9-29-1957 age 69
                                       burial 10-11-1957 cremated
      George A, 1867-1936   res. Fowlerville
                                       d-Aug. 26, 1936 age 69

Section "Two"   Greenwood cemetery
lot #
93   LAYTON-EMMONS-SHERWOOD (wide lot)
      Ralph L Emmons   res. Kalamazoo Co.
      1898-1969   d- 3-9-1969 age 70
      Maude R, 1879-1935   (Rose M Layton) res. Howell twp.
                                       d-Nov. 11, 1935 age 56, cancer

      John C, 1878-1961 (masonic)   no record
      Flora Belle, 1897-1968 (Star)   (Flora Belle Layton)
                                       burial 4-19-1968

      on monument-Layton
                                       (John Layton)
                                       burial 1-8-1896 from old cemetery

      double stone;-Emmons
      Amos, 1896-1976   res. Livingston Co.
                                       d- 9-30-1976 age 80(listed lot One-93)
      Fern, 1899-19-   not listed
      double stone;-Sherwood
      Eva, 1919-   not listed
      Garth, 1914-1968 (masonic)   res. Grosse Pointe, Mi.
                                       d- 4-20-1968 age 54
                                       (Terry Lee Berry)
                                       d- 7-6-1965 stillborn

94   HADLEY
      double stone;-Hadley
      Hazel, 1894-1935   res. Howell
                                       d-Nov. 29, 1935 age 43, heart
      Louis, 1893-1968   "Louis E" res. Howell
                                       d- 9-23-1968 age 70

95   SMITH
      Temple F, 1889-1944 (masonic)   res. Handy
                                       d- Dec. 26, 1944 age 55 in Detroit
      Julia A, 1890-1980 (Star)   burial 5-5-1980
      on monument-Smith
96   PARKER
      double stone;-Parker
      Peter Dow, 1876-1960   b-Mi.   res. Livingston Co.
                                       d- 11-15-1960 age 84
      Mabel E, 1883-1968   res. Fenton, Mi.
                                       d- 12-7-1968 age 85
97   RUTTMAN
      August Ruttman "father"   res. Iosco twp.
      1879-1963   d- 1-21-1963 age 83
      Mary G Ruttman "mother"   res. Iosco
      1887-1937   d-Feb. 14, 1937 age 49, pnue.
      Ernest L White   "Ernest Leslie" b-Mi. res. Marion
      1903-1959   d- 11-8-1959 age 56
      on monument-Ruttman
98   HART--PHELPS
      Burton M Hart   res. Detroit
      1878-1937   d-June 23, 1937 age 58, cancer
      Clarissa R Hart   res. Howell
      1883-1950   d-Feb. 2, 1950 age 67

Section "Two"   Greenwood cemetery
lot #
98 continued
     Gladys Hart McKiddie   (Gladys H McKiddy)b-Mi.
     1916-1961   burial 6-30-1961 cremated
                                   res. Wayne Co.
                                   (Victor Russell Phelps) res. Detroit
                                   d-7-28-1981 age 84, bur-ashes

99   RIDER--MILETT
     double stone;-Rider
     Charley A, 1874-1959   b-Mi.   res. Livingston Co.
                                   d- 4-23-1959 age 84
     Hattie, 1874-1956   b-Mi.   res. Livingston Co.
                                   d- 6-18-1956 age 82
     C Cecil Rider   "Clarence Cecil" res. Handy
     1913-1940   d-Sept. 11, 1940 age 27
     double stone;-Milett
     Hattiebelle, 1871-1947   res. Durand
                                   d-May 14, 1947 age 75
     Joseph, 1866-1948   "Jos. A" res. Durand, Mi.
                                   d-April 10, 1948 age 82
100 BELL
     no stones   (Malinda Bell) res. Fowlerville
                                   d-Nov. 16, 1937 age 78, cancer
                                   (Eugene Bell) res. Fowlerville
                                   d-Aug. 15, 1939 age 79
                                   (Grace Bell) res. Fowlerville
                                   d-Feb. 27, 1943 age 38
                                   (Helen Bell) res. Fowlerville
                                   d- 9-23-1964 age 71

101 WRUCK (wide lot)
     double stone-Wruck
     Carl O, 1896-1935 "husband" (masonic)   res. Detroit
                                   d-April 11, 1935 age 37
                                   (listed as Ruck, bur. 4-15-35)
     Frances, 1899-19-   "wife"   not listed
102 GROVER
     double stone;-Grover
     George T, 1888-1971   res. Livingston Co.
                                   d- 5-12-1971 age 82
     Lena, 1889-1958   b-Mi.   res. Howell
                                   d- 6-20-1958 age 68
103 GROVER
     double stone;-
     Joann L Johnson   "Joann Lucille" res. Fowlerville
     1943-1968   d- 11-10-1968 age 25
104 HUNRICH--RENN
     Carl Raymond Humrich
     Jan. 4, 1942-Oct. 15, 1950   d-age 8, fractured skull
                                   burial Oct. 18, 1950
     double stone;-Renn
     Bertha, 1913-1977   "Bertha H"
                                   d- 4-2-1977 age 64
     Carl, 1905-   not listed

Section "Two"   Greenwood cemetery
lot #
105 REINMANN
     Charles Reimann   res. Handy
     Michigan Wagr. 330 Fld. Arty. 85 Div. World War 1
     Oct. 4, 1887-Nov. 10, 1949   d-age 62
                                        (Grace Reinmann) res. Handy
                                        d- 10-10-1965 age 54

106 FRANKS--TUCKER
     double stone;-Franks
     Nelson, 1866-1957   "Nelson B" b-Mi. res. Iosco
                                        d- 1-22-1957 age 90
     Louisa, 1874-1947   "Louisa C" res. Handy
                                        d-March 22, 1947 age 72
                                        (Dusty Donald Franks)b-Mi.
                                        d- 10-14-1956 age 2 mo. sufficated

     double stone;-Tucker
     Elma M, 1885-1948   "Elma Mary" res. Fowlerville
                                        d-Oct. 20, 1948 age 63
     John W, 1876-1958   b-Mi.   res. Livingston Co.
                                        d- 12-1-1958 age 82
                                        (Caroline Jean Culver)res. Iosco
                                        d-April 22, 1951, premature
                                        (Russell Henry Mitchell)
                                        d- 3-4-1967 age 63

107 JENSEN
     Swen W, 1899-1941 "husband"   b-Sweden, res. Iosco twp.
                                        d-June 24, 1941 age 41
     Julia M, 1905-19-   "wife"   not listed
     Patricia A Conklin   res. Ingham Co.
     1928-1978   d- 8-19-1978 age 50
     on monument-Jensen
108 HOISINGTON
     Gale O Hoisington   not listed
     1895-19-
     Pearl H Hoisington   res. Fowlerville
     1899-1946   d-Oct. 4, 1946 age 47
     Meredith G Hoisington   res. Cohoctah
     1922-1938   d-age 16, auto accident
                                        burial 3-19-1938
     Kendall D Hoisington   res. Washtenaw Co.
     1919-1981   d- 5-2-1981 age 61
     Shirley E Hoisington   not listed
     1919-
     Nancy Lee Hoisington "baby"   res. Cohoctah
     Oct. 24-1940-Dec. 5   d-age 6 weeks, bur. 12-7-1940
     on monument-Hoisington
109 METZ--TRUHN
     Temple Bruce Metz (masonic)
     Dec. 17, 1920-Aug. 26, 1982   d-age 61
     Mary L Metz   "Mary Lee" res. Livingston Co.
     Lt. U S Navy, World War 11
     Dec. 4, 1919-March 9, 1981   d-age 61, burial Mar. 18, cremated

Section "Two"   Greenwood cemeter
lot #
109 continued
     double stone;-Metz
     Eva M, 1888-1960   b-Mi.   res. Livingston Co.
                                     d- 8-27-1960 age 72 of burns

     John G, 1885-1962   "John George" b-Liv. Co. res. Liv.
                                     d- 2-17-1962 age 76

110 O'DONNELL--GROMMON (wide lot)
     double stone;-O'Donnell
     Frank E, 1882-1937   res. Webberville
                                     d-July 29, 1937 age 56

     Ola M, 1882-1965   "Iva Viola" res. Grand Rapids, Mi.
                                     d- 3-6-1965 age 82

     double stone;-Graham Jr.
     Nellie M, 1875-1968   (Nellie Mae Graham)res. Hubbardston
                                     d- 9-14-1968 age 92

     George E Jr. 1876-1965   (Geo. Elmer Graham Jr.)res. Ionia)
                                     d- 4-16-1965 age 88

     double stone;-Grommon
     Josephine, 1879-1970   res. Washtenaw Co.
                                     d- 10-5-1970 age 91

     Fred, 1877-1939   "Frederick" res. Ann Arbor
                                     d-Nov. 10, 1939 age 62

111 BROWER   (wide lot)
     Willis A Brower "father" (masonic)   b-Mi. res. Kent Co.
     1865-1955   d- 12-2-1955 age 90
     Caroline V Brower   res. Fowlerville
     1862-1936   d-May 16, 1936 age 73
     Leland P Brower   res. Wayne Co.
     1900-1944   d-June 7, 1944 age 44
     Charles H Truman (masonic)   "Chas. Henry" b-Mi.
     1884-1960   d- 4-27-1960 age 75
                                     res. Ft. Lauderdale, Florida

112 BRISTOL--JOHNSON
     double stone;-Bristol
     William W, 1875-1938   b-Fowlerville, res. Fowl.
                                     d-age 63, burial 11-22-1938
     Maude A, 1822-1931   d-Dec. 20, 1931 age 49, pnue.
     double stone;-Johnson
     Josephine E, 1906-   not listed
     J C, 1903-1973   "J C" male, res. Livingston Co.
                                     d- 1-31-1973 age 69

113 RICKETT--HORTON
     double stone;-Rickett
     S Reynolds, 1854-1944   "Stephen R" res. Conway twp.
                                     d-April 13, 1944 age 89
     Jennie G, 1866-1933   res. Conway twp.
                                     d-Jan. 5, 1933 age 66

     double stone;-Horton
     Bessie M, 1897-1976   res. Livingston Co.
                                     d- 5-14-1976 age 78

     Roy D, 1894-1983   res. Ingham Co.
                                     d- 7-10-1983 age 89

Section "Two"   Greenwood cemetery
lot #
114 GRISWOLD
     double stone;-Griswold
     Burt W, 1864-1935   res. Fowlerville
                                      d-May 6, 1935 age 71, stroke

     Edna M, 1882-1969   no record
115 JENSEN
     Patty Ann Lozo   "Patricia" res. Fowlerville
     1926-1932   d-Aug. 16, 1932 age 8, pnue.
     double stone;-Jensen
     Olga, 1897-1977   res. Oklahoma
                                      d- 9-28-1977 age 80
     Henry S, 1897-19- (med. insignia)   not listed
     William Jensen   res. Fowlerville
     1881-1964   d- 9-8-1964 age 83
116 MILLETT
     Edward B Millett "father"   res. Perry, Mi.
     1879-1935   d-May 21, 1935 age 56, heart
117 ELLIOTT--ALLBRIGHT
     Nettie Rose Elliott   res. Lansing
     Sept. 27, 1862-July 6, 1932   d-age 69
     double stone;-Allbright
     Wayne E,   not listed
     May 17, 1900-
     Gertrude M,   "Gertrude C" res. Wayne Co.
     Sept. 2, 1903-Oct. 17, 1972   d-age 69, buried from Detroit
                                      (James H Allbright)res. Fowl.
                                      d-Jan. 23, 1936 age 76
                                      (Ida R Allbright)b-Liv. Co.
                                      d- 10-10-1961 age 92, res. Gratiot Co.

118 THORNBURY--PIKE
     double stone;-Thornbury
     Albert J, 1852-1934   res. Handy
                                      d-Oct. 17, 1934 age 82

     Cynthia A, his wife   res. Handy
     1860-1939   d-June 20, 1939 age 79
     double stone;-Pike
     Pearl E, 1890-1975   res. Livingston Co.
                                      d- 9-13-1975 age 85

     Glen H,1890-1941   res. Handy
                                      d-Jan. 18, 1941 age 50
119 (wide lot)
     empty
120 HARDY
     Mariah Hardy "mother"   "Maria H" res. Lansing
     1861-1935   d-June 9, 1935 age 74
121-122
     empty
123 RUSSELL
     Halsey, 1902-1969   (Halsey Edward Russell)res. Liv. Co.
                                      d- 10-23-1969 age 67

     on monument-Russell

Section "Two"   Greenwood cemetery
lot #
124 RUSSELL
     Timothy Wayne Russell "our son"   res. Handy twp.
     Nov. 10, 1952-Nov. 12, 1952   d-age 2 days of heart condition
125 HORTON
     Gerald E Horton   "Gerald Edward" res. Handy
     1947-1949   d-April 13, 1949 age 1, lukemia
126 KLEE--CASADY
     double stone;-Klee
     Robert W, 1896-1946   res. Jackson
                                   d-Nov. 26, 1946 age 48
                                   burial June 16, 1948 from Jackson

     Hazel B, 1898-19-   (Star)   not listed
     double stone;-Casady
     Lillian H, 1874-1961   b-Mi.   res. Livingston Co.
                                   d- 1-9-1961 age 86

     Amos B, 1871-1966 (masonic)   res. Fowlerville
                                   d- 1-26-1966 age 95

127 CASADY
     double stone;-Casady
     Frank J, 1886-1978   res. Livingston Co.
                                   d- 4-18-1978 age 91

     Maggie, 1887-1967   res. Fowlerville
                                   d- 5-31-1967 age 80

     Ross M Casady   res. Conway twp.
     1920-1935   d-June 23, 1935 age 14
     Wanda Jo "my darling"   (Wanda J Schultz)res. Fowl.
     May 7, 1964   d5-7-1964 age 1 minute
128 DIETRICH--JOHNSON
     double stone;-Dietrich
     Herbert C, 1892-1972   res. Livingston Co.
                                   d- 1-27-1972 age 79

     Winnie B, 1888-1951   b-Conway twp. res. Fowlerville
                                   d-Dec. 29, 1951 age 63

     double stone;-Johnson
     Cora Dell, 1869-1952   b-Conway, res. Livingston Co.
                                   d-Feb. 15, 1952 age 82

     Edward, 1872-1953   b-Mi.   res. Fowlerville
                                   d- 12-1-1953 age 81

129 DIETERLE--DRIVER
     double stone;-Dieterle
     Julia, 1910-   not listed
     Walter, 1902-1950   res. Lansing
                                   d-Aug. 14, 1950 age 47
129 DRIVER-WELLS-DIETERLE-CARLSON (wide lot)
     double stone-Driver
     George, 1878-1956   "Geo. W" b-Mi. res. Fowlerville
                                   d- 8-16-1956 age 78

     Edna, 1879-1949   res. Handy twp.
                                   d-Nov. 7, 1949 age 70

     double stone;-Wells
     George W, 1882-1950   res. Fowlerville
                                   d-Aug. 1, 1950 age 68

     Louise M, 1885-1964   "Louise Mary" res. Oakland Co.
                                   d- 9-7-1964 age 79

Section "Two"   Greenwood cemetery
lot #
129 continued
    John W Carlson   "John Werner" b-Sweden, res. Howell
    1870-1954   d-Dec. 6, 1954 age 84
130 SHOWERS--CARR
    Maude M Benjamin   "Maude May" b-Fowl. res. Fowl.
    1875-1940   d-Nov. 14, 1939 age 63
    Mattie L Showers   res. Washtenaw Co.
    1877-1969   d- 11-11-1969 age 92
    Harry B Showers   b-Mi.   res. Fowlerville
    1874-1955   d-Jan. 9, 1955 age 80
    Erwin P Carr   (masonic)   b-Mi.   res. Fowlerville
    1867-1952   d- 10-30-1952 age 85
    Fame Carr   "Fame Benjamin" b-Mi. res. Liv.Co.
    1873-1960   d-11-10-1960 age 87
131 MATTHIESEN
    double stone;-Matthiesen
    John F, 1872-1955   "John Frederick"b-Mi. res. Ingham Co.
    Luna M, 1878-1962   "Luna Mae" b-Liv. Co. res. Ingham Co.
                                d- 1-14-1962 age 83

    Double stone;-Matthiesen
    Leon J, 1901-   not listed
    Ella Marie, 1908-   not listed
132 BROWER-MATTHIESEN
    double stone;-Brower
    Rose M, 1895-19-   not listed
    David, 1887-1970   res. Livingston Co.
                                d- 10-3--1970 age 70
    Leo Matthiesen   res. Lansing
    Oct. 14, 1936   burial 10-16-1936 age 0
    double stone;-Matthiesen
    Agnes B, 1902-   not listed
    Clifford H, 1903-   not listed
133 CHAPPEL
    Margurite, 1893-1931   "Margaret"
                                burial 6-9-1936,
                                removed from Catholic cemetery
    Dale R, 1893-1965   "Dale Richard" res. Stockbridge
                                d- 10-28-1965 age 72
    Louise, 1893-1964   "Louise A" res. Stockbridge, Mi.
                                d- 5-10-1964 age 71

    on monument-Chappel
134 MAXWELL
    double stone;-Maxwell
    Clara E, 1888-1971   "Clara Edith" res. Oceola twp.
                                d- 6-13-1971 age 82
    Ray R, 1887-1957   b-Mi.   res. Livingston Co.
                                d- 7-3-1957 age 70

Section "Two"   Greenwood cemetery
lot #
135 HAIST--BAKER
     double stone;-Haist
     Arthur W, 1910-1975   "Arthur Winfield" res. Lansing
                                    d- 7-28-1975 age 65,
                                    burial from Charlotte, Mi.

          married July 29, 1935
     Beulah E, 1912-   "Beulah Edna" res. Eaton Co.
                                    d- 5-8-1983 age 71
                                    (Charles Baker) res. California
                                    d- 3-23-1972 age 70
                                    burial from LaPuento, California

136 HAIST
     Arist H Haist   "Arist Harpel" res. Detroit
     1918-1943   d-Aug. 27, 1943 age 24
                                    (Nelson Frederick Haist)b-Liv. Co.
                                    d- 9-18-1961 age 80, res. Liv. Co.
                                    (Maude Haist) res. Livingston Co.
                                    d- 10-29-1975 age 87

137 VAN POLEN
     Robert E Van Polen "son"   "Robt. Ernest" res. Fowlerville
                                    d-March 26, 1943 age 17

138 WINEGAR
     Gilbert Henry Winegar   res. Florida
     1880-1963   d- 3-3--1963 age 82
     Minnie Ann Winegar   b-Florida, res. Pinellas Co. Fla.
     1878-1960   d- 12-11-1960 age 82
     Fred Winegar   "Fredrick" res. Howell
     1905-1937   d-March 27, 1937 age 30, accident
139 HAARER
     Ernesr G Haarer "father"   (listed on lot 132)
     1870-1939   d-Sept. 20, 1939 age 68, cancer
     Estella M Haarer "mother"
     1875-1934   burial 9-3-1934
140 BUGARD--LANTIS
     double stone;-Bugard
     Jesse A, 1878-1960   "Jesse Anthony" b-Mi. res. Liv. Co.
                                    d- 3-29-1960 age 82
     Violet S, 1891-1951   b-Detroit, res. Cohoctah twp.
                                    d-Nov. 10, 1951 age 60, cancer
     Joe M Lantis   "Joseph M" b-Kansas, res. Howell
     1888-1951   d-Oct. 26, 1951 age 58
141 HALE--AUSTIN
     double stone;-Hale
     Albert E, 1910-1958   "Albert Ellis" b-Mi. res. Liv. Co.
                                    d- 11-22-1958 age 48
     Anita I, 1912-1981   res. Livingston Co.
                                    d- 2-17-1981 age 68

     double stone;-Austin
     Frances L, 1883-1974   res. Clare, Mi.
                                    d- 2-2-1974 age 90
                                    burial from Owasso, Mi.
     Spencer W, 1883-1958   b-Mi.   res. Fowlerville
                                    d- 9-17-1958 age 75

Section "Two"   Greenwood cemetery
lot #
142 HARRIS
     double stone;-Harris
     Clara V, 1894-1954   b-Mi.   res. Fowlerville
                                  d- 1-26-1954 age 59

     Bernie G, 1890-1972   res. Livingston Co.
                                  d- 8-12-1972 age 82

143 WRIGHT--KING
     Eva E Wright "mother"   "Eva Elizabeth" res. Liv. Co.
     1916-1962   d- 12-8-1962 age 46
     double stone;-King
     Gerald F, 1902-1978   res. Liv. Co.
                                  d- 11-22-1978 age 76

     Gladys E, 1902-   not listed
144 PHILLIPS--PARKER
     double stone;-Phillips
     Viola V, 1907-19-   not listed
     Theron A, 1900-1956   b-Mi.   res. Brighton
                                  d- 8-9-1956 age 55

     double stone;-Parker
     Mayme, 1881-1960   "Mayme H" b-Mi. res. Genessee Co.
                                  d- 11-21-1960 age 79

     Emerson D, 1879-1962   res. Livingston Co.
                                  d- 10-1-1962 age 83

145 MORLOCK--SMITH
     double stone;-Morlock
     Floyd D, 1901-1964   res. Fowlerville
                                  d- 11-14-1964 age 63

     Ruth E, 1898-1960)Legion Aux.)b-Mi.   res. Livingston Co.
                                  d- 5-7-1960 age 62

     triple stone;-Smith
     Dorothy, 1904-19-   not listed
     Kate, 1877-1969   "Catherine" res. Liv. Co.
                                  d- 7-17-1969 age 92

     Rollie, 1874-1959 (vet)   b-Mi.   res. Livingston Co.
                                  d- 11-15-1959 age 85

146 GROMMON--HAYWARD
     Foyer R Grommon   "Faye R" female, b-Mi. res. Wayne
     Marine Corps
     1910-1960   d- 12-28-1960 age 50
     Ernest D Grommon   b-Mi.   res. Whitmore Lake, Mi.
     T/Sgt. U S Army
     1902-1955   d-March 30, 1955 age 52
                                  (Linda Lee Hayward)b-Mi. res. Howell
                                  d-March 17, 1955 age 1 day
                                  (Donna Kay Hayward)b-Mi. res. Lansing
                                  d- 4-7-1956 age 3 hours. premature

147 SHARPE
     Vern Sharpe (vet)   b-Mi.   res. Conway twp.
     1899-1959   d- 10-21-1959 age 60

Section "Two"   Greenwood cemetery
lot #

148 TOBIN
     Patrick B Tobin   b-Fowlerville, res. Brighton
     1898-1941   d-July 25, 1941 age 43
     double stone;-Tobin
     Rose E, 1878-1949   res. Brighton
                                     d-Oct. 8, 1949 age 72

     Edward, 1867-1944   res. Brighton twp.
                                     d-April 24, 1944 age 76

149 SHOOTER
     double stone;-Shooter
     Rose D, 1919-1954   indian, b-Mi. res. Howell
                                     d- 1-19-1954 age 34
     Oscar A, 1914-19-   not listed
                                     (baby, Shooter)res. Liv. Co.
                                     d- 2-3-1962 stillborn

150 LYNN-GALBRAITH-SUTTON
     double stone-Lynn
     Jessie W, 1876-1954   b-Mi.   res. Fowlerville
                                     d- 2-12-1954 age 77, pnue.
     George W, 1879-1957   b-Mi.   res. Livingston Co.
                                     d- 7-5-1957 age 78
                                     (baby, Lynn)b-Mi. res. Fowl.
                                     d- 3-25-1954 age 0
     Pearl E Galbraith (legion Aux.)"Pearl Esther" res. Fowlerville
     1897-1968   d- 3-6-1968 age 70
     William W Galbraith   "Wm. Wayne" b-Illinois, res. Ill.
     1891-1956   d- 9-7-1956 age 64(listed lot 64)
151 OESTERLE
     Charles C, 1888-1981   (Chas. C Osterle) res. Handy
                                     d-Dec. 25, 1931 age 42, typhoid
     Asenath B, 1893-1943   (Asenath Wilson) res. Kalamazoo
                                     d-Sept. 8, 1943 age 49

     Charles E Hearrington   res. Handy twp.
     1852-1939   burial 8-7-1939 age 86
     Barbara A Hearrington   res. Handy
     1852-1944   d-Jan. 31, 1944 age 91, bur 2-8-44
     on monument-Oesterle
152 MALEITZKE
     August J Maleitzke   res. Handy
     1890-1933   d-March 17, 1933 age 42, cancer
     Ruth C Maleitzke Jacobs
     1897-19-   not listed
     Brad Coy Maleitzke "our baby"   res. Ingham Co.
     May 7, 1955-May 13   d-May 13, 1955 age 6 days, premature
153 MASTIC
     double stone;-Mastic
     William B, 1893-1957   "Wm. Bertie" b-Mi. res. Liv. Co.
                                     d- 1-3-1957 age 63
     Alice M, 1904-1948 (legion aux.)"Alice Mae" res. Fowlerville
                                     d-Oct. 26, 1948 age 44

Section "Two"   Greenwood cemetery
lot #
154 ALBERT
     double stone;-Albert
     Carolyn J, 1951-1952   b-Mi.   res. Lansing
                                   d- 4-10-1952 age 7 months

     Karen A, 1948-1950   "Karen Ann" b-Mi. res. Lansing
                                   d-Feb. 18, 1950 age 1 year
                                   moved from lot Two-44, April 16, 1952

155 GENNRICH
     Wendy Ann Gennrich "our baby" b-Mi.   res. Saginaw
     Apr. 27, 1953-July 27, 1953   d-age 3 months
156 BESSERT--SKYM
     double stone;-Bessert
     Albert, 1892-1970   res. Livingston Co.
                                   d- 6-3-1970 age 78

     Eva I, 1889-1963   "Eva Isabell" res. Fowlerville
                                   d- 5-21-1963 age 73

     Carol Ann Skym   res. Livingston Co.
     1946-1963   d- 1-27-1963 age 16, carbon monoxide
157 HUCK--BROWN
     double stone;-Huck
     Winnie O, 1897-1954   b-Mi.   res. Howell twp.
                                   d-Oct. 24, 1954 age 57

     Wilbur E, 1893-1956   b-Mi.   res. Livingston Co.
                                   d- 10-11-1956 age 63
                                   (listed on lot Two-268-no such lot)

     triple stone;-Brown
     Laura, 1884-1959   "Laura Ann" b-Mi. res. Handy
                                   d- 7-26-1959 age 75

     Joseph, 1877-1956   "Jos. C" b-Mi. res. Liv. Co.
                                   d- 10-24-1956 age 79(listed lot 63)

     Gerald, 1914-   not listed
158 SOULE--RAYMER
     double stone;-Soule
     George C, 1897-1973 (masonic) res. Livingston Co.
                                   d- 12-21-1973 age 76

     Ruby E, 1899-19-   not listed
     Marilyn Marie Soule   "Murlon" res. Fowlerville
     1922-1935   d-Jan. 17, 1935 age 12, pnuemonia
     double stone;-Raymer
     Clarissa L, 1870-1948   res. Conway twp.
                                   d-Feb. 10, 1948 age 77

     Lester E, 1875-1952   no record
159 McILWAIN--WILSON
     donald G McIlwain   res. Brighton
     1903-1935   d-May 16, 1935 age 32, auto accident
     Theodore R McIlwain   res. Livingston Co.
     1905-1969   d- 11-4-1969 age 64
     double stone;-Wilson
     Stuart J, 1892-1974 (vet)   res. Livingston Co.
                                   d- 2-19-1974 age 81

     Marie T, 1897-1975   res. Macomb Co.
                                   d- 10-8-1975 age 77

Section "Two"   Greenwood cemetery
lot #
160 LILLARD
     double stone;-Lillard
     Clarence G, 1902-   not listed
     Lolabell, 1910-1978   res. Fenton
                                        d- 4-3-1978 age 68

161 AUSTIN-WHITFORD-BELL
     double stone;-Austin
     Anna, 1929-   not listed
     Joseph W, 1903-1970   res. Lansing
                                        d- 8-21-1970 age 67
     Edith M Van Riper, wife of Gerald Whitford,b-Mi. res. Ingham Co.
     1907-1960   d- 12-24-1960
162 HESS-- PHILLIPS
     double stone;-Hess
     Hilton E, 1903-1970   "Hilton Earl"
                                        d- 8-30-1970 age 67,shot wound
     double stone;-Phillips
     Foster J, 1897-1975   d- 7-3-1975 age 77
     Lena A, 1900-1962   res. Livingston Co.
                                        d- 4-22-1962 age 62

163 LEWIS
     Randy Edwin Lewis "our baby"   res. Livingston Co.
     June 21, 1959-Dec. 17, 1959   d-age 6 months
     Melvin L Lewis (masonic-FLT-VFW)   res. Fowlerville
     March 29, 1926-July 29, 1964   d-age 38, heart trouble
     Helen L Lewis "mother"   not listed
     Decemeber 14, 1903-
     Chester L Lewis "father"   res. Livingston Co.
     February 8, 1901-September 3, 1977   d-age 76
     on monument-Lewis
164 MUSOLF--ANDERSON
     Amy Sue Musolf "our daughter"   res. Washtenaw Co.
     5-18-1968 7-18-1969   d- 7-21, 1969 age 1
165 BRIGGS--HAMLIN
     double stone;-Briggs
     Herbert J, 1880-1963   res. Livingston Co.
                                        d- 2-11-1963 age 82
     Minnie, 1886-19-   no record
     double stone;-Hamlin
     Rose U, 1912-   not listed
     Willard J, 1910-1962   res. Livingston Co.
                                        d- 3-26-1962 age 51

166 MUNRO-SOMMER-
     Irma Josephine Munro   res. Ingham Co.
     1889-1975   d- 3-31-1975 age 83
                                        (Merril W Munro)res. Lansing
                                        d- 11-11 age 64 age 73

     double stone;-Sommer
     Hilda A, 1899-19-   not listed
     Louis H, 1887-1966   "Louis Henry" res. Fowlerville
                                        d- 3-22-1966 age 79

     Jerry (carved on a rock)   (Geraldine Frances Smith)
                                        d- 4-30-1983 age 37, res. Ingham Co.

Section "Two"   Greenwood cemetery
lot #
167 MALEITZKE
     Phyllis Lynda Maleitzke   res. Wayne Co.
     1954-1964   d- 7-29-1964 age 10, pnuemonia
168 KING
     Agnes A Corse   res. Detroit
     Mar. 6, 1887-Nov. 27, 1975   d-age 88, burial from Brighton
169
     empty
170 NASS--JENSEN
     double stone;-Nass
     Margaret M, 1914-   not listed
     Arnold A, 1911-1968   res. Livingston Co.
                                    d- 4-20-1968 age 56

     Dorothy M Jensen   not listed
     1932-
     Henry Rober Jensen   "Henry Robert" res. Washtenaw Co.
     Michigan AIC U S Air Force, Korea
     July 22, 1929-July 10, 1970   d-age 40
171 LEWIS
     double stone;-Lewis
     Harold K, 1895-1979 masonic-vet)
                                    d-age 83, burial 5-31-1979
     Mabel Mann, 1893-1979 (OES)   (Mabel Lewis) res. Liv. Co.
                                    d- 8-8-1979 age 85
172 double stone;-Rolfe
     Floyd A,   res. Ingham Co.
     Mar. 4, 1903-Nov. 28, 1970   d-age 67
     Wilma A,   res. Ingham Co.
     Jan. 3, 1913-Apr. 17, 1972   d-age 59
173 PEARSON--KETCHUM
     Meta M Pearson "mother"   "Mattie M" b-Mi. res. Ingham Co.
     1874-1960   d- 11-18-1960 age 86
     double stone;-Ketchum
     Virginia, Jan. 26, 1917-   not listed
     Arthur H,   "Arthur Henry" res. Ingham Co.
     July 21, 1912-Feb. 15, 1972   d-age 59, burial from Williamston
174 ANCEL
     Jimmy Ancel "our baby"   b-Mi. res. Livingston Co.
     May 10, 1958   d-May 10, 1958 age 12 hours, prem.
175
     empty
176 BOGAN
     Gerald F Bogan   b-California, res. Los Angeles, Cal.
     Michigan AVN Cadet, Army Air Forces, World War 11
     July 26, 1925-March 16, 1958   d-age 33
     Frank Jay Bogan "our son"   b-Detroit, res. Wayne Co.
     1940-1946   d- 10-11-1946 age 6
                                    bur. 4-29-1958, removed from
                                    Evergreen cemetery in Detroit
     Elvah M Bogan "our beloved mother"   res. Livingston Co.
     1900-1969   d- 1-7-1969 age 68
                                    (Wm. Charles Bogan)res. Detroit
                                    d- 12-11-1976 age 76-cremated

Section "Two"   Greenwood cemetery
lot #
177 WEGIENKA
     double stone;-Wegienka
     John S, 1896-1967   "John Stanley" b-Fowlerville
                                    d- 10-18-1967 age 71

     Audrey E, 1909-1979   "Audrey Elaine" res. Georgia
                                    d- 10-10-1979 age 70
178
     empty
179 WINEGAR
     double stone;-Winegar
     John S, 1900-1983   res. Oakland Co.
                                    d- 4-9-1983 age 82

          married Dec. 22, 1923
E Marie, 1905-   not listed
     Richard H Winegar   "Richard Henry"
     Jan. 13, 1930-July 14, 1972   d-age 41 at VA hospital, at
     25th Div. 65th Eng.   Battle Creek, Mi.
180 GEISTER
     Robert L Geister   res. Iosco
     June 21, 1931-Aug. 2, 1975   d-age 44
                                    (Alice Geister)
                                    burial 8-5-1975

181 EBERT--MacINTOSH
     double stone;-Ebert
     Heinrich, 1897-1977   res. Livingston Co.
                                    d- 1-9-1977 age 79

     Margaret, 1896-1975   res. Livingston Co.
                                    d- 10-6-1975 age 79

     double stone;-MacIntosh (DFD_IAF of F)
     Erdean L, 1918-   res. Livingston Co.
                                    d- 1-3-1984 age 65

     Vaughn L, 1912-1972   res. Livingston Co.
                                    d- 2-20-1972 age 59
                                    burial from Detroit

182 ROLFE--BAKER
     double stone-Rolfe
     Edmund, 1898-1977   d- 3-4-1977 age 78
     Marian, 1920-   not listed
     Crystal J Baker, nee Rollins
     1923-1982   d-age 53, burial Jan. 27, 1982
182
     empty

- - - - - - - - - - - -
End

SECTION "3"

GREENWOOD CEMETERY

Veterans' Memorial

Section 3

Section "Three"   Greenwood cemetery
lot #
1 to 4 are the Veterans' section (vet monument in middle)
    (lots listed in two rows, from left to right)
    Donald B Wyzlic   res. Washtenaw Co.
    T Sgt. U S Air Force
    Feb. 15, 1927-Oct. 30, 1974   d-age 47
    Ralph P Lyons Jr.
    Tec 5, U S Army, World War 11
    1920-1977   d- 4-4-1977 age 56
    Howard J Goetterman   res. Roseville, Mi.
    Sn. U S Navy, Vietnam
    Sep. 22, 1945-Aug. 23, 1980   d-age 34
    William E Boyce   "Wm. Earl" res. Livingston Co.
    Pfc. U S Army, World War 11
    Mar. 13, 1913-Nov. 16, 1980   d-age 67
    Ernest F Boyce   res. Washtenaw Co.
    U S Army, World War 11
    Nov. 23, 1918-July 24, 1982   d-age 63
    Robert D Behringer   res. Howell, Mi.
    Michigan S 1, USNR, World War 11
    July 30, 1923-Jan. 12, 1969   d-age 45
    Richard E Fredenburg   res. Howell
    Michigan Sp 4, U S Army, Vietnam
    April 20, 1943-Aug. 25, 1973   d-age 30
    Andrew Lindquist   res. Saginaw
    Pvt. U S Army, World War 1
    Jul. 22, 1893-Dec. 17, 1975   d-age 82
    Paul A Binando   res. Los Angeles, California
    Sp 4, U S Army, Vietnam
    1943-1978   d- 1-30-1978 age 34
    Thomas Rankin   res. Livingston Co.
    Pvt. U S Army, World War 1
    May 27, 1896-Feb. 20, 1978   d-age 81
    Spencer L Crawford   no record
    U S Navy
    Mar. 2, 1942-May 11, 1980
    Harry E Haskins   b-Mi.   res. Livingston Co.
    born Sept. 23, 1923, died Dec. 5, 1958   d-age 35
    Alvin E McPherson   b-Mi.   res. Livingston Co.
    Michigan Cpl. Co. F, 18 Infantry, World War 1
    May 10, 1892-June 22, 1960   d-age 68
    Thomas W Wright   b-Mi.   res. Livingston Co.
    Michigan Pvt. 91 Infantry Division, World War 11
    Sept. 27, 1898-June 3, 1961   d-age 62
    Dale R Hefner   res. Hawaii
    EO 3, U S Navy
    Jul. 31, 1961-Nov. 7, 1981   d-age 20, accident in Navy
                                   burial 11-16-1981
    Albert E Hefner   "Albert Edwin" res. Liv. Co.
    Michigan Pvt. 110 Inf. 28 Inf Div.
    July 3, 1911-Dec. 22, 1968   d-age 57

Section "Three"   Greenwood cemetery
lot #
        veterans' lots continued
        Edward Marvin Hiner
        Michigan A2c, 37 Air Ddef. Msl. Sq. AF
        March 2, 1943-May 11, 1964   d-age 21, airplane crash in
                                      Phillipine islands
        Norman W Vermillion   res. Parkers Corners
        Michigan A3c, U S Air Force
        Nov. 8, 1941-June 18, 1963   d-age 21
        John Zuzisky   res. Livingston Co.
        Michigan Cpl. Hq. Co, 126 Infantry, World War 1
        Dec. 25, 1889-Dec. 25, 1962   age 72
        Biron W Bradley   "Brian W" res. Somerset, Pa.
        Cpl. U S Marine Corps
        Sep. 11, 1961-Feb. 12, 1982   d-age 20, skull fracture
        on monument-
        "In memory of those who so gallantly served in the wars of our
        country" Village of Fowlerville, Handy township, Conway township,
        Iosco township. Dedicated May 30, 1958.
5   HYST-KREMSKI-LUCAS
        double stone;-Hyst
        Stanley, Dec. 19, 1921-   not listed
            (married?)May 1, 1950
        Natalie I,   res. Washtenaw Co.
        Dec. 14, 1929-Dec. 22, 1980   d-age 51
        double stone;-Kremski
        Albert, 1925   "father"   not listed
        Janette E, "mother"   (listed as Jack Lucas sister)
        1927-1980   burial 2-6-1980
6   VAN SLYKE--BOHN
        double stone;-Van Slyke
        William J, 1896-1981   res. Livingston Co.
                                       d- 10-29-1981 age 84
        Edythe M, 1896-19-   not listed
        double stone;-Bohn
        Georgia, 1896-1974 (OES)   res. Livingston Co.
                                       d- 7-23-1974 age 78
        Cecil, 1892-1977 (masonic)   "Julius C" res. Washtenaw Co.
                                       d- 6-7-1977 age 85
7   HARDY--SOBER
        double stone;-Hardy
        Maude M, 1892-1958   "Maude May Louise" b-Mi. res. Liv. Co.
                                       d- 2-24-1958 age 65
        Purl C, 1887-1958 (masonic)   b-Mi. res. Handy
                                       d- 7-10-1958 age 71
        double stone;-Sober
        Carrie B, 1879-1966   "Carrie Bush" res. Handy
                                       d- 8-18-1966 age 87
        Orson W, 1884-1958   b-Mi. res. Livingston Co.
                                       d- 1-13-1958 age 72

Section "Three"   Greenwood cemetery
lot #
8   SMITH--BENJAMIN
     double stone-Smith
     Neva Maud, 1893-1980   res. Ingham Co.
                                   d- 11-26-1980 age 87
                                   burial from Lansing

              married Dec. 6, 1919
     Yaple Enoch, 1886-1967 (vet) res. Holland, Mi.
                                   d- 6-1-1967 age 81

9   WALLENMAIER
     multi-stone;-Wallenmaier
     William W, 1891-1968   res. Fowlerville
                                   d- 11-26-1968 age 77
     Bertha L, 1897-1968   res. Fowlerville
                                   d- 7-23-1968 age 70
     Amil W, 1917-1975   res. Livingston Co.
                                   d- 10-3-1975 age 58
     Edith M, 1921-   not listed
10- KILLINGER
     double stone;-Killinger
     Laura, 1891-1975   "Laura E" res. Liv. Co.
                                   d- 4-29-1975 age 84
     Arwin, 1890-1965   "Arwin T" res. Conway twp.
                                   d- 12-16-1965 age 75

11   RADDATZ--KRUMM
     double stone;-Raddatz
     Nellie M, 1894-1977   res. Livingston Co.
                                   d- 8-14-1977 age 83
     Carl W, 1893-1968   "Carl Wm." res. Fowlerville
                                   d- 2-6-1968 age 74,frac. skull

     double stone;-Krumm
     Della M, 1901-   not listed
     Charles, 1906-1973   res. Livingston Co.
                                   d- 5-8-1973 age 66

12   GASS--HAYTER
     double stone;-Gass
     Beulah G, 1886-1967   no record
     Arthur, 1896-19-   not listed
     double stone;-Hayter
     Margaret J, 1907-19-   not listed
     John W, 1909-1957   b-Mi. res. Ingham Co.
                                   d- 12-16-1957 age 48

13   DARE
     Peter Joseph Dare "our son"   res. Fowlerville
     1961-1969   d- 1-27-1969 age 7
14
     empty
15   GOETTERMAN
     Howard W Goetterman   res. Livingston Co.
     Pfc. U S Army, World War ll
     Dec. 7, 1926-Mar. 11, 1981   d-age 54

Section "Three"   Greenwood cemetery
lot #
16   RADDATZ
      double stone;-Raddatz
      Margaret M, 1913-1980   res. Ingham Co.
                                     d- 6-9-1980 age 67
      Ralph W, 1911-1978   res. Washtenaw Co.
                                     d- 4-6-1978 age 66

17   WEGIENKA
      triple stone;-Wegienka
      Charles, 1922-1983 "son"   res. Fowlerville
                                     d- 2-10-1983 age 61, pnue.
      Viola, 1898-   "mother"   not listed
      George, 1894-1967 "father"   "Geo. F" res. Fowlerville
                                     d- 2-28-1967 age 72

18   HETCHLER
      Goldie B Hughes, 1908-   not listed
      Rose A Hetchler   res. Handy twp.
      1885-1964   d- 1-26-1964 age 78
      Henry J Hetchler   res. Livingston Co.
      1883-1983   d- 5-11-1983 age 99
      on monument-Hetchler

19   CROFOOT
      small multi stone;-Crofoot
      Raymond, June 5, 1954   "Ray Arthur" d-age 6
      Leonard, May 17, 1955   "Leonard Wayne" d-age 5
      Edward, Sept. 4, 1956   "Edward Marvin" d-age 3
      Alan, January 10, 1959   "Alan Dale" d-age 1
                                     (all above d-8-21-1960 in a fire)
      Mitchell Ray, 1952-1957   (Mitchell Ray Crofoot)b-Mi.
                                     d- 10-27-1957 age 5, car wreck
                                     removed from lot ONe-36 in 1960
      Judy Lynn, 1957-1957   res. Livingston Co.
      children of George & Rita Crofoot   d- 10-31-1957 stillborn
                                     (both Mitchell & Lynn killed
                                     in a car wreck)
                                     (Penny Crofoot) res. Handy twp.
                                     d- 11-10-1963 age 2½ mo. of shock

20   CRESSWELL
      double stone;-Cresswell
      Caleb, 1884-1968 "father"   res. Fowlerville
                                     d- 9-19-1968 age 84
      Mary, 1883-1966 "mother"   "Mary Bell" res. Howell
                                     d- 12-2-1966 age 83

21   DOUGLASS
      Dororthy I, 1913-   not listed
      Stirling C, 1913-   not listed
      on monument-Douglass
22   BROOKLAND
      Lillie Brookland "loving mother"   b-Mi. res. Fowl.
      1895-1958   d-10-18-1959 age 63
      Floyd C Brookland "dear father""F Charles" b-Mi. res. Fowl.
      1889-1959   d- 7-14-1959 age 70
                                     (Raymond C Brookland)res. Shia. Co.
                                     d- 1-7-1978 age 63
                                     burial from Owasso.

Section "Three"   Greenwood cemetery
lot #
23   SPALDING
     double stone;-Spalding
     Mable E, 1896-1983   res. Livingston Co.
                                     d- 7-18-1983 age 87
     Roscoe C, 1889-1972   res. Livingston Co.
                                     d- 10-2-1972 age 83
                                     (David Lynn Spalding)b-Mi.
                                     d- 12-6-1958 age 3 days
                                     burial at foot of Roscoe C.
                                     res. Ann Arbor, Mi.
24   SLANKER
     Karl J Slanker "son"   "Karl Jr." b-Mi. res. Fowl.
     1937-1959   d- 2-22-1959 age 21
25   HILL
     Gary Lee Hill "our darling baby"   res. Colorado Springs
     March 19, 1969   d- 3-21-1969 stillborn
     double stone;-Hill
     Julia M, June 14, 1920-   not listed
     James B, Oct. 8, 1913-   not listed
26   BOWEN
     double stone-Bowen
     Carl D, Nov. 9, 1922   not listed
          married May 27, 1946
     Frances A,   "Frances Adeline" res. Howell
     Aug. 17-1924-Dec. 25, 1978   d-age 54
27   BOHM
     empty
28
     empty
29   DALY
     double stone;-Daly
     Wayne E, USN (vet)   res. Ingham Co.
     1914-1982   d- 8-1-1982 age 68
     Helen A, 1916-   not listed
30   (used for part of well-house site)
31   SLANKER--VOGT
     Frank Slanker   b-Mi. res. Livingston Co.
     1876-1959   d- 11-12-1959 age 83
     Goldie Slanker   res. Eaton Co.
     1878-1972   d- 5-13-1972 age 93
     double stone;-Vogt
     Leora D, 1910-   not listed
     Rollin F, 1906-1961   "Rollin Fred" b-Mi. res. Ingham Co.
                                     d- 3-18-1961 age 55
32   KLEIN--LINTEMUTH
     double stone;-Klein
     Clara A, 1880-1972   res. Howell
                                     d- 1-19-1972 age 92
     Daniel C, 1875-1967   "Dan Charles" res. Fowl.
                                     d- 10-28-1967 age 92

Section "Three"   Greenwood cemetery
lot #
32 continued
    double stone;-
    Viola L, 19o4-   not listed
    Marshall L, 1908-1982   res. Livingston Co.
                                            d- 7-30-1982 age 73

    on monuemnt-Lintemuth
33 PALMERTON
    double stone;-Palmerton
    Eva Jean, 1918-   not listed
    Glenn, 1908-1976   res. Livingston Co.
                                            d- 2-3-1976 age 67

34 PALMERTON
    double stone;-Palmerton
    Zadie, 1873-1963   "Zadie Jane" res. Fowlerville
                                            d- 8-28-1963 age 90
    Fred H, 1867-1937   "Harvey F" res. Fowlerville
                                            d-May 18, 1937 age 69
                                            removed from lot A-66, 1963

35 BRAUN
    double stone;-Braun
    Edward C, 1899-1965   "Ed. Clinton" res. Fowlerville
                                            d- 3-6-1965 age 66
    Luella E, 1910-   not listed
    Rodney C Braun "our baby"   "Rodney Clinton" res. Fowl.
    7-17-67   9-15-67   d- 9-17-1967 age 2mo, heart
36 JEFFREY
    Anna Marie Jeffrey   (Anna M Newkirk)res. Liv. Co.
    1943-1962   d- 10-15-1962 age 19, auto accident
    double stone;-Jeffrey
    Ethel M, 1910-1972   d- 5-17-1972 age 62. res. Liv. Co.
    Lyle G, 1905-1979   "Lyle Emerson" res. Howell
                                            d- 6-1-1979 age 74

37 COLL--SMITH
    double stone;-Coll
    LeMoine M, 1915-1976   res. Livingston Co.
                                            d- 8-31-1976 age 60
    Charles L, 1915-   not listed
    double stone;-Smith
    Hubert T, 1901-1977   res. Livingston Co.
                                            d- 7-27-1977 age 76

    Laura, 1904-   (OES)   not listed
38 BROOKS
    double stone;-Brooks
    Roland A, (masonic)
    1891-1965   burial 8-11-1965
    Nellie V, 1892-19-   not listed
    Donald Lee Bates "beloved husband"   res. Genessee Co.
    1947-1976   d- 12-10-1976 age 29,carbon Monox.

Section "Three"   Greenwood cemetery
lot #
39   BESSERT
     double stone;-Bessert
     Ernest H, 1901-1961   b-Mi.   res. Livingston Co.
                                      d- 9-15-1961 age 59

     Bernice M, 1908-   not listed
40   BROCKMILLER--SCHAFER
     double stone;-Brockmiller
     Vern, 1905-   not listed
     Fred E,   (masonic)   res. Livingston Co.
     1894-1978   d- 6-20-1978 age 83
     double stone;
     Joseph H Schafer (masonic)   res. Oakland
     1895-1962   d- 4-7-1962 age 76
     Florence M Schafer (Star)   res. Livingston Co.
                                      d- 5-21-1977 age 84
41   (used for part of well-house site)
42   GIEGLER--WALTERS
     double stone;-Giegler
     Graham L, 1910-   not listed
            married Sept. 26, 1934
     Kathleen, 1912-   not listed
     John E Walters   res. Livingston Co.
     Pfc. U S Army, World War 11
     Aug. 15, 1925-Nov. 5, 1979   d-age 54
43   KING--GEER
     Marvin J King   res. Fowlerville
     Cpl. U S Army, Korea
     Aug. 14, 1928-Nov. 2, 1982   d-age 54
     Victor H Geer   (vet)   res. Livingston Co.
     1918-1982   d- 7-16-1982 age 64
44 & 45
     empty
46   FISHER--ADDISON
     double stone;-Fisher
     Blanche E, 1905-   not listed
     Harvey C,   (vet)   res. Livingston Co.
     1905-1979   d- 10-11-1979 age 73
     double stone;-Addison
     Edward C,   res. Ingham Co.
     Jan. 25, 1888-June 6, 1976   d-age 88
     Grace M,   res. Livingston Co.
     Feb. 17, 1890-May 14, 1974   d-age 84
                                      (Daniel D Sancho)res. Wash. Co.
                                      d- 2-2-1984 age 18

47   BOZARTH--ALSTOTT
     double stone;-Bozarth
     Luther W,   "Jim"   res. Livingston Co.
     1906-1982   d- 8-14-1982 age 75
            married June 16, 1935
     Bernice V, "Bea" 1904-   not listed
     Roger W Alstott "father"
     1953-1971   d- 9-18-1971 age 18 of burns
                                      (A MacDonalds) d-age 75, bur. ?

Section "Three"   Greenwood cemetery
lot #
48   McCONNELL-BENJAMIN-HAMMOND
     Leslie Hugh McConnell   res. Livingston Co.
     Sgt. U S Army, World War ll
     Jan. 19, 1922-May 25, 1981   d-age 59
                                    (Virginia Mae Stickney)
                                    d- 1-13-1982 age 77, res. Ann Arbor
                                    (Georgia Hammonds mother)
49
     empty
50   HOUSTON
     Kimberly Jo Houston   res. Detroit
     June 23, 1963   d-stillborn
51   TOMION
     Flora A, 1899-   not listed
     S Walter   "Samuel Walter"
     1899-1977   d- 9-26-1977 age 78
     Lois E, 1875-1957   no record
     Samuel J, (masonic)   res. St. Petersburg, Florida
     1876-1973   d- 1-27-1973 age 96
     on monument-Tomion
52   CAMPBELL
     double stone;-Campbell
     W Bruce, (masonic)   "Wm. Bruce" res. Livingston Co.
     1913-1962   d- 4-8-1962 age 48
     Lois W, 1912-19-   not listed
53   KLEIN
     Ruth W, 1905-1962   res. Livingston Co.
                                    d- 6-14-1962 age56
     Harold D, 1904-   not listed
     on monument-Klein
54   NYGREN
     W William Nygren "beloved father"   "Walker Wm."
     1920-1974   d- 9-16-1974 age 54, res. Wash. Co.
     Robert W Mechanico (FFA)   res. Livingston Co.
     1946-1963   d- 1-27-1963, carbon monoxide
     double stone;-Nygren
     Louis L, "father"   res. Livingston Co.
     1893-1982   d- 8-18-1982 age 89
     Hazel E, "mother"   res. Livingston Co.
     1900-1970   d- 7-12-1970 age 69
     Ella M Ferrington   "Ella May" res. Livingston Co.
     1871-1963   d- 9-13-1963 age 91
55   HENDREN--LEPARD
     double stone;-
     Lida Rainey   (OES)   no record
     Sept. 27, 1893-
     Jesse Jones   (vet)   res. Lansing
     Feb. 14, 1893-July 16, 1971   d-age 71
     on monument-Hendred
     Mary E, 1910-   not listed
     Cecil L,   (Cecil L Lepard) res. Fowl.
     1910-1969   d- 1-17-1969 age 58
     on monument-Lepard

Section "Three"   Greenwood cemetery
lot #
56   ROBERTS--CURTIS
     double stone;-Roberts
     Alma V, 1900-1982   res. Houghton Lake, Mi.
                                    d- 8-7-1982 age 82
                                    burial from Prudenville, Mi.
     J D, 1900-1967   "John D"
                                    d- 5-14-1967 age 66
     double stone;-Curtis
     Bessie B, 1889-1967   res. Fowlerville
                                    d- 3-18-1967 age 77
     Clyde H, 1880-1965   d- 1-13-1965 age 84
57   HILL--LUDTKE
     double stone;-Hill
     Anna M, 1904-19-   not listed
     Ralph C, 1908-1970   no record
     double stone;-Ludtke
     Edna M, 1893-1967   "Edna Mae" res. Fowlerville
                                    d- 11-18-1967 age 74
     Chris O, 1889-1966   res. Fowlerville
                                    d- 7-29-1966 age 77
58   WOODS--PLUMMER
     double stone;-Woods
     Thomas G, 1894-1973 (masonic-vet)   res. Liv. Co.
                                    d- 5-17-1973 age 78
     Besse E, 1898-19-   not listed
     Anna E Alger "mother"   b-Mi.   res. Fowlerville
     1865-1959   d- 9-8-1959 age 94
     double stone;-Plummer
     Betty G, 1923-   not listed
     G Glendon, 1922-1972 (vet)   "Gerold Glendon" res. Ingham Co.
     1922-1972   d- 5-23-1972 age 50
59   BENJAMIN
     double stone;-Benjamin
     Frances E, 1922-   not listed
     Charles N, 1918-1969 (vet)   res. Livingston Co.
                                    d- 6-19-1969 age 51
60   ALSTOTT
     double stone;-Alstott
     Webster N, 1908-1979 (masonic) burial 12-15-1979 age 71
     Edith F, 1909-   not listed
     double stone;-Alstott
     Forrest L, 1913-   not listed
     Alys E, 1917-   not listed
     Irene B Alstott
     1907-1971   d- 8-13-1971 age 64
61   NIXON--ALSTOTT
     double stone;-Nixon
     Clark D, 1889-1980   res. Livingston Co.
                                    d- 12-17-1980 age 91
     Hathe M, 1896-1978   "Hathe May" res. Livingston Co.
                                    d- 5-13-1978 age 81

Section "Three"   Greenwood cemetery
lot #
61 continued
        double stone;-Alstott
        Elbert M, 1917-   not listed
        Marguarette T, 1916-   not listed
                                           (Webster Noah Alstott)res. Liv. Co.
                                           d- 12-12-1979 age 71

62   VOGT
      no stones   (Hilda M Vogt) res. Wayne Co.
                                           d- 2-4-1981 age 55
                                           (Anna Popa) res. Livingston Co.
                                           d- 2-9-1984 age 76

63   BURLEY
      double stone;-Burley
      Floyd E, 1902-   not listed
      Charlotte K, 1902-1981   res. Charlotte, Mi.
                                           d- 9-5-1981 age 79

64   HASTINGS--BURLEY
      empty
65   SCHADDT--CARSON
      empty
66   JOHNSON--MORRELL
      double stone;-Johnson
      Albert E, 1903-1982   res. Fowlerville
                                           d- 9-11-1982 age 78

      Bessie, 1915-   not listed
      double stone;-Morrell
      Francis J, 1914-   not listed
      Rose K, 1907-   not listed
67   WRIGHT--COPELAND
      double stone;-Wright
      Frank E, Sr. (masonic)   "Frank Elwood" res. Liv. Co.
      1911-1974   d- 8-12-1974 age 62
              married Oct. 6, 1934
      Juanita G, 1916-   not listed
      double stone;-Copeland
      Virginia M, 1914-1980   res. Washtenaw Co.
                                           d- 8-7-1980 age 66
      Russell H, 1910-1972   res. Fowlerville
                                           d- 11-17-1972 age 62
68   FULLER--BURLEY
      Judith Ann, "daughter"   no record
      June 23, 1944
      Milburn Wells Fuller "father   res. Livingston Co.
      Jan. 11, 1905-Dec. 14, 1979   d-age 74
      Ethel B Burley Fuller "mother"   not listed
      July 12, 1907-
      on monument-Fuller
      double stone;-Burley
      Arnold N, 1903-1963   res. Fowlerville
                                           d- 6-17-1963 age 59

      Oso Mau, 1904-   not listed

Section "Three"   Greenwood cemetery
lot #
69   HALL--MONROE
     James B Hall   (vet)   "James Burton" res. Manistee, Mi.
     1927-1963   d- 4-29-1963 age 36, airplane crash
70   KETCHUM
     double stone;-Ketchum
     Frances M, 1913-   not listed
     Theodore N, (masonic)   res. Livingston Co.
     1912-1963   d- 4-30-1963 age 50
71   GROSTIC--McLEAN-CLARK
     double stone;-Grostic
     Rosanna L, 1885-1966   "Roasanna Lavinia" res. Genoa twp.
                                     d- 7-9-1966 age 81
     Charles J, 1878-1963   res. Genoa twp.
                                     d- 9-30-1963 age 85
     double stone;-McLean
     Charles W, 1884-1963   res. Handy
                                     d- 12-4-1963 age 79
     Helen A, 1884-1970   res. Livingston Co.
                                     d- 7-21-1970 age 86
                                     (Wm. H Clark) res. Fowlerville
                                     d- 1-22-1969 age 79
                                     (Jane Elizabeth Clark)res. Fowl.
                                     d- 1-16-1968 age 69

72   CLARK--EPLEY
     double stone;-Clark
     Charles J, MD "father"   "Chas. Jr." res. Genoa twp.
     1905-1965   d- 9-21-1965 age 60
             married May 31, 1936
     A Lucille, "mother   not listed
     1910-
     double stone;-Epley
     Cleo F, 1918-1982 (OES)   res. Washtenaw Co.
                                     d- 12-4-1982 age 64
     Victor B, 1922-   (masonic)   not listed
73   BERTOLASI--PETERS
     Joseph L Bertolasi "father"   res. Winnebago Co. Illinois
     1912-1965   d- 12-29-1964 age 51
     Helen M Bertolasi "mother"   b-Mi.   res. Handy
     1911-1959   d- 8-30-1959 age 48
     Gus H Peters   (Hans Heinrick Peters)res. Fowl.
     Apr. 2, 1883-May 20, 1967   d-age 84
74   DeFOREST--PETERSON
     double stone;-DeForest
     Mabel I, 1900-1961   "Mabel Irene" b-Mi. res. Liv. Co.
                                     d- 5-27-1961 age 61
     Ernest J, 1897-1980   burial 2-9-1980
     double stone-Peterson
     Hulda, 1888-1961   b-Mi.   res. Livingston Co.
                                     d- 6-18-1961 age 73
     Reinhold, 1889-1961   res. Ingham Co.
                                     d- 9-21-1974 age 85

Section "Three"   Greenwood cemetery
lot #
75   SMITH
     double stone;-Smith
     Eda A, 1911-   not listed
     Harold L, 1904-1980   burial 4-14-1980 age 76
                                           (Corey Allen Smith)
                                           d- 4-17-1977, premature

76   LARSEN
     double stone;-Larsen
     Jeanette E, 1911-1961   "Emma Jeannette" b-Liv. Co.
                                           d- 12-6-1961 age 50, res. Liv. Co.
     William P, 1892-1965   res. Handy twp.
                                           d- 7-11-1965 age 73

77   FULKERSON
     double stone;-Fulkerson
     Lois M, 1898-1982   res. Livingston Co.
                                           d- 9-5-1982 age 84
     Ezra A, 1896-1971   res. Livingston Co.
                                           d- 2-6-1971 age 74

78   WALLACE-LOUNSBERRY-ROGERS
     double stone;-Wallace
     Paul F, 1903-1976   res. Howell twp.
                                           d- 3-31-1976 age 72
                                           burial 4-13-1976 ashes
     Rosemond M, 1908-   not listed
     double stone;-Lounsberry
     Dorothy M, 1921-   (OES)   not listed
     Clare C, 1913-1974 (masonic)   res. Lansing
                                           d- 3-14-1974 age 60

     double stone;-Rogers
     Carmen M, 1915-   not listed
           married June 11, 1938
     Myron D, 1909-1973   "Myron Daniel" res. Liv. Co.
                                           d- 5-4-1973 age 63
79   HALL
     Margaret L Hall   res. Royal Oak, Mi.
     1887-1977   d- 11-19-1977 age 90
     (on metal tag)Herbert Billings Maxwell   res. Liv. Co.
               born Feb. 23, 1897, died Aug. 7, 1983 age 86
                             (Helen E Hall)res. Liv. Co.
                             d- 10-16-1983 age 73

80
     empty
81   GIBSON
     empty
82   MEAD
     double stone;-Mead
     Leo B, 1908-   not listed
     Mary P, 1917-1976   res. Washtenaw Co.
                                           d- 11-17-1975 age 59, bur. 1975.

Section "Three"   Greenwood cemetery
lot #
83 LARSEN-HEARL-VOSS
    Minnie Ronschke   res. Liv. Co. (mother of Gert. Voss)
    1888-1974   d- 7-31-1974 age 86
    double stone;-Larsen
    Ralph H, 1905-1980 (masonic)   "Ralph Henry"
                                   burial 12-18-1980 age 75
    Lilah C, 1910-1980   (OES)   "Lilah Cynthia" res. Liv. Co.
                                   d- 7-6-1980 age 69
    double stone;-Hearl
    Leah E, 1910-   not listed
            married Aug. 15, 1936
    Donald, 1911-   not listed
84 DeMARAIS
    Caleb R DeMarais   no record
    Pvt. U S Army, World War 1
    Jan. 26, 1904-May 10, 1980
    M Agnes DeMarais   not listed
    Feb. 14, 1912-
85 GALBRAITH--SIMICH
    triple stone;-Galbraith
    Clinton R, 1891-1979 (vet)   res. Livingston Co.
                                   d- 10-7-1979
    Florence G, 1892-1965   res. Handy twp.
                                   d- 2-20-1965 age 73
    James W, 1918-   not listed
    double stone;-Simich
    Mary L, 1887-1963   res. Handy
                                   d- 11-16-1963 age 76 in Florida
    Luke, 1885-19-   not listed
86 KELLY-HUGHES-REDINGER
    double stone;-Kelly
    Garland B, 1897-1965   res. Arkansas
                                   d- 7-29-1965 age 67
    Marvel E, 1901-1963   "Marvel Elnice" res. Liv. Co.
                                   d- 2-2-1963 age 61
    Blanche A Hughes   res. Fowlerville
    1894-1969   d- 10-22-1969 age 75
    double stone;-Redinger
    Florence A, 1904-1962   res. Livingston Co.
                                   d- 10-31-1962 age 58
    Lyle C, 1901-19-   not listed
87 FLADOM--ANDERSON
    Emil Fladom   (Emil Fladam) res. Iosco
    Michigan Cook, Med. Det. 42 Mg Bn, World War 1
    Dec. 29, 1892-Dec. 10, 1962   d-age 69
    double stone;-Anderson
    Ida, 1882-1967   (listed on section One-87) see
    Frank H, 1879-1962   res. Livingston Co.
                                   d- 8-13-1962 age 83
88 CHASE
    double stone;-Chase
    Florence W, 1911-   not listed
    E Carleton, 1906-1960   "Eugene Carleton" b-Mi. Res. Liv. Co.
                                   d- 1-10-1960 age 53

Section "Three   Greenwood cemetery
lot #
89   WINEGAR--ESCH
     double stone;-Winegar
     F Claude, 1886-1963   res. Livingston Co.
                                      d- 4-9-1963 age 76
     Marion E, 1911-   not listed
     double stone;-Esch
     Norman M,   "Norman Martin" res. Leroy twp.
     July 16, 1923-Dec. 30, 1964   d-age 41, burial 1-2-1965
     Betty J,   not listed
     Nov. 25, 1925-
90   JONES-ANDERSON-PARSONS
     double stone;-Jones
     LaRainne F, 1918-   not listed
     Sam D, 1913-1965   res. Fowlerville
                                      d- 12-9-1968 age 55
                                      (Franklin Anderson) res. Howell
                                      d- 8-4-1963 age 74
                                      (Blanche Anderson) res. Howell
                                      d- 2-2-1971 age 78
                                      (Robert Warren Parsons)res. Conway
                                      d- 5-11-1966 age 46

91   HARFORD--COLL
     double stone;-Harford
     Alice, 1870-1958   (Alice L Hartford)b-Mi.
                                      d- 12-8-1958 age 87
     George, 1867-1963   res. Howell
                                      d- 6-25-1963 age 95
     double stone;-Coll
     Ruby L, 1893-1975   "Ruby Lorena" res. Liv. Co.
                                      d- 10-15-1975 age 82
     Basil L, 1889-1958   b-Mi.   res. Plymouth
                                      d- 10-1-1958 age 69
92   OTT--HAMILTON
     Kelly E Ott "our baby"   female, res. Liv. Co.
     Jan. 28, 1962-Mar. 10, 1962   d-age 6 weeks
     double stone;-Hamilton
     Romine G, 1909-1961 (masonic)   b-Livingston Co. res. Washtenaw Co.
                                      d- 10-9-1961 age 51

93   EATON--FRAZIER
     double stone;-Eaton
     Gladys H, 1898-1969   res. Livingston Co.
                                      d- 9-2-1969 age 70
     Wm. Leslie, 1893-1974   res. Howell
                                      d- 5-24-1974 age 80
     Leslie George Eaton, DVM   res. Warren, New Jersey
     1921-1969   d- 11-23-1969 age 48
     James W, (masonic-vet)   (James W Frazier)res. Liv. Co.
     1927-1962   d- 2-15-1962 age 34, burned in
                                      airplane crash

     on monument-Frazier

Section "Three"   Greenwood cemetery
lot #
94   DORRANCE--DAVIS
     Amy L Allen "mother"   "Amy Louella" b-Liv. Co.
     1906-1962   d- 3-12-1962 age 55, res. Liv. Co.
                                    burial on Dorrance lot
95   LINE
     double stone;-Line
     Gertrude V, 1909-   not listed
     W Donald, 1905-1973   "Wm. Donald" res. Liv. Co.
                                    d- 5-1-1973 age 68
96   JENKINS
     Thomas R Jenkins "dear son-brother"
     Oct. 16, 1959-Oct. 14, 1978   d-age 18 of injury
97   LIECHTI
     Howard F Liechti "son"   res. Livingston Co.
     1935-1975   d- 3-21-1975 age 39, pnuemonia
     double stone;-Liechti
     Vera V, 1916-   not listed
     Howard W, 1912-1973   d- 10-27-1973 age 61
98   GIBSON--HARGROVE
     Arnold Gibson   res. Ann Arbor, Mi.
     1923-1975   d- 8-29-1975 age 52
     Wilson Hargrove   res. Kalkaska   (listed lot 97)
     Michigan U S Marine Corps, World War 11
     Dec. 6, 1924-Jan. 17, 1974   d-age 49, self inflicted gunshot
99   WESTPHAL
     Fred C, "dad"   (vet)   "Frederick" res. Howell
     1929-1980   d- 8-13-1980 age 50
     Rosemary, "mom" 1934-   not listed
100 LASKEY-CLAY-WESTPHAL
     empty
101 JENKINS--DENIKE
     Woodrow R Jenkins   res. Luna Co.
     Pfc. U S Army, World War 11
     Sep. 12, 1915-Aug. 6, 1982   d-age 66, burial from New Mexico
     double stone-Denike
     Doris L, 1912-   "mother"   not listed
     Henry W, 1911-1978 "father"   burial 12-15-1987 ashes
102 ZIMMERMAN
     double stone;-Zimmerman
     Minnie E, 1886-1969   "Minnie Ethel" res. Liv. Co.
                                    d- 10-5-1969 age 83
     Neail H, 1886-1977   res. Livingston Co.
                                    d- 12-7-1977 age 91
103 MILLER
     double stone;-Miller
     Emory E, 1884-1964   res. Oakland Co.
                                    d- 8-30-1964 age 79
     Mina E, 1891-1980   res. Livingston Co.
                                    d- 10-8-1980 age 89

Section "Three"   Greenwood cemetery
lot #
104 BARTON--TAIT
    Charles K, 1889-1957   "Chas. Kester" b-Mi.
                                    d- 11-17-1957 age 67
                                    res. Hollywood, Florida

    Merle D, 1894-19-   buried ?
    Evely Velmure Haas, 1902-   buried-?
    on monument-Barton
                                   (Gladys Tait)res. Livingston Co.
                                   d- 10-13-1979 age 80
                                   (Wm. Bradford Hoskins)
                                   burial 1-12-1962

105 TAIT
    Lillian Bradford Hoskins, mother of Gladys L Tait   b-Mi.
    1874-1962   d- 1-10-1962 age 87, res. Wayne
    Gladys L Tait   no record
    1899-1979
    George R Tait   "Geo. Sr." res. Fowlerville
    1902-1975   d- 7-22-1975 age 73
    on monument-Tait "love is reflected in love"
106 TAIT
    empty
107 ALTON--TAIT
    double stone;-Alton
    James T, Sr. "father"
    1876-1960   d- 10-30-1960 age 84
                                    burial 4-27-1982 ashes
    Gertrude R, "mother"   (both ashes brought in by Don. Alton)
    1879-1968   d- 12-21-1968 age 89
                                    burial 4-27-1982 ashes

108 HAVILAND
    Alberta M, 1936-1960   b-Mi.   res. Livingston Co.
                                   d- 6-13-1960 age 23

    on monument-Haviland
109 CARUSI
    no stones   (baby girl, Caruso)res. Liv. Co.
                                   d- 5-28-1962 age 0

110 HANSON--ANCEL
    double stone;-Hanson
    Elva A, 1882-1971   "Elva Aurelia" res. Charlotte, Mi.
                                   d- 8-11-1971 age 89
    Charles F, 1885-1974   res. Eaton Co.
                                   d- 9-16-1974 age 89
                                   burial from Pinckney

    double stone;-Ancel
    Edwin J, 1893-1982   res. Livingston Co.
                                   d- 2-3-1982 age 88
    Lottie A, 1890-1968   "Lottie Agnes" res. Fowl.
                                   d- 2-7-1968 age 77

Section "Three"
lot #
111 FOSTER--JUDD
    double stone;-Foster
    Alice E, 1899-   not listed
    Wesley B, 1892-1966   res. Leelanau Co. Mi.
                                 d- 8-5-1966 age 74

    double stone;-Judd
    Kenneth, 1903-1975   "Charles K" res. Howell
                                 d- 7-30-1965 age 71
    Edith M, 1906-1965   res. Fowlerville
                                 d- 4-27-1965 age 58, fell downstairs

    Norma E Hanson
    1912-   not listed
112 WESTPHAL--TITMUS
    double stone;-Westphal
    Helen V, "mom"   res. Ingham Co.
    1912-1981   d- 5-30-1981 age 69
          married Mar. 12, 1928
    Ira C, "dad"   "Ira Cranston" res. Lesberg, Fla.
    1905-1976   d- 3-30-1976 age 70
    (behind, a double stone) Westphal
                        Helen V, 1912-1981
                        Ira C, 1905-1976

    double stone;-Titmus
    L B, 1890-1975   res. Grandville, Mi.
                                 d- 8-10-1975 age 84
    Edna S, 1894-1966   res. Lansing
                                 d- 10-22-1966 age 72
                                 burial from Lansing

113 HOLEMS
    empty
114 CHAMBERS--LUCAS
    double stone;-Chambers
    Milos S, 1908-1982   res. Livingston Co.
                                 d- 7-11-1982 age 73
    Ruby A, 1904-   not listed
    double stone;-Lucas
    James R, 1916-   not listed
    Helen F, 1914-1975   res. Wayne Co.
                                 d- 12-29-1975 age 61

115 HARMON
    empty
116 CHOATE--MARTIN
    triple stone;-Choate
    Rodney R, 1902-1981   res. Livingston Co.
                                 d- 4-1-1981 age 78(listed lot 115)
    Jane E, 1880-1982   res. Wayne Co.
                                 d- 5-14-1982 age 102
    Rodney S, 1883-1979   res. Livingston Co.
                                 d- 8-18-1979 age 96
    Richard Martin "husband"
    1901-1980   burial 2-11-1980

117 ENGELBRECHT--WESTPHAL
     double stone-Engelbrecht
     Edward, 1885-1978   res. Livingston Co.
                                      d- 4-27-1978 age 78

     Amalia, 1891-1980   res. Livingston Co.
                                      d- 7-1-1980 age 89

     double stone;-Westphal
     Johanna, 1912-1976   res. Livingston Co.
                                      d- 8-19-1976 age 64

     Arthur, 1908-1983   res. Livingston Co.
                                      d- 4-13-1983 age 74

118 CASADY
     double stone;-Casady
     Ruth E,   not listed
     Clarence B, 1896-1982   res. Livingston Co.
                                      d- 11-22-1982 age 86

119 ELDRIDGE
     double stone;-Eldridge
     John F, 1921   not listed
     Dora I, 1921-   not listed
     Carrie Ellen Eldridge   no record
     Nov. 1, 1950-Nov. 5, 1950

120 LANG--GANTON
     Teresa M Lang "our little darling"   res. Fowl.
     1964-1966   d- 1-15-1966 age 1, scalded
     double stone;-Ganton
     Jessie L, 1896-1965   "Jessie Louise" res. Fowl.
                                      d- 12-19-1965 age 69

     Oakley M, 1896-1981   res. Livingston Co.
                                      d- 3-17-1981 age 85

121 PAETSCH
     double stone;-Paetsch
     Walter E, 1900-1974   res. Howell
                                      d- 5-2-1974 age 74

     L Olga, 1900-1966   res. Fowlerville
                                      d- 4-21-1966 age 66

122 MUNSELL
     empty
123 MUNSELL
     Helen L, 1904-1964   res. Florida
                                      d- 12-17-1964 age 60

     George G, 1906-1979   res. Bakefield twp.
                                      d- 10-3-1979 age 73

     Raymond G, 1931-1971   res. Columbus, Ohio
                                      d- 10-4-1971 age 40 (listed lot 122)

     E Mae, 1937-   not listed
     on monument-Munsell (lot 122-123)
124 ALLISON
     double stone;-Allison
     Mamie 1, 1897-19-   not listed
     James R, 1889-1980 (surveyors emblem)   "James Ray"
                                      burial 1-7-1980 age 90

Section "Three"   Greenwoood Cemetery
lot #
125 ROSEN
     Jack Rosen   res. Detroit
     1900-1966   d- 2-26-1966 age 65
     on monument-Jack Rosen family

                                        (Henry Rosen)res. Wayne Co.
                                        d- 12-12-1969 age 67

126 PETERSON--KREEGER-TIMMERMAN
     Carl E Peterson   res. Denedin, Florida
     Cpl. U S Army, World War ll
     Oct. 1, 1917-Nov. 11, 1978   d-age 61,heart failure
     double stone;-Kreeger
     Lillian V, 1896-19-   not listed
     Charles A, 1893-1967   res. Dansville, Mi.
                                        d- 4-29-1967 age 74
                                        (Fred Timmerman)res. Oakland Co.
                                        d- 10-23-1983 age 81

127 WATTERS
     triple stone;-Watters
     Lavern, 1934-   not listed
     Judith, 1941   not listed
     Frederick, 1936   not listed
     Russell, 1890-1967   (Anson Russell Watters)res. Fowl.
                                        d- 3-26-1967 age 76
     Estella, 1903-1975   (Estella Watters)res. Liv. Co.
                                        d- 2-24-1975 age 71

     father
     mother
128 WESTMORELAND--WILLIAMS
     double stone;-Westmoreland
     Elwin, 1915-1971   res. Ingham Co.
                                        d- 3-19-1971 age 55

     Dorothy, 1923-   not listed
     double stone;-Williams
     Viola C, 1902-1966   "Viola Clara" res. Howell
                                        d- 10-27-1966 age 64
     Arthur D, 1894-1970   res. Washtenaw Co.
                                        d- 8-29-1970 age 75

129 WINNIE-WILSON-CARPENTER
     Wilson H Winnie   res. Washtenaw Co.
     Michigan S Sgt. 397 Mil. Police Bn. World War ll
     April 24, 1925-Oct. 29, 1969   d-age 46, kidney trouble
     double stone;-Wilson
     Irene C, 1907-19-   not listed
     Howard R, 1908-1971 (vet)   d- 8-23-1971 age 62
130 VAN VLACK-BOSSARD
     double stone;-
     Jessie Van Vlack "mother"   res. Ypsilanti, Mi.
     1893-1978   d- 12-5-1978 age 85
                                        burial from Howell, Mi.

     Max A Thorp "son"   "Max Albert" res. Liv. Co.
     1921-1976   d- 10-13-1976 age 54

Section "Three"   Greenwood cemetery
lot #
130 continued
      double stone;-Bossard
      Harriet M, 1898-19-   not listed
      Glenn D, 1886-1972   res. Livingston Co.
                                      d- 9-25-1972 age 86
131 GAMBER--GARNIER
      empty
132 NELSON
      empty
133 RUTTMAN
      Byron August Ruttman, twin son of Tom & Carol
         8-8-76   d- 8-8-1976 age 0, res. Liv. Co.
134 DRIVER--WILSON
      double stone;-Driver
      Marcella, 1908-   not listed
      Clayton, 1905-1971   "Clayton M" res. Florida
                                      d- 1-9-1971 age 65

      double stone;-Wilson (back of stone on lot 120)
      Mary C, 1908-19-   not listed
      Leon J, 1897-1982   "Leon James" res. Howell
                                      d- 11-10-1982 age 85

135 PLUMMER--McCLELLAN
      double stone;-Plummer
      Alfred H, 1912-1982   res. Livingston Co.
                                      d- 4-18-1982 age 69
      Wanetta L, 1902-1977   res. Livingston Co.
                                      d- 4-26-1977 age 74
      Jay D McClellan   res. Livingston Co.
      1942-1977   d- 3-24-1977 age 35
136 HISSONG-BARTIG-PICHA
      Joe S Hissong "grandpa" (Moose emblem)   "Sylvester" res. Liv. Co.
      1910-1981   d- 7-2-1981 age 70
      double stone;-Bartig
      Marymae, 1910-   not listed
      Rutherford B, 1902-1968   res. Fowlerville
                                      d- 2-7-1968 age 65, gun wound
      Arthur E Picha "father"   "Arthur Emil" res. Brighton
      1914-1966   d- 11-21-1966 age 52
                                      (Robert E Bartig)res. Ingham Co.
                                      d- 7-14-1971 stillborn
137 MILLER
      Russell A Miller "father"   "Russell Andrew" res. Conway twp.
      1914-1966   d- 11-7-1966 age 52
138 ROSEN--RUSSELL (wide lot)
      Henry Rosen   listed on lot 125-see
      1902-1969
      double stone;-Russell
      Daisy E, 1909-1978 (Aux. emblem)res. Ingham Co.
                                      d- 5-6-1978 age 68
            married April 14, 1958
      Don G, 1912-1977   "Don Graves" res. Liv. Co.
                                      d- 10-21-1977 age 65

Section "Three"   Greenwood cemetery
lot #
139 WOOD-BOWLING-CREECH (wide lot)
     triple stone;-Wood
     Russell W, 1925-   not listed
     Steven W, 1951-1969   "Steven Wayne" res. Fowlerville
                                      d- 1-20-1969 age 17

     Bebe L, 1929-   not listed
     double stone;-Bowling
     Wilda F, 1904-   "mother"   not listed
     Yancie Sr. 1903-1971 "father"   res. Livingston Co.
                                      d- 4-29-1971 age 68

     double stone;-Creech
     Letha, 1915-   not listed
     Otis, 1915-1968   "Otis S" res. Fowlerville
                                      d- 1-30-1968 age 52

140 GOUGH--ELLIOTT
     double stone;-Gough
     Priscilla, 1889-1969   res. Livingston Co.
                                      d- 7-31-1969 age 80

     Arnold, 1891-1970   (Arnold Gaugh)res. Liv. Co.
                                      d- 7-13-1970 age 78

     Allen F Elliott   "Allen Floyd" res. Fowlerville
     Sgt. U S Army, World War 11
     May 17, 1923-Aug. 18, 1967   d-age 44
141 GODFREY--STAGE
     double stone;-Godfrey
     Daisy E, 1903-19-   not listed
     Kenneth G, 1903-1968   "Ken Guy" res. Fowlerville
                                      d- 1-14-1968 age 64

     triple stone;-Stage
     Lunette, 1902-   "mother"   not listed
     Theodore, 1949-1967 "son"   "Theo. Wm." res. Fowlerville
                                      d- 11-11-1967 age 18, auto accident

     Gleason, 1901-   "father"   not listed
142 HOUSE
     double stone;-House
     Florence J, 1890-1972 (OES)   res. Livingston Co.
                                      d- 7-30-1972 age 81

     Rex B, 1890-1970 (masonic)   res. Livingston Co.
                                      d- 9-22-1970 age 80

143 WILSON
     double stone;-Wilson
     Nina L, 1917-   not listed
     Rex W, 1913-1972   res. Livingston Co.
                                      d- 9-2-1972 age 59
                                      (Crystal Lynn Wilson)res. Ingham Co.
                                      d- 2-5-1978 stillborn

144 PLUMMER--DODSON
     Robert J Plummer Jr. "son"
     December 27, 1960-December 26, 1979   d-age 18
     Ada Elizabeth Crain   not listed
     Sept. 18, 1904-
     (grave?)   (Glenda M Dodson)res. Liv. Co.
                                      d- 2-19-1981 age 44

Section "Three"   Greenwood cemetery
lot #
145 ANDERSON
     double stone;-Anderson
     Erma L, 1912-   not listed
          married Oct. 15, 1938
     Carl G, 1908-1982   res. Livingston Co.
                                          d- 8-6-1982 age 73

146 GRANET
     double stone;-Granet
     Marlene, 1934-   not listed
     Edmund, 1930-1975   res. Detroit
                                          d- 4-25-1975 age 44

147 YAGO
     double stone;-Yago
     Charles E, 1905-1983   "Chas. Edward" res. Arizona
                                          d- 6-23-1983 age 78

               married April 8, 1926
     Ethelyn A, 1906-   not listed
148 DIEHL
     (grave?)   (Patricia Rose Diehl)res. Wash. Co.
                                          d- 9-13-1983 age 52, heart failure

149 KENT
     double stone;-Kent
     Doris A, 1913-   not listed
     DuWayne F, 1913-1968   res. Fowlerville
                                          d- 1-5-1968 age 54

150 SWORTHWOOD--McKNIGHT
     double stone;-Swarthwood
     Ernest H, 1902-1968 (vet)   (Ernest Henry Swarthout)res. Fowl.
                                          d- 11-19-1968 age 66, spinal injury
     Elsie G, 1910-   not listed
     Joseph McKnight   no record
     July 4, 1896
151 DeFOREST
     double stone;-DeForest (back of stone on lot 140)
     Susan M, 1915-   (OES)   not listed
     Grant H, 1912-   (masonic) not listed
152 PARTLO--COSELMAN
     Edward H Partlo   "Ed. Harvey" res. San Bernardino, Cal.
     Tec 5, U S Army, World War ll
     1922-1980   d- 9-29-1980 age 58
     Anna L Coselman   "Anna Louise"
     March 1, 1919-June 8, 1967   d- age 48, burial 6-12-1967
     Harold J Coselman   res. Livingston Co.
     May 15, 1913-Jan/ 25, 1983   d-age 69
153 NYGREN
     double stone;-Nygren
     Pearley E,   "Pearly Elizabeth" res. Liv. Co.
     Jul. 17, 1927-Feb. 8, 1977   d-age 49
     Bernard L,   not listed
     Apr. 2, 1923-

Section "Three"   Greenwood cemetery
lot #
154 ST. CHARLES--JOHNSON
     Cecil D St. Charles, husband & father   "Cecil David"
     1931-1972   d- 1-19-1972 age 40, res. Ann Arbor
                                    burial from Brighton
     (grave?)   (Frances A Johnson)res. Mecosta Co.
                                    d- 4-27-1983 age 71,

155 DREXEL--EBRIGHT
     Edna G Drexel   res. Lakewood
     1904-1969   d- 1-8-1969 age 65, bur. 1-13-69
     George B Ebright   res. Lansing
     Michigan Pvt. U S Army, World War 1
     June 30, 1895-Jan. 12, 1972   d-age 76, burial from Lansing

156 BURNIE-FUESLEIN-KALLEK
     double stone;-Burnie
     Violet E, 1910-1969   res. Livingston Co.
                                    d- 10-15-1969 age 59
     G Douglas, 1905-1976   "Gordon Douglas" res. Liv. Co.
                                    d- 10-1-1976 age 71
                                    (Jonathan Burnie)res. Liv. Co.
                                    d- 1-6-1983 stillborn
                                    (was son of Mary & Douglas Burnie)
                                    (Edmund Kallek) res. Fowl.
                                    d- 9-8-1967 age 70

157 HUSCHKE--FUESLEIN
     Fredrick R, 1910-1968
     Veteran of World War 11   burial 6-21-1968 from Saginaw
     on monument-Huschke
     double stone;-Fueslein
     Virgiline, 1910-   not listed
     John V, 1898-1976   "John Vern" res. San Andreas, Cal.
                                    d- 2-20-1976 age 77 (listed lot 156)
                                    (Ralph Charles Hill)res. Liv. Co.
                                    d- 3-18-1970 age 61

158 GREEN--PATTEN
     Bertha Belle Green   res. Lansing
     Mar. 10, 1915-May 4, 1974   d-age 59, burial from Lansing
     Ralph Patten   res. Pontiac
     Michigan Tec 5, Ordance Dept. World War 11
     Sept. 2, 1913-Sept. 20, 1969   d-age 56
159 ALBAUGH--WEIR
     Lawrence G Albaugh
     Sgt. U S Army, World War 11
     Jan. 26, 1914-Jan. 30, 1980
     Agnes I Albaugh, wife of Lawrence   not listed
     March 8, 1915-
     Frances M Weir "mother"   res. Handy (dau. is AnnaEastman)
     1916-1980   d- 7-27-1980 age 64
160-161
     empty
162 HOODLEY--BENNETT
     empty

Section "Three"   Greenwood cemetery
lot #
163 BENNETT--DRIVER
     no stones

                                         (Otis H Bennett)res. E. Lansing
                                         d- 5-29-1982 age 80
                                         (Jeffery Thomas Driver)
                                         d- 1-26-1969 age 3, res. Liv. Co.

164 RAMBO--HALE
     Michael J Rambo   "Michael Jeffery"
     1955-1977   d- 12-28-1977 age 22,skull injury
     Kim E Hale   "Kim Elizabeth" res. Fowlerville
     Jan. 12, 1962-June 4, 1963   d-age 1
165 BANDKAU
     double stone;-Bandkau
     Amelia, 1906-1968   res. Washtenaw Co.
                                         d- 4-22-1968 age 61
     Erwin H, 1904-   not listed
166 DeFOREST
     Natashia T DeForest "buddy"   res. Livingston Co.
     Nov. 9, 1976-Sept. 3, 1982   d-age 5
167 HUCK
     Terri Lee Huck Jr.   "Terry Lee" male, res. Liv. Co.
     Mar. 6, 1969-Mar. 16, 1970
168 BUGARD
     double stone;-Bugard
     Ruth L, 1914-   not listed
     William E, 1913-1971   d- 9-4-1971 age 57
169 RIFE--SCOON
     double stone;-Rife
     Jennie, 1912-1973   "Jennie Diane" res. Howell
                                         d- 2-6-1973 age 61, heart trouble
     Herman, 1910-   not listed
     Edith M Scoon (Aux. emblem)
     March 24, 1917-June 29, 1974   d- age 57
170 ALLHOUSE--ORWELLER
     double stone;-Allhouse
     Ardale L, 1916-   not listed
     George C, 1912-1969   res. Livingston Co.
                                         d- 1-8-1969 age 56

     double stone;-Orweller
     Marjorie I, 1910-1980   (Marjorie Oreweller)
                                         burial 2-10-1980
                                         res. Ingham Co.
     Edward M, 1907-1972   d- 2-14-1972 age 64
                                         (Harold K Lewis)res. Brighton
                                         d- 5-28-1979 age 83

171 ALLHOUSE
     empty

{339}

Section "Three"   Greenwood cemetery
lot #
172 MANNING
     double stone;-Manning
     Donna M, 1905-1977   res. Livingston Co.
                                  d- 3-6-1977 age 71
     Freeman E, 1890-1968   res. Fowlerville
                                  d- 10-29-1968 age 78

173 MILLER
     Norman C Miller   res. Alaska
     Michigan Major, 21 Opr. Sq. AF AM-AFCM (helicopter emblem)
     October 23, 1933-June 3, 1967 d-age 33, drowned
     Alice, 1910-1979   (Alice Cummings Miller)
                                  d- 12-26-1979 age 69, res. Austin, Tx.
     Hollis, 1906   not listed
     on monument-Miller
174 EDWARDS--LURGES
     Lester B Edwards   res. Livingston Co.
     A2C, U S Air Force, Korea
     1930-1979   d- 1-3-1979 age 48
     Peter C Lurges "father"   res. Livingston Co.
     1929-1970   d- 5-28-1970 age 41
                                  (Peter Lurges)res. Detroit
                                  d- 3-2-1976 age 89

175-176
     empty

- - - - - - - - - - - -
                        End

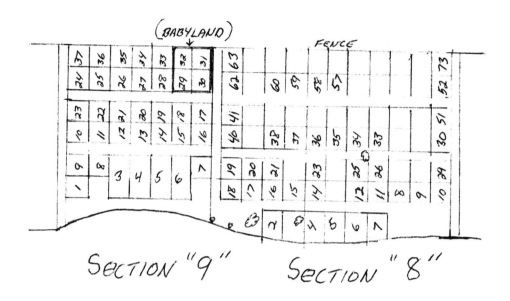

(BABYLAND)

FENCE

SECTION "9"   SECTION "8"

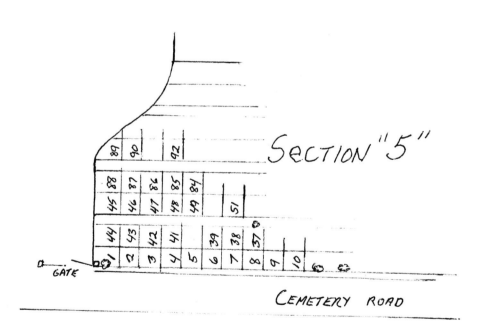

SECTION "5"

GATE

CEMETERY ROAD

Section "Five"   Greenwood cemetery

        Section number "Five" is a newer section having 294 lots.
        Only the first 100 lots are used at this time of which several
        have not been sold.
lot #
1   LEBERFINGER--VAN AMBERG
     double stone;-Leberfinger
     Eleanor M, 1913-   not listed
     Sebold J, 1910-   not listed
     double stone;-Van Amberg
     Dorothy E, 1923-1976   res. Livingston Co.
                                   d- 11-6-1976 age 53

     Leo R, 1916-   not listed
2   McCLURE
     Alexander G Dieterle   res. Livingston Co.
     1904-1976   d- 12-18-1976 age 72
3   HUGHES--TIMMINS
     double stone;-Hughes
     Donna J, 1934-   (Star)   not listed
          married Aug. 6, 1954
     Floyd T, 1932-1981 (masonic) res. Farmington
                                   d- 11-24-1981 age 49, heart
     (behind stone above) Floyd T Hughes
                     Pfc. U S Army, Korea
                     Jul. 14, 1932-Nov. 24, 1981
     Viola M Timmins   "Viola Mae" res. Liv. Co.
     1910-1979   d- 9-25-1979 age 69
4   YATES--COLL
     double stone;-Yates
     Clara B, 1914-   not listed
     Emmette W, 1911-1982   Emmette Wilson" res. Lakeland, Fla.
                                   d- 10-28-1982
     Donald R Coll   no record
     Tec 5, U S Army, World War 11
     Mar. 8, 1921-May 7, 1980
5   CRAWFORD-GABLER-LaMARSH
     double stone-Gabler
     Homer L, 1894-1981 WW-1   res. Calhoun Co.
                                   d- 1-9-1981 age 86

          married Aug. 15, 1927
     Esther E, 1906-   not listed
     double stone;-LaMarsh
     Fern M, 1921-   not listed
          married July 6, 1940
     Charles F, 1916-1980   res. Livingston Co.
                                   d- 11-1-1980 age 64
     double stone;-Crawford (on lot 5 & 6)
     Ileen M, 1922-   not listed
           married Aug. 23, 1941
     William H, 1918-   not listed
6   CRAWFORD
     empty

Section "Five"   Greenwood cemetery
lot #
7   KUEHN
     double stone;-Kuehn
     Lawrence J, 1907-1976   res. Ingham Co.(listed lot Two-7)
                                    d- 9-12-1976 age 69

     Ruth M, 1918-   not listed
8   LUCAS
     (grave)   (Betty Marie Lucas)res. Grand Is. Fla.
                                    d- 1-30-1983, bur. from Eustis, Fla.

9   TANNER
     no stones   (baby girl, Tanner)res. Ingham Co.
                                    d- 11-23-1977 premature

10   Tanner
     empty
11 to 37
     empty
38   GROVER
     double stone;-Grover
     Lyle J, 1907-1982 (masonic)   res. Washtenaw Co.
                                    d- 7-17-1982 age 75

     L Ruth, 1910-   (OES)   not listed
39   GROVER
     double stone;-Grover
     Donnie N, 1933-   not listed
     Duane H, 1932-1980   burial 2-2-1980

40
     empty
41   BACH--FOX
     double stone;-Bach
     Helen B, "mother"   not listed
     June 28, 1920-
     Leroy W, "father"   res. Washtenaw Co.
     Nov. 19, 1919-Mar. 13, 1983   d-age 63
     (grave)   (Francis A Fox)res. Lansing
                                    d- 7-19-1983 age 69

42   SIMKO
     double stone;-Simko
     Ruth H, 1914-   not listed
     James J, 1914-   not listed
43   COPELAND--MARSHALL
     double stone;-Copeland
     Patricia R, 1937-1982   res. Wayne Co.
                                    d- 10-6-1982 age 44

     Robert L, 1936-   not listed
     (grave)   (Katherine Marshall)res. Wash Co.
                                    d- 8-10-1983 age 61
                                    (see metal tag on lot 46)

44   KREBS
     Francelia Krebs "our baby daughter"   res. Liv. Co.
         1981   d- 4-28-1981 stillborn
     double stone;-Krebs
     Lillian M, 1923-   not listed
     Walter L, 1922-   not listed

Section "Five"   Greenwood cemetery
lot #
45   WAKEMAN
     Mark A Wakeman "son"   "Mark Allen" res. Fowlerville
     July 2, 1958-June 11, 1973   d-age 14, brain injury
46   DeFOREST
     double stone;-DeForest
     Eva L, 1910-1976   res. Ingham Co.
                                       d- 11-6-1976 age 66
     Arthur, 1906-   not listed
     (on metal tag near stone above)Katherine I Marshall
                                       born 1922, died 1983 age 61
                                       (listed as buried lot 43) see
47   DONAL
     Dennis J Donal   res. Livingston Co.
     Jan. 19, 1945-Dec. 31, 1977   d-age 32, carbon monoxide
48   GARVER
     double stone;-Garver
     Vivian F, 1920-   not listed
     Leo W, 1914-1982 (vet)   (Charles Wm. Leo Garver)res. Liv. Co.
                                       d- 6-18-1982 age 67
49   SHORMAN
     empty
50
     empty
51   GRILL--GLOVER
     empty
52 to 83
     empty
84   ARMSTRONG
     (grave)   (Debra A Armstrong)res. Mustang, Ok.
                                       d- 1-17-1983 age 15, accidental
85   HEVER
     no stones   (Virginia C Hever)res. Trenton, Mi.
                                       d- 12-16-1983 age 73
                                       (Philip H Breslin)res. Liv. Co.
                                       d- 12-23-83 age 84
86   EDDY
     double stone;-Eddy
     Harold B,   not listed
     Jan. 29, 1914-
     Helen E,   not listed
     Sept. 23, 1915-
87   EDDY--MAURER
     John Charles Eddy "son"   res. Ingham Co.
     June 1, 1944-Feb. 20, 1982   d-age 37, hemmorage
     Henry Maurer   res. Livingston Co.
     Pvt. U S Army, World War 1
     Oct. 10, 1889-Dec. 2, 1979   d-age 90

Section "Five"   Greenwood cemetery
lot #
88   ROWE--HARRISON
      Rickey R Rowe "son"   res. Ingham Co.
      Aug. 8, 1951-Nov. 27, 1974   d-age 23, gunshot wound
89
      empty
90   CRAFT
      double stone;-Craft
      Vera M, 1914-   not listed
      Walter K, 1904-1974   res. Howell
                                        d- 11-17-1974 age 69
91
      empty
92   LITTKE
      Steven Ward Littke "our baby son"   res. Ingham Co.
      Nov. 20-21, 1974   d-age 1 day
93 to 221
      empty
                        - - - - - - - - - - - -
                              End

        Section number "Eight" is a newer section in the back.
        It has 73 lots of which several have not been sold.
lot #
1
      empty
2   SPENCER
      double stone;-Spencer
      A James, 1917-   not listed
      Marvel D, 1917-   not listed
3
      empty
4   IVERSON
      double stone;-Iverson
      Myrtie A, 1902-1969   res. Kent Co. Mi.
                                  d- 3-9-1969 age 66
      Ernest I, 1901-   not listed
5   PHILLIPS--CARBARY
      no stones   (Dwight D Phillips)res.Columbus, Oh.
                                  d- 11-3-1972 age 2
6   SHERWOOD
      double stone;-Sherwood
      Gertrude M,   not listed
      Feb. 6, 1893-
      John T,   res. Livingston Co.
      June 22, 1889-Sept. 4, 1978 d-age 89
7 to 13
      empty
14   KONOPASKA
      empty
15   KONOPASKA--TINSLEY
      double stone;-Konopaska
      Frederick C,   res. Ingham Co.
      Sept. 2, 1915-Nov. 3-1974   d-age 59
      Rosalie H,   not listed
      Mar. 2, 1914-
      double stone;-Tinsley
      Wm. Emmitt, 1907-1972   res. Livingston Co.
                                  d- 3-25-1972 age 64
      Nannie M, 1907-1969   no record
16   MARTIN--HERBERT
      double stone;-BEHR
      Herbert C, 1904-1974   res. Howell
                                  d- 4-7-1974 age 69
      Lois B, 1910-   not listed
      Gust A Martin   not listed
      1902-19-
17   PETSCH-BOWLSBY-SIMMONS
      Walter A Petsch   res. Washtenaw Co.
      Michigan Pvt. 23 Engeneers, World War 1
      April 16, 1898-May 23, 1969 d-age 71
                                  (Emily Petsch)res. Liv.Co.
                                  d- 4-16-1983 age 83

Section "Eight"   Greenwood cemetery
lot #
17 continued
    James M Bowlsby   res. Livingston Co.
    Michigan Sp5, U S Army, Vietnam
    Feb. 27, 1948-Nov. 25, 1972   d-age 24
    Richard D Simmons "son"   res. Livingston Co.
    1952-1973   d- 7-3-1973 age 21, pnuemonia
18 SIMMONS
    empty

19

    empty
20 HANSON--NUNN
    double stone;-Hanson
    Crystal I, 1914-   not listed
    Donald G, 1921-   not listed
    double stone;-Nunn
    Juanita L, "mother"   not listed
    1915-
            married Apr. l4, 1834
    Ray L, "father"   res. Howell
    1908-1979   d- 11-9-1979 age 71
21 HAYWARD
    double stone;-Hayward (on back of Behr stone, lot 16)
    Robert J, 1926-1977   d- 4-24-1977 age 50
    Nancy I, 1928-   not listed
22
    empty
23 MILLER
    Dorothy R Miller   not listed
    1915-
    Charles H Miller   res. Shiawassee Co.
    1912-1976   d- 5-21-1976 age 64
                                   burial from Ovid, Mi.

    on monument-Miller
24
    empty
25 MORRIS
    Marie Morris "mother"   res. Livingston Co.
    1902-1979   d- 11-14-1979 age 77
26 HELLWEGE--Brown
    William J Brown   res. Brighton
    ENFA, U S Navy
    May 12, 1961-Aug. 23, 1981   d-age 20, accident
27 to 32
    empty
33 MYERS
    double stone;-Myers
    Viola R,   not listed
    Edward T, 1905-1973 (masonic) res. Ingham Co.
                                   d- 6-26-1973 age 68
34 SHEPARD
    no stones   (Larry Douglas Shepard)res. Fowl.
                                   d- 8-13-1968 age 4, heart failure

Section "Eight"   Greenwood cemetery
lot #
35   HARMON
     double stone;-Harmon
     Elmer, 1898-1973 (fire Dept. City of Det. #702 emblem)
                                  d- 8-6-1973 age 75, res. Liv. Co.

     Ann, 1902-   not listed
36   PICKERING
     double stone;-Pickering
     Carl E, 1911-1982   res. Tampa, Florida
                                  d- 9-11-1982
     Dolores P, 1912-1976   res. Southfield twp. Oakland Co.
                                  d- 3-27-1976 age 63
37   RYAN
     (grave?)   (infant boy, Ryan)res. Liv. Co.
                                  d- 12-2-1981,newborn

38   BISHOP
     double stone;-Bishop
     Willis E, 1905-1981   "Rev." res. Livingston Co.
                                  d- 9-24-1981 age 75
     Mary Belle, 1908-   not listed
39 t0 56
     empty
57   TOTH
     double stone;-Toth
     Lawrence, 1902-1977   res. Livingston Co.
                                  d-9-9-1977 age 75
     Julia Ann, 1899-1976   res. Livingston Co.
                                  d- 1-18-1976 age 76
58   MALCOLM
     Carrie L Malcolm   res. Ann Arbor, Mi.
     1959-1975   d- 8-8-1975 age 16, head injury
59   FOSTER
     Steven E Foster "our son"   res. Lansing
     1964-1981   d- 8-21-1981 age 17, accident
60   CHINN--BOOKBORN
     double stone;-Chinn
     William J, Jr. 1935-1983   "Wm. James" res. Fowlerville
                                  d- 1-21-1983 age 48
     Mary A, 1935-   not listed
     double stone;-Bookborn
     Howard E, 1914-1979   (Howard Bookham?)res. Liv. Co.
                                  d- 6-28-1979 age 65
     Frances A, 1915   not listed
61 to 73
     empty
              - - - - - - - - - - - - -
                      End

Section number "Nine' is a newer section in the back,
left of sec. 8, and contains 37 lots.
"Babyland is in the back row lots of sec. 9 and at present
consist of lots #29 to 31. Each grave has it own number.

lot #
1
    empty
2   FRANKLIN
    double stone;-McCullom
    Edgar, 1866-1947   res. Fowlerville (listed lot Two-9)
                                  d-Feb. 7, 1947 age 81

    Mary, 1866-1948   "Mary C" res. Lansing
                                  d- July 9, 1948 age 82

    (grave?)   no record
3   GARDNER--PICHA
    double stone;-Gardner
    Fred B, 1898-1948   res. Ann Arbor
                                  d- Oct. 8, 1948 age 50, pnue.
    Ruth M, 1902-   b-Mi.   res. Montcalm city, Mi.
                                  d- 11-23-1958 age 56
    Pearl E Picha   "Pearl Ethel)res. Howell twp.
    1895-1950   d-April 13, 1950 age 54
    Emil G Picha   "Emil George" res. Howell
    1889-1966   d- 7-24-1966 age 77
                                  (Mary E Franklin)
                                  burial May 19, 1945

4 to 28
    empty
29 to 32 "Babyland"
#63 no stone   (Jacob Paul Watkins)res. Wayne
                                  d- 3-8-1982 newborn
#64 Keeley E O'Neil "our daughter" "Keeley Elizebeth"
     Jan. 19, 1982   d-stillborn, res. Lansing Gen. Hosp.
#66 Joseph M Marquette "our son" res. Livingston Co.
     Oct. 13, 1980   d-age 2 hours, premature
#67 Dale L Wolverton   "Dale Lee" res. Livingston Co.
     1979   d- 8-6-1979 age 45 minutes
? no stone   (baby boy, Marquette)res. Liv. Co.
                                  d- 10-22-1981 premature
? no stone   (Craig Percival)res. Wash. Co.
                                  d- 2-3-1971 age 2 weeks
33 to 37
    empty
            - - - - - - - - - - - -
                   End

The MAUSOLEUM

On June 21, 1915 Merritt N Cook sold a 66 by 100 foot piece of land to the Howell Mausoleum Company for $250. Later after the mausoleum had been built the whole thing was transferred through Mr. R E Corbin, agent for the Howell concern to the Fowlerville mausoleum group for the consideration of One dollar with Fred Kuhn acting as their trustee.

On Feb. 26, 1923 the property was turned over to the village of Fowlerville with all its assets. Stipulation was made that the village forever care and maintain the building.

The mausoleum is a fine old style cement block building covered by a red tile roof and contains two rows of crypts stacked four high with a large hall down through the middle and a fine stained glass window at the rear. The floor of the hall is covered with thin white marble tiles.

The Mausoleum record book shows that George L Fisher was chairman when the building was turned over to the Fowlerville association. The officers were Pres. Eugene Bush, Vice president C Smith, secretary G L Fisher and treasurer John M Bradley. Trustees were Fred Kuhn, F G Rounsville and Andrew J Wickman. The mausoleum had been dedicated July 30, 1916. The O J McBride Company supplied the crypts. A small vault room was built that same year. The last meeting of the Fowlerville company was Dec. 9 of 1922.

When the mausoleum property was turned over to the village of Fowlerville its assets were $10,455.

Mausoleum   Greenwood cemetery

Vault #
1   John M Bradley
     born Aug. 22, 1853, died May 24, 1932
2   Catherine Bradley
     born Nov. 11, 1852, died May 9, 1917
3   Lewis H Westphal
     born May 25, 1864, died Oct. 5, 1941
4   Mary Westphal
     born May 20, 1864, died May 5, 1929
5
6   R C Smith   (masonic)   res. Iosco
     born Dec. 12, 1861, died Aug. 4, 1951   d-age 89
7   Emma Smith   (OES)
     born Sept. 3, 1864, died Apr. 17, 1918
8   Elbert L Grover   (USWV & masonic)   res. Howell
     born July 11, 1882, died May 16, 1949   d-age 66
9   Ada E Grover   (USWV & Ladies auxillery United)res. Howell
     born Aug. 29, 1880, died Jan. 15, 1948   d-age 67
10   Frank D Nichols (masonic)   res. Fowlerville
     1871-1947   d-Oct. 27, 1947 age 75
11   Ada J Nichols (Star)   "Ada Julia Anna" res. Liv. Co.
     1878-1971   d- 12-30-1971 age 93
12   Freeman C Peterson
     May 30, 1848-July 7, 1918
13   Zora Peterson
     Jan. 5, 1851-Nov. 21, 1921
14   Gale F Peterson
     Aug. 29, 1877-July 8, 1955
15   Helen E Peterson   b-Mi.   res. Fowlerville
     April 22, 1877-Nov. 11, 1925 d-age 48
16   Katherine B Render
     Jan. 16, 1879-Feb. 8, 1934
17   Walter E Render
     May 30, 1882-Oct. 9, 1940
18   Dr. F C Jewell "son-father"   res. Grosse Pointe city
     March 28, 1911-June 29, 1979
19
20   Nelson G Swarthout (FLT emblem)
     Mar. 28, 1855-Aug. 22, 1929
21   Mary E Swarthout
     Apr. 17, 1856-Dec. 2, 1935
22   Edgar D Defendorf (masonic) res. Fowlerville
     born Apr. 28, 1876, died July 25, 1949   d-age 73
23   Jessie M Defendorf   b-Mi.   res. Fowlerville
     born July 5, 1875, died October 24, 1952   d-age 77
24
25   Maria L Benjamin
     born Sept. 5, 1847, died Mar. 19, 1925
26   H C Benjamin
     born Mar. 7, 1845, died June 26, 1929

Mausoleum   Greenwood cemetery

Vault #
27   Clyde S Wimbles   "Clyde Spencer" b-Mi. res. Liv. Co.
      1875-1955   d- 11-15-1955 age 80
28   Edwina A Wimbles   res. Fowlerville
      1876-1967   d- 6-17-1967 age 91(listed in crypt)
29   mother & Claudie
      Phebe, wife of Frederick Copeland   b-England, res. Fowl.
      b-Oct. 6, 1851, d-June 15, 1915   d-age 65, cancer
      Claudie
      b- Mar. 29, 1882, d-Nov. 9, 1888
30   Frederick Copeland
      b-Jan. 2, 1845, d-June 28, 1931
31
32
33   Julian B Fuller, 1857-1932
34   Matilda H Fuller, 1859-1937
35   Fobes C Jewell "father"
      June 10, 1864-April 7, 1932
36   Mattie E Jewell "mother"   (Matie Jewel)b-Mi. res. Liv. Co.
      Aug. 3, 1863-July 12, 1960   d- 7-12-1960 age 91
37   G A Marsh (masonic & FLT)
      Dec. 24, 1849-May 6, 1930
38   Susan Marsh (OES)
      Feb. 22, 1849-May 6, 1931
39   Eugene A Bush
      born Sept. 16, 1846, died Dec. 19, 1926
40   Amanda M Bush
      born Oct. 20, 1846, died May 1, 1920
41   Eugene A Defendorf   b-Mi.   res. Livingston Co.
      born Oct. 13, 1904, died July 8, 1960   d-age 55
42   Elizabeth Worden
      born Aug. 19, 1849, died Mar. 15, 1924
43   Charles Worden
      born Dec. 26, 1846, died July 17, 1919
44   Ruel Curtis
      Sept. 26, 1849-Apr. 21, 1925
45   Merritt N Cook, 1872-1941
46   Josephine M Cook, 1879-1927
47   Alonzo G Phillips "father"
      Oct. 8, 1857-Dec. 17, 1921
48   Laura Phillips "mother"
      Jan. 21, 1865-Oct. 18, 1928
49   Cornelius W Davis
      born May 6, 1850, died March 19, 1920
50   Mary E Davis   res. Fowlerville
      born Feb. 6, 1854, died Jan. 16, 1941   (d-Dec. 17, 1941?)
                                         burial Jan. 19, 1941 age 86
51   (Charles H Van Verst)res. Detroit
                                         d- 6-10-1967 age 92
52
53

Mausoleum   Greenwood cemetery

Vault #
54   Carsten Damman
      born Sept. 12, 1845, died Aug. 3, 1920
55   Metta Damman
      born Oct. 22, 1842, died Mar. 25, 1924
56   Carl Damman
      born Jan. 15, 1875, died June 18, 1928
57   Minnie Damman
      born Apr. 29, 1875, died April 7, 1932
58   Henry Damman
      born Aug. 27, 1873, died Sept. 16, 1943
59
60   Otto R Steiner (masonic)
      Oct. 21, 1883-May 6, 1920
61   (Margaret J Fisher)
                                       d-Oct. 14, 1936
62   Andrew H Fisher
      Jan. 27, 1861-March 2, 1925   (d-Mar. L, 1925)
63   Carrie B Murningham   b-Marion, res. Marion twp.
      July 2, 1876-Dec. 20, 1950   d-age 74
64   Francis W Murningham   b-Mi.   res. Oceola
      Jan. 13, 1871-July 1956   d- 7-19-1956 age 85
65   Helen Virginia, dau. of Gale & Helen Peterson
      Mar. 25, 1904-Dec. 31, 1918
66
67
68
69
70   Ethel Newman Pearson DO (Star) "Ethel B" b-Mi. res. Liv. Co.
      born Aug. 10, 1896, died Feb. 7, 1960   d-age 63
71   Thomas G Sharp (masonic)
      born Sept. 9, 1852, died March 26, 1925
72   Emma Sharp   (OES)
      born July 9, 1860, died April 23, 1946
73   Frank H Westmoreland
      born Jan. 7, 1857, died March 13, 1921
74   Esther Westmoreland
      born Oct. 9, 1859, died April 28, 1927
75   Frank S Riley   res. Pontiac
      born Oct. 5, 1879, died Sept. 28, 1949   d-age 69
76   Grace Riley
      born Dec. 23, 1875, died-
77   Fred J Steiner   res. South Lyon, Mi.
      born Feb. 25, 1872, died Jan. 29, 1947   d-age 74
78   Josie E Steiner
      born Dec. 25, 1875, died May 19, 1917
79   R E Grover, 1853-1935
80   Helen Grover, 1857-1937
81   C H Chapman
      born May 16, 1840, died Sept. 18, 1917
82   Helen E Chapman
      born Mar. 16, 1842, died May 2, 1922

Mausoleum   Greenwood cemetery

Vault #
83   Cora L Rudolph   "Cora Lillian" res. Liv. Co.
     born Oct. 16, 1872, died Apr. 16, 1969   d-age 96
84   C F Rudolph   "Christopher Frederick"res. Cohoctah
     born June 28, 1863, died Oct. 17, 1950   d-age 87
85
86   George A Newman (masonic& FLT)
     born Sept. 13, 1863, died June 15, 1938
87   Mary E Newman (OES)   "Mary Ellen" b-Mi. res. Liv. Co.
     born Feb. 25, 1865, died July 2, 1958   d-age 93
88   Richard T Kilpatrick, 1874-1936
89   Harriet A M Kilpatrick   res. California
     1874-1965   d- 9-17-1965 age 90
90   Frank M Miner (masonic)
     born June 14, 1849, died April 9, 1928
91   Addie I Miner
     born Aug. 22, 1852, died Mar. 12, 1923
92   James Converse   b-Mi.   res. Fowlerville
     born Sept. 30, 1838, died Feb. 20, 1917   d- age 78
93   Emily A Converse
     born Sept. 29, 1844, died Feb. 7, 1934   (d-Feb. 1917/)
94   Robert Glover, 1919-1923
95   Florence Hetchler   (Florence E Glover)
     1875-1921   d-May 16, 1921
96   B F Hoag (FLT)
     Oct. 14, 1840-June 12, 1924
     Corp. Co. H, 5th Mich. Inf.
97   Martha E Hoag
     April 17, 1851-Nov. 22, 1926   (d-Aug. 1938?)
98   M T Graham (FLT)
     Apr. 7, 1871-Aug. 9, 1938
99   Ella M Graham
     Sept. 14, 1869-   d-2-27-1963, bur. in crypt of Maus.
100 Lt. A W Messenger (masonic)
     born Aug. 31, 1837, died Oct. 23, 1917
     Co. B, 26 Mich. Vol.
101 Amelia Ward Messenger
     Aug. 1, 1847-Dec. 2, 1915
102
103 Fred Kuhn (masonic)
     born Sept. 7, 1854, died July 2, 1928
104 Mary Kuhn (OES)
     born June 11, 1856, died March 31, 1934
105 Andrew J Wickman
     Apr. 14, 1845-Jan. 29, 1916
     Co. H, 22nd Mich. Inf.
106 Harriet L Wickman
     July 24, 1848-Oct. 14, 1935

Mausoleum   Greenwood cemetery

Vault #
107 Ernest D Benjamin (masonic)   b-Mi.   res. Livingston Co.
     1881-1957   d- 7-21-1957 age 76
     Floss A Benjamin   res. Fowlerville
     1879-1946   d-July 8, 1946 age 66
109 Cecil A Dey
     born Oct. 2, 1876, died Sept. 13, 1919
110 Elda B Dey
     born Oct. 4, 1873, died Mar. 25, 1949
111 Geo. L Fisher
     Feb. 7, 1839-May 2, 1930
     Sergt. Co. K, 9th Mich. Inft.
112 Ella B Fisher   (Ella B Smith)b-Mi. res. Fowl.
     July 11, 1851-Dec. 31, 1917   d-age 66
113 Jessie N Elliott
     born Aug. 5, 1851, died Feb. 26, 1918
114 Josephine Elliott
     born Oct. 28, 1863, died Mar. 2, 1934
115 Charley L Benjamin   b-Mi.   res. Fowlerville
     born Dec. 4, 1849, died April 23, 1918   d-age 68
116 Mary A Benjamin
     born Sept. 5, 1853, died May 22, 1939   d-age 85
117 Millie Wilhelm   "Mildred E" b-Mi. res. White Oak
     Nov. 29, 1886-Oct. 22, 1955   d- age 68
118 Vern Wilhelm   "Vernon E" res. Ingham Co.
     Oct. 30, 1885-Nov. 10, 1972   burial from Williamston, Mi.
119
120 Etha B Smith   "Etha Beatrice"
     born May 18, 1892, died Nov. 2, 1936
121 Augusta C Smith
     born Sept. 14, 1888-
122 John Fellows Lewis (masonic)
     Mar. 28, 1833-Apr. 25, 1918
123 Alice Preston Lewis
     Apr. 22, 1832-May 12, 1920
124 Wirt I Stowe
     born Nov. 7, 1861, died June 9, 1936
125 Alice J Stowe
     born Nov. 14, 1862, died Jan. 2, 1929
126 Clarence C Stowe   b-Iosco, res. Fowlerville
     born Apr. 27, 1856, died Jan. 4, 1951   d-age 94
127 Clara E Stowe
     born Oct. 7, 1859, died Jan. 15, 1933
128 Frank P Smith
     born Nov. 24, 1858, died Mar. 2, 1928
129 Agness H Smith
     born Oct. 1, 1856, died Dec. 22, 1916
130 Albert Wilhelm
     Aug. 28, 1856-Feb. 2, 1932
131 Elizabeth A Wilhelm
     Nov. 17, 1855-Aug. 28, 1918

Mausoleum   Greenwood cemetery

Vault #
132 Julius Carr
     born Aug. 3, 1855, died Feb. 6, 1939
133 Amarilla Carr
     born Aug. 27, 1854, died June 3, 1922   (d-June 4, 1922?)
 ?   (Elizabeth Mary Henry)b-England
                                      d- March 14, 1924 age 74, res. Fowl.

Listed as buried in the "Vault" in the office records

     Julia Pardy   d-Sept. 26, 1897

     Emma D Miner   burial 5-26-1898

     Julia Ostrom   b-New York, res. Fowl.
                                  d- Feb. 22, 1900 age 49

     Mrs. Winifred "Agnes Rantall b-Mi. res. Handy
                                   d- 2-13-1917 age 43

GREENWOOD CEMETERY

Civil War Monmument

LIST OF OLD SOLDIERS BURIED IN SECTIONS "A" "B" "1" "2"
·(this list made about 1960)

Section "A"

M M Abbott	217	J Walters	182
Charles Lyman Adams	336	William C Wert	?
Marvin Benjamin	282	George W Whitney	287
Richard Bristol	239	Fred Wickman	183½
Dewitt Carr	336	Charles Williams	175
Justus Colburn	239	John D Williams	194
Dr. Cooper	200	W Williams	?
G M Crawford	286	Brazil Wilson	157
Isaia Crippen	6		
Henry Curtis	318		
Elyah Dunn	250	**Section "B"**	
Elias Durfee	106	Franklin Abbott	395
John Elliotte	310	William Edward Allen	390½
Earl Henry Fields	191	Zaccheus Armstrong	208
Dan Ferrin	136	Orin Barber	22
J G Gould	193	Albert D Benjamin	102
Glen R Hankins	183½	Hiram Bowen	47
A G Hause	336	James Bowers	226
E A Hause	336	Cornelius Cadwell	134
Sanford Hause	336	G W Chaplin	197
C C Hayner	290	Marcus Childs	309
Isaac Horton	285	Lewis Coblen	2
William Horton	343	Clifford W Coleman	189½
Charles Hiram Jackson	112	James L Collins	74
James Kleckner	73	J L Cook	301
Harry Lane	325	Albert Cooper	390
Emil M Lauterbock	67½	Harold M Craig	119
Calvin Lockwood	305	John M Craig	49
James Lockwood	306	Alonzo R Dakins	43
Levi Manning	147	Stillman Davenport	37
M H McManus	231	Robert M Davis	188
Theron Metcalf	322	Laurence P Eddy	275½
S B Minich	251	H C Elliott	134
Melvin Munson	?	Henry J Elliott	134
Albert Nichols	178	Sylvester Feagles	295
E C Plumb	279	Daniel W Foster	14
Milton H Pullen	114	Garland S Glover	118
William Pullen	221	Richard Gott	252
O C Rathburn	338	William Gott	161
James Reese	308	Charles W Graham	107
George W Rife	54½	Thomas H Graham	80
J S Rose	230	James Grant	341
George Ruel	348	George D Hamilton	70
J M Ruggles	235	Edward Harris	161
Samuel Scripture	321	James L Hawley	76
Cleve Tanner	209	George Jones	236
John Tucker	213	R M Jones	188
Lewis Vogts	205	Isaac Loree	61

LIST OF OLD SOLDIERS BURIED IN SECTION "A" "B" "1" "2"

Section "B"

Robert McCall	402	Howard Soules Jr.	168
Hugh E MacMillen	270½	George E Thomas	228
Isaac Page	51	Hugh Van Gilder	126
Erwin Osborne	217	Lavern Clyde Van Gorder	25
Edgar Rathburn	347		
Edward R Reed	78		
Andrew B Roberts	260	**Section "2"**	
Clem Roberts	260	Joseph R Allen	143
R W Roff	137	Gerold Bogan	176
Orson A Rose	160	Joseph Burrell	81
Oscar D Rose	160	Joyce Ellis Curtis	49
Hal M Schlaack	202	William Galbraith	64
Oliver P Showers	198	Ernest D Gromman	52
Ray L Skutt	61	Arist Harpel Haist	136
Alfred H Smith	275	Ray Hillman	54
Ray Thompson	205	William Berlie Mastic	153
Emory Vreeland	162	Frank Moore	61
William B Walker	387	George Palmer	18
Jay E Walton	300	Jack Peck	68
Galen J Westmoreland	153	Deak Richmond	78
Henry White	378	Charles Riemann	105
Charles Wilkinson	339	Henry E Tiedman	2
Andrew Woll	361	Patrick B Tobin	148
Gaylon O Worthington	216	Marian L Yerkes	89
Earl D Wright	267½		

Section "1"

Louis E Boyce	146	
Luellan S Chalker	215	**Mauseleum**
Roland Cheney	70	George L Fisher
Charles H Coll	34	Albert F Grove
Merritt K Cook	136	Benjamin Hoag
John A Crofoot	61	Albert Messenger
David DeWaters	80	Andrew Wickman
Fred H Dillingham	104	
Columbus H Fluria	229	
Martin R Foster	200	
Robert Marshall Gates	106	
Charles Hoag	69	
Ralph Holmes	112	
Floyd Roy Moore	167	
Robert L Oliver	67	
Ernest J Palmer	77	
Ralph Plummer	244	
Melvin Richmond Jr.	25	
Norman Roberts	5	
Edward Seymour	273	
Felix Smith	48	

Miscellaneous and Unknown lots   Greenwood cemetery

Julia A Benjamin   b-Mi.   res. Fowlerville
                                    d-Jan. 4, 1926 age 77, cancer

Mary M Bliss   removed from vault at Plainfield
                                    cemetery, April 1894.

Emerson Bowen   b-Mi.   res. Pontiac
                                    d-April 17, 1923 age 67

Julia E Chalker   b-Locke twp.   res. Locke
                                    d-age 10, removed from old cem.

Annie Finley?   b-Ireland res. Fowlerville
                                    d-Sept. 1, 1862 age 32, consumpt.

Susan, wife of M R Foster   (stone laying near garage in back)
died June 21, 1898 aged 78ys & 8rs (see lot One-200)

Thomas J Flynn   b-Mi.   res. Fowlerville
                                    d- 8-14-1917 age 4.

Annie Gimley?   (same as Annie Finley)
                                    listed page 18 of old cem. book

David K Harris   b-Fairfield, Ohio
                                    d-Nov. 9, 1882 age 45

Henry Jane Schooley   burial 12-27-1891

daughter of A West   b-Mi.   res. Locke, Ingham Co.
                                    d- 8-4-1912 stillborn

Lewis C __?__   1857-1921   (stone found laying near garage
                                    in back of cemetery.)

MOUNT OLIVET CEMETERY
of
St. Agnes Roman Catholic Church
in Fowlerville, Michigan

General View

Mt. Olivet Catholic Cemetery of Fowlerville, Michigan

    Mount Olivet cemetery is located east of the village
of Fowlerville and north of Grand River avenue on the
Cemetery road. It lies on the east side of section 11,
Handy township, directly across from the old section "A"
of Greenwood cemetery. The burial ground is the property
of St. Agnes Catholic church of Fowlerville.

    The records for this cemetery consist mainly of an
old plat map with some lot owner's names and a small
amount of index cards containing a few burial dates. It
is said that some of the sextons for the cemetery, in the
past, kept the records in their heads and did not leave
any written records at all.

                    - - - - - -

            HISTORY of Mt. Olivet Cemetery

    Catholics of Handy and Iosco township were served by
a mission priest in the early days of the townships.
Most of these pioneers were of German descent. They had
their own cemetery ground in Iosco township, now known
as the Eisele cemetery.

    In 1891 Father Ryan organized St. Agnes parish in the
village of Fowlerville and soon built a church. About
this time Mr. E A Metcalf sold a 16 rod piece of land
for a Catholic cemetery to H Loughlin and others. Later
Francis J Shields, a lawyer turned over the land to Rev.
Michael J Gallagher, Bishop of Detroit, dated August 30,
1920 for the consideration of one dollar.

    It was stated at this time that the land had been
donated originally to the church by James McCarthy and
his wife Mary of Fowlerville in a deed given the Bishop
but the deed had been lost.

                    — — — — — —

    The present sexton of the cemetery is Jim Sober of
Handy township. The village of Fowlerville began to
record the burials in Mt. Olivet cemetery around 1959
among its records of burials in Greenwood cemetery.

The tombstone transcriptions have been recorded in three sections for the purpose of easier location of the family lots.

The LEFT section is to the left of the circle drive as you enter the cemetery.

The RIGHT section is to the right of the drive as you enter the cemetery.

The CENTER section is contained inside the circle drive-way path.
The transcription was done in the spring of 1984.

Mt. Olivet Catholic Cemetery

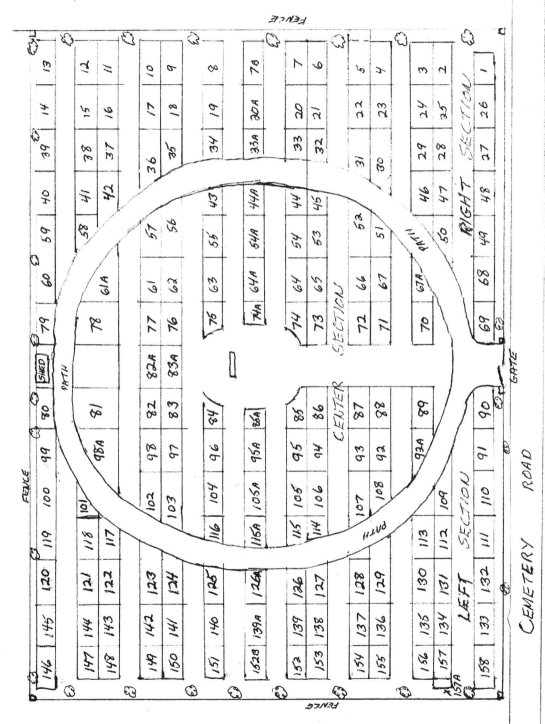

INDEX of tombstone names in Mt. Olivet cemetery

INDEX of tombstone names in Mt. Olivet cemetery

family name   lot

family name	lot	family name	lot
Kovacs	19	Salatowski	115
Kropik	8	Sariscsany	134,156
Kuch	44a	Schellenberg	18
Kuyda	74a	Scollon	55
		Segun	54a
Lako	127	Sessions	81,98,117
Lennon	130	Shields	71
Lockwood	75	Smith	7,19,33
Loughlin	142		91,92,132
Lynch	118	Smyth	7
		Sober	132,133,158
Maas	32	St. Charles	120
MacKenzie	128	Stopa	102
Mahan	83	Sutton	136
Maloney	20a	Swidriski	121,143
Mathews	83a	Szymanski	6
McCarty	71	Tock	107
McDonald	110	Tokman	5
McDonough	34	Trowbridge	53
McGuire	21, 108,113	Turnbull	126
McKight	94		
Merchand	141	Unterbrink	23
Meyer	138,148		
Milett	26,67,104	Westergren	147
Miller	18	White	103
Miner	142	Wilcox	154
Monks	75	Wines	87
Monroe	61a	Winiarski	126
Moran	64	Wyzlic	144
Mulvaney	69,122,131		
Newton	95		
O'Brien	45		
Outwater	76		
Parris	83a		
Peterson	141		
Pierce	53		
Quinn	51		
Raymer	52,66		
Rector	34		
Robben	7		
Roy	2		
Rushing	2		

Left section   Mt. Olivet cemetery

Row 1
lot 158   double stone-SOBER
             Gertrude I, 1920-1981
                       married June 22, 1940
             Anthony A, 1915-

lot 133   double stone-SOBER
             Gerald F & Jerome J, "our twins"
             March 10-11, 1953

lot 132   double stone-SOBER
             Lawrence O, 1890-1964
             Lena F, 1890-1978

             double stone-SMITH
             Pauline F-1917-1967
             Elmer R, 1918-

Lot 111   Charles S Driver, 1909-1910

             Daniel L Driver, 1899-1900

             Lucille I Driver, 1903-1918

             Catherine Driver, 1897-1916

             Margaret Driver, 1879-1909

             Samuel Driver, 1867-1924

lot 110   Paul G McDonald, 1902-1921

             on monument-COLLOTON

             Thomas J, 1877-1950 "son"

             Catherine, 1882-1916 "daughter"

             Elizabeth, 1844-1917 "mother"

             Thomas, 1846-1890 "father"

lot 91   on monument-
             Mary, wife of Albert L Smith, 1876-1907

             Mary

lot 90   double stone-GEHRINGER
             Theresa, 1872-1946 "mother"
             Leonard, 1850-1924 "father"

Left section   Mt. Olivet cemetery

Row 2
lot 157a   John Wilbur Gerych, SP4, U S Army, Vietnam
                Aug. 30, 1949-Aug. 11, 1983

lot 157   William J Eisele, 1936-1950 "son"

                double stone-EISELE
                Thelma E, 1898-1970
                            married August 11, 1919
                Wilbur F, 1895-1962

                (behind stone above) Wilbur F Eisele
                                Michigan Pvt. Co 1, 340 infantry
                                World War 1
                                March 26, 1895-June 18, 1962

lot 134   Steve J Sariscsany, 1918-1975 (vet)

                Lawrence Sariscsany, 1947-1952

                on monument-SARISCSANY

lot 131   double stone-MULVANEY
                James B, 1879-1949
                Mabel, 1887-1972

lot 112   multi-stone-FLYNN
                Thos. W, 1913-1917
                Chris L, 1879-1951
                Rosa P, 1883-1912
                Gertrude, 1909-1918
                Alma, 1885-1968

lot 109   Bernard J Flynn, Pfc U S Army, World War 2
                April 9, 1917-Oct. 8, 1966

                double stone -GRILL
                Nick, 1909-1952
                Madelyn, 1914-

Row 3
lot 156   double stone-SARISCSANY
                Anna B, 1886-1944 "mother"
                John, 1883-1950 "father"

lot 135   Imogene, wife of Matt Dillingham, 1923-1959

                double stone-DILLINGHAM
                Mott, 1911-19-
                Irene, 1911-1942

lot 130   double stone-LENNON
                Julia, 1870-1941
                William, 1872-1950

Left section   Mt. Olivet cemetery

Row 3 cont.-
lot 113   double stone-McGUIRE
                Thomas, 1882-1961
                Ellen, 1883-1940

                Marjorie Ann McGuire "daughter"
                May 2, 1942-July 6, 1955

Row 4
lot 155   Hellen M Hoffman, 1880-1951 "wife"

lot 136   David D Sutton, 1931-1962 (vet)

Row 5
lot 154   Thelma Defendorf Wilcox, 1902-

lot 137   Myron T Dunham, Michigan Pvt. 1 Co. Armd Recp Tng Cen
                             World War 2   (grave partly on lot 154)
                Oct. 3, 1907-Jan. 21, 1962

                "baby" Deschamps 1964

                double stone-HUGHES
                Agnes, 1886-1970
                Joseph, 1885-1970

lot 128   double stone-MacKENZIE
                Donald N, 1922
                Anna L, 1916-

Row 6
lot 153   double stone-JENEY
                Lousi , 1887-1952
                Rosī, 1872-1959

lot 138   double stone-DAY
                Hollis, 1885-1961 "husband"
                Vina, 1892-1971 "wife"

                double stone-MEYER
                H F, 1873-1965
                Pauline M, 1880-1964

lot 127   double stone-LAKO
                Mary, 1888-1958
                George, 1882-1975

Left section   Mt. Olivet cemetery

Row 7
lot 152   triple stone-FRITZ
               Matilda M, 1889-1976
               Gerome, 1916-1920
               Jack E, 1889-1954

lot 139   multi-stone-DAILEY
               Thomas T, 1887-1958 (vet)
               May R, 1893-1974
               Gerald T, 1916-1984
               Beulah B,

lot 126   Robert J Turnbull, Michigan Pvt. 19 Inf. 24 Inf. Div.
                                 Korea A-4
               Oct. 7, 1931-Nov. 4, 1950

               Anna Winiarski, 1883-1963

Row 8
lot 152b   Russell Leo Brennan, 1898-1983

lot 139a   double stone-HAAS
               J Rea, 1906-
               Earnest V, 1902-1976

lot 126a   no stones

Row 9
lot 151   no stones

lot 140   Helen Marie Cox, 1920-1966 (vet)

lot 125   double stone-HEATON
               Mary, 1896-1979
               Frank, 1891-1975

               (behind stone above)Frank R Heaton, Sgt. Air Service
                                 Oct. 15, 1891-Sep. 1, 1975

               Celinda Marie Bulger, 1898-1970

Row 10
lot 150   double stone-GUZIEL
               Rose, 1910-1974

lot 141   double stone-MERCHAND
               Lucille,
               Ted A, 1908-1968

               double stone-Peterson
               Wayne F, 1913-1968 (vet)
               Mary A, 1913-

Row 10 cont.-
lot 124   double stone-GLOVER
              Joan, 1920
              Russell, 1919-1972

Row 11
lot 149   Thomas Mathew Cowles, Feb. 24, 1958-Dec. 1, 1973

              Martha C Cieslak, 1899-1973

lot 142   double stone-LOUGHLIN
              Mary A, 1908-1972
              John G, 1909-

              double stone-MINER
              Lucille E, 1914-1974
              William H, 1911-1978

              double stone-BIALKE
              John H, Jan. 27, 1910-Jan. 17, 1970 (vet)

Lot 123   double stone-HALL
              Gloria E, Apr. 19, 1930-Jan. 20, 1977 "mother"
              Rober D, Sept. 13, 1930-   "father"

              Donald Rosco Baughn, Pvt U S Army, World War 2
              Jan. 30, 1916-Mar. 24, 1980

Row 12
lot 148   on monument-MEYER

              Anthony A Meyer Jr. Cpl Army Air Force, World War 2
              1920-1975

lot 143   Marie Chrzaszcz, 1888-1979 "mother"

              triple stone-SWIDRISKI
              Olga, 1897-1977
              Adam, 1895-1969

lot 122   double stone-JUDD
              Eileen, 1911-
              Hulett, 1907-1977

              double stone-MULVANEY
              Madeline A, 1914-
              Bernard H, 1909-1972

              (behind stone above)Bernard H Mulvaney
                          Michigan 1st Lt. U S Army, World War 2
                          Mar. 15, 1909-Dec. 6, 1972

Left section   Mt. Olivet cemetery

Row 12 cont.-
lot 117   triple stone-SESSIONS
             Wayne M, 1953-1980
             Elizabeth A, 1932-
             Robert J, 1931-

Row 13
lot 147   (on metal tag) Margaret K Westergren
                        born 9-29-1910, died 1-16-1984, age 73

             double stone-BACKHAUSEN
             Margaret, 1908-
             Gerold J Sr., 1902-1983

lot 144   double stone-WYZLIC
             Laura, 1907
             Bernard, 1903-1975

lot 121   double stone-SWIDRISKI
             Kathleen, 1928
             Anthony, 1923-1979

             double stone-EPLEY
             Margaret M, 1921-
             Robert J, 1916-

lot 118   a new slab (?)

             James V Lynch, Pvt U S Marine Corps, World War 2
             Dec. 13, 1922-July 10, 1980

lot 101   David Thomas Beddow, June 2, 1955-Oct. 30, 1983 "father"

Row 14
lot 146   no stones

lot 145   a footstone (?)

             Clare A Cavender, Michigan Pfc Medical Department
                        Wotld War 2
             Sept. 16, 1900-Feb. 18, 1961

lot 120   double stone-St. CHARLES
             Clare E, Mar. 30, 1902-Nov. 18, 1974
             Eli H, Oct. 22, 1890-Aug. 23, 1976

             (on a wood cross) Delmar, Sept. 27, 1938-Oct. 6, 1938

             (a small wood cross-recent grave)?
Lot 119, 100, 99 and 80
             no stones

Row 3
lot 92a   double stone-DAILEY
               Mary J, 1853-1940
               Frank E, 1855-1933

lot 89   no stones

lot 70   on monument-BROWN
               William Brown, 1845-1922
               Mary Brown, 1856-1931
               Maggie Brown, 1884-1902
               William Brown Jr. 1879-1959

lot 67a   double stone-KENNEDY
               John D, 1889-1957
               Lula Belle, 1891-1967

Row 4
lot 108   on monument-McGUIRE
               James, 1852-1929
               Sarah, 1855-1921

lot 92   triple stone-SMITH-GROVER
               Roy, 1900
               Anna, 1899
               infant 1925

lot 88   Clement J Gannon, 1871-1939

               Carrie B Gannon, 1873-1954

               Agnes L Gannon, 1914-1979

               Gertrude M Gannon, 1908-

lot 71   Mary McCarty, 1842-1916

               James McCarty, 1839-1904

               Thomas F Shields, 1846-1906

               on monument-McCARTY

lot 67   Bertha Milett, 1889-1915

               Austin Milett, 1833-1913 "father"

               Jane Milett, 1839-1907 "mother"

               Sarah Milett, 1865-1929

               Lena Milett, 1879-1940

               on monument-MILETT

Center section   Mt. Olivet cemetery

Row 4 cont.-
lot 51   double stone-QUINN
              E Maxine, 1916-
              John E, 1900-1979

Row 5
lot 107   on monument-TOCK

              Grace S, 1884-1944

              William H, 1858-1928

              Sarah, 1856-1897

lot 93   double stone-FINLAN
              Helen, 1884-1954 "mother"
              John, 1881-1952 "father"

lot 87   double stone-WINES
              George R, 1872-1944 "father"
              Margaret E, 1873-1933 "mother"

lot 72   on monument-CONNER

              James, 1858-1903

              Minnie Conner, 1864-1931

lot 66   (RAYMER lot)
              Francis W, Apr. 23, 1855-June 1, 1923

              Veronica, May 9, 1873-Sept. 25, 1966

              Margaret M, Feb. 5, 1858-Aug. 11, 1916

              John, Feb. 24, 1853-Aug. 11, 1911

              Wm. F, July 15, 1860-Aug. 11, 1906

lot 52   on monument- RAYMER

              double stone-RAYMER
              Leo, 1914-1975
              Mable, 1918-1972

              double stone-RAYMER
              Lewis F, 1908-
              Hazel V, 1902-1955

Center section   Mt. Olivet cemetery

Row 6
lot 114   no stones

lot 106   no stones

lot 94   Angela Britten Grover, Feb. 19, 1974-Aug. 25, 1977

               Mary M McKnight, 1900-1977

               Joann L Colwell, Nov. 1, 1978-Nov. 3 "our baby"

               Catherine Barle, born April 22, 1822, died July 30, 1904

lot 86   on monument-DOHERR

               Freda Doherr, 1883-1971

               Julia Doherr, 1862-1942

               Emil Doherr, 1856-1935

lot 73   on monument-KANE

               Agnes Kane, 1868-1946

               Thomas, 1882-1902

               Catherine, 1839-

               Michael, 1870-1917

               Thomas Kane, 1865-1938

               Margaret Kane, 1863-1941

lot 65   on monument-GANNON

               Daniel Gannon, 1843-1918

               Anne, wife of Daniel Gannon, 1843-1909

               Joseph D, 1879-1883, son of D & A Gannon

               Marge F Gannon, Apr. 13, 1892-Jan. 3, 1981

               Casper H Gannon, 1883-1973

               Mary B Gannon, 1873-1954

Center section   Mt. Olivet cemetery

Row 6 cont.-
lot 53   double stone-TROWBRIDGE
             William H, 1840-1928
             Susan, 1846-1906, his wife

             father

             mother

             double stone-PIERCE
             Edward, 1874-1955
             Bertha S, 1887-1956

             Horace J Pierce, Michigan Pvt Co A, 802 MP Bn
                              ·   World War 2
             Aug. 20, 1909-June 5, 1969

lot 45   Lucy A O'Brien, 1857-1921 "mother'

Row 7
lot 115   Francis Salatowski, 1875-1936 "dear husband-father"

             Frances Salatowski, 1874-1945 "dear mother"

             Joanna Salatowski, 1902-1934 "dear daughter"

lot 105   footstone (a grave?)

             Eunice Barber Brady, 1908-1937

             triple stone-BARBER
             Jay R, 1880-1956
             Rose A, 1883-1963
             Ellen A, 1923-1974

lot 95   Mathew Heeney, 1867-1913 (vet)

             Jane Sarah Newton, 1870-1948

             Patrick Heeney, 1827-1914

             James Heeney, 1861-1925 (Span. Amer vet)

             Michael Heeney, 1863-1924 (vet)

lot 85   on monument-BURLEY

             Edward, 1852-1927

             Maggie, 1851-1937

Center section   Mt. Olivet cemetery

Row 7 cont.-
lot 74   John Kane, 1881-1946

              DeEtte Kane, 1886-1941

              Mary Kane, 1857-1941

lot 64   on monument-MORAN

              John, 1841-1920

              Catherine, 1849-1914

              Edward, 1868-1939

              Agnes, 1882-1971

lot 54   on monument-CURTIS

              Joan F, 1947-1958 "daughter"

lot 41   on monument-BRANDELL

              Elizabeth E, 1855-1941 "mother"

              Charles, 1847-1922 "father"

              Bernard H A, 1883-1958 "son"

Row 8
lot 115a   double stone-KNICKERBACKER
              Guy F, 1934-
              M Catherine, 1935-

lot 105a   Francis C Eisele, 1924-1977

              John F Eisele, Pfc U S Army, World War 2
              Sept. 9, 1905-May 20, 1981

              Francis C Eisele, 2nd Lt. U S Army, World War 2
              Sep 29, 1924-Jan. 28, 1977 (same as 1st stone above)

              Charles F Eisele, Michigan Pvt U S Army, World War 1
              April 8, 1897-Sept. 17, 1973

lot 95a   double stone-EISELE
              Charles F, 1897-1973
              Martha J, 1897-1980

              double stone-KANE
              Thomas L, 1909-1975
              Viola E, 1911-

Center section   Mt. Olivet cemetery

Row 8
85a   on monument-DILLINGHAM

             double stone-
             Mary N, 1925-
             Gale D, 1924-

In center of center section a large monument
          "in memory of Alfons DeCang"

lot 74a   double stone-KUYDA
             Ellen,
             Bernard,

             Vera DeWitt, 1896-19-   "mother"

64a   double stone-FURMONEK
             Louise, 1906-1980
             Joseph W, 1901-

             a grave (?)

54a   double stone-SEGUN
             Louise M, 1908-

             Francis J, 1904-1981

             double stone-EASTMAN
             Mary E, 1926-
             Gerald F, 1924-1981

             (behind stone above) Gerald F Eastman, Cpl U S Marine Corps
                                   World War 2
                                   May 29, 1924-Feb. 27, 1981

lot 44a   double stone-KUCH
             Mike P, 1913-
             Esther M, 1919-

Row 9
lot 116   double stone-DEVINE
             Patrick, 1840-1926
             Mary, 1830-1912

lot 104   multi-stone-MILETT
             Josephine C, 1899-19-
             Austin E, 1873-1958
             infant son, 1934
             infant daughter 1938

lot 96   double stone-FINLAN
                Thomas, 1883-1965
                Lyra E, 1893-1977

lot 84   no stones

lot 75   on monument-MONKS-FINLAN

                Winifred, 1878-1906

                Donald E Lockwood, Michigan AE3, U S Navy
                June 15, 1930-March 16, 1957

                William Finlan, 1869-1940

lot 63   no stones

lot 55   on monument-SCOLLON

                James, 1857-1932 "father"

                Isabella, 1861-1918 "mother"

lot 43   on monument-C?MISKEY

                Sarah, 1850-1921 "mother"

                John, 1839-1934 "father"

Row 10
lot 103   double stone-WHITE
                Frank J, 1884-1965
                Delia M, 1881-1960

                double stone-CARUSI
                Eleanor L, 1886-1961 "wife" (ladis Aux.)
                John, 1877-1958 "husband"

lot 97   on monument-KASUDA

                Joseph, 1878-1956 "father"

                Carolina, 1884-1939 "mother"

                Raymond, 1919-1939 "son"

                Edmond, 1937-1939 "grandson"

                double stone-
                Concella, 1911-
                Walter, 1908-
                parents of Edmond

Center section   Mt. Olivet cemetery

Row 10 cont.-
lot 83   (large old slab-for monument?)

                Frances C Mahan, 1891-1962 "mother"

lot 83a   Elizabeth Lavey Mathews, 1895-1982

                Lois J Parris, 11-22-45 10-15-76 "mother"

lot 76   double stone-OUTWATER
                Garret O, 1882-1973
                Mary G, 1890-1956

lot 62   double stone-DOHERR
                Paul E, 1890-1950
                Rosa M, 1892-19-

                Dorothy Agnes Doherr, born April 13, 1921 (on small stone)
                                   died Aug. 15, 1921

                Mary Lucane Doherr, born Nov. 2, 1916 (on small stone)
                                   died Nov. 9, 1916

lot 56   Leon R Gaffney, 1909-1964

                triple stone-GAFFNEY
                Mary, 1877-1957
                William, 1866-1948
                mae, 1899-1918

Row 11
lot 102   large double stone-STOPA
                Joyce Elaine, Feb. 28, 1940-Feb. 13, 1966
                James Robert, Aug. 12, 1939-Feb. 13, 1966 (vet)

lot 98   double stone-SESSIONS
                Elizabeth, 1920-1922 "daughter"
                William, 1914-1915 "son"

                Sessions, "in memory of Pfc Gordon, 1926-1945
                USMC, killed on Okinawa while serving his country"

                double stone-SESSIONS
                Clarence, 1888-1956 "father"
                Mary, 1893-1975 "mother"

Row 11 cont.-
lot 82 double stone-ALLEN
     James, 1882-1969
     Clara, 1902-1982

     Joseph R Allen, Michigan Pvt, Field Artillary
          World War 2
     March 26, 1927-Nov. 29, 1956

     triple stone-BOEVE
     Emma, 1886-1981
     Pfc Homer, 1917-1945 killed in Germany
     Henry, 1881-1953

lot 82a Mary Ann Behringer, April 15, 1956-Sept. 9, 1974

lot 77 no stones

lot 61 Wm. H Jacoby, 1864-1936

     Julia C Jacoby, 1882-1949

     Hilda M Coe, 1906-1930

     James A Jacoby, 1911-1919

     Mary Coe Henderson, 1927-1964

lot 57 no stones

Row 12 & 13
lot 98a no stones

lot 81 double stone-SESSIONS
     Victor F, 1918-   (vet)
     Lillian P, 1924-1983

lot 78 (a pot and a artificial flower)?

lot 61a Jesse J Monroe, Oct. 19, 1980-Nov 23 "our little angel"

Right section   Mt. Olivet cemetery

Row 1
lot 69   on monument-MULVANEY

              John, 1832-1921

              Jane, 1843-1912

              James, 1834-1899

              John, 1873-1953

              Michael, 1868-1943

lot 68   no stones (Mulvaney lot)

lot 49   triple stone-GERMAIN
              Henry, 1881-1956 "father"
              Clementine, 1892-1979 "mother"
              Peter, 1917-   "son"

              Alphonse Germain, 1915-1916

lot 48   on monument-BUSHEY

              Joel, 1841-   a Sgt Co K, 15 NY Arty (vet)

              Celia, 1847-1916

lot 27   Gamiel Germain, 1873-1942

              Alma M Germain, 1887-1964

lot 26   on monument-MILETT
              Nancy H Milett, May 7, 1945 "baby"
              Suzanna C Dutkiewicz, Mar. 26, 1960 "baby"
              John Thomas Milett, 1869-1947 "father"
              Harold T Milett, 1909-   "husband"
              Helen L Milett, 1911-   "wife"

lot 1   no stones

Row 2
lot 50   John D Haltinner Jr. Michigan Pfc, 144 Ord Ammo Co.(vet)
              April 1, 1938-Aug. 7, 1960

              A J Kane, 1915-1958

Row 2 cont.-
lot 47   Chris A Gehringer, 1880-1962

              Rose McGuire Gehringer, 1885-1926

              double stone-GEHRINGER
              Lillian A, 1893-1978
              George J, 1884-1979

lot 28   George V DeCang, May 24, 1933-Sept. 12, 1942 "son"

              triple stone-DeCANG
              Gabriele, 1902-1957
              Al, 1890-1964
              Mary, 1929-1965

lot 25   no stones

lot 2   Louis J Roy, 1887-1961 "husband"

              D Anseline Roy, 1899-1929

              August J King, 1881-1953

              Josephine Roy, 1855-1929

              double stone-RUSHING
              Clara, 191801966 "mother"
              William, 1912-1979 "father"

Row 3
lot 46   no stones

lot 29   double stone-HOLZINGER
              Edward, 1907-1970
              Carrie, 1906-1981

lot 24   no stones

lot 3   no stones

Row 4
lot 30   John Dale Brower, 1934-1980 "son"

              Lewis Brower, 1889-1974 "father"

              Frances Brower, 1898-1938 "mother"

              Carl Brower, 1929-1939 "son"

Right section   Mt. Olivet cemetery

Row 4 cont.-
lot 23   (a large cement cross)?

            double stone-UNTERBRINK
            Laurence W, 1911-1980
            Helen I. 1913-

            double stone-EISELE
            Alma, 1883-1981
            Joseph L, 1877-1955

lot 4   no stones

Row 5
lot 31   Edward C Heinrich, 1916-1925

            Elizabeth M Bauerle, 1908-1924

            Michael Bauerle, 1904-1923

lot 22   Edward Heinrich, 1879-1953

            Mary A Heinrich, 1881-1961

lot 5   double stone-CRUGHER
            Agnes B, 1884-1965
            Lewis, 1881-1950

            Lucy Tokman, 1900-1965 "mother"

            Eleanor Bozyk (Tokman) "sister-aunt"
            Sep. 24, 1919-Nov. 25, 1966

5a   George A Tokman, Pfc U S Army, World War 2
            1918-1977

Row 6
lot 32   Frank J Maas, 1884-1948

            Bernard M Maas, 1926-1942

            Frances Maas, infant

lot 21   Robert E McGuire 2, 1950-1971 "son"

            Lucille May McGuire, June 21, 1965 "daughter"

Right section   Mt. Olivet cemetery

Row 6 cont.-
lot 6   Harry Dombecker, 1910-1949

             Hester C Baker, 1877-1960 "mother"

             John Szymanski, 1887-1963

Row 7
lot 33   (an old slab)?

             Sarah A Smith, 1861-1907

             double stone-FLOOD
             Philip-, 1862-1952
             Catherine Heeney, 1865-1935

             Catherine E Flood 3-6-1902 7-15-1902

lot 20   double stone-FITZGERALD
             Mary Agnes, 1900-1962
             Lea J, 1898-1979

             double stone-BLOSCOVICH
             Dolly, 1928-1962

lot 7   William J Smith, 1891-1951

             Charles Hammill, 1869-1942 "uncle" (vet)
             (erected by W J Smyth)

             double stone-ROBBEN
             Paul H, 1896-1965 (vet)
             Fern E, 1902-

Row 8
lot 33a   no stones

lot 20a   double stone-MALONEY
             Harold J, 1927-1981
             Mary N,

             (behind stone above)Harold J Maloney
                          Pvt U S Army, World War 2
                          Mar. 28, 1927-Feb. 26, 1981

lot 7b   (a wood cross-childs grave?)

             Jerold E Delaney, Sgt U S Army, Korea
             Mar. 31, 192_, Jul. 9, 1977

Right section   Mt. Olivet cemetery

Row 9
lot 34   double stone-McDONOUGH
             Ann, 1858-1949
             John, 1852-1926

             double stone-RECTOR
             Port T, 1855-19-
             Margaret, 1855-1927

lot 19   Charles L Kovacs, Pfc U S Army, World War 2
             1926-1976

             double stone- COX
             Timothy L, 1909-1977 "father"
             Dorothy W, 1916-1979 "mother"

             Margaret Mary Smith, Jan. 31, 1912-Dec. 17, 1982 "mother"

lot 8   Gregory Joel Kropik "beloved sonshine"
             July 30, 1961-Feb. 21, 1980

             Joseph O Couture "dad"
             12-26-90 6-20-71

Row 10
lot 35   no stones

lot 18   Merle H Schellenberg, 1938-1981

             Tracey Anne Miller "our beloved daughter"
             July 24, 1963-Aug. 23, 1981

lot 9   no stones

Row 11
lot 36   no stones

lot 17   (a new grave)(vet)

lot 10   no stones

No burials in Rows 12, 13 and 14

RECORDS of MT. OLIVET CEMETERY

(Taken from the official card file and plat map of the cemetery
kept by the sexton at his home.)

lot 4a   Julius "Joe" Dyonckheer, 12-4-67
         Joseph A Sachy, 7-22-69 (Wysocki)

5a   Bozyk lot
      Mrs. Louis Tokman
      Eleanor Bozyk, 12-2-66
      George Tokman, 1977

6a   Hester Baker
      John Szymanski

7a   Paul Robben

7b   John M Kozdron, 12-4-80
      Jerrard Delaney, July 19_7

8   Gregory Kropik, 2-26-80
      Joseph O Courture

9   Earl Wolff, 2-3-?

18   Schellenberg, 11-10-81
      Tracey Miller, 8-25-81

19   Charles Kovacs
      Timothy Cox
      Dorothy Cox, 8-21-79
      Margaret Smith, 12-21-82

20   Mary Fitzgerald

20a   Harold Maloney, 3-2-81

21   Robert Jr. 9-15-71 (McGuire)
      Lucille Mary McGuire, 9-15-71 at foot of #6

23   Alma Eisele, 7-22-81
      Joe Eisele, 1955

25   baby, #6

26   Nancy Milet, May 45
      John T Milet, Dec. 6, 47
      Suzanne C, March 26, 60

29   Ed Holzinger, 4-1-70
      Carrie Holzinger, 2-20-81

RECORDS of MT. OLIVET CEMETERY

lot 30   John Dale Brower "80"

35   (crossed out) Hiram Tobin, 4-5-6

49   Henry Germain, 1956
          Clementine Germain, 11-17-79

51   4-28-79

52   Thomas Lea, 9-8-81
          Leo, Jan. 3, 1975
          Mable, June 5, 1972
          Hazel

53   Wm. Harrison Trowbridge, 1928
          Susan Trowbridge, 1906
          Edward Pierce, 1955
          Bertha Pierce, 1956

54a   Francis Seguin, 2-14-81
          Robert Bonday, 5-16-83
          Gerald Eastwood, 3-3-81

61a   baby lots
          Hanes, 1-13-66
          St. Charles, 2-3-66
          Darnell, 8-5-67
          Schlehuber, 10-25-67
          Wilson twins, 1-14-70
          Jesse J Monroe, 11-25-80
          Hetrick, 9-12-76

64a   Louise Furmanek, 8-23-80
          Clayton Cousina, 10-22-80

66   Francis   (Raymor lot)
          Veronica
          Mary
          Margaret
          John
          William

69   Mulvaney lot
          John, 1921
          Jane, 1912
          James, 1899
          John, 1851
          Michael, 1943

76   Outwater lot
          Garrett, 1973
          Mary, 1956

RECORDS of MT. OLIVET CEMETERY

lot 81   Lillian Sessions, 1-18-83
          Roger Cahaney, 4-5-6

82   Allen lot
          James, 12-6-69
          Clara, 4-10-82
          Joseph, 56
          Emma Boeve, 6-4-81
          Henry Boeve
          baby

82a   Mary Ann Berhinger, 1974

83   Elizabeth Matheus, 12-27-82

83a   Lois J Parrish

85   Burley lot
          Howard
          Maggie

88   Clem Gannon
          Mrs. Clem Gannon
          Agnes Gannon, 11-6-79

94   Angela Dawn Britten, 8-29-77
          Jeann Coldwell, infant, 11-4-78
          Mrs. McKnight, 6-1-77

95a   Charles Eisele
          Martha Eisele, 9-26-80
          Tom Kane, 12-11-75

96   Tom Finlan
          Lyra Finlan

98   Mrs. Clarence Session, 1975

102   James Stopa
          Joyce Stopa

105a   John Eisele, 5-27-81
          Frances Eisele, 1977

108   James McGuire
          Sarah McGuire

109   Bernard Flynn
          Alex "Nick" Grill

{389}

RECORDS of MT. OLIVET CEMETERY

lot 112   Thomas
          Alma, 1-15-68
          Chris, 1951
          Rosa
          Gertrude

117   Wayne Sessions, 5-14-80

120   Clara St. Charles, 1974
      Eli St. Charles, 1976
      Dalmar St. Charles, 38

121   James Lynch, 7-14-80

122   Hulett Judd, 8-27-77
      Bernard Mulvaney, 11-72

123   Don Baughn, 3-26-80

124   Russell Glover, 2-26-72

125   Frank Heaton
      Celinda M Bulger, 4-27-70

127   Mrs. George Lako
      George Lako, Nov. 1975

132   Laurence Sober, 4-20-64
      Lena Sober, 4-5-78
      Pauline Smith, 12-6-67

134   Steve Sariscsany
      Lawrence Sariscsany

136   David

137   Bo Dunham
      Agnes Hughes, 2-13-70

139   Tom Dailey
      May (Dailey) DeForest, 1974

139a Robert Lieber
      John Schoreder
      Earnest Haas, 5-4-76

RECORD of MT. OLIVET CEMETERY

lot 140   Cox lot
           Helen

141   Ted Merchand, 3-7-68
           Wayne Peterson, 12-21-68

142   Mary Laughlin
           Lucille Miner, Dec. 1974
           John Bialke, 1-21-70

143   Marianna Chrzaszcz "mother" May 1979
           Olga
           Adam S Swidriski, 10-7-69

144   Bernard Wyzlie

147   Gerald Bockhausen, 7-30-83

148   Anthony A Meyer, 8-5-75

149   Thomas Cowles, 12-4-73
           Martha, 801-73

150   Rose Guziel, 5-25-74

152   Matilda, 9-10-76
           Wm. J Lieber, 11-21-79 from Grand Blanc
           John

157   son
           Thelma, 1-14-70
           Wilbur

157a   John Gerzck, 8-13-83

158   Sober lot
           Gertrude, 7-11-81

BURIALS in Mt. Olivet cemetery
(abstracted from burial book of Village of Fowlerville)

name	death	age	burial	residence at death
Clara A Allen	4-7-82	79	4-10-82	Ingham Co.
James Thomas Allen	12-4-69	87	12-6-69	Liv. Co.
Ellen A Barber	7-22-74	51	7-23-74	Ingham Co.
Mary Ann Behringer	9-9-74	18	9-12-74	Fowlerville
John H Bialke	1-17-70	59	1-20-70	Liv. Co.
Gerold J Bockhausen	7-28-83	81	7-30-83	Liv. Co.
Robert Bonday	5-12-83	84	5-16-83	Liv. Co.
Emma E Bowe	6-1-81	94	6-3-81	Liv. Co.
Russell Lee Brennon	2-22-83	84	2-24-83	Handy twp.
Angela Britton	8-25-77	3	8-29-77	Washtenaw Co.
John Dale Brower	5-30-80	26	5-14-80	Liv. Co.
Louis Brower	8-12-74	84	8-15-74	Ingham Co.
Celinda M Bulger	4-23-70	71	4-25-70	Liv. Co.
Marianna Chrzaszcz	5-18-79	91		Liv. Co.
Martha C Cieslak	7-30-73	74	8-1-73	Liv. Co.
Joann L Colwell	11-3-78	2d	11-4-78	Liv. Co.
Joseph Courture	6-20-71	80	6-24-71	Detroit
Thomas M Cowles	12-1-73	15	12-4-73	Liv. Co.
Dorothy W Cox	8-18-79	62	8-20-79	Liv. Co.
Timothy L Cox	4-25-77	67	4-29-77	Liv. Co.
Vina M Day	11-9-71	79	11-11-71	Trenton
Mary Ruth Deforest	8-29-74	80	9-2-74	Howell
Lillian Ann Dehringer	1-26-78	84	2-2-78	Shiawassee Co.
Jerald E Delaney	7-9-77	48	7-12-77	Ingham Co.
Freda Katherine Doherr	5-15-71	86	5-17-71	Ingham Co.
Gerald F Eastwood	2-27-81	56	3-3-81	Liv. Co.
Alma M Eisele	7-19-81	98	7-21-81	Ingham Co.
Charles F Eisele	9-17-73	90	9-20-73	Liv. Co.
Francis C Eisele	1-28-77	52	1-29-77	Liv. Co.
Martha J Eisele	9-23-80	83	9-26-80	Handy twp.
Thelma E Eisele	1-14-70	71	1-14-70	Liv. Co.
Lyra E Finlan	7-15-77	84	7-18-77	Liv. Co.
Leo J Fitzgerald	5-5-79	80	5-8-79	Liv. Co.
Louise Furmanek	8-20-80	73	8-23-80	Howell
Agnes Gannon	11-3-79	65	11-6-79	Kalamazoo
Casper H Gannon	8-9-73	90	8-11-73	Liv. Co.
George J Gehringer	11-3-79	95	11-6-79	Owasso
Clemintine Germain	11-5-79	87	11-17-79	Liv. Co.
John W Gerych	8-11-83	34	8-13-83	Liv. Co.
Russell E Glover	2-23-72	52	2-26-72	Liv. Co.
Rose Guziel	5-19-73	63	5-23-73	Howell

BURIALS in Mt. Olivet cemetery
(abstracted from burial book of Village of Fowlerville)

Name		Age		Place
Gloria C Hall	1-20-77	46	1-24-77	Liv. Co.
Frank R Heaton	9-1-75	83	9-4-75	Oakland Co.
Mary M Heaton	3-28-79	82	3-31-79	Liv. Co.
Carrie L Holzinger	2-17-81	74	2-20-81	Ingham Co.
Edward Holzinger	3-29-70	66	4-1-70	Liv. Co.
Agnes E Hughes	2-10-70	83	2-13-70	Liv. Co.
Joseph G Hughes	6-19-70	84	6-22-70	Liv. Co.
Judd Hulett	8-25-77	69	8-27-77	Liv. Co.
Thomas L Kane	12-5-75	66	12-9-75	Liv. Co.
Charles L Kovacs	9-30-76	49	10-2-76	Liv. Co.
John M Kozdron	12-1-80	9	12-3-80	Liv. Co.
George Lako	11-7-75	93	11-10-75	Oakland Co.
Mary A Laughlin	6-7-72	64	6-10-72	Ingham Co.
William J Lieber	11-18-79	28	11-12-79	Flint
James V Lynch	7-10-80	57	7-14-80	Liv. Co.
Michael T M ?	12-23-82	87	12-27-82	Oakland Co.
Harold J Maloney	2-27-81	53	3-2-81	Ann Arbor
*Lucille May McGuire	?	0	6-21-65	
Robert McGuire	9-12-71	21	9-15-71	Byron
Mary M McKnight	5-28-77	76	5-31-77	Liv. Co.
Anthony A Meyer Jr.	8-2-75	55	8-5-75	Howell twp.
Tracey Anne Miller	8-23-81	18	8-25-81	Liv. Co.
Lucille E Miner	12-31-74	60	12-28-74	Washtenaw Co.
William H Miner	5-23-78	67	5-26-78	Liv. Co.
Jesse J Monroe	11-23-80	5w	11-25-80	Howell
Agnes A Moran	6-6-77	82	6-9-77	Oceola twp.
Bernard H Mulvaney	12-6-72	63	12-9-72	Liv. Co.
Mabel D Mulvaney	2-26-72	82	4-1-72	Liv. Co.
Mutch boy & girl(twins)	5-28-70	0	5-30-70	Wayne Co.
Garrett O Outwater	6-20-73	90	6-23-73	Unadilla twp.
Lois J Parris	10-15-76	30	10-19-76	Liv. Co.
Horace Pierce	6-5-69	59	6-7-69	Battle Creek
John E Quinn	4-25-79	78	4-26-79	Liv. Co.
Leo H Raymer	9-4-81	39	9-8-81	Plymouth
Mable G Raymer	6-5-72	53	6-8-72	Wayne Co.
Willie Rushing	12-7-79	28	12-10-79	Mecosta, Mi.
Steve J Sariscsany	11-30-75	56	12-3-75	Washtenaw Co.
Merle H Schalenberg	11-10-81	58	1-18-83	Liv. Co.

*burial in lot 75, then reburied lot 21, 9-15-71

BURIALS in Mt. Olivet cemetery
(abstracted from burial book of Village of Fowlerville)

Lillian B Sessions	1-15-83	58	1-18-83	Liv. Co.
Mary Ann Sessions	3-17-75	81	3-19-75	Liv. Co.
Wayne M Sessions	5-11-80	26	5-14-80	Liv. Co.
Francis J Sequin	2-10-81	76	2-14-81	Washtenaw Co.
Margaret M Smith	12-17-82	69	12-21-82	Liv. Co.
Gertrude J Sober	7-9-81	60	7-11-81	Ingham Co.
Lena F Sober	4-1-78	87	4-5-78	Liv. Co.
Clara E St. Charles	11-18-74	72	11-21-74	Handy twp.
David M St. Charles	1-17-83	40	1-19-83	Ingham Co.
Eli St. Charles	8-23-76	85	8-25-76	Washtenaw Co.
Joseph A Suchy	7-19-69	85	7-22-69	Liv. Co.
Adam S Swidriski	10-4-69	74	10-7-74	Liv. Co.
Anthony Swidriski	6-9-79	55	6-11-79	Liv. Co.
Olga Swidriski	12-18-77	80	12-21-77	Liv. Co.
Marguerite F Tannon	1-3-81	88	1-5-81	Oakland Co.
George A Tokman	2-9-77	46	1-24-77	
Lawrence W Unterbrink	12-25-80	69	12-29-80	Flint
Merritt P Welley	11-19-56	86	11-21-56	Liv. Co.
Margaret K Westergren	1-16-84	73	1-19-84	Liv. Co.
Wilson boys (twins)	1-11-70	0	1-14-70	Ingham Co.
Bernard Wyzlic	10-29-75	72	10-31-75	Liv. Co.

ADDITIONS AND CORRECTIONS